FOUNDATION 2　　HIGHER 1

MASTERING ~~ATICS~~

FOR
EDEXCEL GCSE

Assessment Consultant:
Keith Pledger

Series Editor: **Roger Porkess**

Gareth Cole, Heather Davis, Sophie Goldie,
Linda Liggett, Robin Liggett, Andrew Manning
Richard Perring, Rob Summerson

Follows the NCETM Mathematics Textbook Guidance,
www.hoddereducation.co.uk/GCSEmasteringmathematics/qualityframework

> **HODDER**
> EDUCATION
> AN HACHETTE UK COMPANY

In order to ensure that this resource offers high-quality support for the associated Edexcel qualification, it has been through a review process by the awarding body to confirm that it fully covers the teaching and learning content of the specification or part of a specification at which it is aimed, and demonstrates an appropriate balance between the development of subject skills, knowledge and understanding, in addition to preparation for assessment.

While the publishers have made every attempt to ensure that advice on the qualification and its assessment is accurate, the official specification and associated assessment guidance materials are the only authoritative source of information and should always be referred to for definitive guidance.

Edexcel examiners have not contributed to any sections in this resource relevant to examination papers for which they have responsibility.

No material from *Mastering Mathematics for Edexcel GCSE Foundation 2 / Higher 1* will be used verbatim in any assessment set by Edexcel.

Endorsement of *Mastering Mathematics for Edexcel GCSE Foundation 2 / Higher 1* does not mean that the book is required to achieve this Edexcel qualification, nor does it mean that it is the only suitable material available to support the qualification, and any resource lists produced by the awarding body shall include this and other appropriate resources.

Photo credits:

p.5 © m-gucci – iStockphoto via Thinkstock; **p.7** © Caitlin Seymour; **p.9** © Jürgen Fälchle – Fotolia.com; **p.13** © pumpuija – Fotolia.com; **p.16** © whitewizzard – iStockphoto via Thinkstock; **p.22** © Marek Kosmal – Fotolia.com; **p.24** scanrail – iStockphoto via Thinkstock; **p.27** © Kurhan – Fotolia.com; **p.35** © Alexander Khripunov – Fotolia.com; **p.40** © Wavebreak Media – Thinkstock; **p.41** © helenedevun – Fotolia.com; **p.50** © Simon Smith/iStockphoto.com; **p.51** © Sasa Komlen – Fotolia.com; **p.55** © Rawpixel – Fotolia.com; **p.61** © ttatty – iStock via Thinkstock; **p.68** © picsfive – Fotolia.com; **p.72** *t* © Sue Hough, *b* © Kate Crossland-Page; **p.74** © Corbis/ Education – image100 RFCD697; **p.78** © Kate Crossland-Page; **p.80** © RTimages – Fotolia.com; **p.86** © Claudio Divizia – Fotolia.com; **p.93** © FotolEdhar – Fotolia.com; **p.101** © Britain On View/VisitBritain / Britain 100 CD001RF; **p.105** *t* © Popartic – iStockphoto via Thinkstock *b* © JaysonPhotography – iStockphoto via Thinkstock; **p.108** © Heather Davis; **p.112** © Robert Churchill – iStockphoto via Thinkstock; **p.115** © Arkady – iStock via Thinkstock; **p.122** © aliafandi - iStock via Thinkstock; **p.138** © Ingram Publishing Limited / Ingram Image Library 500-Food; **p.143** © Kate Crossland-Page; **p.145** © bloomua – Fotolia.com; **p.148** © Kate Crossland-Page; **p.149** © Sue Hough; **p.151** © alanstenson – Fotolia.com; **p.158** © MADDRAT – Fotolia.com; **p.175** © Alexandra Officer; **p.180** © Jupiterimages – Pixland via Thinkstock; **p.193** © arturas kerdokas – Fotolia.com; **p.204** © Tupungato – iStock via Thinkstock; **p.214** © Heather Davis; **p.222** © Francesco Scatena – iStockphoto via Thinkstock; **p.232** *t* © Minerva Studio – Fotolia.com *b* © Imagestate Media (John Foxx) / Education SS121; **p.244** © oriontrail – Fotolia.com; **p.254** © loreanto – Fotolia.com; **p.264** © Nitiruj – iStockphoto via Thinkstock; **p.266** © yasar simit -Fotolia.com; **p.282** © ratselmeister – Fotolia.com; **p.294** © highwaystarz – Fotolia.om; **p.302 © Boggy – Fotolia.com; p.307** © eyjafjallajokull – iStock via Thinkstock; **p.309** © iriska – Fotolia.com; **p.324** *t* © blvdone – Fotolia.com, *bl* © Kate Crossland-Page, *br* © Caitlin Seymour; **p.333** *t* © AKS – Fotolia.com *b* © Kate Crossland-Page; **p.341** © rusty Elliott – Fotolia.com; **p.342** © Kate Crossland-Page; **p.351** © cherezoff – Fotolia.com; **p.360** *t* © kreizihorse – Fotolia. com *bl* © VRD – Fotolia.com *br* © magann – Fotolia.com; **p.370** ©HelenaT – iStockphoto via Thinkstock.

Although every effort has been made to ensure that website addresses are correct at time of going to press, Hodder Education cannot be held responsible for the content of any website mentioned. It is sometimes possible to find a relocated web page by typing in the address of the home page for a website in the URL window of your browser.

Orders: please contact Bookpoint Ltd, 130 Milton Park, Abingdon, Oxon OX14 4SB. Telephone: (44) 01235 827720. Fax: (44) 01235 400454. Lines are open 9.00–17.00, Monday to Saturday, with a 24-hour message answering service. Visit our website at www.hoddereducation.co.uk

© Cornwall Learning, Gareth Cole, Sophie Goldie, Linda Liggett, Robin Liggett, Andrew Manning, Keith Pledger, Roger Porkess, South Dartmoor Community College, Rob Summerson, Hodder & Stoughton

With contributions from Mark Dawes

First published in 2015 by

Hodder Education

An Hachette UK Company,

338 Euston Road

London NW1 3BH

Impression number	5	4	3	2	1
Year	2019	2018	2017	2016	2015

Cover photo © agsandrew - Fotolia

Typeset in ITC Avant Garde Gothic Std Book 10/12 by Integra Software Services Pvt. Ltd., Pondicherry, India

Printed in Italy

A catalogue record for this title is available from the British Library

ISBN 9781471839894

Contents

This is the second book in the Mastering Mathematics for Edexcel GCSE series. Opportunities to refresh and extend Units covered in the first book are provided through the Moving on sections at the start of each strand.

How to use this book   vi

NUMBER

Strand 1 Calculating   1

Units 1–9 Moving on   2

Strand 2 Using our number system   3

Units 1–6 Moving on   4
Unit 7 Calculating with standard form   5

Strand 3 Accuracy   11

Units 1–6 Moving on   12
Unit 7 Limits of accuracy   13

Strand 4 Fractions   18

Units 1–6 Moving on   19

Strand 5 Percentages   20

Units 1–5 Moving on   21
Unit 6 Reverse percentages   22
Unit 7 Repeated percentage increase/decrease   27

Strand 6 Ratio and proportion   33

Units 1–3 Moving on   34
Unit 4 The constant of proportionality   35
Unit 5 Working with inversely proportional quantities   41

Strand 7 Number properties   48

Units 1–3 Moving on   49
Unit 4 Index notation   50
Unit 5 Prime factorisation   55
Unit 6 Rules of indices   61

Contents

ALGEBRA

Strand 1 Starting algebra — 66

Units 1–6 Moving on — 67
Unit 7 Working with more complex equations — 68
Unit 8 Solving equations with brackets — 74
Unit 9 Simplifying harder expressions — 80
Unit 10 Using complex formulae — 86
Unit 11 Identities — 93

Strand 2 Sequences — 99

Units 1–4 Moving on — 100
Unit 5 Quadratic sequences — 101
Unit 6 Geometric progressions — 108

Strand 3 Functions and graphs — 113

Units 1–4 Moving on — 114
Unit 5 Finding equations of straight lines — 115
Unit 6 Quadratic functions — 122
Unit 7 Polynomial and reciprocal functions — 128

Strand 4 Algebraic methods — 137

(Unit 1 Trial and improvement is not required for GCSE)
Unit 2 Linear inequalities — 138
Unit 3 Solving pairs of equations by substitution — 145
Unit 4 Solving simultaneous equations by elimination — 151
Unit 5 Using graphs to solve simultaneous equations — 158

Strand 5 Working with quadratics — 165

Unit 1 Factorising quadratics — 166
Unit 2 Solving equations by factorising — 172

GEOMETRY

Strand 1 Units and scales — 177

Units 1–10 Moving on — 178
Unit 11 Working with compound units — 180

Strand 2 Properties of shapes — 188

Units 1–8 Moving on — 189
Unit 9 Congruent triangles and proof — 193
Unit 10 Proof using similar and congruent triangles — 204

Strand 3 Measuring shapes | 211

Units 1–4 Moving on	212
Unit 5 Pythagoras' theorem	214
Unit 6 Arcs and sectors	222

Strand 4 Construction | 230

Units 1–2 Moving on	231
Unit 3 Constructions with a pair of compasses	232
Unit 4 Loci	244

Strand 5 Transformations | 253

Units 1–6 Moving on	254
Unit 7 Similarity	256
Unit 8 Trigonometry	266
Unit 9 Trigonometry for special angles	276
Unit 10 Finding centres of rotation	282

Strand 6 Three-dimensional shapes | 291

Units 1–6 Moving on	292
Unit 7 Constructing plans and elevations	294
Unit 8 Surface area and volume of 3D shapes	302

Strand 7 Vectors | 308

Unit 1 Vectors	309

STATISTICS

Strand 1 Statistical measures | 318

Units 1–4 Moving on	319

Strand 2 Draw and interpret statistical diagrams | 321

Units 1–4 Moving on	322
Unit 5 Displaying grouped data	324
Unit 6 Scatter diagrams	333
Unit 7 Using lines of best fit	341

Strand 3 Collecting data

(This is not required for GCSE)

Strand 4 Probability | 348

Units 1–3 Moving on	349
Unit 4 Estimating probability	351
Unit 5 The multiplication rule	360
Unit 6 The addition rule	370

Index | 378

How to get the most from this book

This book covers the content for the Edexcel GCSE that is common to both Foundation and Higher tiers.

Sometimes the level of problem-solving in a question might mean a question becomes too difficult for the Foundation Tier. These questions are flagged with (Higher tier only).

The material is split into 21 'strands of learning':

Number Strands	Algebra Strands	Geometry Strands	Statistics Strands
Calculating	Starting algebra	Units and scales	Statistical measures
Using our number system	Sequences	Properties of shapes	Draw and interpret statistical diagrams
Accuracy	Functions and graphs	Measuring shapes	Probability
Fractions	Algebraic methods	Construction	
Percentages	Working with quadratics	Transformations	
Ratio and proportion		Three-dimensional shapes	
Number properties			

Each strand is presented as a series of units that get more difficult as you progress (from Band b to Band k). This book mainly deals with units in Bands f to h. In total there are 45 units in this book.

Getting started

At the beginning of each strand, you will find a 'Progression strand flowchart'. It shows what skills you will develop in each unit in the strand. You can see:

• what you need to know before starting each unit
• what you will need to learn next to progress.

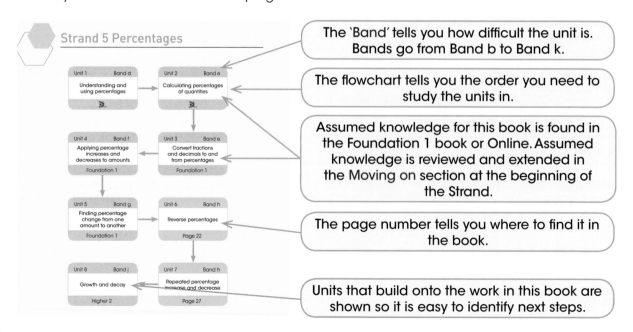

When you start to use this book, you will need to identify where to join each Strand. Then you will not spend time revisiting skills you have already mastered.

If you can answer all the questions in the 'Reviewing skills' section of a unit then you will not have to study that unit.

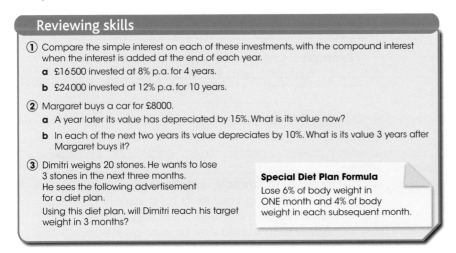

Reviewing skills

① Compare the simple interest on each of these investments, with the compound interest when the interest is added at the end of each year.

  a £16500 invested at 8% p.a. for 4 years.

  b £24000 invested at 12% p.a. for 10 years.

② Margaret buys a car for £8000.

  a A year later its value has depreciated by 15%. What is its value now?

  b In each of the next two years its value depreciates by 10%. What is its value 3 years after Margaret buys it?

③ Dimitri weighs 20 stones. He wants to lose 3 stones in the next three months. He sees the following advertisement for a diet plan.

  Using this diet plan, will Dimitri reach his target weight in 3 months?

Special Diet Plan Formula
Lose 6% of body weight in ONE month and 4% of body weight in each subsequent month.

When you know which unit to start with in each strand you will be ready to start work on your first unit.

Starting a unit

Every unit begins with some information:

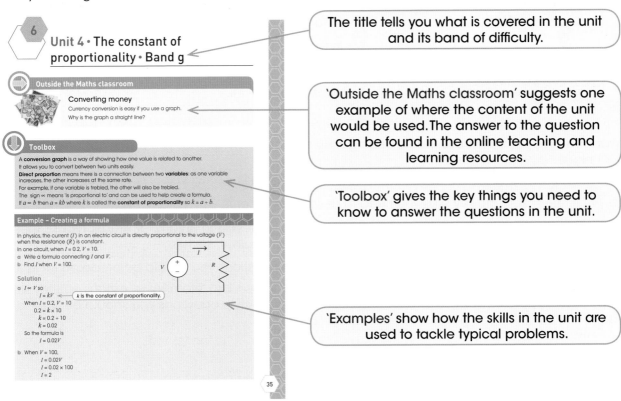

The title tells you what is covered in the unit and its band of difficulty.

'Outside the Maths classroom' suggests one example of where the content of the unit would be used. The answer to the question can be found in the online teaching and learning resources.

'Toolbox' gives the key things you need to know to answer the questions in the unit.

'Examples' show how the skills in the unit are used to tackle typical problems.

Now you have all the information you need, you can use the questions to develop your understanding.

Practising skills

① The number A is 6000.
   a A is increased by 10% to give B. What is number B?
   b B is increased by 10% to give C. What is the number C?
   c C is increased by 10% to give D. What is the number D?
   d What is the percentage increase from A to D?

② Asaph buys a field for £6000. For each of the next 3 years it increases in value by 10%.
   a What is its value at the end of 3 years?
   b What is the percentage increase in its value since Asaph bought it?
   c Explain why the increase is greater than 30%.

③ The number P is 5000.
   a P is decreased by 20% to give Q. What is the number Q?
   b Q is decreased by 20% to give R. What is the number R?
   c R is decreased by 20% to give S. What is the number S?
   d What is the percentage change from P to S?

> **'Practising skills' questions are all about building and mastering the essential techniques that you need to succeed.**

> **'Examples' take you through how to answer typical questions step-by-step.**

Developing fluency

① Peter invests £500 at 6% per annum.
   a How much interest does Peter receive at the end of the first year?
   b He reinvests the £500 but not the interest. What is his total investment at the end of the first year?
   c His reinvestment earns interest for another year at 6%. How much interest does he receive at the end of the second year?

② Interest is paid on the following investments but not reinvested.
   a How much interest is received in total on
      i £1000 at 5% p.a. for 2 years
      ii £2000 at 10% p.a. for 5 years
      iii £500 at 3.5% p.a. for 3 years?
   b Now find the interest paid on these investments when the interest is reinvested each year.

③ A riverbank has been colonised by mink. They are an alien species that attacks local wildlife. The river authority traps the mink and removes them. Each year it reduces the number of mink by 60%.
   What percentage of mink remain after
   a 1 year   b 2 years   c 3 years   d 4 years   e 5 years?

> **'Developing fluency' questions give you practice in using your skills for a variety of purposes and contexts, building your confidence to tackle any type of question.**

Problem solving

① The thickness of an A4 sheet of paper is 0.1 mm.
   Bill cuts an A4 sheet of paper in half and places the two halves on top of each other. He then cuts the two halves in half and places these two halves on top of each other. He repeats this a further 4 times.
   a Work out the height of the pile of paper formed.
   b Explain why it would be very difficult for Bill to do this a further 10 times.

② Daniel is a free-range pig farmer. The diagram shows his field. Its shape is a trapezium.
   Daniel gives each pig an area of $2 \times 5^3 m^2$ of land. Work out the greatest number of pigs that Daniel can put in this field.

③ In a game of 'Double Your Money', contestants are asked a number of questions.
   Contestants who answer the first question correctly win £1. If they answer the second question correctly, their winnings are doubled to £2, and so on.
   Monica is a contestant on 'Double Your Money'. She answers 10 questions correctly.
   a How much money had she won after answering the 10 questions? Give your answer using index notation.
   b Work out the minimum number of questions she would have to answer correctly to win over £1 million.

> **'Problem solving' questions give examples of how you will use the Maths in the unit together with problem solving skills in order to tackle more demanding problems:**
> - **in the real world**
> - **in other subjects**
> - **within Maths itself.**

When you feel confident, use the 'Reviewing skills' section to check that you have mastered the techniques covered in the unit.

You will see many questions labelled with **Reasoning** or **Exam-style**

Reasoning skills are key skills you need to develop in order to solve problems.

They will help you think through problems and to apply your skills in unfamiliar situations. Use these questions to make sure that you develop these important skills.

Exam-style questions are examples of the types of questions you should be prepared for in the exam. Exam-style questions that test problem solving will often be unfamiliar questions, so they are impossible to predict. However, if you can answer the exam-style questions you should be able to tackle any question you get in the exam.

About 'Bands'

Every unit has been allocated to a Band. These bands show you the level of difficulty of the Maths that you are working on.

Each Band contains Maths that's of about the same level of difficulty.

This provides a way of checking your progress and assessing your weaker areas, where you need to practise more.

Moving on to another unit

Once you have completed a unit, you should move on to the next unit in one of the strands. You can choose which strand to work on next but try and complete all the units in a particular Band before moving on to the next Band.

A note for teachers

Lower Bands have been assigned to units roughly in line with the previous National Curriculum levels. Here they are, just to help in giving you a reference point.

Band	Approximate Equivalent in terms of Old National Curriculum Levels
b	Level 2
c	Level 3
d	Level 4
e	Level 5
f	Level 6
g	Level 7
h	Level 8
i, j, k	No equivalent

Answers and Write-on sheets

Write-on sheets to aid completion of answers are denoted by 👆. These and answers to all the questions in this book are available via **Mastering Mathematics 11–16 Teaching and Learning Resources for Edexcel GCSE** or by visiting www.hoddereducation.co.uk/MasteringmathsforEdexcelGCSE

Strand 1 Calculating

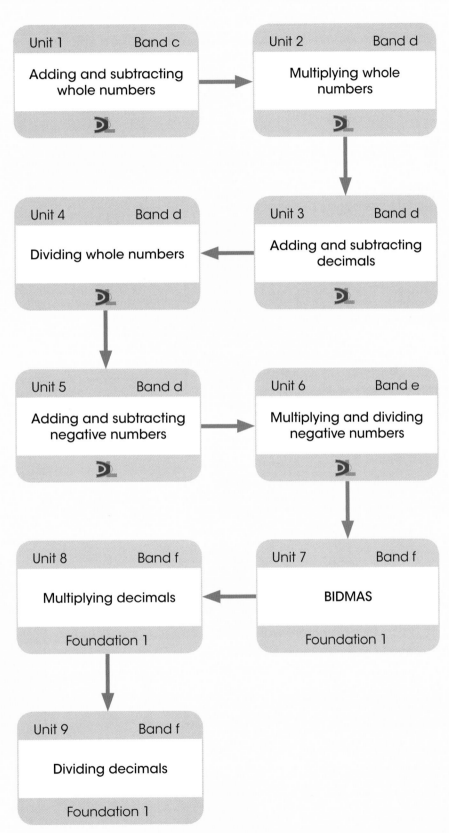

| Unit 1 | Band c |
| Adding and subtracting whole numbers |

| Unit 2 | Band d |
| Multiplying whole numbers |

| Unit 4 | Band d |
| Dividing whole numbers |

| Unit 3 | Band d |
| Adding and subtracting decimals |

| Unit 5 | Band d |
| Adding and subtracting negative numbers |

| Unit 6 | Band e |
| Multiplying and dividing negative numbers |

| Unit 8 | Band f |
| Multiplying decimals |
| Foundation 1 |

| Unit 7 | Band f |
| BIDMAS |
| Foundation 1 |

| Unit 9 | Band f |
| Dividing decimals |
| Foundation 1 |

This strand is assumed knowledge for this book. The skills are reviewed and extended in the Moving on section on page 2.

Knowledge and skills from these units are used throughout the book.

Units 1–9 • Moving on

The questions in this section should be answered *without* the use of a calculator.

1 Miss Smith has £26 in her bank account. She carries out the following transactions:

Payment to Food4U	£60
Payment for shoes	£41
Wages	£125
Payment for mobile phone	£32
Payment for diesel	£70
Birthday money	£55

Copy and complete this bank statement for Miss Smith.

Transaction	Credit	Debit	Balance
			£75
Payment to Food4U		£60	
Payment for shoes			

2 What is the difference between 7^2 and $(-4)^2$?

3 Find the two answers to each of these:

a $\sqrt{25}$ b $\sqrt{121}$ c $\sqrt{196}$

4 Graham and Susan each work out this sum.

$$3 \times 2 + 9 - 3 \div 3$$

Graham says the answer is 4.

Susan says the answer is 8.

a They are both wrong. Find the correct answer.

b Use brackets to show how they got their answers.

5 Here are some numbers and some symbols.

(1   9   +   –   ×   2   5   )

Arrange them to form a statement that gives an answer of 3.

Each symbol and number must be used exactly once.

6 Richard is going to cover a bathroom wall with tiles.

The wall is in the shape of a rectangle.

The wall is 2.1 m long and 2.4 m high.

The tiles are squares with sides of 0.3 m.

There are 12 tiles in a box. Richard buys 4 boxes of tiles.

Will he have enough tiles to cover the wall in his bathroom?

2.1 m

2.4 m

7 Here are two rectangles.

The areas of the two rectangles are the same.

Work out the value of x.

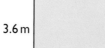

5.2 m

3.6 m

2.4 m

x m

Strand 2 Using our number system

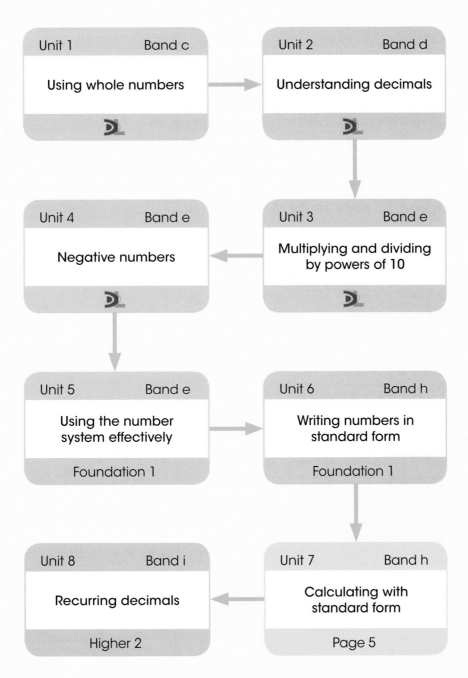

Unit 1 — Band c	Unit 2 — Band d
Using whole numbers	**Understanding decimals**

Unit 4 — Band e	Unit 3 — Band e
Negative numbers	**Multiplying and dividing by powers of 10**

Unit 5 — Band e	Unit 6 — Band h
Using the number system effectively	**Writing numbers in standard form**
Foundation 1	Foundation 1

Unit 8 — Band i	Unit 7 — Band h
Recurring decimals	**Calculating with standard form**
Higher 2	Page 5

Units 1–6 are assumed knowledge for this book. They are reviewed and extended in the Moving on section on page 4.

Knowledge and skills from these units are used throughout the book.

2 Units 1–6 • Moving on

1 $54 \times 142 = 7668$

  a Write down the value of

    i 5.4×14.2 **ii** 54×0.142 **iii** $7668 \div 1420$ **iv** $7.668 \div 1.4$.

  b Adjust the calculation in the box so it gives an answer of

    i 766.8 **ii** 0.7668 **iii** 1420 **iv** 0.54.

2 Choose the number from the box that best completes each statement.

> 6.371×10^{3} 1.99×10^{-23}
> 5×10^{-2} 1.49×10^{11}

  a The mass of an atom of carbon is ☐ grams.

  b The average distance to the Sun is ☐ metres.

  c The radius of the Earth is ☐ kilometres.

  d The diameter of a human hair is ☐ millimetres.

3 The numbers in the box are written in standard form.

> 9.32×10^{-4} 9×10^{4} 4.2×10^{-3}
> 1.2×10^{-5} 2.41×10^{5} 5.71×10^{3}

  a **i** Write down the smallest number.

    ii Write your answer as an ordinary number.

  b **i** Write down the largest number.

    ii Write your answer as an ordinary number.

4 Which of the following numbers are in standard form? Convert those that are not into standard form.

  a 23.4 **b** $23\,400\,000$ **c** 0.0234

  d 0.0234×10^{4} **e** 0.0234×10^{-4} **f** 2.34×10^{4}

  g 23.4×10^{-4} **h** 2.34

5 Write the numbers in the following statements in standard form.

  a The thickness of a crystal is $0.000\,000\,045\,\text{m}$.

  b The population of china is about 1400 million.

  c A human cell measures about 0.00005 metres.

  d The Earth's atmosphere extends upwards to about $650\,000$ metres from the Earth's surface.

Unit 7 • Calculating with standard form • Band h

 Outside the Maths classroom

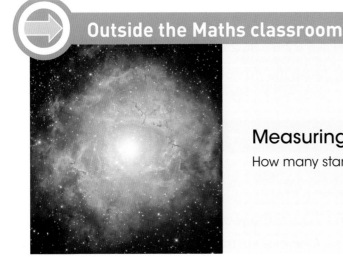

Measuring space

How many stars are there in our galaxy?

Toolbox

Adding or subtracting numbers in standard form is straightforward if the power of ten is the same.

Five million added to three million is eight million, which can be written as $5 \times 10^6 + 3 \times 10^6 = 8 \times 10^6$.

If the powers of ten are not equal rewrite them so they are.

Then the same strategy can be used.

$6 \times 10^9 + 5 \times 10^8 = 60 \times 10^8 + 5 \times 10^8$ ⟵ Making the powers of 10 the same.

$= 65 \times 10^8$ ⟵ Adding.

$= 6.5 \times 10^9$. ⟵ Rewrite the number in standard form.

When multiplying (or dividing) two numbers in standard form, work with each part of the number separately.

$5 \times 10^7 \times 3 \times 10^4 = 5 \times 3 \times 10^7 \times 10^3$ ⟵ $5 \times 3 = 15, 10^7 \times 10^3 = 10^{10}$

$= 15 \times 10^{10}$ ⟵ Note: This is not standard form.

$= 1.5 \times 10^{11}$

⟵ The *number* must be between 1 and 10.

5

Example – Multiplying large and small numbers

The mass of a grain of sand is about 3.5×10^{-10} kg.

It is thought that there are about 7.5×10^{18} grains of sand on the Earth.

Use the figures above to calculate the mass of all of the sand on Earth. Give your answer in standard form.

Solution

$3.5 \times 10^{-10} \times 7.5 \times 10^{18} = 26.25 \times 10^{8}$ ⟵ $3.5 \times 7.5 = 36.25, 10^{-10} \times 10^{18} = 10^{8}$

$= 2.625 \times 10^{9}$ kg ⟵ Make the *number* between 1 and 10.

Example – Subtraction and division of small numbers

A loaf of bread contains 5×10^{-3} kg of yeast and 1×10^{-2} kg of salt.

a How much do the salt and yeast weigh in total?

b How much greater is the mass of the salt than the mass of the yeast in kg?

c How many times is the mass of the salt greater than the mass of the yeast?

Solution

a $1 \times 10^{-2} + 5 \times 10^{-3} = 10 \times 10^{-3} + 5 \times 10^{-3}$ ⟵ Converting to the same power of ten.

$= 15 \times 10^{-3}$ kg

$= 1.5 \times 10^{-2}$ kg ⟵ In standard form.

b $1 \times 10^{-2} - 5 \times 10^{-3} = 10 \times 10^{-3} - 5 \times 10^{-3}$

$= 5 \times 10^{-3}$ kg

The salt weighs 5×10^{-3} kg more than the yeast.

c $\dfrac{\text{mass of salt}}{\text{mass of yeast}} = \dfrac{1 \times 10^{-2}}{5 \times 10^{-3}}$

$= 0.2 \times 10^{-2-(-3)}$

$= 0.2 \times 10^{1}$

$= 2 (\times 10^{0})$

There is twice as much salt as yeast.

Do the questions in this unit without a calculator first. Use your calculator to check your answers.

Practising skills

(1) Work out the values of the following, giving your answers in standard form.

a $3.2 \times 10^{5} + 4.6 \times 10^{5}$ b $6.8 \times 10^{-2} - 5.1 \times 10^{-2}$ c $8000 + 700$

d $6.4 \times 10^{3} + 2000$ e $1.8 \times 10^{-3} + 2.2 \times 10^{-3}$ f $6.4 \times 10^{-2} - 0.033$

(2) Work out the following, giving your answers in standard form.

a $7.2 \times 10^{5} + 4.6 \times 10^{5}$ b $7.2 \times 10^{5} + 4.6 \times 10^{4}$ c $7.2 \times 10^{5} + 4.6 \times 10^{6}$

d $7.2 \times 10^{5} - 4.6 \times 10^{5}$ e $7.2 \times 10^{6} - 4.6 \times 10^{5}$ f $7.2 \times 10^{5} - 4.6 \times 10^{6}$

③ Without using a calculator work out the value of the following. Give your answers in standard form.

    a $3 \times 10^5 \times 2 \times 10^7$ **b** $2 \times 10^3 \times 4 \times 10^5$ **c** $2 \times 10^5 \times 5 \times 10^2$

    d $3 \times 10^{-5} \times 3 \times 10^7$ **e** $5 \times 10^{-7} \times 2 \times 10^5$ **f** $9 \times 10^{-6} \times 7 \times 10^{-4}$

④ Without using a calculator work out the value of these calculations.

    a $6 \times 10^5 \div 2 \times 10^3$ **b** $8 \times 10^9 \div 4 \times 10^8$ **c** $6 \times 10^7 \div 2 \times 10^3$

    d $3 \times 10^7 \div 2 \times 10^3$ **e** $2 \times 10^5 \div 4 \times 10^3$ **f** $2 \times 10^6 \div 8 \times 10^8$

⑤ Using standard form, write down a number that is between:

    a 6×10^5 and 6×10^4 **b** 6×10^{-3} and 6×10^{-2}

    c 7.1×10^2 and 7.1×10^3 **d** 7.1×10^{-6} and 7.1×10^{-7}

⑥ Coley says:

> When you're multiplying numbers in standard form you have to multiply the two numbers at the front together and write down what that comes to, then write '×10' and finally add the two powers together and write that down.

Explain why Coley's method won't always give the correct answer in standard form.

Developing fluency

① Work out the following, giving your answers in standard form.

    a $3.204 \times 10^2 + 4 \times 10^{-1}$ **b** $3.204 \times 10^2 - 4 \times 10^{-1}$

    c $3.204 \times 10^2 \times 4 \times 10^{-1}$ **d** $3.204 \times 10^2 \div 4 \times 10^{-1}$

② The speed of light is 3×10^8 metres per second and there are roughly 3×10^7 seconds in a year.
A light year is the distance travelled by light in one year.
Approximately how many metres is a light year?
Give your answer in standard form.

③ The masses of some of the planets in our Solar System are:

Jupiter 1.9×10^{27} kg   Mercury 3.3×10^{23} kg

Saturn 5.7×10^{26} kg   Earth 6×10^{24} kg.

    a Place the planets in order of mass.

    b How many times greater than the mass of the Earth is the mass of Jupiter?

    c How many times greater than the mass of Mercury is the mass of Jupiter?

    d How many time greater than the mass of Mercury is the mass of the Earth?

Reasoning

Exam-style

④ Some approximate masses are:

caffeine molecule 3.2×10^{-25} kg

eyebrow hair 7×10^{-8} kg

average human cell 1×10^{-12} kg

water molecule 3×10^{-26} kg.

a How many water molecules weigh the same as an eyebrow hair?

b How many water molecules weigh the same as one caffeine molecule?

c How many times greater than the mass of a water molecule is the mass of an eyebrow hair?

⑤ A hydrogen atom weighs 1.67×10^{-27} kg.

An oxygen atom weighs 2.67×10^{-26} kg.

What is the mass of a molecule of water?

Problem solving

① The mass of a spacecraft is 7.8×10^{4} kg.

The spacecraft is carrying equipment with a total mass of 2.4×10^{3} kg.

The spacecraft docks with a space station.

The mass of the space station is 4.62×10^{5} kg.

The commander of the space station does not want the total mass on docking to be greater than 5.43×10^{5} kg.

Is the total mass within this limit?

② Jenny is making a scale model of the Solar System.

She wants the distance from Earth to Saturn to be 20 cm on her scale model.

The real distance from the Earth to Saturn is 1.25×10^{9} kilometres.

a Find the scale of the model in the form $1 : n$ where n is written in standard form.

Jenny wants to put the position of a spacecraft on the scale model.

The real distance of the spacecraft from Earth is 8.5×10^{8} kilometres, correct to 2 significant figures.

b Work out the distance of the spacecraft from Earth on the scale model.

③ Karim is trying to find out the thickness of a piece of paper.

He has a box of paper which contains 3000 sheets of paper positioned on top of each other.

The height of the paper is 0.3 m.

a Work out the thickness of each sheet of paper.

Give your answer in metres, in standard form.

Karim also wants to know the weight of each sheet of paper.

He weighs the box containing the paper, then he weighs the box when it is empty.

The mass of the box and paper is 54 kg.

The mass of the empty box is 500 g.

b Work out the mass of each piece of paper.

Give your answer in kilograms, in standard form.

(4) Elaine is estimating how far away a thunderstorm is from her home.

The speed of sound is estimated at 3.3×10^2 metres per second.

The speed of light is estimated at 3.0×10^8 metres per second.

a The thunderstorm is 6 km away and Elaine sees a flash of lightning.

She hears the clap of thunder x seconds later.

Work out the value of x.

Give your answer to the nearest whole number.

b The length of time between seeing the next flash of lightning and hearing the clap of thunder is 3 seconds.

How far away is the thunderstorm now?

State any assumptions that you have made.

(5) Lynn is carrying out a survey on the living space per person in five different countries.

The table shows the information that she has collected.

Country	Area (in km²)	Population	Area (in km²) per person
Australia	3.0×10^6	2.2×10^7	
Brazil	8.5×10^6	2.0×10^8	
China	9.6×10^6	1.4×10^9	
Germany	3.6×10^5	8.3×10^7	
UK	2.4×10^5	6.4×10^7	
USA	9.8×10^6	3.2×10^8	

She wants to find out which country has the greatest land area per person.

Copy and complete the table and compare the five countries.

(6) Rod is a keen physicist interested in the wavelengths of sound waves.

Rod wants to find the difference between the wavelength of his favourite radio station and the wavelength of his dad's favourite radio station.

Rod listens to FM Capital Radio which has a frequency of 102 MHz.

Rod's dad listens to AM Radio 5 Live which has a frequency of 909 kHz.

1 MHz = 10^6 waves per second. 1 kHz = 10^3 waves per second.

To find the wavelength (in m), Rod uses the formula:

wavelength = 3×10^8 ÷ frequency (in waves per second)

Work out the difference between the wavelength of Rod's favourite radio station and the wavelength of his dad's favourite radio station.

Reviewing skills

① Work out

a $8.48 \times 10^4 + 8.4 \times 10^3 - 3 \times 10^2$

Give your answer in standard form.

b Write the following as ordinary numbers.

   i 8.48×10^4 **ii** 8.4×10^3 **iii** 3×10^2

c Use your answers to part **b** to check your answer to part **a**.

② Work out the following, giving your answers in standard form.

a $6000 \times 1.5 \times 10^9$ **b** $1.6 \times 10^{-4} \times 2 \times 10^{-3}$ **c** $2.3 \times 10^6 + 3$ million

d $0.0052 - 3.2 \times 10^{-3}$ **e** $7.6 \times 10^2 \times 2 \times 10^{-1}$ **f** $7.6 \times 10^2 \div 2 \times 10^{-1}$

③ A human body contains roughly 1×10^{12} bacteria and there are about 7×10^9 people on the planet.

How many bacteria are there in total within all of the people?

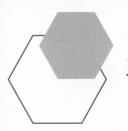

Strand 3 Accuracy

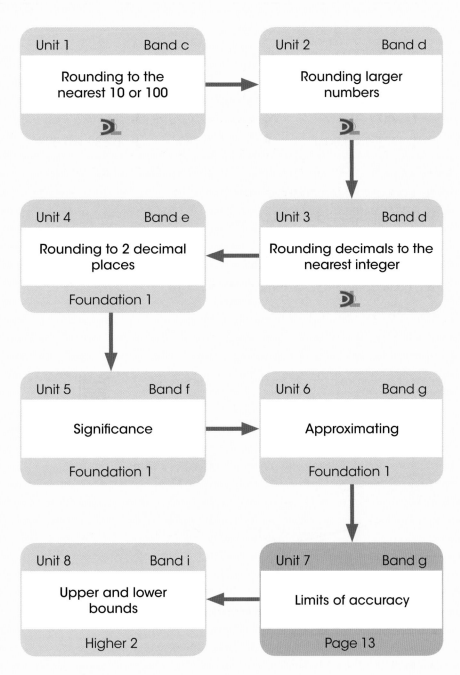

Unit 1	Band c
Rounding to the nearest 10 or 100	

Unit 2	Band d
Rounding larger numbers	

Unit 4	Band e
Rounding to 2 decimal places	
Foundation 1	

Unit 3	Band d
Rounding decimals to the nearest integer	

Unit 5	Band f
Significance	
Foundation 1	

Unit 6	Band g
Approximating	
Foundation 1	

Unit 8	Band i
Upper and lower bounds	
Higher 2	

Unit 7	Band g
Limits of accuracy	
Page 13	

Units 1–6 are assumed knowledge for this book. They are reviewed and extended in the Moving on section on page 12.

3 Units 1–6 • Moving on

Exam-style

① Do the following calculations on your calculator.
Give your answers to 2 decimal places.

   a $22 \div 7$ **b** $23 \div 6$ **c** $10 \div 3$ **d** $\sqrt{34}$

   e $9 \div 7$ **f** $\sqrt{57}$ **g** $55 \div 3$ **h** $11 \div 27$

   i $3.14 \div 8$ **j** 223.6×0.0048 **k** 32.7×0.259 **l** 0.682×0.097

② Which of the following are correct? Find the correct answer where it is wrong.

   a 3.4567 is 3.45, correct to 2 decimal places.

   b 3.405 67 is 3.405, correct to 2 decimal places.

   c 3.405 67 is 3.4, correct to 1 decimal place.

   d 0.345 67 is 0.3 correct to 1 decimal place.

   e 0.0034 567 is 0.0034 correct to 2 decimal places.

③ Jack rounds 365.5768 to 2 decimal places.
Jill rounds 365.5768 to 3 decimal places.
What is the difference between their values?

④ Gareth has just had a swimming pool built in his garden.
The diagram shows the shape of the pool and its dimensions.

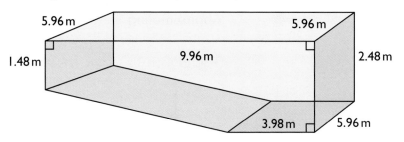

Gareth fills the pool with water using a hosepipe.

The hosepipe delivers water at a rate of $980\,\text{cm}^3$ per second.

Gareth turns on the hosepipe at 10 a.m. on Monday morning.

Estimate when the swimming pool is full of water.

⑤ Bob is building a conservatory at his home.
The diagram shows a plan of its base.

The base will be made of concrete and will be 20 cm thick.

Bob is going to have ready-mixed concrete delivered.

The cost of the concrete is £84 per m^3 plus a £40 delivery charge.

Bob has budgeted £400 for the concrete.

Will Bob overspend on his budget for the concrete?

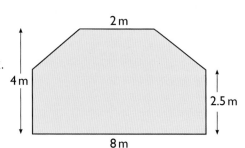

Exam-style

Higher tier only

Unit 7 • Limits of accuracy • Band g

Buying in bulk

Each of these bags should contain 25 kg of coffee. What is the minimum mass you would expect a bag to have?

Toolbox

To say how accurate a measurement is, give its lower and upper bounds.
The length of a line is l, recorded as 36 cm to the nearest centimetre.

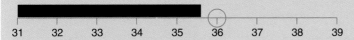

All lines between 35.5 cm and 36.499 999... cm are rounded to 36 cm.
35.5 cm is called the **lower bound.**
36.499 999 is effectively 36.5 cm so 36.5 cm is called the **upper bound**.
This is written as
$$35.5 \leqslant l < 36.5$$
Another way of writing it is
$$l = 35 \pm 0.5 \text{ cm}$$

Example – Recognising the effect of bounds on a result

Stella draws a square with a side length of 21 cm to the nearest centimetre.
a   What are the upper and lower bounds of the side length of the square?
b   What are the upper and lower bounds of the perimeter of the square she has drawn?

Solution

a   Upper bound is 21.5 cm
    Lower bound is 20.5 cm

b   Upper bound of perimeter = 4 × 21.5 = 86 cm
    Lower bound of perimeter = 4 × 20.5 = 82 cm

Practising skills

① Write down the lower and upper bounds for each of these measurements.

a 80 cm (to the nearest cm)

b 80 cm (to the nearest 10 cm)

c 300 g (to the nearest g)

d 300 g (to the nearest 100 g)

② Write down the lower and upper bounds for each of these measurements.

a 5000 m (to the nearest m)

b 5000 m (to the nearest 10 m)

c 5000 m (to the nearest 100 m)

d 5000 m (to the nearest 1000 m)

③ Write down the lower and upper bounds for each of these measurements.

a 600 m (to the nearest 10 m)

b 600 m (to the nearest 5 m)

c 600 m (to the nearest 100 m)

d 600 m (to the nearest 50 m)

④ The mass of a bag of potatoes is m kg. To the nearest kg the mass is 6 kg.
Copy and complete this statement.

$$\Box \leq m < \Box$$

⑤ The length of a pencil is l cm. To the nearest cm the length is 9 cm.
Copy and complete this statement.

$$\Box \leq l < \Box$$

⑥ Each of these measurements is rounded to 1 significant figure. Write down the lower and upper bound for each measurement.

a 3 m   **b** 60 m   **c** 0.4 mg   **d** 0.07 km

⑦ Each of these measurements is rounded to 2 significant figures. Write down the lower and upper bound for each measurement.

a 24 ml   **b** 360 g   **c** 0.83 kg   **d** 0.019 m

⑧ Copy and complete this table.

	Number	Lower bound	Upper bound
a	4 (to nearest whole number)		
b	70 (to nearest 10)		
c	600 (to nearest 10)		
d	0.3 (to 1 decimal place)		
e	0.06 (to 2 decimal places)		
f	80 km (to 1 significant figure)		
g	68 mg (to 2 significant figures)		
h	0.032 (to 2 significant figures)		

Developing fluency

① The capacity of a pot of paint is 300 ml, to the nearest 10 ml.
Thabo buys 5 pots. The total volume of paint is V ml.
Copy and complete this statement.

$\square \leqslant V < \square$

② Mel runs 8 km, to the nearest km, every day.
What is the least possible distance she runs in a week?

③ Ann draws a square with a side length of 14 cm, to the nearest cm.
The area of the square is A cm^2.
Copy and complete this statement.

$\square \leqslant A < \square$

④ A bag of flour weighs 250 g, to the nearest 10 g. Val needs 740 g of flour for a recipe.
Will three bags of flour definitely be enough?
Explain your answer.

⑤ A rectangle has length 80 m, to the nearest 10 m, and width 40 m, to the nearest 5 m.
Its perimeter is p m and its area is A m^2.
Copy and complete these statements.

a $\square \leqslant p < \square$

b $\square \leqslant A < \square$

⑥ Which is the odd one out among these statements about a length l m?

i $l = 50$ to the nearest 5.

ii $47.5 \leqslant l < 52.5$

iii $l = 50 \pm 5$

iv The upper and lower bounds of l are 52.5 and 47.5.

⑦ The number n is 680, correct to 2 significant figures.
Copy and complete these statements about n.

a $n = 680 \pm \square$

b $\square \leqslant n < \square$

c The upper and lower bounds of n are $\square$ and $\square$ respectively.

d n is 680 to the nearest $\square$

Problem solving

① The directors of a golf club issue the following statement about membership.

'The membership of the club to the nearest 5 members will be 650.'

At present there are 648 members of the golf club.

10 people have applied to become members of the golf club.

How many of these 10 people will definitely not be successful?

② The measurements of this photograph are accurate to the nearest centimetre.

Jo has 100 photographs of this size to stick in her photograph album. The measurements of each page of the album are exactly 38 cm by 18.5 cm. There are 9 empty pages in Jo's album.

Is there definitely enough space in Jo's photograph album for these 100 photographs without overlapping?

9 cm

6 cm

③ The following people want to travel in a lift.

David 65 kg	Brian 92 kg
Bronwen 74 kg	Pat 54 kg
Peter 86 kg	Bruce 95 kg
Ahmed 89 kg	Mark 93 kg

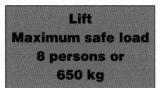

Lift
Maximum safe load
8 persons or
650 kg

a Explain why it might not be safe for these people to travel together in the lift.

b Eight different people get in the lift. They all have the same mass to the nearest kilogram. What is the largest that their mass can safely be?

④ A particular paperback book is 2.6 cm thick, measured to the nearest tenth of a centimetre. Tom has 50 of these paperback books. His bookshelf is 1.30 m in length to the nearest centimetre.

What is the greatest possible number of these books Tom can definitely put on his bookshelf?

Reviewing skills

① Write down the lower and upper bounds for each of these measurements.

    a 40 ml (to the nearest ml)

    b 40 ml (to the nearest 10 ml)

    c 700 kg (to the nearest 100 kg)

    d 700 kg (to the nearest 10 kg)

② Write down the lower and upper bounds for each of these measurements.

    a 650 m (to the nearest m)

    b 650 m (to the nearest 10 m)

    c 650 m (to the nearest 50 m)

    d 650 m (to the nearest 5 m)

③ The mass of a fish is m g. To the nearest 10 g, the mass is 320 g.

    Copy and complete this statement.

    $\square \leqslant m < \square$

④ Each of these measurements is rounded to 1 significant figure. Write down the lower and upper bounds for each measurement.

    a 900 cm   **b** 2000 km   **c** 0.2 g   **d** 0.005 m

⑤ Each of these measurements is rounded to 2 significant figures. Write down the lower and upper bounds for each measurement.

    a 7100 m   **b** 49 cm   **c** 520 mm   **d** 0.0028 km

⑥ Eve has made a square cake with sides of length 20 cm, to the nearest cm. She wants to put a ribbon round the sides. Her piece of ribbon is 80 cm to the nearest cm. Does she definitely have enough ribbon for the cake? Explain your answer.

Strand 4 Fractions

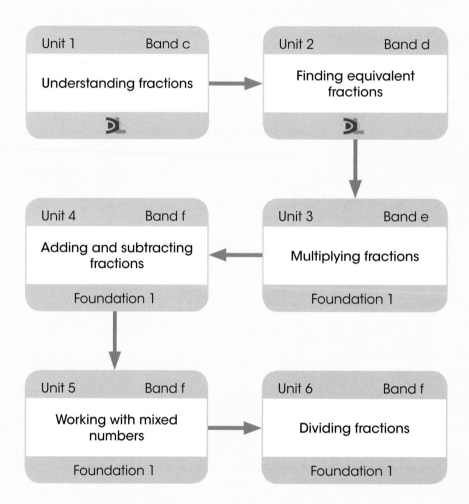

Unit 1	Band c
Understanding fractions	

Unit 2	Band d
Finding equivalent fractions	

Unit 4	Band f
Adding and subtracting fractions	
Foundation 1	

Unit 3	Band e
Multiplying fractions	
Foundation 1	

Unit 5	Band f
Working with mixed numbers	
Foundation 1	

Unit 6	Band f
Dividing fractions	
Foundation 1	

This strand is assumed knowledge for this book. The skills are reviewed and extended in the Moving on section on page 19.

4

Units 1–6 • Moving on

The questions in this section should be answered *without* the use of a calculator.

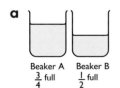

Exam-style

① Libby is planning a party. She has a budget of £300.

Libby spends $\frac{1}{4}$ of her budget on drinks.

She spends $\frac{2}{5}$ of the remaining budget on food.
The rest of the budget is spent on hiring the venue.

How much does the venue cost?

Exam-style

② A manager of a small factory carries out a survey to find out how each employee gets to work.
The manager finds:

$\frac{1}{3}$ of the employees come by car

$\frac{1}{4}$ of the employees come by bus

the rest of the employees walk.

What fraction of the employees walk to work?

Exam-style

③ Peter marks some lengths on a piece of wood that is 5 m long.
Find the value of x.

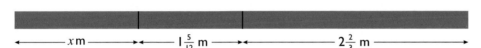

④ Kate is baking flapjacks to sell at a fete. | 1 lb = 16 ounces |
She has 6 lb of oats, 5 lb of butter, 4 lb of sugar and 7 lb of golden syrup.

Each flapjack needs $\frac{4}{5}$ ounce of oats, $\frac{2}{3}$ ounce of butter, $\frac{1}{3}$ ounce sugar and $\frac{1}{2}$ ounce of golden syrup.

How many flapjacks can she make?

⑤ Work out the following.

a $\frac{3}{5}$ of 25 g.   **b** $\frac{5}{6}$ of 30 m.   **c** $\frac{5}{9}$ of 45 gallons.   **d** $\frac{4}{7}$ of 420 miles.

⑥ Rajiv uses the water in beaker A to fill up beaker B.
Work out how much water is left in beaker A for each of these.

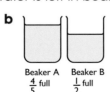 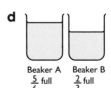

a   **b**   **c**   **d**

Beaker A   Beaker B   Beaker A   Beaker B   Beaker A   Beaker B   Beaker A   Beaker B
$\frac{3}{4}$ full $\frac{1}{2}$ full $\frac{4}{5}$ full $\frac{1}{2}$ full $\frac{7}{10}$ full $\frac{3}{5}$ full $\frac{5}{6}$ full $\frac{2}{3}$ full

⑦ Sandra has a shelf 55 cm long. How many $2\frac{3}{4}$ cm wide books can she fit on the shelf?

Strand 5 Percentages

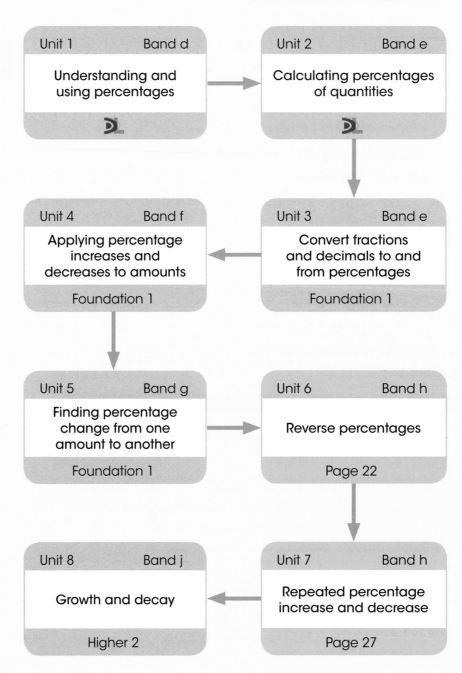

Unit 1	Band d
Understanding and using percentages	

Unit 2	Band e
Calculating percentages of quantities	

Unit 4	Band f
Applying percentage increases and decreases to amounts	
Foundation 1	

Unit 3	Band e
Convert fractions and decimals to and from percentages	
Foundation 1	

Unit 5	Band g
Finding percentage change from one amount to another	
Foundation 1	

Unit 6	Band h
Reverse percentages	
Page 22	

Unit 8	Band j
Growth and decay	
Higher 2	

Unit 7	Band h
Repeated percentage increase and decrease	
Page 27	

Units 1–5 are assumed knowledge for this book. They are reviewed and extended in the Moving on section on page 21.

Units 1–5 • Moving on

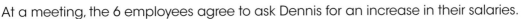

Exam-style

(1) Harry is taking an accountancy course. If he passes he will get a promotion. In his first assignment, Harry gets 36 out of 50. In the next one he gets 56 out of 80.

   a Which is his better score?

   b The last assignment is out of 80. Across all three assignments, he must have scored an average of 75% to pass. What mark will he need on the last assignment?

(2) Dennis owns a small company which employs 6 people.

Dennis earns £60 000 a year. Harry is the works manager and he earns £40 000 a year. Two skilled workers each earn £30 000 a year. Three unskilled workers each earn £20 000.

At a meeting, the 6 employees agree to ask Dennis for an increase in their salaries.

Dennis says that there is only £21 000 to spare.

Harry asks for an increase of 10% for everybody.

Is there enough money for everybody to have a 10% increase in their salaries?

(3) Bill is a sheep farmer. He has 350 female sheep on his farm.

This year each female sheep had on average 2 lambs.

Bill sold 65% of these lambs for £58 each. The selling price of lambs then increased by 3%. Bill sold the rest of his lambs at this increased price.

Work out the total amount that Bill sold his lambs for.

(4) Jodie is taking an accountancy course. If she passes she will get a promotion. In her first assignment, Jodie scores 36 out of 50. In the next assignment she scores 56 out of 80.

   a Which is her better score?

   The last assignment is out of 80. Across all three assignments, she must have scored an average of 75% to pass.

   b What mark will she need on the last assignment?

(5) Amita paid £12 500 for her car 3 years ago. It is now worth £7500.

Sadie paid £9500 for her car 3 years ago. It is now worth £6250.

   a Whose car has depreciated by the lower percentage?

   Both cars are expected to depreciate by 20% next year.

   b How much will they then be worth?

(6) In 2010, Nicole invested £12 000 in a savings account for 3 years.

The investment was compounded each year at a different rate.

The rate of interest for the first year was 2%.

The rate of interest for the second year was 3.5%.

At the end of the third year, Nicole's investment had become £12 858.43.

   a Work out the percentage increase in Nicole's investment after 3 years.

   b Work out the rate of interest paid in the third year.

Higher tier only

Unit 6 • Reverse percentages • Band h

Outside the Maths classroom

Reclaiming VAT

Resources cost £600 including VAT at 20%.

Beth says the VAT is 20% of £600. Why is Beth wrong?

Toolbox

Sometimes you know the value of something and the percentage change but not the original value. Finding the original value involves reverse percentages, as in this example.

A coat costs £45 in a sale. It has been reduced by 10%. What was its original cost?

This percentage bar shows what you know and what you need to find out.

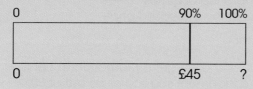 

Alternatively,

90% is £45

1% is $\frac{45}{90} = 0.5$

100% is 0.5×100

$= £50$

The original cost was £50.

Example – When an amount is reduced

The sale price of a pair of designer sunglasses is £96.

a The reduction in the sale is 20%. What percentage of the original price is the sale price?

b Find the original price.

Solution

a The sale price is 80% of the original price.

b 80% is £96 $\boxed{100\% - 20\% = 80\%}$

  1% is $\frac{96}{80} = £1.20$

  100% is 1.2×100

      $= £120$

So the original price was £120.

23

Example – When an amount is increased

A shop sells boots for £56 a pair. The shop makes a profit of 40%.
What price did the shop pay for the boots?

Solution

Cost price = 100%; profit = 40% so the selling price = 140%.

140% is £56

1% is $\frac{56}{140}$ = £0.40

100% is 0.4 × 100

$\qquad$ = £40

so the shop paid £40 for the boots.

Practising skills

(1) A shirt costs £48 which includes VAT at 20%. This means 120% = £48.
Work out the cost of the shirt without VAT.

(2) A tie costs £12 following a reduction of 20%. This means 80% = £12.
Work out the cost of the tie before the reduction.

(3) A lamp costs £27 following a reduction of 10%.
Work out the cost of the lamp before the reduction.

(4) A table costs £138 which includes VAT at 20%.

    a Work out the cost of the table without VAT.   **b** How much VAT was paid?

(5) Work out the original length for each of these.

    a ☐ cm was increased by 30% to give 91 cm.   **b** ☐ m was reduced by 25% to give 96 m.

    c ☐ km was reduced by 14% to give 387 km.   **d** ☐ m was increased by 4% to give 5.2 m.

    e ☐ km was reduced by 38% to give 527 km.

(6) **a** Increase £200 by 15%.

    b An amount was increased by 15% to give £200. What was the original amount?

    c Increase your answer to part **b** by 30%. Is your answer the same as in part **a**? Explain your answer.

Developing fluency

(1) The table shows the sale price and the percentage discount for some items.
Work out the original price of each item.

	Item	Sale price	Discount	Original price
a	Necklace	£63	10%	
b	Watch	£102	15%	
c	Bracelet	£57	5%	
d	Earrings	£12	40%	

2 The table shows the cost of some household bills. Each bill includes VAT at 20%.
Work out the cost without VAT.

	Bill	Cost with VAT	Cost without VAT
a	Telephone	£96	
b	Satellite TV	£21.60	
c	Insurance	£210	
d	Carpet	£1500	

3 The contents of a carton of juice have been reduced by 12%.
The contents are now 792 ml. What was the original content?

4 A nurse worked 52 hours this week. This was an increase of 30% compared to last week.
How many hours did the nurse work last week?

5 Joseph got a reduction of 15% on the cost of his new car. He paid £7990.
What was the original cost?

6 House prices have risen by 3% this year compared to last year.
A house is valued at £185 400 this year. What was its value last year?

7 A jeweller buys a watch and makes 55% profit when he
sells it for £124. How much profit did he make?

8 A photocopier printed 1131 pages this month. This was a reduction of 22% compared to the previous month. How many fewer pages were printed this month compared to last month?

9 Ned travelled 60% more miles in September than he did in August. He travelled 2240 miles in September. What was his total mileage for August and September?

10 Naomi bought a computer for £432, a TV for £270 and a mobile phone for £138. All three items included VAT at 20%. How much VAT did she pay in total?

Problem solving

① Exam-style Ken shops at CashLimited wholesale warehouse where all items are priced without VAT. Ken buys a box of printing paper, 4 ink cartridges and a pack of folders.

A box of printing paper is priced at £11.00; a pack of folders is priced at £9.00 and there is no price on the ink cartridges.

Including VAT, at 20%, Ken pays £84.

Work out the price of an ink cartridge.

② Exam-style Morgan and Rowan buy identical cars. Morgan buys his car from Car Market Sales and Rowan buys his car from Jeff's Autos.

Car Market Sales offers Morgan a 12% reduction on the showroom price for the car. Morgan accepts the offer and buys the car.

At Jeff's Autos, Rowan buys the identical car for £6250.

Morgan pays £86 more than Rowan.

What was the showroom price of the car at Car Market Sales?

③ Exam-style In a sale there is 20% off all items.

Siobhan buys these three items of clothing. The diagram shows the sale prices of two of them.

Siobhan pays €137 for these three items. What was the original price of the shoes?

A

B

€65

C

€32

④ Exam-style Robert buys and sells antique furniture. At an auction, Robert buys a grandfather clock.

As well as the price he bids, he pays an additional 15% commission to the auction house.

He later sells the grandfather clock for £1288 making a 40% profit on what he paid at the auction house.

How much did Robert bid for the clock?

⑤ Exam-style As a result of an economic crisis in 2010, Tony and his wife Sarah have to take a cut in salary.

Tony's salary is reduced by 10%.

Sarah's salary is reduced by 5%.

After the cuts, Tony's salary is £28 800 per annum and Sarah's salary is £42 750 per annum.

Tony needs to know the total percentage cut in the sum of their salaries. Sarah says the total percentage cut is 7.5%, their average reduction.

Show that Sarah is wrong.

Exam-style

Higher tier only

6 Ace Parking owns two car parks, one at Franton and one at Bickles.

Ace Parking wants to increase the capacity of their car parks.

Franton is to increase by 20%.

Bickles is to increase by 25%.

The capacity of the car park in Bickles will be twice that of the car park in Franton.
In total there will be 1800 places to park vehicles.

How many more spaces are there now at Bickles than there are at Franton?

7 Gordon wants to reduce his annual energy bill. Wall insulation reduces annual heating costs by 15%. The cost to install wall insulation for his house is £1620.

After he insulated the walls of his home, Gordon's annual heating cost was £765.

How many years will it take for Gordon to save enough money to cover the cost of installing wall insulation?

8 This article appeared in the local newspaper in the Algarve, Portugal in August 2014.
It went on to say that the rainfall in July 2014 was an increase of 460% on the July average.

> **The wettest July since records began**
>
> With a total rainfall of 5.6 cm, it has been the wettest July since records began. In 2012, just 0.9 cm of rain fell in the month of July.

Compare the rainfall in July 2012 to the average rainfall for the month of July.

Reviewing skills

1 An electricity bill is £126, which includes VAT at 5%.

  a Work out the cost of the bill before VAT was included.

  b How much VAT was paid?

2 Thabo's parents measure his height every birthday. On his 14th birthday his height is 147 cm. His father says 'You grew 5% last year.'

  a How tall was Thabo on his 13th birthday?

  b How much did he grow when he was 13 years old?

3 This year there are 204 registered players in a cricket league. This is a reduction of 15% compared to last year.

  a How many registered players were there last year?

  b What is the reduction in the number of registered players?

4 There is 10% off coats and 25% off shirts in T.C. Clothing. Neil paid £54 for a coat and £48 for a shirt when the offers were on. How much in total did he save?

Unit 7 • Repeated percentage increase/decrease • Band h

Compound Interest

A savings account pays interest at a rate of 2%. John invests £500 for 3 years and Amid invests £1500 for 1 year. Do they have the same amount of money at the end of each of these periods?

Toolbox

A common use of repeated percentage increase is for savings where interest is added to an account and the next year's interest is calculated on the new balance. **This is called compound interest.**

A common use of percentage decrease is for depreciation. Assets such as cars reduce in value each year by a percentage of their value at the start of the year.

It is important to recognise when to use these techniques.

Example – Repeated percentage increase

£2000 is invested at 3.5% interest. Calculate the amount at the end of four years when

a   The interest is not added to the investment

b   The interest is added to the investment.

Solution

a 3.5% of £2000 $= \dfrac{3.5}{100} \times 2000$

$= £70$

This is the interest earned each year.

At the end of four years, the total amount received is the original amount plus four years of interest:

£2000 + 4 × 70 = £2280

b   Each year the investment increases by 3.5% i.e. 103.5% of the investment at the start of that year.

Year 1 103.5% of $2000 = \dfrac{103.5}{100} \times 2000$

$= £2070$

Year 2 103.5% of $2070 = \dfrac{103.5}{100} \times 2070$

$= 2142.45$

Year 3 103.5% of $2142.45 = \dfrac{103.5}{100} \times 2142.45$

$\qquad\qquad\qquad\qquad\qquad = 2217.44$

Year 4 103.5% of $2217.44 = \dfrac{103.5}{100} \times 2217.44$

$\qquad\qquad\qquad\qquad\qquad = £2295.05$

> This can be done in one calculation:
>
> $2000 \times \left(\dfrac{103.5}{100}\right)^4 = £2295.05$

Practising skills

(1) The number A is 6000.

    a A is increased by 10% to give B. What is number B?

    b B is increased by 10% to give C. What is the number C?

    c C is increased by 10% to give D. What is the number D?

    d What is the percentage increase from A to D?

(2) Asaph buys a field for £6000. For each of the next 3 years it increases in value by 10%.

    a What is its value at the end of 3 years?

    b What is the percentage increase in its value since Asaph bought it?

    c Explain why the increase is greater than 30%.

(3) The number P is 5000.

    a P is decreased by 20% to give Q. What is the number Q?

    b Q is decreased by 20% to give R. What is the number R?

    c R is decreased by 20% to give S. What is the number S?

    d What is the percentage change from P to S?

(4) Pepe buys a car for £5000. For each of the next 3 years the car decreases in value by 20%.

    a What is the value of Pepe's car at the end of 3 years?

    b What is the percentage decrease in its value since Pepe bought it?

    c After how many more years is Pepe's car worth less than £2000?
       (It continues to depreciate at 20% per year.)

(5) Match these percentage changes with the decimal multiplier.

% change	Decimal multiplier
20% increase	× 1.5
60% decrease	× 0.88
12% increase	× 1.2
12% decrease	× 0.4
150% increase	× 1.12

Reasoning

Reasoning

6 Start with the number 200.

    a Increase it by 50%.
       Then decrease the answer by 40%.
       Then decrease that answer by 10%.

    b Find the percentage change from 200 to the final answer in part **a**.

    c Work out $200 \times 1.5 \times 0.6 \times 0.9$

    d What do you notice about the answers to parts **a** and **c**? Explain the connection.

Developing fluency

1 Peter invests £500 at 6% per annum.

    a How much interest does Peter receive at the end of the first year?

    b He reinvests the £500 but not the interest. What is his total investment at the end of the first year?

    c His reinvestment earns interest for another year at 6%. How much interest does he receive at the end of the second year?

2 Interest is paid on the following investments but not reinvested.

    a How much interest is received in total on
       i £1000 at 5% p.a. for 2 years

       ii £2000 at 10% p.a. for 5 years

       iii £500 at 3.5% p.a. for 3 years?

    b Now find the interest paid on these investments when the interest is reinvested each year.

3 A riverbank has been colonised by mink. They are an alien species that attacks local wildlife. The river authority traps the mink and removes them. Each year it reduces the number of mink by 60%.

    What percentage of mink remain after

    a 1 year   **b** 2 years   **c** 3 years   **d** 4 years   **e** 5 years?

4 Hannah buys her first car for £3000.

    a After she has owned it for a year, she is told that its value has depreciated by 20%.
       i How much is the car worth after 1 year?

       ii How much value has the car lost in the first year?

    b The rate of depreciation continues at 20% per year from the start of the second year.
       i Show that after two years the car is worth £1920.

       ii How long will it be before Hannah's car is worth less than £500?

Exam-style

5 One Monday, 100 people have a highly infectious disease.
    The number of people with the disease increases by 20% each day.
    How many have the disease the following Monday?

6 In 2002, Mike bought a house for £87 000. The house appreciated in value by 6% per year from the start of the year.

   a How much was the house worth in 2003?

   b How much was the house worth in 2004?

   c In which year did the value of the house become greater than £100 000?

7 **'The world is now losing its tropical forest at the rate of 7% per year.'**

   a If this trend continues, what percentage of the existing tropical forest will be left in 5 years' time?

   b Show that 10 years from now, just under half of the tropical forest will have disappeared.

   c How much tropical forest will remain after 50 years?

   d How much tropical forest will remain after 100 years?
   You may find a spreadsheet useful.

8 Look at this information about compound interest rates.

Allied Avon savings accounts compound interest rates	
Standard saver	6% p.a.
Junior saver	7.5% p.a.
Super saver	11% p.a.

Find the amount and the compound interest paid on each of the following.

   a £580 invested for 3 years in a standard savings account.

   b £1650 invested for 4 years in a junior savings account.

   c £24 000 invested for 10 years in a super savings account.

9 Nathan increases the number of kilometres he runs each day by 25%. He went running on Monday, Tuesday and Wednesday. On Wednesday he ran 18.75 km. How far did he run on the previous two days?

Problem solving

1 Keith and Mary organised a closing-down sale in their clothes shop. They reduced the prices of all the items in the shop by 30%. Two weeks before the end of the sale, Keith reduced the prices by a further 20%.

Mary said that all the prices had then been reduced by 50%. Keith said that all the prices had been reduced by over 50%.

Who was right?

2 In 2012, the population of a country is 36 million. If the population decreases at an annual rate of 2.5%.

   a What was the population in 2010?

   b What will the population be in 2015?
   Write your answers to the nearest thousand.

③ In 2010, the total number of crimes recorded in the town of Blitston was 1250. 40% of these crimes were robberies.

In 2011, the number of robberies recorded decreased by 8%. In 2012, the number of robberies recorded increased by a further 10% on the numbers in 2011. In 2013, there were 30 more robberies recorded in Blitston than in 2011.

The Chief of Police in Blitston has to give details about the robberies committed in 2013. What will she be able to say about the percentage change in the number of robberies committed in 2013 in Blitston, compared with the previous year?

④ In 2013, a young footballer playing in the Premier League was earning £30000 per week. At the end of 2013, he signed a new 2-year contract, giving him an increase of 25% in the first year and a further increase of 30% in the second year.

He tells his mum that by the end of 2015, he will have earned over £4 million in these two years. Is he correct?

⑤ Dan wants to invest £5000 for 3 years in the same bank.

At the end of 3 years, Dan wants to have as much money as possible.

Which bank should Dan invest his £5000 in?

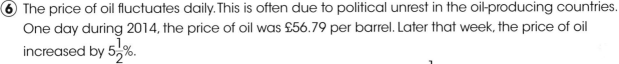

The International Bank
Compound interest
4.5% for the first year
1% for each extra year

The Friendly Bank
Compound interest
5.8% for the first year
0.5% for each extra year

⑥ The price of oil fluctuates daily. This is often due to political unrest in the oil-producing countries. One day during 2014, the price of oil was £56.79 per barrel. Later that week, the price of oil increased by $5\frac{1}{2}$%.

During the following week, after the price of oil had decreased by $5\frac{1}{2}$%, a newspaper headline read 'The price of oil is back to what it was last week.'

Explain why this headline is incorrect.

⑦ Miguel owns a Spanish villa with a swimming pool. On Monday, the depth of the swimming pool was 1.5m. As a result of the hot weather, the depth decreased each day for 4 days, by 1.5% of the depth on the previous day.

On Friday, Miguel had to refill the pool to a depth of 1.5m. The surface area of the water in the pool is 200m².

Work out the amount of water that Miguel had to use to fill the pool.

⑧ Tina invests £1500 in a bank account for 4 years. The bank pays compound interest at an annual rate of 2.5% for the first year and 1.5% for the next 3 years.

Andy also invests £1500 in a bank account for 4 years. Andy's is a variable rate compound interest account. The interest is 2% for the first year, 1.8% for the second year and 1.7% for the third and fourth years.

Who has made the better investment?

9 Jodie buys a painting for £800. The painting increases in value by 12% in the first year and then by a further 10% in the second year.

Jodie says that after two years, the value of the painting has increased by 22%.

Is she right?

10 Leonie invests £800 at compound interest at 8% p.a. The interest is added to the balance each year.

a Copy and complete this table.

Year	Principal	Interest	Amount at end of year
1	£800	£64	£864 ←
2	£864 ←		
3			

Use this amount as the next principal.

Amount from year before.

b The amount, £A, can also be calculated by using the formula

$$A = P\left(1 + \frac{R}{100}\right)^T$$

Use the formula with $P = 800$, $R = 8$ and $T = 1, 2$ and 3 to check your answers to part **a**.

c Explain why the formula works.

d Use the formula to find the final amount in these cases.

  i £900 invested for 5 years at 7.5% p.a. compound interest.

  ii £650 invested for 4 years at 3.9% p.a. compound interest.

  iii £110 invested for 18 months at 5.4% p.a. compound interest.

Reviewing skills

1 Compare the simple interest on each of these investments, with the compound interest when the interest is added at the end of each year.

  a £16 500 invested at 8% p.a. for 4 years.

  b £24 000 invested at 12% p.a. for 10 years.

2 Margaret buys a car for £8000.

  a A year later its value has depreciated by 15%. What is its value now?

  b In each of the next two years its value depreciates by 10%. What is its value 3 years after Margaret buys it?

3 Dimitri weighs 20 stones. He wants to lose 3 stones in the next three months. He sees the following advertisement for a diet plan.

Using this diet plan, will Dimitri reach his target weight in 3 months?

Special Diet Plan Formula

Lose 6% of body weight in ONE month and 4% of body weight in each subsequent month.

Strand 6 Ratio and proportion

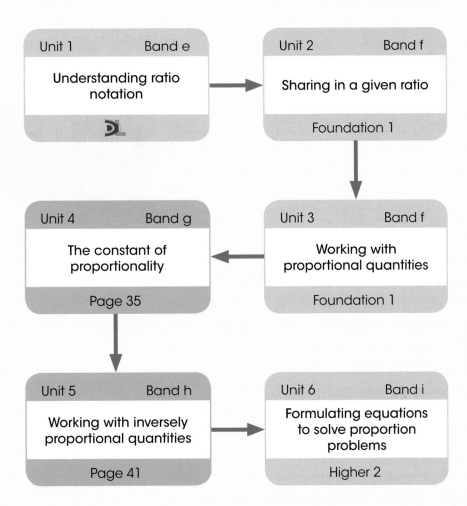

Unit 1 Band e	Unit 2 Band f
Understanding ratio notation	Sharing in a given ratio
	Foundation 1

Unit 4 Band g	Unit 3 Band f
The constant of proportionality	Working with proportional quantities
Page 35	Foundation 1

Unit 5 Band h	Unit 6 Band i
Working with inversely proportional quantities	Formulating equations to solve proportion problems
Page 41	Higher 2

Units 1–3 are assumed knowledge for this book. They are reviewed and extended in the Moving on section on page 34.

Units 1–3 • Moving on

1 Cheese snacks are sold in two sizes of box.
While shopping, Alan saw this offer.

Alan said that the offer was just a gimmick and
that the larger box was the better buy.

Show that Alan is right.

2 Marc sees a flash of lightning and starts counting.

He counts 8 seconds before hearing the thunder.

The speed of sound is 340.29 metres per second.

Two minutes later, Marc counts 4 seconds between seeing another flash of lightning and hearing the thunder.

The thunderstorm is moving directly towards Marc.

At what speed is the thunderstorm moving?

3 There are 32 500 seats in a football stadium. The football club allocates tickets between the home and away team in the ratio 3 : 1.

a How many tickets does each team receive?

For one match, the away team returns half its tickets, which the home team then sells.

b In what ratio are the tickets sold this time?

4 Sunita drives 148 miles on 17 litres of petrol to reach her holiday destination.
While she is there, she travels a further 58 miles.
On the way home she visits her friend, which means she needs to travel an extra 53 miles.
Sunita has budgeted for 50 litres of petrol.

a Will she be under or over her budget?

b Use you answer to part **a** to calculate by how much she will be under or over budget.

5 A new TV channel broadcasts chat shows, reality shows and soaps. They are committed to broadcasting these in the ratio 4 : 3 : 2.
The channel is currently on air for only 12 hours a day.

a How many hours of each type of programme do they broadcast?

b Next month, they plan to increase Saturday broadcasting to 18 hours a day. How many extra minutes of each programme type will they have to broadcast?

6 A football club allocates tickets between the home and away team in the ratio 3 : 1.
There are 32 500 seats in the stadium.

a How many tickets does each team receive?

b For one match, the away team returns half its tickets, which the home team sells. In what ratio are the tickets sold?

Unit 4 · The constant of proportionality · Band g

Outside the Maths classroom

Converting money

Currency conversion is easy if you use a graph.

Why is the graph a straight line?

Toolbox

A **conversion graph** is a way of showing how one value is related to another.

It allows you to convert between two units easily.

Direct proportion means there is a connection between two **variables**: as one variable increases, the other increases at the same rate.

For example, if one variable is trebled, the other will also be trebled.

The sign $\propto$ means 'is proportional to' and can be used to help create a formula.

If $a \propto b$ then $a = kb$ where k is called the **constant of proportionality** so $k = a \div b$.

Example – Creating a formula

In physics, the current (I) in an electric circuit is directly proportional to the voltage (V) when the resistance (R) is constant.

In one circuit, when $I = 0.2$, $V = 10$.

a Write a formula connecting I and V.

b Find I when $V = 100$.

Solution

a $I \propto V$ so

$$I = kV \quad \longleftarrow \boxed{k \text{ is the constant of proportionality.}}$$

When $I = 0.2$, $V = 10$

$$0.2 = k \times 10$$
$$k = 0.2 \div 10$$
$$k = 0.02$$

So the formula is

$$I = 0.02V$$

b When $V = 100$,

$$I = 0.02V$$
$$I = 0.02 \times 100$$
$$I = 2$$

Example – Drawing a conversion graph

One day, £6 is worth the same as €9.

a Draw a conversion graph between pounds (£) and euros (€).

b An ice-cream costs £1.40.

How much is this in euros?

Solution

a You need two points to plot the graph. However it is good practice to use at least one more point as a check.

Make a table.

£	6	0	3
€	9	0	4.5

This is the check point.

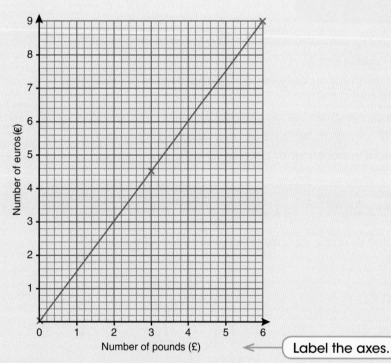

Label the axes.

b Reading from the graph, £1.40 = €2.10.

Practising skills

① **a** Use the graph to complete the table of values.

x	1		2.5	
y		12		7

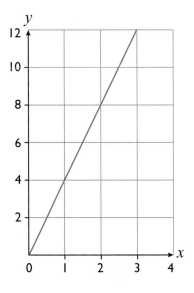

b Find the value of k in the equation $y = kx$ connecting y and x.

c Complete these statements

   i The straight-line graph shows that y is directly ⬚ to x.

   ii k is called the ⬚ of ⬚.

② Write down a formula involving a constant k for each of these.

   a m is directly proportional to n

   b $y \propto x$

   c A is directly proportional to B

   d P varies as Q

   e $T \propto d$

   f C is directly proportional to d

③ y is proportional to x. When $x = 2$, $y = 10$.

> People often shorten statements such as 'y is directly proportional to x' to just 'y is proportional to x'.

   a Write down the value of y when

     i $x = 4$

     ii $x = 6$

     iii $x = 10$

     iv $x = 1$

   b Write down the constant of proportionality.

   c Write down a formula connecting y and x.

④ D is proportional to w. When $w = 4$, $D = 12$.

   a Write down the value of D when

     i $w = 8$

     ii $w = 12$

     iii $w = 1$

     iv $w = \dfrac{1}{3}$

   b Write down the constant of proportionality.

   c Write down a formula connecting D and w.

⑤ V is proportional to n.

   a Write down a formula involving the constant k.

When $n = 6$, $V = 3$.

   b Find the value of k.

   c Find the value of V when $n = 2$.

⑥ y is proportional to x.

   a Write down a formula connecting y and x.

When $x = 3$, $y = 30$.

   b Find the value of y when $x = 5$.

   c Find the value of x when $y = 12$.

⑦ C is proportional to d.

   a Write down a formula connecting C and d.

When $d = 4$, $c = 10$.

   b Find the value of C when $d = 6$.

   c Find the value of d when $C = 25$.

⑧ Write down the odd one out in each of these.

   a | $P = 3L$ | $P = 15$ when $L = 5$ | $P = 27$ when $L = 7$ | P is directly proportional to L | $P \propto L$ |

   b | $A = 4B$ | $A \propto B$ | $A = 12$ when $B = 2$ | A varies as B | $A = 3$ when $B = 0.5$ |

   c | $M \propto N$ | $M = 8$ when $N = 4$ | $M = 4$ when $N = 8$ | M is proportional to N | $M = 0.5N$ |

Developing fluency

① Decide if the following statements are true or false.

   a $V \propto d$ means V is proportional to d

   b y is proportional to x means x is proportional to y

   c $T = 2n$ is the same as $n = 2T$

② M is proportional to e.

$M = 2$ when $e = 8$.

Find the value of e when $M = 1.5$.

③ x and y are variables and are directly proportional to each other. Blaise and Bobby are given data to work out the formula connecting x and y. Blaise works it out to be $y = 2x$. Bobby works it out to be $x = \frac{1}{2}y$.

Can they both be correct? Explain your answer.

④ V is proportional to x. Copy and complete the table of values.

x	8	12	
V	10		45

Reasoning

⑤ T is proportional to n. There is one error in the table of values. What is it?

n	14	6	10
T	60	27	45

Exam-style

⑥ Seth wants to know if h and t are proportional. He draws a table for some values of h and t.

h	51	96	105
t	34	64	70

Are h and t proportional? Explain how you know.

Problem solving

Exam-style

① Tracey sells paintings in an art exhibition.

The graph shows the profit, £p, that she makes when she sells n paintings.

a Write down a formula connecting p and n.

b Tracey has just booked a holiday costing £3500. How many paintings does she need to sell to pay for the holiday?

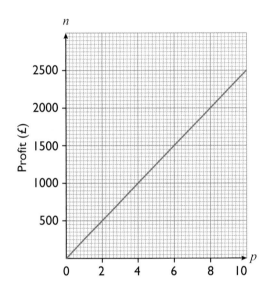

Exam-style

② A ship travels s kilometres in t hours.

s is directly proportional to t.

a What does this tell you about the movement of the ship?

After 30 minutes, the ship has travelled 10 km.

b Find the constant of proportionality.

c How far has the ship travelled after 75 minutes?

Exam-style

③ Anwar draws a number of stars. They are all the same shape but different sizes. He measures the diameter, d cm, and perimeter, p cm, of each star.

The table shows some of his results.

Diameter (d cm)	5	10	15
Circumference (c cm)	16.5	33	49.5

a Find a formula for c in terms of d.

b What is the value of the constant of proportionality?

c What is the perimeter of a star with diameter 30 cm?

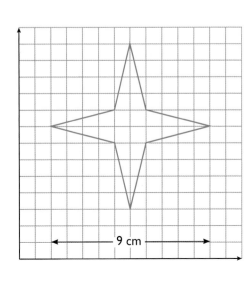

9 cm

39

Exam-style

④ Michaela wants to paint the walls in her bedroom.

Their area is $75\,\text{m}^2$. The paint costs £6.80 a litre and 2 litres of paint cover $30\,\text{m}^2$.

Write down a formula connecting the area of wall, $A\,\text{m}^2$, and the number of litres of paint needed, L. Use it to work out the cost of painting the walls in Michaela's bedroom.

Exam-style

⑤ Clear plastic bottles can be recycled. The value, £V, of the bottles is in direct proportion to their mass, $m\,\text{g}$. 1 tonne of clear plastic has a value of £260.

Ann collects clear plastic bottles, weighing $40\,\text{g}$ each. She wants to buy a game for her computer. The cost of the game is £25.99.

How many bottles does Ann need to collect to buy this game?

Reviewing skills

① t is proportional to d.

When $d = 5$, $t = 35$

   a Find the value of t when

      i $d = 10$

      ii $d = 15$

      iii $d = 20$.

   b Find the constant of proportionality.

   c Write down the formula connecting t and d.

② y is proportional to x.

   a Write down a formula connecting y and x.

When $x = 4$, $y = 24$.

   b Find the value of y when $x = 7$.

   c Find the value of x when $y = 30$.

③ s is directly proportional to t. The constant of proportionality is 70.

Copy and complete this table.

s		210	35		
t	1			8	$\frac{1}{10}$

Unit 5 • Working with inversely proportional quantities • Band h

Outside the Maths classroom

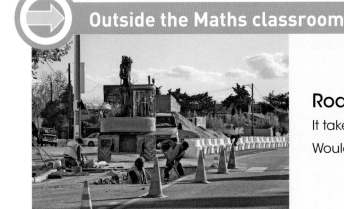

Road works

It takes 3 men 4 hours to repair this road.

Would 6 men take half the time?

Toolbox

Inverse proportion means there is a connection between two **variables**: as one variable **increases**, the other **decreases** by the same proportion.

For example, if one variable is doubled, the other will be halved.

The sign $\propto$ means 'is proportional to'. Inverse proportion is represented using the reciprocal. Where a and b are inversely proportional, then ab is a constant.

$a \propto \dfrac{1}{b}$ means a is inversely proportional to b.

So $ab = k$ where k is a constant.

Example – Solving problems involving inverse proportion

A company is testing four electric cars on a journey from Edinburgh to London.

All the cars travel the same route.

a One car travels for 6 hours at an average speed of 60 miles per hour.
   How long is the route from Edinburgh to London?

b The second car travels at an average speed of 30 miles per hour.
   How long does the journey take this car?

A formula connecting the speed (s) and the time (t) taken for this journey is

$$st = 360$$

c The third car took 9 hours to complete the journey.
   Use the formula to find its average speed.

d The fourth car had an average speed of 50 miles per hour.
   Use the formula to find the time taken.

Solution

a In 1 hour the car travels 60 miles so, in 6 hours the car travels $60 \times 6 = 360$ miles.
The route from Edinburgh to London is 360 miles.

b At 30 mph the journey takes $360 \div 30 = 12$ hours.
Notice that this is a case of inverse proportion.
Travelling at half the speed takes twice as long. $\longleftarrow$ | 2×6 hours = 12 hours |

c $st = 360$
$s \times 9 = 360$ $\longleftarrow$ | The car takes 9 hours. |
$\qquad s = 360 \div 9$ $\longleftarrow$ | Dividing both sides by 9. |
$\qquad s = 40$

The third car travelled at an average speed of 40 miles per hour.

d $st = 360$
$50 \times t = 360$ $\longleftarrow$ | Average speed was 50 mph. |
$\qquad t = 360 \div 50$ $\longleftarrow$ | Dividing both sides by 50. |
$\qquad t = 7.2$

0.2 hours $= 0.2 \times 60 = 12$ minutes
The fourth car takes 7 hours 12 minutes to complete the journey.

Example – Looking for inversely proportional relationships

The table shows values for two variables, c and d.

c	8	12	24
d	30	20	10

Martin thinks that $c \propto \dfrac{1}{d}$.

Is Martin correct?
Explain how you know.

Solution

If c and d are inversely proportional, then $cd = k$. $\longleftarrow$ | This is the same as $c = k \times \dfrac{1}{d}$ or $d = k \times \dfrac{1}{c}$ |

$\quad 8 \times 30 = 240 \qquad 12 \times 20 = 240 \qquad 24 \times 10 = 240$

In each case the answer is the same, 240, so c and d are indeed inversely proportional.

Practising skills

1 Look at this curve. One of the points marked on it is (4, 3).

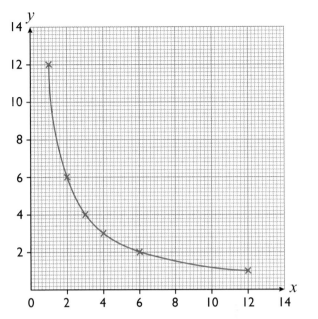

  a Show that at (4, 3), $y = \dfrac{12}{x}$.

  b Five other points are marked on the curve. Show that at each of these $y = \dfrac{12}{x}$.

  c Say whether each of the following equations is a rearrangement of $y = \dfrac{12}{x}$.

   i $xy = 12$ ii $x + y = 12$

   iii $y - x = 12$ iv $x = \dfrac{12}{y}$

  d Say whether each of the following statements is true or false.

   i y is directly proportional to x.

   ii y is inversely proportional to x.

   iii y is directly proportional to $\dfrac{1}{x}$.

   iv x is inversely proportional to y.

2 Write down a formula involving the constant k for each of the following.

  a y is proportional to x.

  b y is inversely proportional to m.

  c T varies as d.

  d M varies inversely as t.

  e $W \propto \dfrac{1}{x}$

  f $C \propto d$

3 Here are some formulae. The letter k is a constant. The rest of the letters used are variables.

$$A = kd \quad M = \frac{k}{n} \quad Ct = k \quad \frac{w}{r} = k$$

  a Write down the formulae that show direct proportion.

  b Write down the formulae that show inverse proportion.

4 y is inversely proportional to x.

  a Write down a formula connecting y and x, involving the constant k.

When $x = 2$, $y = 5$.

  b Work out the value of k.

  c Find the value of y when

   i $x = 2$

   ii $x = 10$.

43

⑤ C is inversely proportional to d.

    a Write down a formula connecting c and d, involving the constant k.

    When $d = 5$, $c = 5$.

    b Work out the value of k.

    c Write down the value of c when

       i $d = 4$ **ii** $d = \dfrac{1}{4}$ **iii** $d = 100$ **iv** $d = \dfrac{1}{100}$

    d Write down the value of d when

       i $c = 25$ **ii** $c = \dfrac{1}{25}$ **iii** $c = 0.1$ **iv** $c = 10$

⑥ M is inversely proportional to t.

    $M = 8$ when $t = 3$.

    a Find a formula connecting M and t.

    b Use your formula to find the value of M when $t = 10$.

    c Use your formula to find the value of t when $M = 6$.

⑦ E is inversely proportional to h.

    $E = 12$ when $h = 3$.

    a Write down a formula connecting E and h.

    b Find the value of E when $h = 12$.

    c Find the value of h when $E = 150$.

Developing fluency

① Say whether these statements are true or false.

    a y is inversely proportional to x means $y \propto \dfrac{1}{x}$.

    b m is inversely proportional to d means $m = kd$, where k is a constant.

    c T is inversely proportional to C means as T increases, C also increases at the same rate.

    d W is inversely proportional to g means $W = \dfrac{k}{g}$, where k is a constant.

    e P is inversely proportional to Q means $PQ = k$, where k is a constant.

② y is inversely proportional to x.

    $y = 12$ when $x = 3$.

    a Write down a formula connecting y and d.

    b Find the value of y when $x = 4$.

    c Is it possible for x and y to have the same value?

③ In a television quiz show there is a fixed amount of prize money.

    At the start there are 6 competitors. Those who answer too many questions wrong leave the show. The prize money is shared equally among those left at the end.

    If 3 people are left at the end, they each get £8000.

    a How much do the winners get if there are only 2 people left at the end?

    b Write down a formula connecting the number of winners, n, and the amount they win, £w.

    c The producer decides to start with 8 competitors rather than 6, but with the same prize money. How does this affect the formula you found in part **b**?

Reasoning

④ In an electrical circuit the current, I amps, is inversely proportional to the resistance, R ohms.
When $R = 24$, $I = 0.5$.

   a Write down a formula connecting I and R.

   b Find the value of I when $R = 6$.

   c Find the value of R when $I = 0.1$.

⑤ A group of m people share the chocolates in a box. Each person gets n chocolates.

   a Copy and complete this table showing some possible values of m and n.

m	6		16
n	8	2	

   b Write down a formula connecting m and n.

   c Describe the relationship between m and n in words.

⑥ C is inversely proportional to m. There is one error in the table of values. What is it?

C	8	400	10
M	40	0.6	32

⑦ Levi thinks h and d are directly proportional. Luke thinks h and d are inversely proportional.
Who is correct? Explain your answer.

h	4	0.8	32
d	10	2	80

⑧ y is directly proportional to x. $y = 40$ when $x = 5$.
x is inversely proportional to z. $z = 2$ when $x = 5$.
Find the value of y when $z = 40$.

Problem solving

① A farmer needs to build a rectangular fence around part of his field.
The length is l metres and the width is w metres.
The fenced-off section needs to have an area of 100 square metres.

   a Make a table of some possible values for l and w.

   b What is the minimum length of fencing needed?

② Look at this table of values, for the curve $y = \dfrac{10}{x}$.

x	1	2	2.5	4	5	10
y	10					

   a Copy and complete the table.

   b Draw the graph, using equal scales for both x and y.

   c What are the values of y when

      i $x = 0.5$ **ii** $x = 0.1$?

   d Describe the shape of the graph.

   e Do all inverse proportion graphs look like this?

Exam-style

Higher tier only

③ Harry is planning to type up his university thesis. The number of pages in the thesis is inversely proportional to the number of characters on each page.

If he types 2000 characters to a page, the thesis will be exactly 186 pages in length.

Harry would like his thesis to be no more than 120 pages. How many characters to a page must Harry type to meet this target?

④ Brampton Council has set aside a fixed sum of money to help people who are having great difficulty paying their heating bills. They will each receive a grant.

Last year 300 people needed a grant and they each received £90.

a How much money has Brampton council set aside?

b Write down a formula for the amount of the grant each person receives, £g, when the money is shared among n people.

c This year 450 people need help with their heating bills. How much grant does each person get?

⑤ The table gives the constant speeds v mph and times t hours of a journey, using different means of transport.

	Car	Bus	Cycle
Speed v mph	52.5	35	14
Time t hours	4	6	15

a Write down a formula connecting v and t.

b Describe how v varies with t.

c What can you say about this journey?

d Delia walks the journey at $3\frac{1}{2}$ mph. How long does she take?

Reviewing skills

① E is inversely proportional to T.

   a Write down a formula connecting E and T, involving the constant k.

  When $T = 2.5$, $E = 4$.

   b Work out the value of k.

   c Work out the value of E when $T = 2$.

   d Work out the value of T when $E = 20$.

② v is inversely proportional to t.

  When $t = 4$, $v = 60$.

   a Find a formula connecting v and t.

   b Use your formula to find the value of v when $t = 3$.

   c Use your formula to find the value of t when $v = 50$.

③ Scott is planning a journey between two places in the Antarctic. It will be slow going but he doesn't know how slow. He says 'It will take me 600 hours if I travel at $\frac{1}{2}$ a kilometre per hour.'

   a Write down a formula that gives Scott's journey time, t hours, when his speed is v kilometres per hour.

   b Use your formula to find how long Scott will take if his speed is

     i 2 km per hour

     ii $\frac{3}{4}$ km per hour.

   c The journey actually takes Scott 200 hours. How fast does he travel?

Strand 7 Number properties

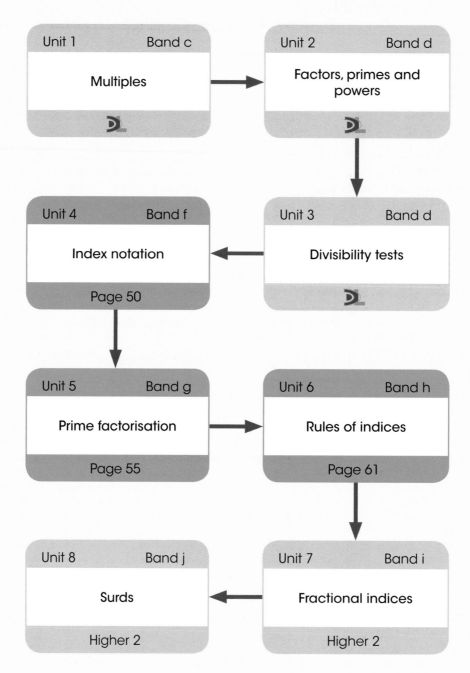

Unit 1	Band c
Multiples	

Unit 2	Band d
Factors, primes and powers	

Unit 4	Band f
Index notation	
Page 50	

Unit 3	Band d
Divisibility tests	

Unit 5	Band g
Prime factorisation	
Page 55	

Unit 6	Band h
Rules of indices	
Page 61	

Unit 8	Band j
Surds	
Higher 2	

Unit 7	Band i
Fractional indices	
Higher 2	

Units 1–3 are assumed knowledge for this book. They are reviewed and extended in the Moving on section on page 49.

7 Units 1–3 • Moving on

1. The diagram shows a regular pentagon and a regular hexagon.

   Corner A of the pentagon and corner B of the hexagon are also shown.

   A and B are at opposite ends of a start line.

   Every second the pentagon rotates by 72° anticlockwise about its centre.

   Every second the hexagon rotates by 60° anticlockwise about its centre.

   The two polygons start at the same time.

   After how many seconds will both A and B be at opposite ends of the start line again?

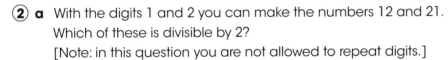

2. **a** With the digits 1 and 2 you can make the numbers 12 and 21.

   Which of these is divisible by 2?

   [Note: in this question you are not allowed to repeat digits.]

   b With the digits 1, 2 and 3 you can make a 3-digit number that is divisible by 3.

   Make as many as you can.

   c How many 4-digit numbers can you find that use the digits 1, 2, 3, 4 and are divisible by 4?

   d What must happen if you want a 5-digit number that uses 1, 2, 3, 4, 5 that is divisible by 5?

   e What must happen if you want a 6-digit number that uses 1, 2, 3, 4, 5 and 6 that is divisible by 6?

3. What is the smallest number that is divisible by all of the numbers from 1 up to 10?

4. **a** Evaluate these powers of 2.

$2^1 = 2$	$2^2 =$	$2^3 =$	$2^4 =$	$2^5 =$
$2^6 =$	$2^7 =$	$2^8 =$	$2^9 =$	$2^{10} =$

   b Calculate the square root of each of your answers in part **a**.

   Which ones have integers (whole numbers) as their answers?

   c Now calculate the cube root of each of your answers in part **a**.

   Which of these have integers as their answers?

   d Can you predict which ones will have integers for answers if you take the fourth root?

   What about the fifth root?

   e Find a number that you could square root, cube root or take the fourth root of and always get a whole number as the answer.

   f Can you find an odd number such that you could take the square, cube and fourth roots of it and always get a whole number?

Unit 4 • Index notation • Band f

Growth patterns

Processing power grows very quickly as technology advances.

How can you describe its growth mathematically?

⬇ **Toolbox**

Repeated multiplications can be written using index notation like this:

- $5 \times 5 \times 5 = 5^3 = 125$.
- $3 \times 3 \times 3 \times 3 \times 3 = 3^5 = 243$.

Numbers written using index notation can be multiplied and divided easily.

To **multiply numbers** written using index notation,

$$3^5 \times 3^4$$
$$= (3 \times 3 \times 3 \times 3 \times 3) \times (3 \times 3 \times 3 \times 3)$$
$$= 3^9 \longleftarrow \boxed{\text{The powers have been added } 5 + 4 = 9.}$$

To **divide numbers** written using index notation,

$$3^5 \div 3^4$$

$$(3 \times 3 \times 3 \times 3 \times 3) \div (3 \times 3 \times 3 \times 3) = \frac{3 \times \not{3} \times \not{3} \times \not{3} \times \not{3}}{\not{3} \times \not{3} \times \not{3} \times \not{3}}$$

$$= 3^1 \longleftarrow \boxed{\text{The powers have been subtracted } 5 - 4 = 1.}$$

$$= 3 \longleftarrow \boxed{\text{Notice that } 3^1 = 3.}$$

Using brackets with index notation means that the powers are multiplied.

$$(3^5)^4 = 3^5 \times 3^5 \times 3^5 \times 3^5$$

$$= (3 \times 3 \times 3 \times 3 \times 3) \times (3 \times 3 \times 3 \times 3 \times 3) \times (3 \times 3 \times 3 \times 3 \times 3) \times (3 \times 3 \times 3 \times 3 \times 3)$$

$$= 3^{20} \longleftarrow \boxed{\text{4 lots of 5 is 20}}$$

Example – Equivalent amounts

Match these cards into pairs of the same value.

4×4^3	$4^9 \div 4^2$
$4^9 \div 4^3$	$4^5 \times 4^2$
$(4^2)^3$	$(4^2)^2$

Solution

Simplify each amount.

$$4 \times 4^3 = 4 \times 4 \times 4 \times 4$$
$$= 4^4$$
$$4^9 \div 4^3 = \frac{\cancel{4} \times \cancel{4} \times \cancel{4} \times 4 \times 4 \times 4 \times 4 \times 4 \times 4}{\cancel{4} \times \cancel{4} \times \cancel{4}}$$
$$= 4^6$$
$$(4^2)^3 = (4 \times 4) \times (4 \times 4) \times (4 \times 4)$$
$$= 4^6$$
$$4^9 \div 4^2 = \frac{\cancel{4} \times \cancel{4} \times 4 \times 4 \times 4 \times 4 \times 4 \times 4 \times 4}{\cancel{4} \times \cancel{4}}$$
$$= 4^7$$
$$4^5 \times 4^2 = (4 \times 4 \times 4 \times 4 \times 4) \times (4 \times 4)$$
$$= 4^7$$
$$(4^2)^2 = (4 \times 4) \times (4 \times 4)$$
$$= 4^4$$
So $4 \times 4^3 = (4^2)^2$
$$4^9 \div 4^3 = (4^2)^3$$
$$4^9 \div 4^2 = 4^5 \times 4^2$$

Practising skills

(1) Write each of these as a power of 3.

   a 3×3 **b** $3 \times 3 \times 3 \times 3 \times 3$

   c $3 \times 3 \times 3 \times 3$ **d** $3 \times 3 \times 3 \times 3 \times 3 \times 3 \times 3$

(2) Write each of these in index form.

   a $5 \times 5 \times 5$ **b** $2 \times 2 \times 2 \times 2 \times 2 \times 2$ **c** $2 \times 5 \times 2 \times 5$

   d $7 \times 7 \times 7 \times 7 \times 7$ **e** $11 \times 11 \times 11 \times 17 \times 17$ **f** $3 \times 3 \times 3 \times 3 \times 3 \times 3 \times 3 \times 3$

   g $2 \times 2 \times 2 \times 2 \times 2 \times 19$ **h** $5 \times 5 \times 7 \times 5 \times 7 \times 7$

(3) Use a calculator to work out the value of these.

   a 5^3 **b** 2^{10} **c** 7^4 **d** 1^{30}

   e 3^6 **f** 6^5 **g** 4.5^2 **h** 8^7

   i 29^1 **j** 15^4 **k** 2^{16} **l** $(-6)^4$

④ Write each of these as a single power of 2.

a $2^2 \times 2^2$ **b** 16 **c** 2×8 **d** 64

e $2^3 \times 2^4 \times 2$ **f** $2 \times 2 \times 2 \div 2$ **g** $2^3 \div 2$ **h** $2 \times 8 \times 16$

⑤ Write each of these as a single power of 3.

a $3^{10} \div 3^2$ **b** $3^7 \div 3^4$ **c** $3^6 \div 3$

d $3^9 \div 3^3$ **e** $3^8 \div 3^2$ **f** $3^{11} \div 3^5$

g $3^{10} \div 3$ **h** $\dfrac{3^6}{3^2}$ **i** $\dfrac{3^9}{3^4}$

⑥ Write each of these as a single power of 5.

a $(5^3)^2$ **b** $(5^2)^4$ **c** $(5^6)^2$

d $(5^4)^3$ **e** $(5^6)^6$ **f** $(5^7)^3$

g $(5^5)^4$ **h** $(5^2)^9$ **i** $(5^8)^4$

Developing fluency

① Write down the equal pairs in this list.

2^{10} 8^3 9^3 2^9 4^5 3^6

② **a** How much greater is 2^6 than 6^2?

b How much smaller is 5^3 than 5^4?

c What is the sum of 2^8 and 3^4?

d What is the product of 6^3 and 1^{10}?

③ Write these in order of size, starting with the smallest.

4^4 7^3 2^9 43×6 3^5

④ Work out the value of these. Give your answers as ordinary numbers.

a $3^2 + 3$ **b** $5^3 - 5$ **c** 4×4^2 **d** $10^3 - 10$

e $7^2 \div 7$ **f** $2^3 + 3^2$ **g** $2^3 \times 3^2$ **h** $2^3 - 3^2$

⑤ Write each of these in index form.

a $2 \times 2 \times 7 \times 7 \times 7$ **b** $6 \times 5 \times 6 \times 6$

c $3 \times 5 \times 3 \times 5 \times 5 \times 5$ **d** $2 \times 3 \times 3 \times 2 \times 3 \times 2 \times 2$

e $7 \times 6 \times 6 \times 2 \times 7 \times 6$ **f** $5 \times 3 \times 7 \times 3 \times 5 \times 7 \times 5$

⑥ Write each of these as a single power of 2.

a $2^3 \times 2^4$ **b** $2^8 \div 2^4$ **c** $(2^4)^2$ **d** $(2^5)^3$

e 2×2^9 **f** $2^{12} \div 2^3$ **g** $\dfrac{2^{10}}{2^2}$ **h** $2^3 \times 2 \times 2^4$

⑦ Write each of these as a single power of 2.

a $\dfrac{2^4 \times 2^5}{2^2}$ **b** $\dfrac{(2^4)^3}{2^3}$ **c** $\dfrac{2^{11} \div 2^3}{2^4}$ **d** $\dfrac{2^{15}}{2^3 \times 2^4}$

e $\dfrac{2^6 \times 2^8}{(2^2)^2}$ **f** $\dfrac{2^9 \times 2^6}{2^5 \div 2^3}$ **g** $\dfrac{2^{10} \div 2^2}{2^7 \div 2^4}$ **h** $\dfrac{2 \times 2^4}{2^2 \times 2^2}$

8 Find the missing numbers.

a $3^4 \times 3^{\square} = 3^{10}$ **b** $7^6 \div 7^{\square} = 7^3$ **c** $(5^{\square})^2 = 5^{12}$ **d** $2^6 = 2^{\square} \div 2$

9 In the men's singles at Wimbledon, the champion has to win 7 matches. How many men play in the first round?

Problem solving

1 The thickness of an A4 sheet of paper is 0.1 mm.

Bill cuts an A4 sheet of paper in half and places the two halves on top of each other. He then cuts the two halves in half and places these two halves on top of each other. He repeats this a further 4 times.

a Work out the height of the pile of paper formed.

b Explain why it would be very difficult for Bill to do this a further 10 times.

2 Daniel is a free-range pig farmer. The diagram shows his field. Its shape is a trapezium.

Daniel gives each pig an area of $2 \times 5^3 \, \text{m}^2$ of land. Work out the greatest number of pigs that Daniel can put in this field.

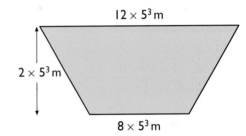

$12 \times 5^3 \, \text{m}$

$2 \times 5^3 \, \text{m}$

$8 \times 5^3 \, \text{m}$

3 In a game of 'Double Your Money', contestants are asked a number of questions.

Contestants who answer the first question correctly win £1. If they answer the second question correctly, their winnings are doubled to £2, and so on.

Monica is a contestant on 'Double Your Money'. She answers 10 questions correctly.

a How much money had she won after answering the 10 questions? Give your answer using index notation.

b Work out the minimum number of questions she would have to answer correctly to win over £1 million.

4 You are given that

$$x = 2^5 \times 8^4$$
$$y = 16^2 \div 4^6$$

and that

$$xy = 2^n$$

Show that $n = 13$.

Exam-style

Higher tier only

⑤ Archie organises a *Ludo* knockout competition. Four people take part in each game and one (the winner) goes through to the next round. There are five rounds in this competition.

    a Work out the number of competitors in this competition. Give your answer using index notation and as an ordinary number.

    b Only 820 people turn up for the competition. Archie gives 68 of them a bye into the second round, so they don't have to play in the first round. Explain how this allows the competition to work out.

⑥ You are given that
$$a = 3 \times 10^5$$
$$b = 5 \times 10^3$$
$$c = 2 \times 10^3$$
Show that $a(b + c) = ab + ac$.

Reviewing skills

① Write each of these in index form.
    a $17 \times 17 \times 17$ **b** $2 \times 2 \times 5 \times 5 \times 5$
    c $3 \times 5 \times 3 \times 3 \times 3 \times 5$ **d** $2 \times 3 \times 3 \times 11 \times 3 \times 11$

② Write each of these as a single power of 2.
    a $2^6 \times 2^4$ **b** 32
    c $2^2 \times 2^5 \times 2^2$ **d** $2 \times 4 \times 8$

③ Work out the value of these. Give your answers as ordinary numbers.
    a $4^3 + 4^3$ **b** $6^3 - 6^2$
    c $2^3 \times 2^2$ **d** $19^2 \div 19^2$

④ Work out the missing numbers.
    a $7^8 \times 7^2 = 7^{\square} \div 7^2$ **b** $3^{\square} \times 3^2 = (3^2)^4$
    c $5^9 \div 5^2 = 5^{\square} \times 5$ **d** $(2^6)^3 = 2^{\square} \div 2^2$

Unit 5 • Prime factorisation • Band g

Outside the Maths classroom

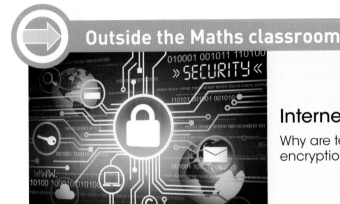

Internet security

Why are telephone numbers used in code encryption?

Toolbox

The factors of a number divide into it exactly.

The factors of 12 are 1, 2, 3, 4, 6 and 12.

Prime factors are the factors of a number that are also prime numbers.

The prime factors of 12 are 2 and 3.

Every number can be written in terms of its prime factors. ← Remember 1 is not a prime number.

$12 = 2 \times 2 \times 3 = 2^2 \times 3$

A factor tree is often used to write a number as a **product of its prime factors**.

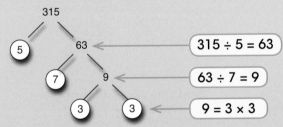

$315 \div 5 = 63$

$63 \div 7 = 9$

$9 = 3 \times 3$

From this diagram, you can see that $315 = 5 \times 7 \times 3 \times 3 = 3^2 \times 5 \times 7$.

Any number's set of prime factors is unique. A different set of prime factors will give a different number.

The **highest common factor (HCF)** of two numbers is the largest factor that they share.

You can find the HCF of two numbers by listing their factors, as in this example for 20 and 30.

Factors of 20 1 2 4 5 ⑩ 20
Factors of 30 1 2 3 5 6 ⑩ 15 30

The highest number in both lists is 10 and this is the HCF. ← The HCF is often quite a small number.

The **lowest common multiple (LCM)** of two numbers is the lowest multiple that they share.

You can find the LCM of two numbers by listing their multiples, as in this example, again using 20 and 30.

Multiples of 20   20   40   60   80   100

Multiples of 30   30   60   90   120   150

The lowest number in both lists is 60 and this is the LCM.

> The LCM is often quite a large number.

Another way of finding the HCF and LCM of two numbers is to place their prime factors in a Venn diagram. In the following example this is done for 315 and 270.

315 = 3 × 3 × 5 × 7   270 = 2 × 3 × 3 × 3 × 5

Placing these factors in a Venn diagram gives

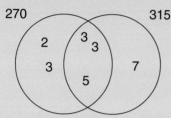

The HCF is found by multiplying the numbers in the intersection:

    3 × 3 × 5 = 45

The LCM is found by multiplying all of the numbers in the diagram:

    2 × 3 × 3 × 3 × 5 × 7 = 1890

Example – Finding prime factors using a factor tree

Write 1540 as a product of its prime factors.

Solution

Using a factor tree:

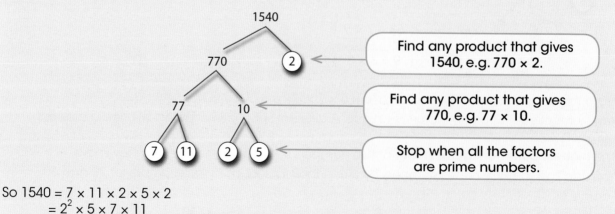

So 1540 = 7 × 11 × 2 × 5 × 2
       = 2^2 × 5 × 7 × 11

Example – Prime factors

Find the HCF and LCM of 24 and 90 by
a using a Venn diagram
b listing factors and multiples.

Solution

a The prime factors of 24 are $2 \times 2 \times 2 \times 3 = 2^3 \times 3$.
The prime factors of 90 are $2 \times 3 \times 3 \times 5 = 2 \times 3^2 \times 5$.
On a Venn diagram these are placed like this.

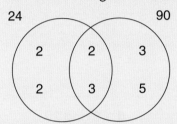

24   90

$HCF = 2 \times 3 = 6$ ← The numbers in the intersection give the HCF.

$LCM = 2 \times 2 \times 2 \times 3 \times 3 \times 5 = 360$ ← All the numbers are needed for the LCM.

b Factors of 24   1   2   3   4   ⑥   8   12   24
Factors of 90   1   2   3   5   ⑥   9   10   15   18   30   45   90

The HCF is 6. ← The highest number which is in both lists is 6.

Multiples of 24   24   48   72   96   120   144   168   192   216   240   264   288
     312   334   ③⑥⓪   384
Multiples of 90   90   180   270   ③⑥⓪   450 ...

The LCM is 360. ← 360 is the first number which is in both lists.

Practising skills

① Find these numbers. They have been written as the products of their prime factors.

   a ☐ $= 2 \times 3 \times 5$ b ☐ $= 2 \times 5 \times 11$ c ☐ $= 2^2 \times 3$ d ☐ $= 2 \times 3^2$

   e ☐ $= 3 \times 5^2$ f ☐ $= 2 \times 5^3$ g ☐ $= 3 \times 5 \times 7^2$ h ☐ $= 3^3 \times 5^2 \times 7$

② Write each of these numbers as a product of its prime factors, in index form.

   a 60   b 126   c 100   d 54

   e 225   f 154   g 105   h 495

   i 300   j 405   k 500   l 624

③ **a** Write down all the factors of 12.

   b Write down all the factors of 20.

   c Which numbers are common factors of 12 and 20?

   d What is the highest common factor (HCF) of 12 and 20?

④ Find the HCF of each pair.

   a 6 and 10   **b** 15 and 20   **c** 24 and 30   **d** 9 and 18

   e 16 and 24   **f** 26 and 52   **g** 40 and 75   **h** 36 and 54

   i 48 and 60   **j** 29 and 37   **k** 66 and 154   **l** 51 and 85

⑤ **a** Write down the first ten multiples of 6.

   b Write down the first ten multiples of 8.

   c Which numbers are common multiples of 6 and 8?

   d What is the lowest common multiple (LCM) of 6 and 8?

⑥ Find the LCM of each pair.

   a 6 and 9   **b** 5 and 8   **c** 7 and 10   **d** 12 and 20

   e 6 and 14   **f** 15 and 30   **g** 16 and 10   **h** 5 and 13

   i 24 and 40   **j** 50 and 60   **k** 18 and 27   **l** 30 and 36

Developing fluency

① Work out the missing numbers in these.

   a $2 \times 3^{\square} \times 7^2 = 882$

   b $2^{\square} \times 3 \times 5^2 = 1200$

   c $3 \times \square^3 \times 11 = 4125$

   d $\square^{\square} \times 7 \times \square = 5824$

② **a** Write 60 as a product of its prime factors.

   b Write 126 as a product of its prime factors.

   c Place the prime factors in a Venn diagram.

   d Find the HCF of 60 and 126.

   e Find the LCM of 60 and 126.

                                  60   126

③ **a** Write 180 as a product of its prime factors.

   b Write 63 as a product of its prime factors.

   c Place the prime factors in a Venn diagram.

   d Find the HCF of 180 and 63.

   e Find the LCM of 180 and 63.

                                180   63

Exam-style

④ Find the HCF and LCM of each set of numbers.

   a 12, 20 and 28   **b** 45, 60 and 90

   c 168, 700 and 1470   **d** 210, 490 and 875

⑤ Amy is in hospital. Her medication consists of:

     paracetamol, 2 tablets to be taken every 4 hours

     antibiotics, 1 tablet every 3 hours

     steroids, 1 injection every 6 hours.

At 8.30 a.m. this morning, Amy had all three of her medications. When will Amy next have all three medications at the same time?

⑥ **a** Work out these numbers.

   i 3×37 **ii** 11×101 **iii** $7 \times 11 \times 13$ **iv** 41×271

   b Write 111 111 as the product of its prime factors.

Problem solving

① Nadir is planning a party. She wants to buy some samosas, some sausage rolls and some cakes. The table shows the quantities and costs of each item.

	Samosas	Sausage rolls	Cakes
Number in a box	24	16	18
Cost per box	£5.80	£2.50	£7.10

Nadir wants to buy exactly the same number of samosas, sausage rolls and cakes so that each of the people at the party will have one of each. She has £120 to spend on this food.

Does she have enough money to buy the food she needs?

② Linda has her car serviced every 6000 miles. Here are some of the checks they carry out.

Check	Required every
Brake fluid	6000 miles
Change oil filter	12 000 miles
Tyres	6000 miles
Wiper blades	18 000 miles
Change timing belt	24 000 miles

How many miles does the car travel before it has a service that includes all five checks?

③ Bradley and Mark cycle around a cycle track. Each lap Bradley cycles takes him 50 seconds. Each lap Mark cycles takes him 80 seconds.

Mark and Bradley start cycling at the same time at the start line. How many laps behind Bradley will Mark be when they are next at the start line together?

④ The map shows the route of a charity walk.

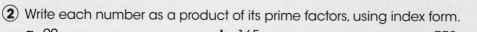

Axford
Start

30 km

Benton
Lunch

18 km

Corr Bridge
Finsh

Marshals stand at equally spaced intervals along the route, including the lunch stop, the start and the finish. The distance between marshals is always a whole number of kilometres.

What is the smallest possible number of marshals?

⑤ Buses to Ashinton leave a bus station every 28 minutes. Buses to Cardsbury leave the same bus station every 35 minutes.

A bus to Ashinton and a bus to Cardsbury both leave the bus station at 08:15. These are the first buses of the day to leave the bus station. The last bus of the day to leave this bus station leaves at 22:45.

How many times during the day will a bus to Ashinton and a bus to Cardsbury leave the bus station at the same time?

⑥ Nomsa is reading a book about numbers. It says, 'Every number has just one set of prime factors.'

Nomsa says, 'That's not true. I can factorise the number 24 871 in two completely different ways. It can be 209 × 119 or it can be 187 × 133.'

Explain the mistake in Nomsa's reasoning.

Reviewing skills

① Work out these numbers. They have been written as the products of their prime factors.

a $2^2 \times 5$ **b** $2^4 \times 5^2$ **c** $2 \times 3 \times 5 \times 7 \times 11$

d $2^2 \times 3 \times 5^2 \times 7 \times 11$ **e** $2^4 \times 3 \times 5^4 \times 7 \times 11$

② Write each number as a product of its prime factors, using index form.

a 90 **b** 165 **c** 770

d 819 **e** 1400 **f** 1750

g 1584 **h** 2912

③ a Write down all the prime factors of 54 and 60, using index form.

b Find the highest common factor (HCF) of 54 and 60.

c Find the lowest common multiple (LCM) of 54 and 60.

Unit 6 • Rules of indices • Band h

Outside the Maths classroom

Estate agents

How big is a house that has a floor area of 151 square metres?

Toolbox

The rules of indices can be used provided the base number is the same in all numbers used.

$$a^m \times a^n = a^{m+n}$$

$$a^m \div a^n = a^{m-n}$$

$$(a^m)^n = a^{mn}$$

Powers are repeated multiplication.

Looking at the pattern helps you to understand what happens if the power is negative.

$$4^3 = 4 \times 4 \times 4 = 64$$

$$4^2 = 4 \times 4 = 16$$

$$4^1 = 4$$

$$4^0 = 1$$

$$4^{-1} = \left(\frac{1}{4}\right)^1 = \frac{1}{4}$$

$$4^{-2} = \left(\frac{1}{4}\right)^2 = \frac{1}{16}$$

$$4^{-3} = \left(\frac{1}{4}\right)^3 = \frac{1}{64}$$

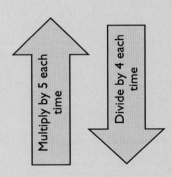

Multiply by 5 each time

Divide by 4 each time

It is helpful to know common square and cube numbers.

$1^2 = 1$	$11^2 = 121$	$1^3 = 1$
$2^2 = 4$	$12^2 = 144$	$2^3 = 8$
$3^2 = 9$	$13^2 = 169$	$3^3 = 27$
$4^2 = 16$	$14^2 = 196$	$4^3 = 64$
$5^2 = 25$	$15^2 = 225$	$5^3 = 125$
$6^2 = 36$		$6^3 = 216$
$7^2 = 49$		$7^3 = 343$
$8^2 = 64$		$8^3 = 512$
$9^2 = 81$		$9^3 = 729$
$10^2 = 100$		$10^3 = 1000$

Example – Using the rules of indices

Calculate the following.

Give your answers using indices.

a $6^4 \times 6^9$

b $6^9 \div 6^4$

c $6^4 \div 6^9$

d $(6^4)^9$

e How many times bigger is your answer to **b** than your answer to **c**?

Solution

a $6^4 \times 6^9 = 6^{(4 + 9)}$
$\qquad = 6^{13}$

b $6^9 \div 6^4 = 6^{(9 - 4)}$
$\qquad = 6^5$

c $6^4 \div 6^9 = 6^{-5}$

d $(6^4)^9 = 6^{(4 \times 9)}$
$\qquad = 6^{36}$

e $6^5 \div 6^{-5} = 6^{(5 - (-5))}$
$\qquad = 6^{10}$

f 6^5 is 6^{10} times bigger than 6^{-5}.

Practising skills

① **a** Copy and complete this table.

Index form	In full	Ordinary number
2^5	$2 \times 2 \times 2 \times 2 \times 2$	32
2^4	$2 \times 2 \times 2 \times 2$	16
2^3		
2^2		
2^1		
2^0		1
2^{-1}	$\dfrac{1}{2}$	$\dfrac{1}{2}$
2^{-2}	$\dfrac{1}{2 \times 2}$	
2^{-3}	$\dfrac{1}{2 \times 2 \times 2}$	

b Write down the value of

i 2^7

ii 2^{-4}.

② **a** Copy and complete this table.

Index form	In full	Ordinary number	In words
10^3	$10 \times 10 \times 10$	1000	One thousand
10^2			
10^1			
10^0		1	
10^{-1}	$\dfrac{1}{10}$	$\dfrac{1}{10}$	
10^{-2}	$\dfrac{1}{10 \times 10}$		
10^{-3}			One thousandth

b Write 10^6 as a number and in words.

c Write 10^{-6} as a decimal and in words.

③ Jasmine is working out $2^2 \times 2^4$.
This is what she writes.

a Use Jasmine's style to write out the answers to these calculations.

i $3^2 \times 3^3$ **ii** $5^4 \times 5^2$ **iii** $10^3 \times 10^4$

b Copy and complete the rule for multiplying numbers in index form,
$a^m \times a^n = \square$

$$2^2 \quad \times \quad 2^4$$
$$2 \times 2 \quad \times \quad 2 \times 2 \times 2 \times 2$$
$$2^6 \qquad \text{Answer}$$

Check
$$\qquad 4 \quad \times \quad 16$$
$$\qquad 64$$
and $\quad 2^6 \;=\; 64\ \checkmark$

Reasoning

④ Multiply the following. Give your answers both in index form and as ordinary numbers.

a $2^3 \times 2^3$ **b** $3^4 \times 3^2$ **c** 5×5^2 **d** $5^5 \times 5^{-2}$

⑤ Niamh is working out $3^5 \div 3^2$.
This is what she writes.

a Use Niamh's style to write out the answers to these calculations.

i $3^6 \div 3^4$ **ii** $5^4 \div 5^3$ **iii** $10^5 \times 10^2$

b Copy and complete the rule for dividing numbers in index form,
$a^m \div a^n = \square$

> $3^5 \quad \div \quad 3^2$
>
> $\dfrac{3 \times 3 \times 3 \times \cancel{3} \times \cancel{3}}{\cancel{3} \times \cancel{3}}$
>
> 3^3 Answer
>
> Check
> $243 \div 9 = 27$
> $3^3 = 27$ ✓

⑥ Carry out these divisions. Give your answers both in index form and as ordinary numbers.

a $2^6 \div 2^3$ **b** $3^4 \div 3^3$ **c** $10^6 \div 10^3$ **d** $5 \div 5^{-2}$

⑦ Sanjay is working out $(7^2)^3$.
This is what he writes.

a Use Sanjay's style to work these out.

i $(2^4)^3$ **ii** $(3^2)^5$ **iii** $(10^3)^2$

b State a rule for simplifying numbers in the form $(a^m)^n$.

> $(7^2)^3$
>
> $7 \times 7 \times 7 \times 7 \times 7 \times 7$
>
> 7^6 Answer
>
> I used my calculator to check.
> Both 49^3 and 7^6 are the same.
> They are 117649 ✓

⑧ Simplify the following. Give your answers both in index form and as ordinary numbers.

a $(2^2)^5$ **b** $(2^5)^2$ **c** $(10^3)^4$ **d** $(10^2)^6$

Developing fluency

① Without using a calculator, decide which numbers in each pair is larger, or whether they are equal in value.

a 2^1 or 1^2 **b** 2^3 or 3^2 **c** 2^4 or 4^2 **d** 2^5 or 5^2

e 2^6 or 6^2 **f** 2^{-1} or 1^{-2} **g** 2^{-3} or 3^{-2} **h** 2^{-4} or 4^{-2}

② You are given that $5^a \times 5^b = 5^{10}$.
How many different pairs of values can you find for a and b if they

a are both positive whole numbers

b can be any whole numbers, positive or negative?

③ Work out the following. Give your answers in index form.

a $3^2 \times 3^4 \times 3^7$ **b** $2^3 \times 2^4 \times 2^5$ **c** $10 \times 10^2 \times 10^3$ **d** $5^4 \times 5 \times 5$

④ Work out the following. Give your answers in index form.

a $6^7 \times 6^4 \div 6^2$ **b** $6^7 \times 6^4 \times 6^{-2}$ **c** $(6^7 \times 6^4)^2$ **d** $(6^{-7} \times 6^{-4} \div 6^{-2})^{-1}$

⑤ Work out the following. Give your answers in index form.

a $\dfrac{3^6 \times 3^7}{3^8}$　　　　b $3^6 \times 3^7 \div 3^{-8}$　　　c $\dfrac{3^3 \times 3^{10}}{3^4 \times 3^4}$　　　d $\dfrac{3^3 \times (3^2)^5}{(3^2)^4}$

⑥ Work out the following. Give your answers in index form.

a $2^3 \times (2^5 - 2^5)$　　b $2^3 \times (2^5 + 2^5)$　　c $2^8 \div (2^5 \div 2^3)$　　d $\dfrac{3^4}{(3^3 + 3^3 + 3^3)}$

⑦ Place these numbers in order of size, largest first. If two or more are the same size, put them together.

a 2^5　　　　　b 5^2　　　　　c 19^0　　　　　d $\dfrac{3^2 \times 3^5}{3^7}$

e $\dfrac{2^4}{2^7}$　　　　f $10^3 \div 10^4$　　g $\left(\dfrac{3^7}{3^6}\right)^3$　　h $\left(\dfrac{3^6}{3^7}\right)^{-3}$

i $\dfrac{2^4 + 2^5}{2^0}$　　j $\dfrac{10^2 \times 10^3}{10^4 \times 10^4}$

⑧ Sarah says, 'I know that 2^{10} is just over a thousand. So 2^{20} must be just over a million and 2^{40} must be just over a billion.'

How much of Sarah's statement is correct? Use the rules of indices to explain your answer.

Problem solving

① Here are some powers of x.

x^{-2}　　x^4　　x^{-1}

a Select two of them (you can have the same one twice if you want) and either multiply them or divide them.

b How many different answers can you make?

c Can you choose another set of three indices that will give you a greater number of different answers?

Reviewing skills

① Work out the following. Give your answers in index form.

a $5^2 \times 5^3 \div 5^4$　　b $\dfrac{5^2 \times 5^3}{5^4}$　　c $5^2 \times 5^3 \times 5^{-4}$

② Work out the following. Give your answers in index form.

a $\dfrac{10^3 \times 10^3}{10^8}$　　b $10^2 \times 10^2 \times 10^3 \times 10^{-8}$　　c $\dfrac{(10^2)^3}{(10^2)^4}$

③ Work out the following. Give your answers in index form.

a $(2^3)^4 \div 2^{10}$　　b $(7^3)^5 \times (7^{-2})^7$　　c $\dfrac{(10^{-6})^2}{(10^{-3})^4}$

④ Use the rules of indices to show that $23^0 = 1$.

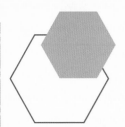

Strand 1 Starting algebra

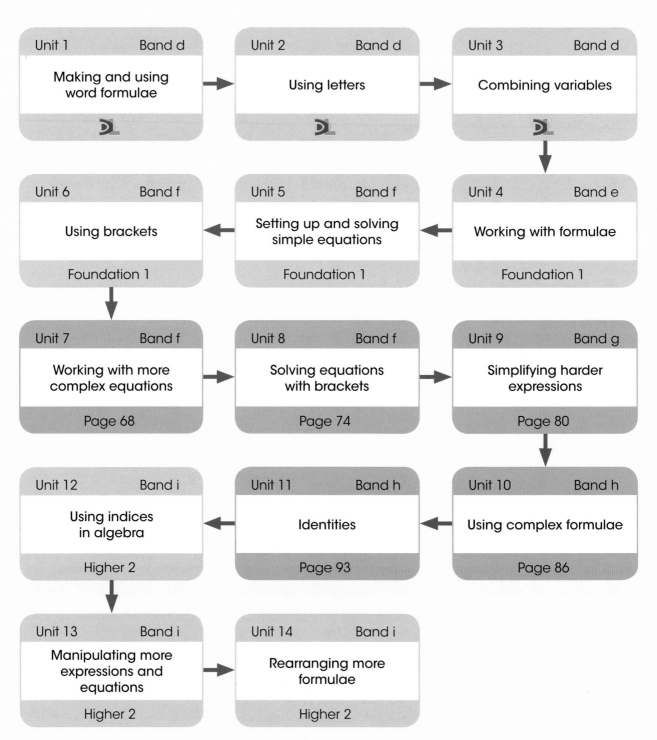

Unit 1	Band d
Making and using word formulae	

Unit 2	Band d
Using letters	

Unit 3	Band d
Combining variables	

Unit 6	Band f
Using brackets	
Foundation 1	

Unit 5	Band f
Setting up and solving simple equations	
Foundation 1	

Unit 4	Band e
Working with formulae	
Foundation 1	

Unit 7	Band f
Working with more complex equations	
Page 68	

Unit 8	Band f
Solving equations with brackets	
Page 74	

Unit 9	Band g
Simplifying harder expressions	
Page 80	

Unit 12	Band i
Using indices in algebra	
Higher 2	

Unit 11	Band h
Identities	
Page 93	

Unit 10	Band h
Using complex formulae	
Page 86	

Unit 13	Band i
Manipulating more expressions and equations	
Higher 2	

Unit 14	Band i
Rearranging more formulae	
Higher 2	

Units 1–6 are assumed knowledge for this book. They are reviewed and extended in the Moving on section on page 67.

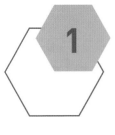

Units 1–6 • Moving on

Exam-style

(1) Ruby makes a pentagonal prism from straws.

The ends of the prism are made from 2 regular pentagons of side x cm.

The lengths of the rectangular faces of the prism are $x + 5$.

The total length of the straws that Ruby used was 1 m.

Find the value of x.

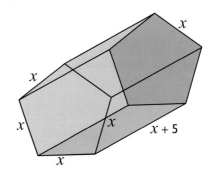

Exam-style

(2) A square has a perimeter of $(40x + 60)$ cm.

A regular pentagon has the same perimeter as the square.

Show that the difference between the lengths of the sides of the two shapes is $(2x + 3)$ cm.

(3) Here is a T shape drawn on part of a 10 by 10 grid.

1	2	3	4	5	6
11	12	13	14	15	16
21	22	23	24	25	26
31	32	33	34	35	36
41	42	43	44	45	46

The shaded T is called T_2 because 2 is the smallest number in the T. T_2 is the sum of all the numbers in the T shape; so $T_2 = 45$.

a Copy and complete this formula for T_n in terms of n.

$T_n = n + (n + 1) + ($ $) + ($ $) + ($ $)$.

b Use the formula to find the value of n for which $T_n = 105$.

c Explain why T_n cannot equal either 39 or 130.

(4) This hexagon is to form part of a tiling design. The angles, x, are to be the same. The remaining two angles, y, need to be 30° larger than x.

a In the diagram, the hexagon has been split into four triangles. Use this to help you form an equation about the total angles in this hexagon.

b Solve your equation to find all the angles in the hexagon.

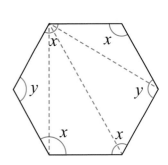

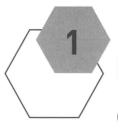

Unit 7 • Working with more complex equations • Band f

Outside the Maths classroom

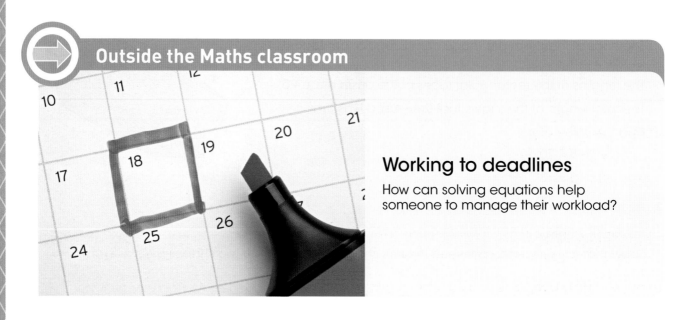

Working to deadlines

How can solving equations help someone to manage their workload?

Toolbox

You can use the **balance method** to solve equations with an unknown on both sides.

The first step is to get all the unknowns onto the same side of the equation:

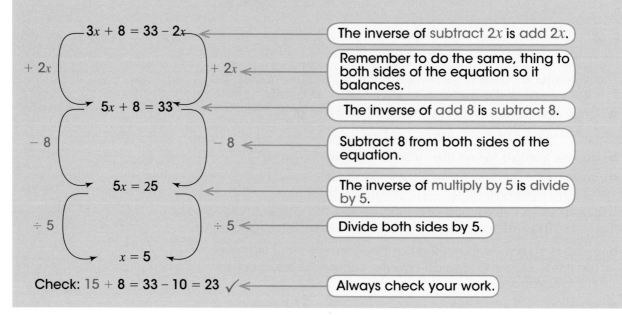

$3x + 8 = 33 - 2x$ — The inverse of subtract $2x$ is add $2x$.

$+ 2x$ $+ 2x$ — Remember to do the same, thing to both sides of the equation so it balances.

$5x + 8 = 33$ — The inverse of add 8 is subtract 8.

$- 8$ $- 8$ — Subtract 8 from both sides of the equation.

$5x = 25$ — The inverse of multiply by 5 is divide by 5.

$\div 5$ $\div 5$ — Divide both sides by 5.

$x = 5$

Check: $15 + 8 = 33 - 10 = 23$ ✓ — Always check your work.

Example – Solving an equation with an unknown on both sides

Solve $3x - 8 = 20 - x$.

Solution

$$3x - 8 = 20 - x$$

$$4x - 8 = 20 \qquad \longleftarrow \boxed{\text{Add } x \text{ to both sides.}}$$

$$4x = 28 \qquad \longleftarrow \boxed{\text{Add 8 to both sides.}}$$

$$x = 7 \qquad \longleftarrow \boxed{\text{Divide both sides by 4.}}$$

Check: $3x - 8 = 20 - x$

$3 \times 7 - 8 = 20 - 7$

$21 - 8 = 13$

$13 = 13$ ✓

Example – Solving word problems

Jamie and Holly both had the same amount of credit on their mobile phones.
Jamie sent 18 texts and has £1.40 credit left.
Holly sent 12 texts and has £2 credit left.
They both pay the same amount for one text.

a Find the cost of one text message.

b How much credit did Jamie and Holly start with?

Solution

a Let t represent the cost of one text message in pence. Change pounds to pence because whole numbers are easier to work with.

Jamie's credit = Holly's credit

$$18t + 140 = 12t + 200 \qquad \longleftarrow \boxed{\text{Subtract } 12t \text{ from both sides.}}$$

$$6t + 140 = 200 \qquad \longleftarrow \boxed{\text{Subtract 140 from both sides.}}$$

$$6t = 60 \qquad \longleftarrow \boxed{\text{Divide both sides by 6.}}$$

$$t = 10$$

So a text message costs 10p.

b Substitute $t = 10$ into the expression for Jamie's credit.

$$18t + 140 = 18 \times 10 + 140$$

$$= 320$$

So Jamie's starting credit was 320p or £3.20
Check that Holly's credit is also 320p:

$$12t + 200 = 12 \times 10 + 200$$

$$= 320 \qquad ✓$$

Practising skills

① Write an equation for each balancing problem and solve it.

a

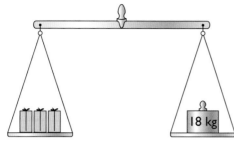

b

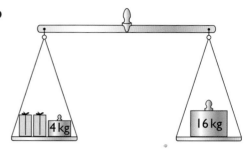

c

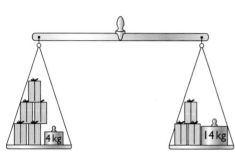

d

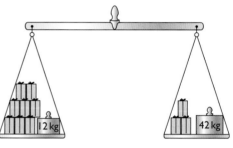

② Solve these equations.

a $6s = 27$	**b** $5x + 14 = 49$	**c** $18 - 3h = 3$	**d** $\dfrac{y}{4} - 6 = 9$
e $12 = 2 - 5m$	**f** $14 = 29 + 6g$	**g** $8 = 5 + \dfrac{1}{2}p$	**h** $-8 = -5 - \dfrac{1}{2}p$

③ Solve these equations.

a $4a + 7 = 3a + 3$ **b** $7f + 3 = 2f + 18$ **c** $7x - 3 = 6 - 2x$ **d** $17 - 2y = 8 - y$

④ Solve these equations.

a $5a + 8 = 7a + 22$ **b** $6b + 15 = -2b - 9$ **c** $5c - 3 = c - 1$ **d** $11 - 2f = 8 - 8f$

Developing fluency

① Julie works out that if she buys 6 apples she will have 20p left over but if she buys only 4 apples she will have 64p over.

a Write an equation to represent this situation.

b Solve the equation to find the cost of an apple.

② Jan tries to solve this equation.

$$11 - 4x = 6x + 5$$

a Here is her attempt.

$$11 - 4x = 6x - 4x$$
$$11 + 5 = 6x - 4x$$
$$16 = 2x$$
$$16 \div 2 = x$$
$$x = 8 \quad \times$$

Explain what she has done wrong.

b Using the same steps as Jan, write out a correct answer.

c Check your solution by substituting it in the original equation.

③ Sally and Tara need to solve this equation.

$$4.1x - 3.7 = 3.6x - 2.2$$

Here is how they start.

Sally

$$4.1x - 3.7 = 3.6x - 2.2$$
$$4.1x - 3.6x = -2.2 + 3.7$$
$$0.5x = 1.5$$
$$x = \frac{........}{........}$$
$$x = ...$$

Tara

Multiply both sides by 10.
$$41x - 37 = 36x - 22$$
$$41x - 36x = 37 - 22$$
....
....
....

a Complete their answers.

b Whose method do you prefer? Say why.

④ Solve these equations.

a $2.1a + 3.6 = 1.1a + 5.7$

b $4.5b - 2.9 = 3.6b + 4.3$

c $3.7 - 2.2c = 1.8c - 5.4$

d $8.5 - 5.3d = 3.6 - 1.8d$

e $2\frac{1}{2}x - 6 = 3 - \frac{1}{2}x$

f $2\frac{1}{2}x - 6 = 3 + \frac{1}{2}x$

g $4.11x - 2 = 4.1x - 1$

h $0.001x - 0.005 = 0.003 - 0.003x$

⑤ Sandra and Zoe are sisters. They are making dresses from the same material. Their parents give them the same amount of money to buy it. The cost of 1 metre of the material is £m.

Sandra gets 3.5 metres and has £4.25 left over.

Zoe gets 2 metres and has £11.00 left over.

a Write this information as an equation for m.

b Solve the equation.

c How much money was each girl given?

⑥ Sam is tiling his bathroom wall. The tiles go part of the way up. Above them the wall is painted.

11 rows of tiles would leave 108 cm of wall to be painted.

14 rows of tiles would leave 72 cm of wall to be painted.

a Write this information as an equation for the height of a tile, w cm.

b Solve the equation.

c How many rows of tiles would cover the whole wall?

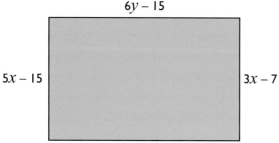

I think of a number.
I multiply it by 5 and take away 8.
My answer is 12 more than if I'd doubled my number and added 10.

⑦

a Write this information as an equation.

b What number did Charlie think of?

Problem solving

①

I think of a number.
I multiply it by 5 and subtract 3.
My answer is 7 more than if I'd multiplied my number by 3.

a Write this information as an equation.

b What number did Ava think of?

② Here is a rectangle. All the measurements are in centimetres.

$6y - 15$

$5x - 15$

$3x - 7$

$2y + 15$

Find the area of the rectangle.

③ Here is part of a polygon.

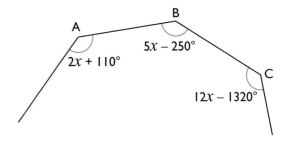

a Angles A and B are equal.
How many degrees are they?

b Show that angle C is also equal to A and B.

c What can you say about the polygon?

④ Jack has £400 which he gives to his 3 grandchildren.
He gives Ellie twice as much as Harry.
He gives Tom £40 less than Harry.
Let £h stand for the amount of money that Harry gets.

a Write down expressions for the amount of money given to

   i Ellie   **ii** Tom

b How much money does Jack give to each grandchild?

⑤ The angles in this triangle are $3a°$, $(5a + 12)°$ and $(96 - 2a)°$.
Show that the triangle is isosceles.

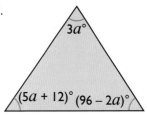

Reviewing skills

① Solve these equations.

  a $8g - 5 = 5g + 40$ **b** $8 + 2d = d + 2$ **c** $9t - 4 = t - 8$ **d** $24 + 5c = 16 - 3c$

② Solve these equations.

  a $23 - 4d = 3d + 2$ **b** $7e + 4 = 18 - 3e$ **c** $17 + g = 6 - g$ **d** $5 - 3h = 1 + h$

③ Solve these equations.

  a $1.4x + 2.1 = 0.5x + 5.7$ **b** $3.88 - 1.02x = 1.38 + 1.48x$

  c $4\frac{1}{4}x + 1\frac{1}{2} = 16\frac{1}{2} - \frac{3}{4}x$ **d** $5 - \frac{3}{4}x = 1\frac{1}{2} - \frac{1}{4}x$

④ Zorro is buying USB pens for his computer. They cost £p each.
Zorro could buy 5 USB pens and have £4.25 change from the money in his pocket.
Instead he buys 2 USB pens and spends £16.50 on a game.
That leaves him with just 20 pence.

a Form an equation for p.

b Solve the equation.

c What is the cost of a USB pen?

d How much money did Zorro have?

Unit 8 • Solving equations with brackets • Band f

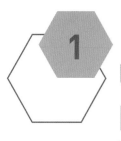

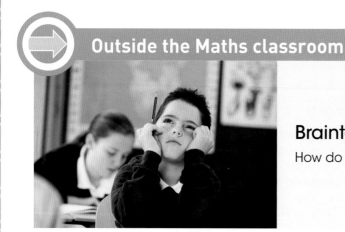

Brainteasers

How do equations help solve brainteasers?

↓ **Toolbox**

When an equation has a bracket it is usually easiest to expand the brackets first.

$5(3x - 6) = 12$

$5 \times 3x - 5 \times 6 = 12$ ← First multiply out the brackets.

$15x - 30 = 12$ ← Add 30 to both sides.

$15x = 42$ ← Divide both sides by 15.

$x = 2.8$

Alternatively you can choose to divide both sides of the equation by the number outside the brackets.

$4(n + 13) = 80$

$n + 13 = 20$ ← Divide both sides by 4.

$n = 7$ ← Subtract 13 from both sides.

Example – Solving equations with an unknown on one side

Solve these equations.

a $6(5a - 2) = 33$ b $5(4b + 3) = -25$

Solution

a
$$6(5a - 2) = 33$$
$$6 \times 5a - 6 \times 2 = 33 \quad \longleftarrow \boxed{\text{First multiply out the brackets.}}$$
$$30a - 12 = 33 \quad \longleftarrow \boxed{\text{Simplify.}}$$
$$30a = 45 \quad \longleftarrow \boxed{\text{Add 12 to both sides.}}$$
$$a = 1.5 \quad \longleftarrow \boxed{\text{Divide both sides by 30.}}$$

b
$$5(4b + 3) = -25$$
$$4b + 3 = -5 \quad \longleftarrow \boxed{\text{It is easiest to divide both sides by 5 first.}}$$
$$4b = -8 \quad \longleftarrow \boxed{\text{Subtract 3 from both sides.}}$$
$$b = -2 \quad \longleftarrow \boxed{\text{Divide both sides by 4.}}$$

Example – Solving equations with an unknown on both sides

Solve $2(3 - x) = 9 + x$.

Solution

$$2(3 - x) = 9 + x$$
$$2 \times 3 - 2 \times x = 9 + x \quad \longleftarrow \boxed{\text{First multiply out the brackets.}}$$
$$6 - 2x = 9 + x \quad \longleftarrow \boxed{\text{You can subtract } x \text{ from both sides or add } 2x \text{ to both sides.}}$$
$$6 = 9 + 3x \quad \longleftarrow \boxed{\begin{array}{c}\text{Subtracting } x \text{ from both sides gives a negative } x \text{ term} \\ \text{so it is easier to add } 2x \text{ to both sides.}\end{array}}$$
$$-3 = 3x \quad \longleftarrow \boxed{\text{Subtract 9 from both sides.}}$$
$$-1 = x \quad \longleftarrow \boxed{\text{Divide both sides by 3.}}$$
$$x = -1 \quad \longleftarrow \boxed{\begin{array}{c}\text{Swap the two sides of the equation} \\ \text{over. } -1 = x \text{ means the same as } x = -1.\end{array}}$$

Check by substituting $x = -1$ back into the original equation.
$$2(3 - x) = 9 + x$$
$$2 \times (3 - -1) = 9 + -1$$
$$2 \times 4 = 8 \quad \checkmark$$

Practising skills

① Solve these equations by expanding the brackets first.

    a $5(2x + 3) = 75$ **b** $3(x + 2) = 33$ **c** $4(5x - 3) = 18$ **d** $8(5 - x) = 16$

② Solve these equations by dividing both sides by the number outside the brackets first.

    a $10(3a + 6) = 180$ **b** $2(5b - 3) = 74$ **c** $5(4c + 7) = 195$ **d** $4(2d - 9) = 52$

③ **a** Copy and complete the table to build an equation to find the number.

Instruction	Algebra
I think of a number, n	n
I multiply it by 5	
I add 6	
I multiply it by 3	
The answer is 123	

    b Solve your equation to find the number.

    c Work through the instructions to check your answer is correct.

④ Solve these equations.

    a $4(x + 6) + 3x = 38$ **b** $2(3x - 5) - 3x + 4 = 6$

    c $5(2x + 1) - x - 3 = 56$ **d** $4x + 9 - 2(x - 4) = 27$

⑤ Solve these equations.

    a $8(x + 3) = 3x - 11$ **b** $2(4x - 2) = 11 - 2x$

    c $3(5x - 6) = 4x + 15$ **d** $10(3x - 5) = 5x$

⑥ Solve these equations.

    a $7(3x - 4) = 4(2x + 3) - 1$ **b** $6(2x - 5) = 3(x + 2)$

    c $5(x + 4) = 3(2x - 8)$ **d** $3(4x + 2) = 4(5x + 2)$

Developing fluency

① Solve these equations. Each answer represents a letter. What word does this spell?

−3	−2	−1	2	3	4	8	24
L	A	T	S	V	E	P	O

    a $2(x + 3) = 10$

    b $3(x - 10) = 2x - 6$

    c $2(6x + 3) = 10(x + 1) - 10$

    d $4(2x + 1) = 2(x + 5) + 12$

    e $5(3x - 2) - 4x = 3(x + 5) + 7$

② The perimeter of this rectangle is 28 cm.

    a Write down an expression for the perimeter of the rectangle.

    b Write down and solve an equation for x.

    c Find the area of the rectangle.

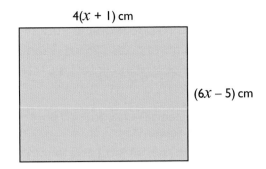

$4(x + 1)$ cm

$(6x - 5)$ cm

③ Isobel thinks of a number, n.

When she subtracts 2 and then multiplies the results by 3 she gets the same answer as when she subtracts her number from 30.

    a Write down an expression for 'subtracts 2 and then multiplies the results by 3'.
Use n for Isobel's number.

    b Write down an equation for n.

    c What number is Isobel thinking of?

    d Show how you can check your answer is correct.

④ The sum of the ages of Peter and his Dad is 42.

    a Peter is p years old now.
Copy and complete this table.

	Age now	Age in 4 years
Peter	p	
Dad		

    In 4 years' time, Peter's Dad will be four times as old as Peter.

    b Write down an equation for p.

    c Solve the equation.

    d How old are Peter and his Dad now?

    e Show how you can check you answer is correct.

⑤ **a** Expand the brackets.

    i $\frac{1}{2}(4x + 2)$ **ii** $\frac{1}{3}(3x + 6)$

    b Solve this equation.

    $\frac{1}{2}(4x + 2) = \frac{1}{3}(3x + 6)$

⑥ **a** Simplify

    i $6 \times \frac{1}{2}(4x + 2)$ **ii** $6 \times \frac{1}{3}(3x + 6)$

    b Multiply both sides of the equation $\frac{1}{2}(4x + 2) = \frac{1}{3}(3x + 6)$ by 6.

    c Using your answer to part **b**, solve the equation $\frac{1}{2}(4x + 2) = \frac{1}{3}(3x + 6)$.

(7) There are 54 people on a coach trip to a theme park.

There are 30 adults on the coach trip.

A child's ticket costs £25 less than an adult's.

The total cost of the tickets is £1560.

How much is a child's ticket for the trip?

(8) The total length of a daffodil is 44 cm. This is made up from three parts: the bulb, the stem and the flower.

The flower is 5 cm long. The length of the stem is three times the length of the flower and bulb together.

Find the lengths of each of the parts.

Problem solving

Exam-style questions that require skills developed in this unit are included in later units.

(1)

I think of a number and call it n.
I add 12 to the number.
I then multiply by 3.
This gives me the same answer as when I subtract n from 60.

   a Write this as an equation for n.

   b What number is Louise thinking of?

(2) Jeremy's present age is y years.

Today, Jeremy's sister, Kate, is twice as old as Jeremy.

Two years ago Kate was three times as old as Jeremy was then.

   a Write this information as an equation for y.

   b Solve your equation. How old are Jeremy and Kate today?

(3) Mr MacDonald has 120 animals on his farm.

He has hens, cows and sheep. The number of cows is c.

The number of hens is 20 more than the number of cows.

He has twice as many sheep as hens.

   a Write this information as an equation for c.

   b How many cows are there on the farm?

   c How many hens and sheep are there?

(4) Here is a quadrilateral.

Show that the quadrilateral is not a square.

$3(3x - 4)$ cm

$2(3x + 5)$ cm

$4(3x - 8)$ cm

Exam-style

⑤ Jody and Ben went to the leisure centre together.

Jody spent 40 minutes in the gym then went for a swim. Jody swam for *m* minutes.

Ben spent all the time swimming. He was swimming for three times longer than Jody.

How long were Jody and Ben in the leisure centre?

Exam-style

⑥ Here is a quadrilateral.

Use the given angles to decide whether or not this quadrilateral is a parallelogram.

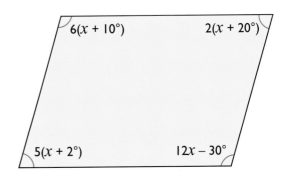

Reviewing skills

① Solve these equations.

a $6(5a - 1) = 114$ **b** $3(2b + 4) = 6$ **c** $5(4c - 3) = 165$ **d** $7(4d - 5) = 0$

② Solve these equations.

a $3(2x - 5) = 5x - 14$ **b** $2(4x + 1) = 7x + 4$

c $5(3x - 4) = 2(5 - x) - x$ **d** $4(2x - 3) = 5(x - 1) + 2$

③ Here is a rectangle.

The perimeter of the rectangle is 136 cm.

What is the area of the rectangle?

$5(x + 4)$ cm

$(4x + 3)$ cm

Unit 9 • Simplifying harder expressions • Band g

Outside the Maths classroom

Designing platform games

Computer games model real-life situations.

Why do games designers need to use formulae?

Toolbox

These are the **laws of indices**.

$$a^n = \underbrace{a \times a \times a \times \ldots \times a}_{n \text{ factors of } a} \qquad \text{So } a^5 = \underbrace{a \times a \times a \times a \times a}_{5 \text{ factors of } a}$$

$$a^1 = a$$

$$a^0 = 1$$

$$a^x \times a^y = a^{x+y} \qquad \text{So } a^5 \times a^7 = a^{5+7} = a^{12}$$

$$a^x \div a^y = a^{x-y} \qquad \text{So } a^9 \div a^4 = a^{9-4} = a^5$$

$$(a^x)^y = a^{x \times y} \qquad \text{So } (a^5)^3 = a^{5 \times 3} = a^{15}$$

When you expand a pair of brackets you multiply every term in the second bracket by every term in the first bracket then simplify your answer.

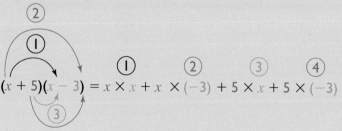

$$(x+5)(x-3) = x \times x + x \times (-3) + 5 \times x + 5 \times (-3)$$

Alternatively, you can use a table

$$= x^2 + (-3x) + (+5x) + (-15)$$

$$= x^2 + \qquad 2x \qquad -15$$

$$= x^2 + 2x - 15$$

	$x + 5$	
x	x^2	$5x$
-3	$-3x$	-15

$$x^2 + 5x - 3x - 15$$
$$= x^2 + 2x - 15$$

Example – Simplify harder expressions

Simplify these expressions.

a $2a^3b^7 \times 4ab^5$

b $\dfrac{12a^4b^3}{4ab^2}$

Solution

a Use the rules of indices: $a^x \times a^y = a^{x+y}$.

$2 \times 4 = 8$

$a^3 \times a = a^3 \times a^1 = a^{3+1} = a^4$

$b^7 \times b^5 = b^{7+5} = b^{12}$

So, $2a^3b^7 \times 4ab^5 = 8a^4b^{12}$

b Use the rules of indices: $a^x \div a^y = a^{x-y}$.

$12 \div 4 = 3$

$a^4 \div a = a^4 \div a^1 = a^{4-1} = a^3$

$b^3 \div b^2 = b^{3-2} = b^1 = b$

So, $\dfrac{12a^4b^3}{4ab^2} = 3a^3b$

Example – Expanding a pair of brackets

Expand $(x - 4)(x - 2)$.

Solution

You can use a grid to help you.

	x	-4
x	x^2	$-4x$
-2	$-2x$	8

Put the contents of one bracket along the top and the other down the side then multiply at each cross-section.

$(x - 4)(x - 2) = x^2 - 4x - 2x + 8$
$= x^2 - 6x - 8$

Then add the results.

Practising skills

1 Write these as single powers.

    a $5 \times 5 \times 5$

    c $(9 \times 9 \times 9 \times 9 \times 9 \times 9 \times 9)^2$

    b $2 \times 2 \times 2 \times 2 \times 2$

    d $(7 \times 7)^5$

2 Write these as single powers.

    a $f \times f$

    c $(d \times d \times d)^2$

    b $g \times g \times g \times g$

    d $(a \times a \times a \times a \times a \times a \times a \times a)^3$

3 **a** Write each of these in index form and work out their values.

    i $x^2 \times x^3$ **ii** $x^3 \times x^2$ **iii** $x^3 \div x^2$

    iv $x^2 \div x^3$ **v** $(x^2)^3$ **vi** $(x^3)^2$

4 Simplify these expressions.

    a $5a^3 \times 4a^2$ **b** $6b^5 \div 3b^4$ **c** $2c^8 \times 3c^6$ **d** $10d^7 \times 3d$

    e $(2e^2)^3 \div 4e^5$ **f** $4f^3g^2 \times 2f^2g^6$ **g** $8m^3p \times 3mp^4$ **h** $10s^8t^5 \div 5s^5t^5$

5 Simplify these expressions.

    a $\dfrac{12a^5}{4a^3}$

    b $20c^{12} \div (5 \times c^5 \times c)$

    c $\dfrac{15(d^3)^2}{3d}$

    d $6(ef^2)^3 \div (2 \times e^2 \times ef)$

6 **a** **i** Copy and complete this grid to expand $(x + 2)(x + 4)$.

×	x	4
x	x^2	
2		

    ii Now add the four terms together and simplify your answer.

    b Copy and complete these grids and add the terms together, simplifying your answers.

    i $(x + 3)(x + 5)$

×	x	5
x		
3		

    ii $(x + 6)(x - 4)$

×	x	−4
x		
6		

    iii $(x - 5)(x - 7)$

×	x	−7
x		
−5		

Developing fluency

① Copy and complete these algebra pyramids.
Each brick is the product of the two beneath it.

a

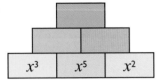

b

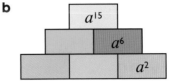

② Match to give six pairs of equivalent expressions.

n^2 $n^4 \times n^2$ n^8 $n^3 \times n^2$

$n^{12} \div n^4$ n^3 $n^3 \div n$ $(n^5)^2$

$n^6 \div n^3$ n^5 n^{10} n^6

③ Expand these expressions and simplify your answers.

a $(x + 2)(x + 9)$ **b** $(x + 5)(x - 3)$

c $(x - 4)(x + 1)$ **d** $(x - 2)(x - 5)$

④ Copy and complete these algebra pyramids. Each brick is the product of the two beneath it.

a

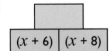

$(x + 6)$ $(x + 8)$

b

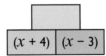

$(x + 4)$ $(x - 3)$

⑤ **a** Tim and Harry have expanded the brackets $(x + 5)^2$.
Tim says the answer is $x^2 + 10x + 25$ and Harry says it is $x^2 + 25$.
Who is correct? What has the other one done wrong?

b Expand these brackets and simplify the answers.

i $(a + 3)^2$

ii $(b + 6)^2$

iii $(c - 4)^2$

⑥ **a** Multiply $(x + 5)$ by $(x + 10)$.

b This rectangle has sides $(x + 5)$ and $(x + 10)$.
It is divided into four parts. One of them is a square of side x.
Copy the rectangle and mark the areas of the four parts on the rectangle.

c Explain the connection between your answers to parts **a** and **b**.

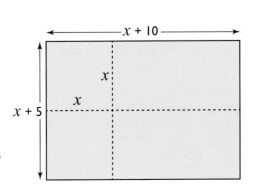

7 The sides of this rectangle are $2x + 4$ cm and $2x$ cm.

   a Find, in terms of x,

     i The area of the whole rectangle

     ii The area that is coloured red.

   b Show that the red and black regions have the same area.

Problem solving

1 A farmer has a field in the shape of a rectangle.

The length of the field is 20 m greater than the width.
Write an expression, in terms of w, for the area of the field.

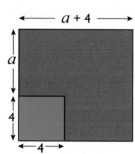

2 Find an expression, in terms of a, for the area shaded red.

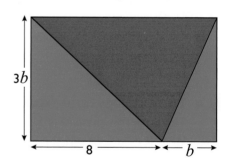

3 Here is a rectangle.

Find an expression, in terms of b, for the area shaded red.

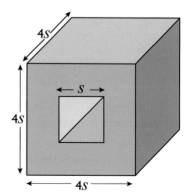

4 A hole in the shape of a square prism is cut through the middle of a cube.

The cube has side $4s$.

The square hole has side s.

Show that the volume of the shape remaining is $60s^3$.

⑤ Find the value of n to make these statements true.

a $a^4 \times a^n = a^{12}$

b $\dfrac{12p^9}{3p^n} = 4p^3$

c $(y^n)^4 = y^{12}$

⑥ All measurements are in cm.

a Find an expression, in terms of x, for the blue area on this flag.

b Show that it is the same as the red area.

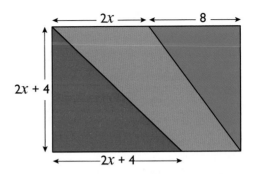

Reviewing skills

① Write these expressions as single powers.

a $a^6 \times a^8$

b $b^{12} \div b^6$

c $c^{16} \div (c^4 \times c^{12})$

d $(d^9)^2$

② Simplify these expressions.

a $6a^4 \times 2a^3$

b $\dfrac{8b^{10}}{2b^5}$

c $\dfrac{3a^2b \times 2ab^2}{6(ab)^3}$

d $\dfrac{30g^{12}h^4}{6g^4h^4}$

③ Expand these expressions and simplify your answers.

a $(a+5)(a+6)$

b $(b-3)(b+7)$

c $(c+1)(c-5)$

d $(d-3)(d-5)$

④ **a** Find the area of the red rectangle in terms of x.
The blue square has sides of x cm.

b Find the areas of each of the three regions in terms of x.

c Find the area of the whole figure in terms of x.

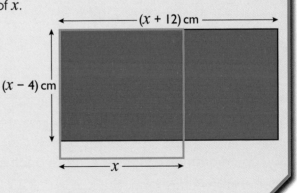

Unit 10 • Using complex formulae • Band h

→ Outside the Maths classroom

Savings plans

What is the difference between compound interest and simple interest?

↓ Toolbox

You can substitute numbers into formulae, these may include negative numbers and decimals.

v^2 is the **subject** of the formula $v^2 = u^2 + 2as$.

Find v when $u = -3$, $a = 9.8$ and $s = 20$.

$$v^2 = u^2 + 2as$$

$$v^2 = (-3)^2 + 2 \times 9.8 \times 20$$ ← Substitute the values given into the formula.

$$v^2 = 9 + 392$$

$$v^2 = 401$$ ← Square root both sides of the formula to find v.

$$v = +20.02 \text{ or } -20.02 \text{ to 2 d.p.}$$ ← Remember that there are two answers when you square root a number, one positive and one negative.

You can **rearrange** a formula to make another letter the subject.

You can use number machines as in Unit 4. A better way is to use a method similar to solving an equation.

You must do the same thing to both sides of the formula to get the variable you want by itself on one side of the formula.

Make s the subject.   Make u the subject.

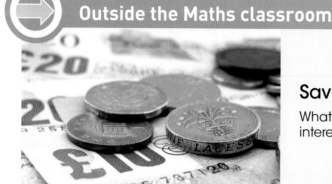

$-u^2 \quad \begin{array}{c} u^2 + 2as = v^2 \\ 2as = v^2 - u^2 \end{array} \Big) -u^2$

$\div 2a \quad \begin{array}{c} \\ s = \dfrac{v^2 - u^2}{2a} \end{array} \Big) \div 2a$

$-2as \quad \begin{array}{c} u^2 + 2as = v^2 \\ u^2 = v^2 - 2as \end{array} \Big) -2as$

$\text{square root} \quad \begin{array}{c} \\ u = \pm\sqrt{v^2 - 2as} \end{array} \quad \text{square root}$

Example – Substituting negative numbers into a formula

Work out the value of a when $b = -2$ in this expression

$$a = \frac{3b^2 - 6}{b + 4}$$

Solution

$$a = \frac{3b^2 - 6}{b + 4}$$

Substitute b = -2 into the expression.

$$= \frac{3 \times (-2)^2 - 6}{(-2) + 4}$$

Note that $(-2)^2$ means -2×-2 which is equal to 4.

$$= \frac{3 \times 4 - 6}{2}$$

$$= \frac{6}{2} = 3$$

Example – Working with formulae

The area of this trapezium is $48 \, \text{cm}^2$.
Work out the height of the trapezium.

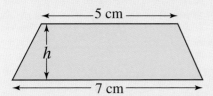

Solution

The formula for the area of a trapezium is

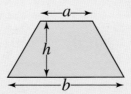

$$A = \frac{1}{2}h(a + b)$$

So $48 = \frac{1}{2}h(5 + 7)$

Substitute $A = 48$, $a = 5$ and $b = 7$ into the formula.

$$\frac{1}{2}h(5 + 7) = 48$$

It is usual to work with the variable on the LHS of the equation.

$$\frac{1}{2}h \times 12 = 48$$

$$6h = 48$$

$$h = 8$$

So the height of the trapezium is 8 cm.

Example – Rearranging a formula

The formula for the perimeter of a rectangle is
$$P = 2(l + w)$$

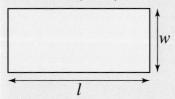

w

l

Rearrange the formula to make *l* the subject.

Solution

Method 1

Look at how Beth and David rearrange the formula:

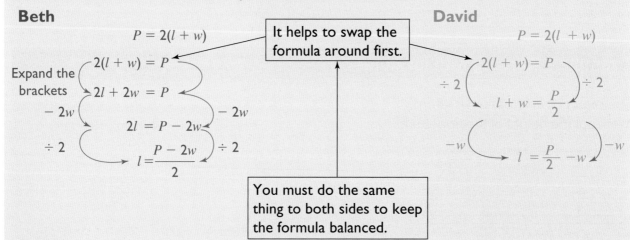

Beth

$$P = 2(l + w)$$

It helps to swap the formula around first.

Expand the brackets

$2(l + w) = P$

$- 2w$ $2l + 2w = P$ $- 2w$

$\div 2$ $2l = P - 2w$

$l = \dfrac{P - 2w}{2}$ $\div 2$

David

$$P = 2(l + w)$$

$\div 2$ $2(l + w) = P$ $\div 2$

$l + w = \dfrac{P}{2}$

$- w$ $l = \dfrac{P}{2} - w$ $- w$

You must do the same thing to both sides to keep the formula balanced.

Method 2

You can also use a function machine.

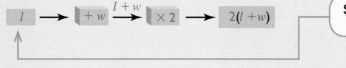

$l \rightarrow \boxed{+ w} \xrightarrow{l + w} \boxed{\times 2} \rightarrow 2(l + w)$

Start with *l*, the letter that you want to make the subject.

$\dfrac{P}{2} - w \leftarrow \boxed{- w} \xleftarrow{\frac{P}{2}} \boxed{\div 2} \leftarrow P$

Starting with the original subject of the formula, find the inverse.

So $l = \dfrac{p}{2} - w$

Practising skills

① Find the value of $5a - 3b + 2c$ when

   a $a = 4, b = 6, c = 5$ **b** $a = 8, b = -3, c = -2$

   c $a = 5, b = -1, c = 6$ **d** $a = 0.5, b = 1.5, c = 2.5$

② Find the value of $6d + 3e - 4f$ when

   a $d = 2, e = 4, f = 1$ **b** $d = 7, e = 3, f = -4$

   c $d = 3, e = -9, f = 2$ **d** $d = 0.1, e = -0.4, f = 0.3$

③ Find the value of $3x^2 - 6x$ when

   a $x = 4$ **b** $x = 5$ **c** $x = -2$ **d** $x = -1$

④ Find the value of $5x(2y - 4)$ when

   a $x = 3, y = 5$ **b** $x = 4, y = 7$ **c** $x = 2, y = -3$ **d** $x = -5, y = -2$

⑤ Make x the subject of the formulae.

   a $y = x - 8$ **b** $y = 3x$ **c** $y = \dfrac{x}{5}$ **d** $y = 2x + 1$

⑥ Make the bold letter the subject of these formulae.

   a $y = \boldsymbol{x} + 4$ **b** $y = 4\boldsymbol{x} - 3$ **c** $a = 6\boldsymbol{b}$ **d** $p = m\boldsymbol{t}$

⑦ Work out the value of $4t^2 - 3w$ when

   a $t = 3, w = 4$ **b** $t = 5, w = -2$ **c** $t = -4, w = 5$ **d** $t = -3, w = -6$

Developing fluency

① Football teams use the formula $3w + d$ to work out the number of points they have, where w is the number of wins and d is the number of draws.

   a Work out the points these teams have.

      i 8 wins and 3 draws

      ii 10 wins and 2 draws

      iii 7 wins and 5 draws

   b Make w the subject of the formula.

   c A team has 20 points. It has drawn 5 matches. How many matches has it won?

② A taxi driver uses the formula $c = 2p + 1.5m$ to work out the fares, where £c is the fare, p is the number of passengers and m miles is the distance travelled.

   a Work out the fares for these journeys.

      i 2 passengers and 6 miles

      ii 1 passenger and 8 miles

      iii 3 passengers and 10 miles

   b Make m the subject of this formula.

   c Find the length of a journey for 3 passengers costing £10.50.

③ A plumber charges £35 per hour plus £18 call-out charge.

   a Write a formula for the cost of a job, £C, lasting h hours.

   b How much does he charge for a job lasting

      i 2 hours   **ii** 6 hours   **iii** 10 hours?

   c Rearrange your formula to make h the subject.

   d How long did the job last if it cost

      i £158   **ii** £438   **iii** £963?

④ The surface area of a sphere is given by the formula $S = 4\pi r^2$ where r is the radius of the sphere. Use the π key on your calculator.

   a Find the surface area of the spheres with radius

      i 6 cm   **ii** 12 m   **iii** 400 km

   b The radius of the Earth is approximately 6400 km. Find its surface area.

   c Rearrange the formula to make r the subject.

   d Find the radius of a marble with surface area 50.265 cm^2.
       Give your answer to 2 decimal places.

⑤ The formula to convert temperatures in Fahrenheit, $F°$, to degrees Celsius, $C°$, is $C = \dfrac{5}{9}(F - 32)$.

   a Convert these Fahrenheit temperatures to degrees Celsius.

      i 32°   **ii** 95°   **iii** 212°   **iv** −40°

   b Make F the subject of this formula.

   c Find the value of F when

      i $C = 0$ **ii** $C = 35$ **iii** $C = 300$ **iv** $C = -40$

⑥ Here is a formula.

$$P = \dfrac{4Mt^2}{h}$$

   a Work out the value of P when $M = 200$, $t = 4$ and $h = 25$.

   b Rearrange the formula to make these the subject.

      i M **ii** t **iii** h

   c Use the appropriate formula to work out the values of

      i M when $P = 4000$, $t = 10$ and $h = 5$

      ii h when $P = 640$, $t = 8$ and $M = 50$

      iii t when $P = 98$, $M = 4$ and $h = 8$.

⑦ Make the bold letter the subject of these formulae.

   a $y = 5\boldsymbol{x} - 6$ **b** $y = 5(\boldsymbol{x} - 6)$ **c** $T = 4m\boldsymbol{p}$ **d** $T = m^2 + 4p\boldsymbol{r}$

Problem solving

① Tara uses the formula $C = 30h + 15$ to work out how much she is going to charge a customer, £C, for working on a car for h hours.

    a How much does she charge for working on a car for 5 hours?

    b Make h subject of the formula.

    c Tara charges Tom £52.50 for working on his car.
       For how long does Tara work on Tom's car?

② The cost, £C, of hiring a cement mixer for d days is given by the formula $C = 12d + 20$.
Rob hires a cement mixer for 7 days.

    a How much does it cost?

    b Make d the subject of the formula.

    c Celia hires a cement mixer and pays £200.
       How many days did Celia hire the mixer for?

③ Jill's monthly bill, £B, for using a mobile phone when she makes c calls and sends t texts is given by the formula $B = \dfrac{10c + 5t}{100} + 15$.

Last month Jill made 120 calls and sent 450 texts.

    a How much was her bill?

    b Make c the subject of the formula.

    c This month Jill's bill was £28. She sent 100 texts. How many calls did she make?

④ The density, d, of a solid object is given by the formula $d = \dfrac{m}{V}$, where m is the mass of the object and V is its volume.

    a Make m the subject of the formula.

    b A packet of butter in the shape of a cuboid has dimensions 10 cm by 6 cm by 4 cm.
       The density of the butter is 1.05 g/cm^3.
       Find the mass of the butter.

⑤ The volume, V, of tomato soup in a can is given by the formula $V = \pi r^2 h$, where r is the radius of the can and h is the height of the can.

    a Make h the subject of the formula.

    b The radius of the can is 3.5 cm and the volume of the soup in the can is 400 cm^3. Find the height of the can.
       Give your answer to the nearest 0.1 cm.

⑥ The area of a trapezium is given by the formula
$A = \frac{1}{2}(a + b)h$

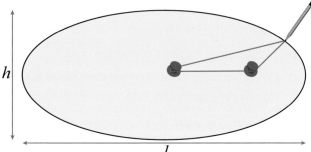
a cm

h cm

b cm

a Find the area of the trapezium when $a = 6$, $b = 10$, and $h = 4$.

b Make h the subject of the formula.

c Find the value of h when $A = 30$, $a = 4.75$ and $b = 7.25$.

d Now make a the subject of the formula.

e Find the value of a when $A = 32.5$, $h = 7$ and $b = 5.28$.

⑦ Dave draws an ellipse on a piece of paper using a piece of string and two drawing pins.

The area of an ellipse is given by the formula $A = \frac{\pi l h}{4}$ where l is the length of the ellipse and h is its height.

h

l

a Find the area of the ellipse when $l = 10$ cm and $h = 4$ cm. Give your answer in terms of π.

b Make l the subject of the formula.

c Dave draws another ellipse. The height of this ellipse is 6 cm, and its area is 15π cm². Find the length of this ellipse.

Reviewing skills

① Make the bold letter the subject of these formulae.

a $d = \boldsymbol{e} + f$ **b** $s = a\boldsymbol{t} + b$ **c** $f = \dfrac{\boldsymbol{g}}{h}$ **d** $v = 4\boldsymbol{w} - 3$

e $C = 2\pi \boldsymbol{r}$ **f** $A = \pi \boldsymbol{r}^2$ **g** $P = \dfrac{M t \boldsymbol{r}}{100}$ **h** $S = 3\boldsymbol{t}^2$

② The final velocity, v, of particles in an experiment is given by the formula $v = u + at$, where a is the acceleration, u is the initial velocity and t is the time of travel.

a Find the value of v when

i $u = 4$, $a = 2$, $t = 3$

ii $u = -10$, $a = 5$, $t = 2$,

iii $u = 20$, $a = -10$, $t = 4$

iv $u = 30$, $a = 0$, $t = 7$

b Make a the subject of the formula.

c A particle accelerates from 10 m/s to 25 m/s in 5 seconds. Calculate its acceleration.

Unit 11 • Identities • Band h

Outside the Maths classroom

Formulae in spreadsheets

Which occupations use spreadsheets?

Toolbox

Here are two formulae:

$$F = \frac{9}{5}C + 32 \qquad u^2 = v^2 - 2as$$

A **formula** is a rule for working something out.
It shows the relationship between the variables.

These formulae both have three **terms**.
A **term** is a single number or variable or a product
of numbers and variables.

> The six terms here are:
> $$F \quad \frac{9}{5}C \quad 32 \quad u^2 \quad v^2 \quad 2as$$

An **expression** is a collection of **terms**, or a single **term**.

> So each of the six terms is an
> expression, but so are
> $$\frac{9}{5}C + 32 \text{ and } v^2 - 2as.$$

Expressions and terms also occur in **equations**
and **identities**.

An **equation** can be solved to find an
unknown quantity.

> The equation $95 = \frac{9}{5}C + 32$ can
> be solved to find the value of C.

An **identity** is **always** true, for all possible
values of the variable.

> $3(x + 2) \equiv 3x + 6$ is an identity.

Conventions for whole numbers

By convention, **n** represents a whole number. This means that:

$2n$ represents multiples of 2, or even numbers and so does **$2n + 2$**.

$2n + 1$ or **$2n - 1$** stands for one more or one less than a multiple of 2, so an odd number.

$3n$ represents a multiple of 3, and so on.

$n + 1$ represents one more than n, so n and $n + 1$ are consecutive integers.

These expressions are useful when making an argument to prove a result.

Example – Using the vocabulary, understanding the concept

n stands for an integer (whole number) in each of these expressions.

$$5n \qquad 3n + 2 \qquad 3n + 2n \qquad 2n + 5 \qquad 10n + 15 \qquad 4n + 1$$

a Which of these expressions are always a multiple of five?

b How do you know which expressions are a multiple of 5 and which expressions are not a multiple of 5?

Solution

a $5n$, $3n + 2n$ and $10n + 15$ are always multiples of five.

b $5n = 5 \times n$ so is a multiple of 5 by definition.

$3n + 2n = 5n$ so is a multiple of 5. ◄——— | It doesn't matter which value of n you use, the result will always be a multiple of 5. |

$10n + 15 = 5(2n + 3)$ so is a multiple of 5.

When $n = 5$: ◄——— | To show something is not true you only have to find one example that is not true. |

$\quad 3n + 2 = 3 \times 5 + 2 = 17$

$\quad 2n + 2 = 2 \times 5 + 2 = 12$

$\quad 4n + 1 = 4 \times 5 + 1 = 21$

So these expressions may equal multiples of five for some values of n but not all.

Example – Proof

a Write expressions for three consecutive integers.

b Prove that the sum of three consecutive integers is always a multiple of 3.

Solution

Consecutive means 'following each other' so 4, 5 and 6 are three consecutive numbers.

a There are several possible answers:

$n, n + 1, n + 2$ is the most often used ◄——— | Call the first number n, the next number is 1 more than n and the third number is 2 more than n. |

$n - 1, n, n + 1$ is another possibility

b Using the answers from a

$\text{sum} = n + n + 1 + n + 2$

$\qquad = 3n + 3$

$\qquad = 3(n + 1)$ which is a multiple of 3. ◄——— | Factorising. |

Or

$\text{sum} = n - 1 + n + n + 1$

$\qquad = 3n$ which is a multiple of 3.

Practising skills

1

an expression	an identity	a term
an equation	a formula	coefficient

Fill in the missing word from the list in the box.

a $5x$ is ☐ of $x^2 + 5x + 7$.

b 5 is the ☐ of x in $x^2 + 5x + 7$.

c $5w - 7$ is ☐.

d $2n$ can be ☐ and ☐.

e $3t - 5 = t + 7$ is ☐.

f $s = 4t - 4.9t^2$ is ☐.

g $a + b = b + a$ is ☐.

Reasoning

2 Which term in the expression $n^2 + 2n - 1$ is always an even number, given that n is an integer? How do you know?

Reasoning

3 One of these is a formula, one is an equation and one is an identity.

$H = x^2 - 6x + 5$ $\quad 0 = x^2 - 6x + 5 \quad$ $(x - 5)(x - 1) = x^2 - 6x + 5$

Which is the equation and which is the identity? How do you know?

4 Show that

a $x + 5 + 3x - 6 = 4x - 1$

b $x(x + 1) - x - 1 = x^2 - 1$

c $4(x - 3) + 3(x + 7) = 7x + 9$

5 Match the expressions to their description, given that n is an integer.

an odd number	a multiple of 3	a multiple of 7
a square number	an even number	

a $2n$

b n^2

c $7n$

d $2n - 1$

e $4n - n$

6 $n^2 + 5$ is even for some values of n.

Choose the values from the list that make $n^2 + 5$ even.

1	6	9	15	24	99

Developing fluency

① Given that n is an integer, say whether these expressions are always odd, never odd or sometimes odd. Give examples to justify your answers.

a $n + 1$ **b** $2n - 1$ **c** $3n + 5$

d $2n + 1$ **e** $6n$

② **a** $7n$ is a multiple of 5 for some values of n. Describe those values of n.

b $2n + 4$ is a multiple of 3 for some values of n. Describe those values of n.

③ **a** Are the following statements true for all values of x, some values of x or no values of x?

    i $5x - 2 = 2 - 5x$ **ii** $5x + 2 = 2 + 5x$ **iii** $x^2 + 5 = 9 + x^2$

    iv $x \div 2 = \frac{1}{2}x$ **v** $x \div \frac{1}{2} = \frac{1}{2}x$ **vi** $x \div \frac{1}{2} = 2x$

b Which of the statements above are identities? Justify your answer.

④ Show that

a $5(x - 2) - 2(x + 3) = 3(2 - x) + 2(3x - 11)$

b $(x + 1)(x - 1) = x^2 - 1$

c $(3x + 1)(5 - 2x) = 1 - 6(x - 4)(x + 1) - 5(x + 4)$

⑤ Prove that

a The sum of two consecutive integers is always odd.

b The sum of five consecutive integers is always a multiple of 5.

c The sum of four consecutive integers is always a multiple of 2.

⑥ Three piles of stones are made up of a total of 45 stones.
The first pile has n stones.
The second pile has twice as many stones as the first one.
The third pile has 5 more stones than the second pile.
Write expressions for the number of stones in each pile.
Use them to work out how many stones there are in each pile.

⑦ The diagram shows part of a city in the United States. It is laid out on a square grid. The roads run north–south and east–west.

Dwight, Gus and Hank set out from O to visit Lil who lives at L. L is x blocks to the east and y blocks to the north of O.

The diagram shows the routes they take. They are all different.

Dwight starts by going a blocks north to A; then he goes b blocks east to B. After that he goes to C and then L.

Hank follows the route OPQRL. OP is p blocks and PQ is q blocks.

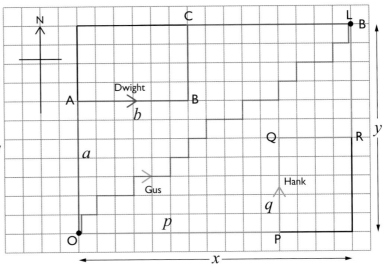

Gus tries to keep as near as he can to a straight line from O to L.

a i Write down expressions for BC and CL.

  ii Write an expression for the total number of blocks in Dwight's total journey.

b i Write down expressions for QR and RL.

  ii Write and expression for the total numbers of blocks in Hank's total journey.

c What do you notice about Dwight's and Hank's journeys?

d What can you say about Gus's journey?

Problem solving

① Look at this triangle.

Pythagoras' theorem tells you that the triangle is right-angled.

$$3^2 + 4^2 = 5^2$$
$$(9 + 16 = 25)$$

Here is a way to find other right-angled triangles with whole-number sides.

Step	Example
Write down an even number	4
Square it	16
Write down the numbers just above and below it	17 and 15
Double your original number	8

The last three numbers you wrote down are the sides of a right-angled triangle.

$$8^2 + 15^2 = 17^2$$

a Check that this works with the following starting numbers.

  i 2   **ii** 6   **iii** 10   **iv** 1000

b Prove that it works with $2n$ as a starting number (where n is any positive whole number).

5 cm
3 cm
4 cm

(2) In the grid six expressions have been written across the top and again down the side.

	3x + 15	4x – 2	F	3(x + 5)	7x – 5	3(x + 2) + 9
3x + 15					equation x = 5	
4x – 2						
F						
3(x + 5)						
7x – 5						
3(x + 2) + 9						

a For each cell in the grid make the side and the top expressions equal to each other. Write in the cell whether they make a *formula*, *equation*, *identity* or *expression*.
The one that has been done for you shows 3x + 15 = 7x – 5 which is an equation.

b What shortcuts helped you to fill in the grid more quickly?

c Why was the answer never 'expression'?

Reviewing skills

(1) Some of the following statements are equations; others are identities.

   i 2x + 6x = 2x + 24

   ii 2(x + 7) + 3 (x + 2) = 5 (x + 4)

   iii x^2 – 8x – 1 = (x – 2) (x – 6) – 13

   iv x(x – 2) – x^2 + 1 = (x – 1)^2 – x^2

  a Say which is an equation and which an identity.

  b Solve the equations and show that the identities are true.

(2) Say whether these statements are true or false, explaining your answers.

  a $(n + 1)^2 > n^2$ for all values of n (positive, zero or negative).

  b An identity in x is true for any value of x.

  c No square number ends in 2.

  d $4n^2 = (2n)^2$

Strand 2 Sequences

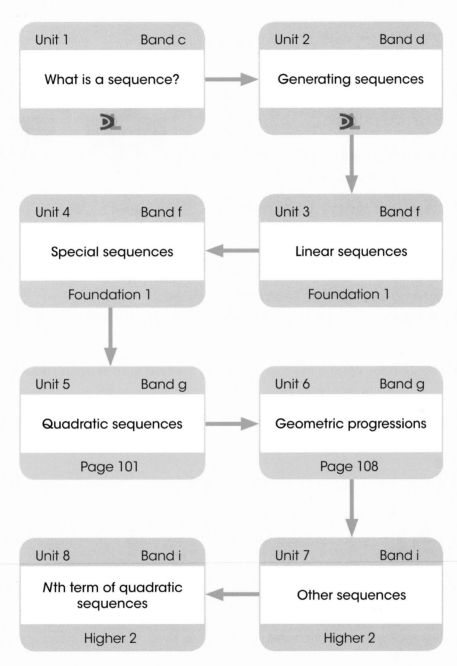

Unit 1	Band c
What is a sequence?	

Unit 2	Band d
Generating sequences	

Unit 4	Band f
Special sequences	
Foundation 1	

Unit 3	Band f
Linear sequences	
Foundation 1	

Unit 5	Band g
Quadratic sequences	
Page 101	

Unit 6	Band g
Geometric progressions	
Page 108	

Unit 8	Band i
Nth term of quadratic sequences	
Higher 2	

Unit 7	Band i
Other sequences	
Higher 2	

Units 1–4 are assumed knowledge for this book. They are reviewed and extended in the Moving on section on page 100.

① Barry makes a tiling pattern using red and blue tiles.

   a Find an expression, in terms of n, for the total number of tiles in pattern n.

   b How many red tiles are there in the nth even-numbered pattern?

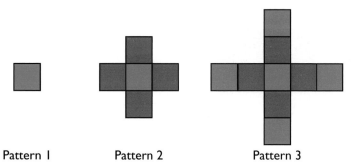

Pattern 1   Pattern 2   Pattern 3

② Here are the first few terms of a sequence.

   11, 29, 47 …

   a Work out the term-to-term rule.

   b Write down the position-to-term formula for the sequence.

   c Find the 50th term.

   d Which position is the term 497?

③ Look at these sequences. What is the rule for finding the next term in each sequence?

   a $\dfrac{1}{2}, \dfrac{3}{4}, \dfrac{9}{8}, \square$ **b** $0, 3, 8, 15 \square$ **c** $-2, -3, -5, -8, \square$

④ In a classroom six people can sit around a single table.

If two tables are put together, 10 people can sit around them.

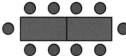

   a Write the position to term rule that will calculate how many people can sit around n tables arranged in a row like this.

Alternatively, two tables can be arranged like this:

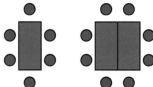

   b What is the position to term rule for this arrangement?

   c Why are the two rules different?

Unit 5 • Quadratic sequences • Band g

Outside the Maths classroom

Building bridges

What shape is the curve on this bridge?

How does knowing the equation of the curve help the engineers build the bridge?

Toolbox

The sequence of **square numbers** begins 1, 4, 9, 16, 25, ...

The differences between these terms are 3, 5, 7, 9, ... and the difference between these differences is constant. In this case, it is 2.

Sequence	1		4		9		16		25 ...
1st difference		+3		+5		+7		+9	
2nd difference			+2		+2		+2		

Such sequences are known as **quadratic sequences** and the expression for the nth term always contain a term in n^2.

For example, the formula for the nth term of a simple quadratic sequence rule might be $n^2 + 1$, which would give 2, 5, 10, 17, 26, ...

To find the rule for a quadratic sequence, look at the relationship between the square numbers (1, 4, 9, 16, 25) and the sequence itself.

Example – Generating terms of a quadratic sequence

Find the fourth and sixth terms of the sequence whose nth term is given by $3n^2 - 8$.

Solution

When $n = 4$,
$3n^2 - 8 = 3 \times 4^2 - 8$

$\qquad = 3 \times 16 - 8$ ← Squaring first.

$\qquad = 48 - 8$ ← Then multiplication.

$\qquad = 40$

When $n = 6$,
$3n^2 - 8 = 3 \times 6^2 - 8$ ← Substitute 6 into the formula.

$\qquad = 3 \times 36 - 8$ ← Squaring first.

$\qquad = 108 - 8$ ← Then multiplication.

$\qquad = 100$

101

Example – Finding the *n*th term of a quadratic sequence

Here is a sequence of patterns.

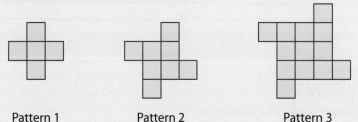

Pattern 1   Pattern 2   Pattern 3

a Draw pattern 4.

b The number of squares in the patterns form a sequence.

What are the first five terms of the sequence?

c Find the *n*th term of this sequence.

Explain how the patterns help you to find the *n*th term of the sequence.

Solution

a

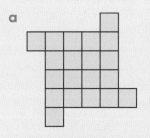

Pattern 4

b From the diagrams, the first four terms are 5, 8, 13, 20.

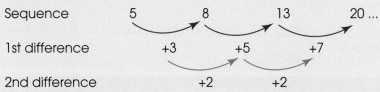

| | Sequence | 5 | 8 | 13 | 20 ... |

1st difference   +3   +5   +7

2nd difference   +2   +2

The next first difference will be 9, so the fifth term is 29.

c The first differences are not the same so the sequence is not linear.

The second differences are the same so this is a quadratic sequence.

Square numbers   1   4   9   16   25   ⟵ [Start with the square numbers.]

+4   +4   +4   +4   +4

This sequence   5   8   13   20   29   ⟵ [To get the required sequence, add 4.]

The *n*th term is therefore $n^2 + 4$.

Look at the pattern.

- The first pattern is a 1 × 1 square plus four single squares.
- The second pattern is a 2 × 2 square plus four single squares.
- The third pattern is a 3 × 3 square plus four single squares.

So the *n*th pattern will be an $n \times n$ square plus four single squares, giving $n^2 + 4$ squares in total.

Practising skills

(1) Write down the first five terms for these sequences.

   a nth term = $5n^2$

   b nth term = $n^2 + 5$

   c nth term = $2n^2 - 1$

   d nth term = $3n^2 + 4$

   e nth term = $10n^2 - 5$

(2) Match each sequence with its position-to-term formula.

   a 9, 8, 7, 6, 5, ...   **i** $n^2 + 10$

   b 90, 80, 70, 60, 50, ...   **ii** $10 - n$

   c 10, 40, 90, 160, 250, ...   **iii** $100 - 10n$

   d 11, 14, 19, 26, 35, ...   **iv** $10n^2$

(3) Find the missing term in each of these sequences and then write down the position-to-term formula.

   a 1, 4, 9, ☐, 25

   b 2, 5, 10, ☐, 26

   c 2, 8, ☐, 32, 50

   d 5, 11, 21, ☐, 53

(4) **a** Copy and complete this table for the sequence with nth term $n^2 + 3$.

     (You may find compiling a spreadsheet useful for this.)

Term	$n^2 + 3$	1st difference	2nd difference
1	4		
2	7	3	
3	12	5	2
4			
5			

   b Repeat part **a** for

     i $n^2 - 1$ **ii** $n^2 + 2$ **iii** $2n^2 - 3$

     iv $5n^2$ **v** $3n^2 + 5$

   c Do all quadratic sequences have the same second difference?

(5) Match each sequence with its position-to-term formula.

   i $2n^2 + 2$ **ii** $n^2 + 2$ **iii** $4n^2 + 6$ **iv** $5n^2 + 5$ **v** $100 - 2n^2$

   a 10, 22, 42, 70, 106, ...

   b 98, 92, 82, 68, 50, ...

   c 4, 10, 20, 34, 52, ...

   d 3, 6, 11, 18, 27, ...

   e 10, 25, 50, 85, 130, ...

6 a Which of these sequences are quadratic?

    i 5, 8, 13, 20, 29, …

    ii 10, 20, 30, 40, 50, …

    iii 3, 12, 27, 48, 75, …

    iv 2, 16, 54, 128, 250, …

    v 5, 11, 21, 35, 53, …

b For the quadratic sequences, write down the position-to-term formula.

Developing fluency

1 Look at this table of sequences.

	1	2	3	4	5	…
A	2	4	6	8	10	…
B	1	4	9	16	25	…
C	0	3	8	15	24	…
D	3	8	15	24	35	…
E	1	3	14	23	34	…

    a Write down the next term in each sequence.

    b Write down the rule for the nth term of sequence **A** and **B**.

    c i How is sequence **C** related to sequence **B**?

      ii Write down the nth term of sequence **C**.

    d i How is sequence **D** related to sequences **A** and **B**?

      ii Write down the nth term of sequence **D**.

    e i Which two sequences are used to make sequence **E**?

      ii Write down the nth term of sequence **E**.

2 Katrina is making a sequence of patterns from square tiles.

    a Draw the next pattern in the sequence.

    b Copy and complete the table.

Pattern	1	2	3	4	5
Number of tiles					

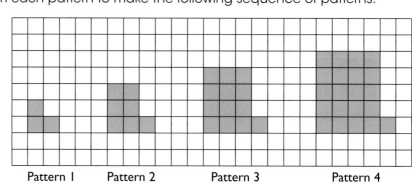

Pattern 1   Pattern 2   Pattern 3

    c Which pattern uses 100 tiles?

    d How many tiles are there in the nth pattern?

Katrina removes some tiles from each pattern to make the following sequence of patterns.

    e i How many tiles does Katrina remove from the 50th pattern?

      ii How many tiles are left in the 50th pattern?

      iii How many tiles are left in the nth pattern?

Pattern 1   Pattern 2   Pattern 3   Pattern 4

3 Here is a pattern made from triangular tiles.

a How many tiles would be needed for Pattern number 8?

b How many tiles are needed for Patter number n?

c Which pattern has 100 tiles?

d Explain why the difference between 2 adjacent pattern numbers is always an odd number.

Pattern number 1   Pattern number 2   Pattern number 3

4 Ben is stacking tins of baked beans.

a How many tins are in stack 5?

The 20th stack needs 210 tins.

b How many tins are needed for the 21st stack?

Ben has 120 tins to stack.

c How many tins should he place in the bottom row?

The nth stack has $\frac{1}{2}n(n+1)$ tins.

d How many tins are in the 100th stack?

Comfort has 169 tins to stack.

e i Can she make one stack out of these tins?
Explain your answer fully.

ii Comfort uses all of the 169 tins to make 2 stacks.
How many tins are in each stack?

Stack 1   Stack 2   Stack 3

5 Look at this Rubik's cube.
It is made up of small cubes around a central mechanism.

a Write down how many cubes have

i 1 sticker   **ii** 2 stickers   **iii** 3 stickers.

b How many cubes have at least one sticker on them?

c You can get different-sized Rubik's cubes.
The smallest is a 2 by 2 by 2 cube. You can also get larger cubes like a 5 by 5 by 5 cube.
Copy and complete this table for different-sized cubes.

Cube size	2	3	4	5	10	n
1 sticker						
2 stickers						
3 stickers						
Total number of stickered cubes						

Reasoning

105

Problem solving

① Here are the first 3 shapes in a rectangular pattern made from dots.

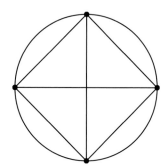

    a How many dots are there in pattern number 6?

    b Find the number of dots in the nth pattern.

    c Find an expression, in terms of n, for the difference in the number of dots between the nth pattern and the $(n + 1)$ pattern.

    d Between which two consecutive patterns is the difference in the number of dots 102?

② Jake draws a circle. He marks points around the circumference of the circle, joining each point to every other point.

Points	Number of lines at each point	Total number of lines
2	1	1
3	2	3
4	3	6
5	4	
6	5	
7	7	
8	8	
n		

    a Copy and complete this table for the number of points around the circle.

    b Mary made a circle pattern by marking points at every 10° from the centre of the circle. How many lines did Mary draw?

③ The nth term of a quadratic sequence is $n^2 + 8$.
The nth term of a different quadratic sequence is $49 - n^2$.
Which numbers are in both sequences?

④ The diagrams show the numbers of diagonals in some regular polygons.

    a Find the number of diagonals in a regular decagon.

    b Find an expression, in terms of n, for the number of diagonals at each vertex of an n-sided polygon.

    c Hence, or otherwise, find the number of diagonals in an n-sided regular polygon.

    d An n-sided polygon has over 100 diagonals. What is the smallest possible value of n?

Reviewing skills

① Find the missing term in each of these sequences and then write down the position-to-term formula.

a 20, 30, 40, 50, 60, □, …

b 3, 12, 27, □, 75, …

c 99, 96, 99, □, 75, …

d 12, 45, 100, □, 276, …

② Copy and complete this table for the sequence with nth term $n^2 + 5$.

(You may find compiling a spreadsheet useful for this.)

Term	$n^2 + 5$	1st difference	2nd difference
1	6		
2	9	3	
3	14	5	2
4			
5			

③ Here are some patterns made from square tiles.

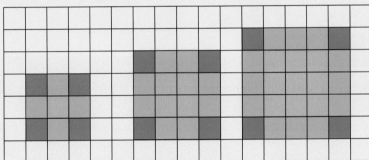

Pattern 1   Pattern 2   Pattern 3

a Draw pattern number 4.

b Copy and complete the table.

Pattern number	1	2	3	4	5
Number of green squares					
Number of blue squares					
Number of red squares					
Total number of squares, S					

c Write down how many of these are in the 10th pattern.

  i green squares   **ii** blue squares   **iii** red squares

  iv Work out the total number of squares in the 10th pattern.

d Write down how many of these are in the nth pattern.

  i green squares   **ii** blue squares   **iii** red squares

e Write down a formula for the total number of squares, S, in the nth pattern.

  Write your formula in two different ways.

Unit 6 • Geometric progressions • Band g

Outside the Maths classroom

 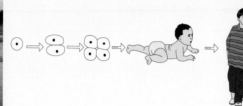

Population change

How might a population of swans change over time?

Toolbox

A **geometric progression** is a sequence where each term is found by multiplying the previous term by the same amount.

The **common ratio** of a geometric progression is the number you multiply each term by to get the next term.

You need to know the first term and **common ratio** to write out a geometric progression.

Sometimes you are not given these but you are given enough information to work them out.

Working out the first term and common ratio is the first step.

A geometric progression has first term $\frac{1}{2}$ and common ratio 4.

First term $= \frac{1}{2}$

Second term $= \frac{1}{2} \times 4 = 2$

Third term $= 2 \times 4 = 8$

Fourth term $= 8 \times 4 = 32$

Fifth term $= 32 \times 4 = 128$

Sixth term $= 128 \times 4 = 512$

Seventh term $= 512 \times 4 = 2048$

The size of the terms increase very quickly.

Geometric progressions have terms that increase or decrease exponentially.
As a result they are used in many contexts.

For example: compound interest, depreciation, population growth or decline, radioactive decay.

Example – Generating geometric progressions

A geometric progression has first term 1 and common ratio 4.
Write down the first five terms of the sequence.

Solution

First term = **1** ← (The first term is 1, to find the next term multiply the previous term by 3.)

Second term = 1 × 3 = **3**

Third term = 3 × 3 = **9**

Fourth term = 9 × 3 = **27**

Fifth term = 27 × 3 = **81**

They are powers of 3. $(3^0, 3^1, 3^2, 3^3, ...)$

Example – Finding the common ratio

Here are two different sequences.

a 1, 4, 9,...

b 10, 4, 1.6...

Decide whether each sequence is geometric and find the common ratio if there is one.

Solution

a Work out the ratios between the terms.

   4 ÷ 1 = 1

   9 ÷ 4 = 2.25

   There is no common ratio between successive terms so the sequence is not a geometric progression.

b Work out the ratios between the terms.

   4 ÷ 10 = 0.4 ← ($10 \times r = 4$ so $r = 4 ÷ 10$)

   1.6 ÷ 4 = 0.4 ← ($4 \times r = 1.6$ so $r = 1.6 ÷ 4$)

   These are the same so the sequence is a geometric progression.

   The common ratio, r, is 0.4. ← (Check: 10 × 0.4 = 4 ✓ and 4 × 0.4 = 1.6 ✓)

Practising skills

① Decide whether each sequence is a geometric progression.

    a 1, 2, 3, 4...

    b 1, 2, 4, 8...

    c 1, 2, 4, 7...

    d 80, 40, 20, 10...

② A geometric progression has first term 3 and common ratio 3.

    a Write down the first four terms of the sequence.

    b Describe these numbers.

③ The sequences are geometric progressions.
Write down the common ratio for each one.

    a 1, 4, 16, 64...

    b 4, 12, 36, 108...

    c 4, 2, 1, $\frac{1}{2}$

    d 10, 1, 0.1, 0.01...

④ The sequences are geometric progressions.
Write down the next two terms for each one.

    a 2, 10, 50, 250...

    b 50, 5, 0.5, 0.05...

    c 8, 12, 18, 27...

    d 6, 1.2, 0.24, 0.048...

⑤ The second and third terms of a geometric progression are 6 and 18.
Work out

    a the common ratio

    b the first term

    c the fifth term.

Developing fluency

① Here are the first three terms of some sequences.

    a Decide whether the numbers below form geometric progressions.

        i 200, 300, 450, ...

        ii 150, 120, 100, ...

        iii 24, 30, 37.5, ...

    In each case

    b Find the ratios between

        i the first two terms.

        ii the second and third terms.

Exam-style

② In each case the first and third terms of a geometric progression are given. You are asked to work out one of the other terms.

  a 1 and 36. Work out the second term.

  b 4 and 1. Work out the second term.

  c 2 and 12.5. Work out the fourth term.

③ The first term of a sequence is 1 and the fifth term is 81.

  Write down the second, third and fourth terms of the sequence if it is a

  a geometric progression

  b linear sequence.

④ £5000 is invested at a compound interest rate of 2%.

  a Work out how much it is worth after 1 year.

  b Work out how much it is worth after 2 years.

  c Work out how much it is worth after 3 years.

  d The amounts form a geometric progression. What is its common ratio?

Exam-style

⑤ The half-life of fermium-253 is 3 days.

  Half of the remaining radioactive atoms in a sample of fermium-253 will decay over a period of 3 days.

  How many days is it before only 6.25% of the original radioactive atoms remain?

⑥ Elsa has a rich but eccentric uncle. She receives the following email from him at the start of the summer.

> Dear Elsa,
>
> I would like to give you a daily allowance for your summer holidays.
> Which of these would you prefer?
> £100 per day,
> or, £10 on day one, £20 on day 2, £30 on day 3 and so on.
> or, 1p on day 1, 2p on day 2, 4p on day 3 and so on.
>
> See you soon!
> Uncle Jim

  a Work out how much would Elsa receive under each option on

  i day 7

  ii day 14

  iii day 28.

  b **i** Which option gives Elsa the most money?

  ii Work out the total amount Elsa receives under this option after 4 weeks.

  (Hint: Find how much Elsa receives after 1 day, 2 days, 3 days and so on. What is special about these numbers?)

Problem solving

Exam-style

① Here is part of Pascal's triangle.

   a The totals of the first three rows are 1, 2, 4. What are the next three terms of this sequence?

   b What is the term-to-term rule for this sequence?

   c What is the position-to-term rule?

   d Which row has a total of 1024?

Row 1				1				
Row 2			1		1			
Row 3		1		2		1		
	1		3		3		1	
	1		4		6		4		1
1		5		10		10		5	1

Exam-style

② Jason bought a new car for £10000.

   Its value depreciated by 10% each year.

   So its value £V, after n years was given by

   $$V = 10000 \times 0.9^n$$

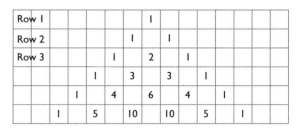

   a Find the value of the car after

   i 1 year   **ii** 2 years   **iii** 3 years.

   b The answers to part **a** give a sequence of values of the car. What is the term-to-term rule for this sequence?

   c After how many years is the value of the car first less than £3000?

③ Payday loan companies offer loans for a short period of time (typically for a few weeks).

   A payday loan company charges interest at 30% per month. To work out how much you owe you need to multiply the previous month's amount by 1.3.

   a If you borrow £100, how much will you owe them after 2 months?

   b The companies are not supposed to lend money to people for a long period of time. How much would you owe if you borrowed £100 and did not pay it back for a year?

   c The amount of money in the world is about three trillion pounds (£3 000 000 000 000). If you borrow £100, roughly how long would it take before you needed to pay back more money than there is in the whole world?

Reviewing skills

① For these geometric progressions
   a Find the common ratio.

   b Write down the next two terms in the progressions below.

   i 3, 6, 12, 24, …

   ii 64, 16, 4, 1, …

② In each case the first and third terms of a geometric progression are given. You are asked to work out two other terms.
   a 3 and 12. Work out the fifth and tenth terms.

   b 5 and 0.2. Work out the second and fourth terms.

Strand 3 Functions and graphs

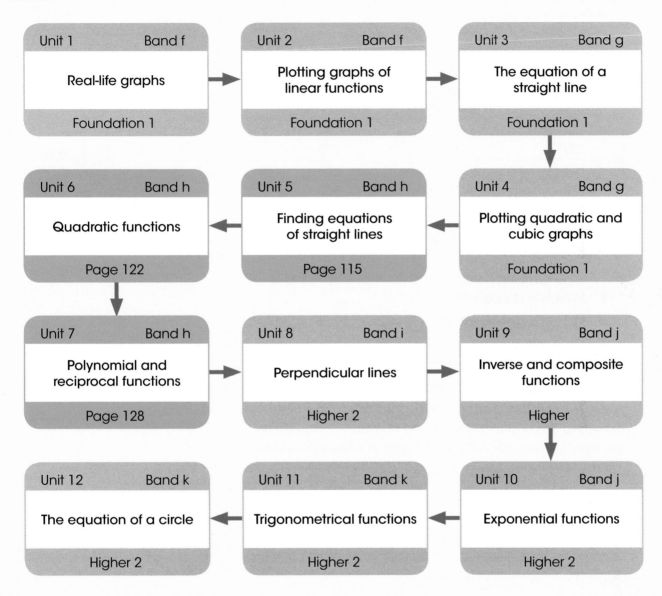

Unit 1	Band f
Real-life graphs	
Foundation 1	

Unit 2	Band f
Plotting graphs of linear functions	
Foundation 1	

Unit 3	Band g
The equation of a straight line	
Foundation 1	

Unit 6	Band h
Quadratic functions	
Page 122	

Unit 5	Band h
Finding equations of straight lines	
Page 115	

Unit 4	Band g
Plotting quadratic and cubic graphs	
Foundation 1	

Unit 7	Band h
Polynomial and reciprocal functions	
Page 128	

Unit 8	Band i
Perpendicular lines	
Higher 2	

Unit 9	Band j
Inverse and composite functions	
Higher	

Unit 12	Band k
The equation of a circle	
Higher 2	

Unit 11	Band k
Trigonometrical functions	
Higher 2	

Unit 10	Band j
Exponential functions	
Higher 2	

Units 1–4 are assumed knowledge for this book. They are reviewed and extended in the Moving on section on page 114.

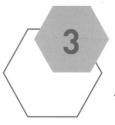

Units 1–4 • Moving on

① Here are the distances it takes a car to stop when it is travelling at speeds from 20 mph to 70 mph.
It shows the stopping distances in dry conditions and in wet conditions.

Speed in mph	Stopping distance in feet (dry)	Stopping distance in feet (wet)
20	40	60
30	75	120
40	120	200
50	175	300
60	240	420
70	315	560

a Draw a graph to show the stopping times in dry and wet conditions.

b Find the stopping distance of a car that is travelling at

   i 35 mph in dry conditions

   ii 45 mph in wet conditions.

c Find the difference in the stopping distances in the dry and in the wet for a car travelling at 75 mph.

② This graph shows the depth of water in a harbour during the first half of one day.
A ship is expected to arrive outside the harbour between 05:00 and 07:00.
It needs a 5 m depth of water in the harbour.
Will there be enough water for the ship to enter the harbour?

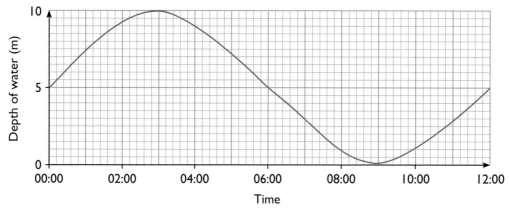

③ Here are the equations of some straight lines.

A $y = \frac{1}{2}x - 3$ **B** $y - 4x = 3$ **C** $y - \frac{1}{2}x = 3$ **D** $x - 2y = 6$ **E** $x + 6 = y$

a Which of these lines are parallel to each other?

b Which of these lines cross the y axis at the same point?

④ A stone is thrown out of a window. Its height, h metres, is given by the equation $h = 20 + 15t - 5t^2$.

a Draw the graph of h against t for values of t (in seconds) from 0 to 4.

b Use your graph to estimate the maximum height the stone reaches.

Unit 5 • Finding equations of straight lines • Band h

Outside the Maths classroom

Calculating acceleration

A tourist simultaneously drops a small coin and a cricket ball from the top of the Leaning Tower of Pisa. Which would land first?

Toolbox

How many different straight lines can you draw through two points, say (3, 6) and (5, 10)? The answer, of course, is one. Two points define a straight line.

It is usual in maths that anything described as a **line** is straight.

If a graph produces something that is not straight then this is usually described as a '**curve**'

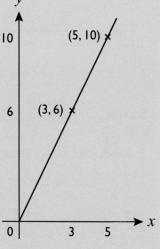

To find the equation of the line, think of the two points as part of a right-angled triangle like this. The line through (3, 6) and (5, 10) goes 2 units across and 4 units up. So the gradient of the line is 2 ÷ 4 or 0.5.

If you know the gradient of a line and a point on that line, then the equation of the line can be found.

$$y = mx + c$$

For example, for a line with gradient of 0.5 that goes through (3, 6) we know that $y = 6$ when $x = 3$.

So, using $y = mx + c$ gives

$$6 = 0.5 \times 3 + c$$
$$6 = 1.5 + c,$$
$$c = 4.5.$$

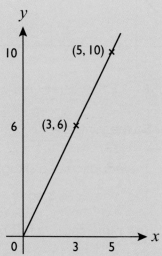

So the equation of the line with gradient 0.5 that goes through (3, 6) is $y = 0.5x + 4.5$.

Example – Using one point and the gradient

A line has a gradient of 3 and passes through the point (1, 8).

a Calculate the y-intercept of the line.

b Find the equation of the line.

Solution

a Here is a sketch of the line.

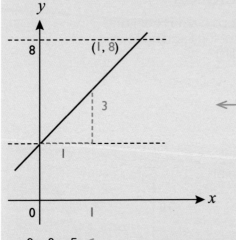

The y-intercept is the point where the graph cuts the y axis.

$8 - 3 = 5$

From $x = 0$ to $x = 1$ the graph goes up 3...

So the y-intercept is at (0, 5).

...so it goes from $y = 5$ to $y = 8$

b The equation of a straight line is $y = mx + c$ where m is the gradient and c is the y-intercept.

The gradient is 3, so $m = 3$.

From the question.

The y-intercept is at (0, 5) so $c = 5$.

From part **a**.

So $y = 3x + 5$.

Example – Using two points

A line goes through $(2, 9)$ and $(3, 7)$.

a Find the gradient of the line.

b Find the equation of the line.

Solution

a

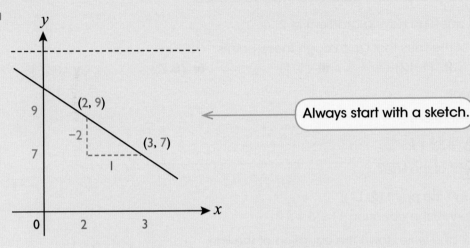

Always start with a sketch.

$$\text{Gradient} = \frac{\text{change in } y}{\text{change in } x}$$

'Downhill lines' have a negative gradient.

$$= \frac{-2}{1}$$

$$= -2$$

b The equation of a straight line is $y = mx + c$.

The gradient is -2 so $m = -2$.

So $y = -2x + c$.

You can find the value of c by substituting the co-ordinates of one point on the line into $y = -2x + c$.

For the point $(2, 9)$:

You could use $(3, 7)$ instead.

substituting $x = 2$, $y = 9$ into $y = -2x + c$

gives $9 = -2 \times 2 + c$

$9 = -4 + c$

$13 = c$

So $c = 13$

The equation of the line is $y = -2x + 13$.

You can write this as $y = 13 - 2x$.

Practising skills

(1) The lines $y = 5x + 2$ and $y = 5x - 2$ are parallel. Match these lines into pairs that are parallel and find the odd one out.

a $y = 3x + 7$ **b** $y = 7x + 3$ **c** $y = -3x + 2$ **d** $y = 7x - 5$

e $y = -5x + 9$ **f** $y = 3x + 9$ **g** $y = -3x - 10$

h Write the equation of a line that is parallel to the odd one out.

(2) All of the lines in this question have a gradient of 2.

a Draw the graphs of the lines that go through these points.

   i (1, 5)   **ii** (1, 12)   **iii** (1, 1)   **iv** (5, 7)   **v** (−2, 1)

b Find their y-intercepts.

c Write down their equations.

(3) A line has equation $y = 3x + k$.

a What is the gradient of the line?

The line passes through the point (2, 11).

b How does this give you the equation $11 = 6 + k$?

c Find the value of k and write down the equation of the line.

d Where does the line cross the y axis?

(4) Find the equation of the line that has a gradient of

a 3 and goes through (1, 1)

b 7 and goes through (2, 5)

c 2 and goes through (10, 1)

d $\frac{1}{2}$ and goes through (2, 2)

e $-\frac{1}{2}$ and goes through (2, 2).

(5) A line goes through the points (2, 1) and (4, 9).

a Show that the gradient of the line is 4.

b Find the equation of the line with gradient 4 that passes through (2, 1).

c Check that (4, 9) lies on your line.

(6) For the following pairs of points

a find the gradient of the line joining them.

b find the equation of the line through them.

c check that both points lie on the lines by substituting x- and y-co-ordinates into the equation.

   i (1, 1) to (5, 7)   **ii** (1, 3) to (5, 7)   **iii** (3, 4) to (5, 7)

   iv (−2, 3) to (5, 7)   **v** (2, 9) to (5, 7)

Developing fluency

① These two lines meet at $(-1, 2)$. One has a gradient of 2 and the other has a gradient of 3.

   a Find the equation of each line.

   b Find the co-ordinates of the points where they cross the y axis.

   c State whether these points are on the red line, the blue line or neither.

      i $(1, 6)$

      ii $(-2, 0)$

      iii $(2, 8)$

      iv $\left(-1\frac{1}{2}, 0\right)$

      v $\left(-\frac{1}{2}, 3\right)$

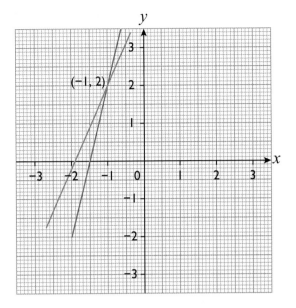

② Write down the equation of a straight-line graph that fits into each section of this two-way table.

	Gradient is 3	Gradient is −7
y-intercept is 6		
y-intercept is −5		

③ The line l goes through the points $(4, 0)$ and $(0, 4)$.
The line m goes through the points $(4, 2)$ and $(0 -2)$.

   a Find the equations of the lines l and m.

   b Draw a graph showing the lines l and m. Use the same scale for both the x axis and the y axis.

   c Find the angle between the two lines.

④ Find the equations of these lines.

   a Through $(1, 2)$ and $(3, 4)$.

   b Through $(1, 3)$ and $(5, 7)$.

   c Through $(1, 5)$ and $(9, 13)$.

   d Through $(5, 9)$ with gradient 1.

   e Gradient 1 and y-intercept 2.

   f

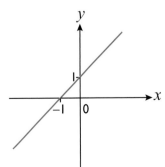

Which lines are the same as each other?

⑤ The co-ordinates of point A are (a, b) and the co-ordinates of point B are (b, a).
Is it always, sometimes or never true that the line through A and B has a negative gradient?
If you think always or never, you must explain how you can be so certain.
If you think sometimes, then you must explain when the statement is and isn't true.

⑥ A triangle is drawn on a co-ordinate grid. It has vertices at (1, 1), (6, 6) and (1, 11).

   a Find the equations of the three lines used to make the triangle.

   b Draw the triangle on graph paper, using the same scales for the x axis and the y axis.

   c Describe the triangle.

   d Find the area of the triangle.

⑦ ABCD is a quadrilateral. The equations of its sides are:

   AB $y = -3x + 7$
   BC $y = 2x - 3$
   DC $y = -2x + 13$
   DA $y = 3x - 17$

   a Draw the four lines on a graph.

   b Find the co-ordinates of A, B, C and D.

   c What sort of quadrilateral is ABCD?

   d The diagonals AC and BD meet at E. What are the co-ordinates of E?

   e What are the equations of AC and BD?

Problem solving

① l and m are two straight lines.
l has a gradient of 2 and crosses the y axis at (0, −1).
m has a gradient of −3 and crosses the y axis at (0, 4).

   a Find the equations of l and m.

   b Draw lines l and m on a graph.

   c Find the co-ordinates of their point of intersection.

② p and q are two straight lines.
p has a gradient of 3 and passes through the point (3, 2).
q has a gradient of −2 and passes through the point (1, −4).

   a Draw lines p and q on a graph.

   b Find the equations of p and q.

   c Write down the co-ordinates of R, the point of intersection of p and q.

   d Show that R lies on the line $y = -4x$

③ A straight line r is parallel to the line $y = x + 3$ and passes through the point (0, 5).
Another straight line s is parallel to the line $x + y = 5$ and passes through the point (0, 1).

   a Find the equations of the lines r and s.

   b Find, by drawing, the co-ordinates of the point of intersection of the two straight lines.

   c Substitute the x- and y-values you found in part **b** into the equations of the lines r and s.
   How does this check your answers?

Exam-style

④ A straight line l is parallel to the line $y = 4x - 3$ and passes through the point $(-1, 2)$.
Another straight line m is parallel to the line $4x + 3y = 2$ and passes through the point $(3, -2)$.

 a Draw the lines l and m on a graph.

 b Find the equations of l and m.

 c Find the point of intersection of l and m.

 d Use your answer to part **c** to check your equation of l and m.

Exam-style

⑤ **a** On the same axes, draw the lines
 p: $y = 1$
 q: $x = 3$
 r: $y = 3x + 1$

 b Write down co-ordinates of the point, C, where line p and line q meet.

 c Line m is parallel to r and passes through C.
 Write down the equation of line m.

 d Find the area of the region bounded by the y-axis and the lines q, r and m.

Exam-style

⑥ Line l passes through the points $(-1, 6)$ and $(1, 2)$.
Line m has equation $y + 2x = 9$.

 a Show that the lines l and m are parallel.

 b Draw lines l and m on the same co-ordinate axes.

 Line n has gradient $\frac{1}{2}$ and the same y-intercept as line l.

 c Find the equation of line n.

 d By substituting for x and y, show that the point $(2, 5)$ lies on both lines m and n.

 e Find the area of the triangle bounded by line m, line n and the y axis.

Reviewing skills

① Find the equations of these lines.

 a Parallel to $y = 2x + 3$ with y-intercept 5.

 b Gradient -1 through the point $(5, 2)$.

 c Through the points $(-1, -4)$ and $(2, 5)$.

② **a** Draw a graph showing the lines $y = 2x + 3$ and $y = -x + 6$.

 b Find the co-ordinates of the point of intersection, P.

 c Show algebraically that the line joining $(0, 7)$ to $(3.5, 0)$ passes through P.

③ A is $(0, 0)$, B is $(3, 4)$, C is $(9, 4)$ and D is $(6, 0)$.

 a Show that the quadrilateral ABCD is a parallelogram, but not a rhombus.

 b Find the equations of the lines AC and BD.

 c Use algebra to show that the point E $(4.5, 2)$ lies on both lines AC and BD.

 d Show points A, B, C, D and E on a graph. Show also the parallelogram ABCD and its diagonals.

Unit 6 • Quadratic functions • Band h

Programming

Why are quadratic functions used in programming platform games?

Toolbox

A **quadratic function** takes the form $y = ax^2 + bx + c$.

Its graph will always take the shape of a **parabola.**

It is symmetrical, and is either ∩-shaped or ∪-shaped.

The **roots** of the equation $ax^2 + bx + c = 0$ are the values of x for which the equation is true.

They are the values of x at which the graph cuts the x axis.

The **line of symmetry** of the graph of a quadratic function is always parallel to the y axis and passes through the **turning point** of the graph.

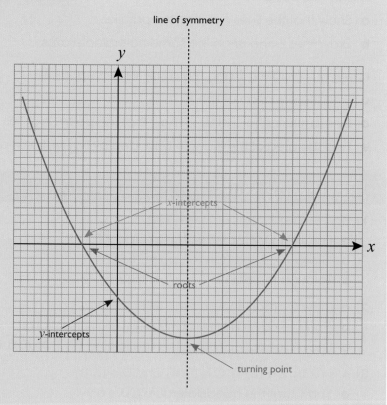

line of symmetry

y

x-intercepts

roots

y-intercepts

x

turning point

The turning point is the name given to the maximum or minimum point on the graph.

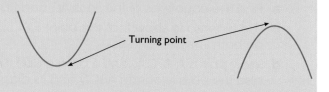

Turning point

Example – Finding intercepts and roots

The graph shows the quadratic function $y = x^2 - 5x + 4$.

a Write down the intercepts with the axes.

b Write down the roots of the equation $0 = x^2 - 5x + 4$.

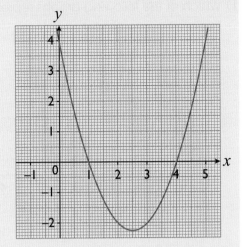

Solution

a The intercept with the y axis is where the graph crosses the y axis.

It crosses at **(0, 4)**.

The intercept with the x axis is where the graph crosses the x axis.

It crosses at **(1, 0)** and **(4, 0)**.

(Don't forget to find all 3 intercepts!)

b The roots of the equation

$0 = x^2 - 5x + 4$ are **1** and **4**.

> The roots are the x co-ordinates of the points where the curve cuts the x-axis.

To check, substitute the numbers into the function and verify that the answer is zero.

$x = 1$

$y = 1^2 - 5 \times 1 + 4$

$= 1 - 5 + 4$

$= 0$

$x = 4$

$y = 4^2 - 5 \times 4 + 4$

$= 16 - 20 + 4$

$= 0$

Example – Using turning points

A quadratic function has a root when $x = -5$ and a turning point at $(1, -12)$.

a Sketch its graph.

b Give the co-ordinate of the other root.

Solution

a

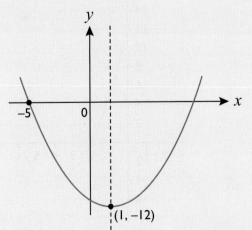

b The line of symmetry goes vertically through the turning point so the line of symmetry is $x = 1$.

Reflecting $(-5, 0)$ in the line of symmetry gives $(7, 0)$. So the second root is when $x = 7$.

Practising skills

① Which of the following graphs represent quadratic functions?
Explain how you know.

a
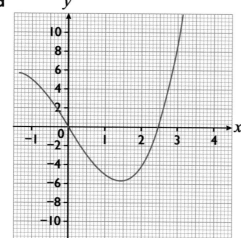

b
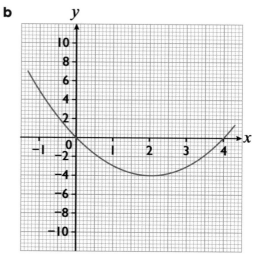

c
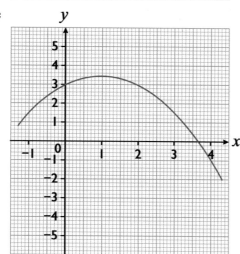

d
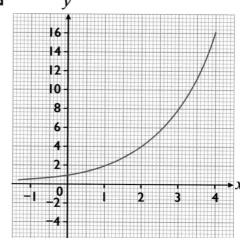

② The graph shows the quadratic function $y = x^2 - 8x + 12$.

   a Write down the intercept on the y axis.

   b Write down the intercepts on the x axis.

   c Write down the roots of $0 = x^2 - 8x + 12$.

   d Write down the equation of the line of symmetry.

   e Write down the co-ordinates of the turning point.

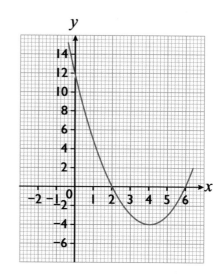

③ A quadratic function has intercepts (0, –3), (–1, 0) and (3, 0).

    a Sketch the function on axes with the x axis from –2 to 5 and y axis from –5 to 10.

    b Write down the roots of the function.

    c What is the equation of the line of symmetry?

④ The graph of a quadratic function crosses the axes at (0, 6), (–3, 0) and (2, 0).

    a Sketch the curve. Take the x axis from –4 to 3 and the y axis from –2 to 8.

    b Write down the roots of the function.

    c What is the equation of the line of symmetry?

⑤ The graph shows the quadratic function $y = -x^2 - 3x + 4$.

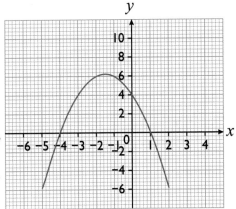

    a Write down the intercept on the y axis.

    b Write down the intercepts on the x axis.

    c Write down the roots of $0 = -x^2 - 3x + 4$.

    d Write down the equation of the line of symmetry.

    e **i** Use your graph to write down the co-ordinates of the turning point.

        ii Check the y co-ordinate of your answer by calculation.

Developing fluency

① Here is a table of values for a quadratic function.

x	–3	–2	–1	0	1	2	3	4
y	6	0	–4	–6	–6	–4	0	6

    a Without drawing the graph, work out

      i the intercepts with the axes

      ii the roots of the function

      iii the equation of the line of symmetry.

    b Estimate the co-ordinates of the turning point.
       What further information do you need to calculate the y co-ordinate of the turning point?

② A quadratic function has the equation $y = x^2 - 3x + 2$.

    a Copy and complete the table of values for the function.

x		–1	0	1	2	3	4
x^2							
$-3x$							
$+2$							
$y = x^2 - 3x + 2$							

    b Plot the points and join them with a smooth curve.

    c Write down the intercepts with the axes.

    d Write down the roots of the equation $x^2 - 3x + 2 = 0$. Call them p and q.

    e Substitute for p and q in $(x - p)(x - q)$. Expand and simplify the expression.
       What do you notice?

③ The graph shows the quadratic function $y = x^2 - x - 2$.

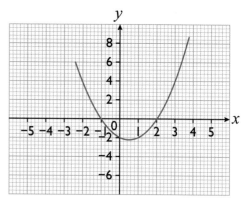

a Write down the intercepts with the axes.

b Write down the roots of the equation $x^2 - x - 2 = 0$. Call them p and q.

c Substitute for p and q in $(x - p)(x - q)$. Expand and simplify the expression. What do you notice?

d Work out the co-ordinates of the turning point. Is it a maximum or minimum value?

④ The path of a cannon ball is described by the quadratic function $y = \frac{1}{2}x - \frac{1}{300}x^2$ where the units are measured in metres.

a Make a table of values for $x = 0, 30, 60, 90, 120$ and 150.

b Draw the cannon ball's path on a graph.

c How far does the ball travel horizontally before hitting the ground?

d What is the maximum height that the cannon ball reaches?

⑤ a Sketch the graph of the function that has a turning point at $(3, 7)$ and one root when $x = -4$.

b Identify the co-ordinates of the second root.

c Sketch a graph of a different function that has a turning point at $(3, 7)$ but no roots.

d Is it possible for a function to have a turning point at $(3, 7)$ but only one root? Explain your answer.

⑥ A quadratic function passes through the points $(2, 4)$, $(3, 15)$, $(1, -3)$, $(0, -6)$ and $(-3, 10)$.

a Draw the graph of the function for values of x from -3 to 3.

b Estimate the turning point of the graph.

c Estimate the roots of the equation.

Problem solving

① A quadratic function passes through the points $(0, 4)$ and $(6, 0)$.
Sketch **two** possible quadratic functions with each of the following properties.

a Two roots and a turning point when $x = 4$.

b Exactly one root.

② At time t seconds, the velocity, v metres per second, of a particle moving along a straight line was measured and recorded in the table.

t	0	1	2	3	4	5	6
v	8	1	-2	-1	4	13	26

a Plot the graph.

b Use your graph to estimate the turning point.

c Describe the movement of the particle at this point.

3 Here are 5 quadratic graphs.

Their equations (not in order) are:

A $y = (x - 1)(x - 3)$

B $y = (x - 1)(x + 1)$

C $y = x(x - 2)$

D $y = (x - 3)(x - 5)$

E $y = (x - 2)(x - 4)$

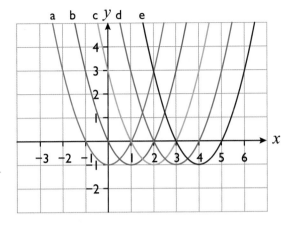

a Match the correct graph to each equation.

b Expand the brackets. What do you notice about the algebra you get?

Reviewing skills

1 The graph shows the quadratic function $y = 4 - x^2$.

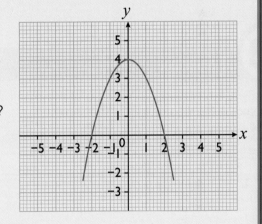

a Write down the intercepts with the axes.

b Write down the roots of the equation $4 - x^2 = 0$; call them p and q.

c Substitute for p and q in $(x - p)(x - q)$. Expand and simplify the expression. What do you notice?

d Work out the co-ordinates of the turning point. Is it a maximum or minimum value?

2 The path of a golf ball is described by the quadratic function $y = \frac{1}{3}x - \frac{1}{540}x^2$ where the units are measured in metres.

a Make a table of values for $x = 0, 30, 60, 90, 120, 150$ and 180.

b Draw the golf ball's path on a graph.

c How far does the ball travel horizontally before hitting the ground?

d What is the maximum height that the ball reaches?

3 The graph of a quadratic function intercepts the axes at just two points, $(0, 4)$ and $(7, 0)$.

a Sketch the graph.

b Identify the co-ordinates of the turning point.

A second quadratic function intercepts the axes at $(0, 4)$, $(7, 0)$ and one other point.

c If the graph has a line of symmetry at $x = 2$, find the roots of the function.

Unit 7 • Polynomial and reciprocal functions • Band h

Outside the Maths classroom

Shapes

This ball follows a parabola as it is thrown into the hoop. Where else might you see parabolas?

Toolbox

By remembering the shape of the positive graph, you can know the shape of the negative graph by reflecting it in the x axis.

Look at these graphs for different powers of x.

Power	Equation	Curve	Turning points
1	$y = 2x - 1$		0
2	$y = x^2 - 2$		1
3	$y = x^3 - x$		2

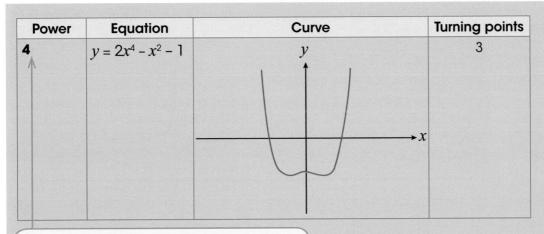

Power	Equation	Curve	Turning points
4	$y = 2x^4 - x^2 - 1$		3

The curves in this unit go up to power 3. This quartic shows how the pattern continues.

They show you that the graph tells you a lot about the equation of a function. In general the power is 1 more than the number of turning points.

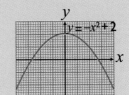

The term with the highest power of x is called the **leading term**. When the leading term is negative, the curve is turned upside down.

Look at the curve $y = -x^2 + 2$. It is still the parabola you get with all quadratics, but is shaped $\cap$ rather than $\cup$.

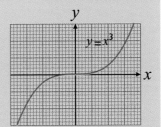

Sometimes a curve flattens out instead of having separate turning points. You can see that in the case of $y = x^3$.

Sometimes the equation of a line may not have y as the subject.

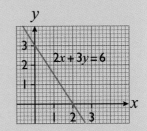

For example the line $y = -\frac{3}{2}x + 3$ would often be written in the form $2y + 3x = 6$.

Substituting $x = 0$ shows you it crosses the y axis at $(0, 3)$.
Substituting $y = 0$ shows you it crosses the x axis at $(2, 0)$.

Another important graph is $y = \frac{1}{x}$. This has two separate branches.
The curve never reaches the y axis. It is called an **asymptote**.
The x axis is also an asymptote.

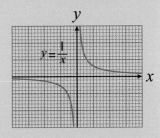

Key words for drawing a graph

Plot means work out the co-ordinates of some of the points and join them up carefully to give a smooth curve (or a straight line).

Sketch means show the main features of a curve. These include where it crosses the x axis and the y axis, and any turning points.

Example – Identifying graphs

Look at this graph.

Which of the following could be the equation of the curve?

$y = 1 - x^3$

$y = -\dfrac{1}{x}$

$y = x^2 - 1$

$y = \dfrac{1}{x} - 1$

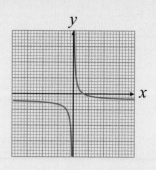

Solution

The graph is a reciprocal graph.

So the equation is either $y = -\dfrac{1}{x}$ or $y = \dfrac{1}{x} - 1$

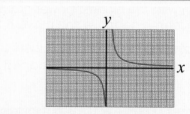

$y = 1 - x^3$ is a **cubic** and $y = x^2 - 11$ is a **quadratic**.

The curve is the same shape as $y = \dfrac{1}{x}$, but 'shifted' down.

So the curve is $y = \dfrac{1}{x} - 1$.

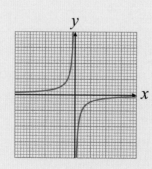

Note: $y = -\dfrac{1}{x}$ will be the 'upside down' version of $y = \dfrac{1}{x}$ and so will be as shown below.

Example – Plotting graphs

a Make out a table of values for $y = x^3 - 6x^2 + 11x - 6$.
Use $x = 0, 1, 2, 3$ and 4.

b Draw the graph.

Solution

a

x	0	1	2	3	4
x^3	0	1	8	27	64
$-6x^2$	0	-6	-24	-54	-96
$+11x$	0	11	22	33	44
-6	-6	-6	-6	-6	-6
y	-6	0	0	0	6

> When $x = 4, x^3 = 4^3 = 64$.

> And $-6x^2 = -6 \times 4^2$
> $= -6 \times 16$
> $= -96$

> And $+11x = +11 \times 4$
> $= 44$

> All the entries in this row are '–6'.

> $64 - 96 + 44 - 6 = 6$
> So when $x = 4, y = 6$

b First plot the points $(0, -6)$, $(1, 0)$, $(2, 0)$, $(3, 0)$ and $(4, 6)$.

> $y = x^3 - 6x^2 + 11x - 6$ is a cubic as the highest power is 3.

Next join the points with a smooth curve.

> The sign in front of the x^3 is positive, so the graph is this way up:

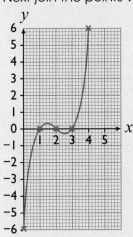

Practising skills

 These equations and their graphs have been muddled up.
Match each graph with its equation.

A $y = \dfrac{1}{x} + x$	**B** $2y - 3x = 4$	**C** $y = x^3 + x^2 - 2x$	**D** $y = x^3$	**E** $2y - 3x + 4 = 0$
F $y = x^2$	**G** $y + 3x - 2 = 0$	**H** $y = x^2 - 3x - 4$	**I** $y = -x^2$	**J** $y = -x^3$
K $y = -x^3 + 5x^2 + 6x$	**L** $y = -\dfrac{1}{x}$	**M** $y = 1 - \dfrac{1}{x}$	**N** $y = \dfrac{2}{x}$	**O** $y = -x^2 - 3x + 4$

(1) 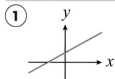 (2) 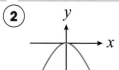 (3) 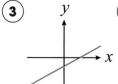 (4) 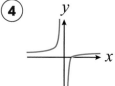 (5)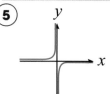

(6) 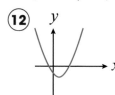 (7) 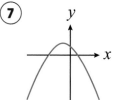 (8) 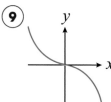 (9) 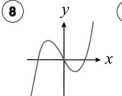 (10)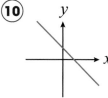

(11) 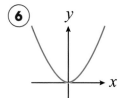 (12) 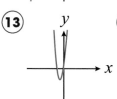 (13) 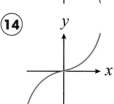 (14) 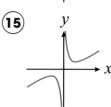 (15)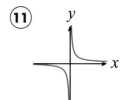

Developing fluency

(1) **a** A curve has the equation $y = x^3 - 2x^2 - 3x$.
Make a table of values for x from –2 to 4.

b Draw the graph of $y = x^3 - 2x^2 - 3x$.

(2) Make a copy of this graph and sketch the following
curves passing through the three points.

a A quadratic.
Say whether the leading term of the quadratic is positive or negative.

b A cubic with positive leading term.

c A cubic with negative leading term.

(3) Which of the following are equations of this straight line?

$$y = -\frac{3}{4}x + 3$$

$$\frac{x}{4} + \frac{y}{3} = 1$$

$$3x + 4y = 12$$

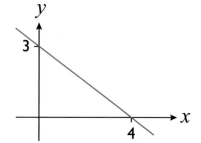

Exam-style

④ **a** Copy and complete this table for $y = x^3 + 2$.

x	-3	-2	-1	0	1	2	3
x^3	-27						
$+2$	$+2$						
$y = x^3 + 2$	-25						

b Draw axes with values of x from -3 to 3 and values of y from -25 to 30.
Draw the curve.

c Use your graph to find the co-ordinates of the points where the curve crosses the x axis and the y axis.

d Describe the symmetry of the graph.

⑤ Here are some graphs and their equations.
For each question decide whether the star is covering a 2 or a 3.

a
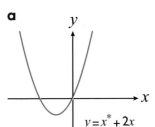
$y = x^* + 2x$

b
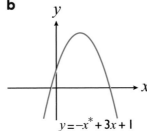
$y = -x^* + 3x + 1$

c
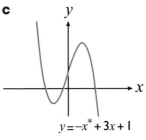
$y = -x^* + 3x + 1$

d
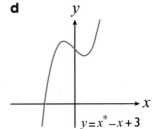
$y = x^* - x + 3$

⑥ Match the following tables with the graphs.

a
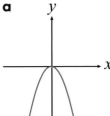

b
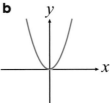

c
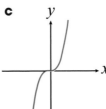

d
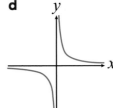

i

x	-3	-2	-1	0	1	2	3	4
y	9	4	1	0	1	4	9	16

ii

x	-3	-2	-1	0	1	2	3	4
y	-9	-4	-1	0	-1	-4	-9	-16

iii

x	-3	-2	-1	0	1	2	3	4
y	$-\dfrac{1}{3}$	$-\dfrac{1}{2}$	-1		1	$\dfrac{1}{2}$	$\dfrac{1}{3}$	$\dfrac{1}{4}$

e One table of values is missing. Write a possible table for x values from -3 to 4.

⑦ **a** Sketch these pairs of curves (or lines) on the same axes as each other.

i $y = x$ and $y = -x$

ii $y = x^2$ and $y = -x^2$

iii $y = x^3$ and $y = -x^3$

iv $y = \dfrac{1}{x}$ and $y = -\dfrac{1}{x}$

b Say what is the same and what is different about your answers to part **a**.

⑧ **a** Find the value of $y = \dfrac{1}{x - 2}$ when

i $x = -2$ **ii** $x = 0$ **iii** $x = 1$ **iv** $x = 4$.

b What happens when $x = 2$?

c Sketch the curve $y = \dfrac{1}{x - 2}$, $x \neq 2$.

d Use your curve to solve the equation $\dfrac{1}{x - 2} = \dfrac{3}{2}$.

Problem solving

① Match each graph to its equation.

a $y = x^3 + x$ **b** $y = 1 - x^3$ **c** $y = x - \dfrac{1}{x}$ **d** $y = \dfrac{4}{x}$

i
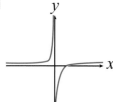

ii
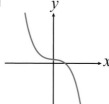

iii
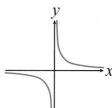

iv
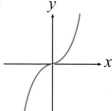

② **a** Draw a pair of axes with x and y values from 0 to 16.
Draw the graph of $y = \sqrt{x}$.

b On the same pair of axes, add the graph of $y = x^2$ for $0 \leqslant x \leqslant 4$.

c Write down the equation of the line of symmetry between the two curves.

③ Chloe is sketching a curve. She plots the point $(2, -3)$.

a Complete each of these to give a possible equation for Chloe's curve.

The missing term in each equation is a constant.

$y = \square - x^2$

$y = \square - x^3$

$y = \dfrac{2}{x} - \square$

b Sketch the curves on the same pair of axes.

c Next, Chloe plots the point $(-2, -3)$ and joins her points.
What is the equation of Chloe's curve?

Exam-style

④ Here are the graphs of $y = x^3 - 4x$ and $y = 4x - x^3$.

  a For which values of x is $y = 4x - x^3$ positive?

  b For which values of x is $y = x^3 - 4x$ negative?

  c Find the values of x when $4x - x^3$ is greater than $x^3 - 4x$.

  d Describe the relationship between the two curves.

  e Describe the symmetry of $y = x^3 - 4x$.

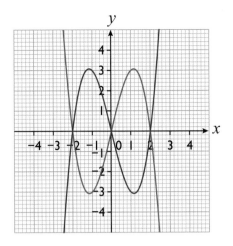

⑤ José makes garden ornaments out of concrete. They stand on a base of radius x cm. The volume of concrete needed for the base, V cm^3 is given by the formula

  $$V = 2x^2 (10 - x)$$

  a Draw a graph of V against x, taking values of x from 0 to 10.

  b A base needs 200 cm^3 of concrete. Use your graph to estimate its radius.

  c One day, José has an order for 5 ornaments of radius 6.2 cm. Use your graph to estimate how much concrete he needs.

⑥ An oil tanker carries a cargo of oil at a speed of v km per hour.

  The cost £C per hour, of carrying the oil is given by the formula

  $$C = 20v + \frac{6000}{v}, \text{ for values of } v \text{ between 5 and the maximum speed of 40 km/hr.}$$

  a Make a table of values.

  b Draw the graph of C against v.

  c Use your graph to estimate the speed at which the value of C is the least.

Reviewing skills

① Plot the graph of $y = x^3 + x^2 - 2x$ when $-3 \leqslant x \leqslant 2$.
Hence solve $x^3 + x^2 - 2x = 0$.

② **a** Complete the table of values for $y = x + \dfrac{1}{x}$

x	−5	−4	−3	−2	−1	−0.5	−0.2	0.2	0.5	1	2	3	4	5
$\dfrac{1}{x}$														
y														

  b Why can't you use $x = 0$?

  c Draw the graph.

  d Use your curve to find values of x for which $x + \dfrac{1}{x} = 3$.

③ **a** Sketch the graph of $y = kx^2$ when $k > 0$.

  b On the same pair of axes sketch $y = kx^2$ when $k < 0$.

  c How do your curves relate to each other?

  d Repeat part **a** for each of the following:

  i $y = \dfrac{k}{x}$

  ii $y = kx^3$.

Strand 4 Algebraic methods

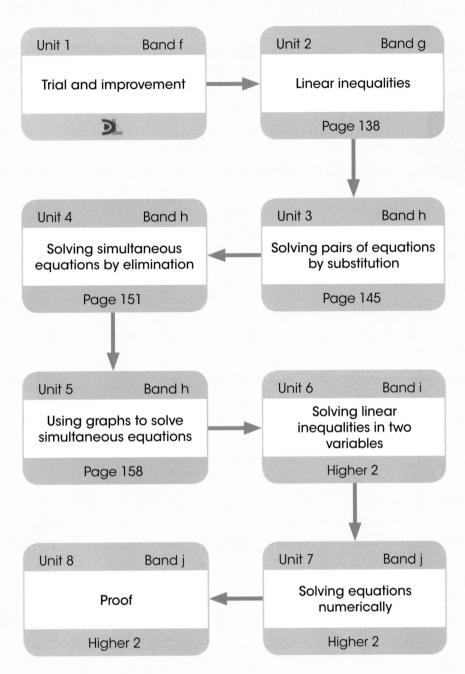

Unit 1 | Band f
Trial and improvement

Unit 2 | Band g
Linear inequalities
Page 138

Unit 4 | Band h
Solving simultaneous equations by elimination
Page 151

Unit 3 | Band h
Solving pairs of equations by substitution
Page 145

Unit 5 | Band h
Using graphs to solve simultaneous equations
Page 158

Unit 6 | Band i
Solving linear inequalities in two variables
Higher 2

Unit 8 | Band j
Proof
Higher 2

Unit 7 | Band j
Solving equations numerically
Higher 2

Unit 1 is not required for GCSE.

Unit 2 • Linear inequalities • Band g

Outside the Maths classroom

Manufacturing constraints

What does a baker need to consider when working out how many of each type of cake she should bake?

How can inequalities help?

Toolbox

You can use a **number line** to show an **inequality**.

This number line represents $-2 \leqslant x < 3$.

$$-4 \; -3 \; -2 \; -1 \; 0 \; 1 \; 2 \; 3 \; 4$$

The integer (whole number) values of x are $-2, -1, 0, 1$ and 2.

These numbers are said to 'satisfy' the inequality.

You solve linear inequalities in the same way that you solve equations, but remember

- keep the inequality sign pointing the same way

$x + 6 < 7$	$x + 6 < 7$	$x + 6 < 7$
$x < 1 \checkmark$	$x = 1 \times$	$x > 1 \checkmark$

- when you multiply or divide by a negative number, turn the inequality sign round.

$-3x > 12$	$-4x > 12$	$-\frac{1}{2}x \leq 2$
$x < -4 \checkmark$	$x > -3 \times$	$x \geq -4 \checkmark$

Example – Solving a word problem with an inequality

An animal shelter has enough kennels to keep 20 dogs.

They never have fewer than 8 dogs.

a Write an inequality for the number of dogs, d, at the shelter.

b Show the inequality on a number line.

Solution

a $8 \leqslant d \leqslant 20$ ⟵ | Use 'less than or equal to' signs to include 8 and 20.

b On the number line, draw circles at 8 and 20 and join them with a straight line.

d can equal 8 and 20, so fill in both of the circles.

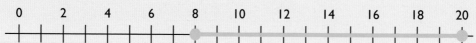

Example – Using a number line

a Show the inequality $-1 \leqslant x < 4$ on a number line.

b Write down the possible integer (whole number) values of x.

Solution

a

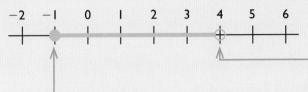

x must be less than 4 so leave this circle open.

x can equal –1, so fill in this circle.

b Include –1, but not 4.

The integer values of x are –1, 0, 1, 2 and 3. ← Remember that 0 is a whole number.

Example – Solving inequalities

Solve these inequalities.

a $5(2x + 3) \geqslant 20$

b $8(x + 1) \leqslant 3x + 18$

c $6 - 3x < 9$

Solution

a $5(2x + 3) \geqslant 20$

$10x + 15 \geqslant 20$ ← Expand the brackets.

$10x \geqslant 5$ ← Subtract 15 from both sides.

$x \geqslant \dfrac{5}{10}$ ← Divide both sides by 10.

$x \geqslant \dfrac{1}{2}$

Check: Let $x = 1$. ← Choose any number greater than or equal to $\dfrac{1}{2}$.

$5(2 \times 1 + 3) \geqslant 20$

$5(2 + 3) \geqslant 20$ ← Calculate the brackets first.

$5 \times 5 \geqslant 20$

$25 \geqslant 20 \checkmark$

b $8(x + 1) \leqslant 3x + 18$

$8x + 8 \leqslant 3x + 18$ ← Expand the brackets.

$5x + 8 \leqslant 18$ ← Subtract $3x$ from both sides.

$5x \leqslant 10$ ← Subtract 8 from both sides.

$x \leqslant 2$ ← Divide both sides by 5.

Check: Let $x = 2$. ← Choose any number less than or equal to 2.

$8(2 + 1) \leqslant 3 \times 2 + 18$

$8 \times 3 \leqslant 6 + 18$

$24 \leqslant 24 \checkmark$ ← Notice that $\leqslant$ means less than or equal to so it is true that $24 \leqslant 24$.

Let $x = 1$. ← Choose another number less then or equal to 2.

$8(1 + 1) \leqslant 3 \times 1 + 18$

$8 \times 2 \leqslant 3 + 18$

$16 \leqslant 21 \checkmark$

c In this inequality there is a negative x term.
There are two methods you can use to deal with this.

Method 1

$6 - 3x < 9$

$-3x < 3$ ← Subtract 6 from both sides.

$x > \dfrac{3}{-3}$ ← Divide both sides by –3 and change the direction of the inequality sign.

$x > -1$

Method 2

$6 - 3x < 9$

$6 < 9 + 3x$ ← Add $3x$ to both sides so the x term becomes positive.

$-3 < 3x$ ← Subtract 9 from both sides.

$\dfrac{3}{3} > x$ ← Divide both sides by 3.

$-1 < x$

$x > -1$ ← Turn the inequality around.

Check: Let $x = 1$. ← Choose a value of x that is greater than –1.

$6 - 3 \times 1 < 9$

$6 - 3 < 9$

$3 < 9 \checkmark$

Practising skills

① Look at the following pairs of numbers.
Put the correct inequality sign, $<$ or $>$ between them.

a 3 ☐ 5

b 7 ☐ 1

c –3 ☐ –5

d –4 ☐ 1

e 1 ☐ –1

f 4.5 ☐ 4.55

g 2.72 ☐ 2.7

h –10 ☐ –8

② Which of these inequalities matches the following statements?

$x < 5$ $x > 5$ $x \leqslant 5$ $x \geqslant 5$ $x > -5$ $x < -5$

a x is bigger than 5

b x is greater than or equal to 5

c x is at most 5

d x is at least 5

e x is lower than –5

f the lowest x can be is –5

g x has a minimum value of 5

h x has a maximum value of 5

3 Write down the inequalities shown on these number lines.

a
```
−7 −6 −5 −4 −3 −2 −1  0  I  2  3  4  5  6  7  8
```

b
```
−7 −6 −5 −4 −3 −2 −1  0  I  2  3  4  5  6  7  8
```

c
```
−7 −6 −5 −4 −3 −2 −1  0  I  2  3  4  5  6  7  8
```

d
```
−7 −6 −5 −4 −3 −2 −1  0  I  2  3  4  5  6  7  8
```

e
```
−7 −6 −5 −4 −3 −2 −1  0  I  2  3  4  5  6  7  8
```

f
```
−7 −6 −5 −4 −3 −2 −1  0  I  2  3  4  5  6  7  8
```

4 Show each of these inequalities on a number line.

a $2 < x < 9$ **b** $6 \leqslant x < 8$ **c** $-4 < x \leqslant -1$ **d** $-2 \leqslant x \leqslant 5$

5 **a** Apply the operation '+ 4' to both sides of the inequality $-2 < 10$.
State whether the new inequality is true or false.

b Now do the same thing using these operations.

i -7 **ii** $\times 3$ **iii** $\times -3$ **iv** $\div 2$ **v** $\div -2$

In each case, state whether the new inequality is true or false.

6 Solve these inequalities.

a $x + 5 < 8$ **b** $x - 2 > -5$ **c** $4x < 20$

d $3x \geqslant -18$ **e** $2x + 1 > 9$ **f** $3x - 5 < 22$

7 For each of these inequalities, list all the possible whole-number values of x.

a $2 < x < 7$ **b** $-3 < x < -1$ **c** $1 \leqslant x \leqslant 4$ **d** $-5 \leqslant x < 2$

Developing fluency

1 Write each of these statements as an inequality.

a The hourly pay rate goes from £7 up to £11.

b To go on this ride you must be at least 18 years old.

c The seniors' ticket is for anyone over the age of 64 years.

d There were over 100 but fewer than 150 people at the show.

e The lift carries a maximum of 16 people.

f To play in the junior league you must be at least 12 but not over 17 years old.

2 You know that $5 < \sqrt{30} < 6$ because $25 < 30 < 36$.
Write each of these square roots between consecutive positive whole numbers.

a $\sqrt{38}$ **b** $\sqrt{90}$ **c** $\sqrt{199}$ **d** $\sqrt{5}$

③ Tom is x years old where x is an integer (whole number).
His brother is twice as old as Tom. Tom's sister is 10 years older than Tom.
The total of their ages is less than 40.

   a Write down expressions involving x for the ages of Tom's brother and sister.

   b Complete this inequality for Tom's age.

      $\square < x \,\square\square$

   c What is the oldest that Tom could be?

   d What is the oldest that Tom's siblings could be?

   e Can Tom's brother and sister be twins?

④ The perimeter of this rectangle is at least 18 cm and less than 42 cm.
The length is double the width.

w cm

   a Write down an expression involving w for the perimeter.

   b Complete this inequality for w.

      $\square \leqslant \square\, w < 42$

   c The width is a whole number of centimetres. Find the minimum and maximum possible area of the rectangle.

⑤ Solve these inequalities.

   a $5x - 3 \geqslant 2x + 9$ **b** $24 + 2x < 30 - 4x$

   c $7(x - 3) < 5(x + 6)$ **d** $3(x + 2) + 2(x + 1) \geqslant 4(x + 5)$

⑥ Solve these inequalities.

   a $4x < 12$ **b** $-4x < 12$ **c** $4x < -12$ **d** $-4x < -12$

⑦ Trish and Wendy are solving the inequality $-2x < 8$.
Trish says the answer is $x < -4$.
Wendy says the answer is $x > -4$.
Who is correct? Explain why.

⑧ **a** **i** Draw the line $x = 3$ on graph paper.
      ii Shade the region $x < 3$.

   b Draw graphs to show these regions.
      i $x > -3$ **ii** $y > 4$ **iii** $y > x$

⑨ Solve these inequalities.

   a $4 - 3x > 19$ **b** $2 - x < -5$ **c** $6 - 4x \leqslant 12$

   d $5(1 - 2x) \geqslant 15$ **e** $2x + 7 < 5x - 5$ **f** $4 + \dfrac{x}{2} > 7$

Problem solving

①

I think of a positive whole number.
I double the number and take away 7.
My answer is less than 5.

a Write this information as an inequality, using n for my number.

b Which numbers could Salman have thought of?

②

I think of a whole number less than 20.
I take 8 away from the number and
double it.
My answer is more than 11.

a Write this information as an inequality.

b Which numbers could Aimee have thought of?

③ Sue is x years old. She is over 2.
Ben is twice as old as Sue.
Ceri is 4 years older than Sue.
The total of their 3 ages is less than 28.

a Write this information as an inequality.

b What age could Sue be?

c What are the corresponding ages of Ben and Ceri?

④ Narinder is x years old.
Rashmi is 2 years older than Narinder.
Bhavinda is twice as old as Rashmi.
The total of their ages is less than 42.

a Write this information as an inequality.

b Solve the inequality.

c What is Rashmi's greatest possible age?
Give your answer as a whole number of years.

⑤ The perimeter of this rectangle is greater than 21 cm and
less than 33 cm. The length is exactly 5 cm more than
the width. The width is x cm.

a Write this information as two inequalities.

b The width is a whole number of centimetres.
Find the range of possible values of the rectangle's area.

⑥ Here is the cost of hiring a van from two companies.

Vans 2 go	**Vans r Us**
£80 fixed cost	£1 a mile
+	No other charges
50p a mile	

Dave wants to drive m miles. Vans 2 go will cost him less.

a Write down an inequality for m.

b Solve it to find m.

⑦ In this diagram, the equation of the green line is $y = x + 1$.

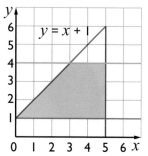

a Write down the equations for the following.

   i the blue line

   ii the red line

   iii the purple line

b Write down the inequalities that fully describe the shaded region. The boundary lines are included in the region.

c Sophie draws a straight line within the region. Its length is l units. Complete this inequality.

   $\Box < l \leqslant \Box$

⑧ Here are four inequalities.

   A $2x + 1 < 15$ **B** $5 - 4x > 3 - 3x$ **C** $4x + 5 > x + 2$ **D** $7 - 4x < 1 - 2x$

a They cannot all be true at the same time. Explain why.

b Find three of them that can all be true. What values can x take?

c How many sets of three of the inequalities work?

Reviewing skills

① Solve these inequalities.

   a $3x + 2 < 14$ **b** $2x - 5 > 17$ **c** $4x - 3 \leqslant 11 - 3x$ **d** $2 - 12x \geqslant 16 - 19x$

② Solve these inequalities.

   a $2(x + 3) - 5 > 3(2 - x)$ **b** $x + 5 < 3x + 9$

   c $3(x - 8) < 5x - 28$ **d** $-12x - 3 > -8x - 23$

③ Abbi is a years old.

Abbi is 5 years older than Cathy.

Bobbi is twice as old as Abbi.

The total of their ages is less than 35.

   a Write this information as an inequality.

   b Solve the inequality.

   c What is Bobbi's greatest possible age?

      Give your answer as a whole number of years.

Unit 3 • Solving pairs of equations by substitution • Band h

Outside the Maths classroom

Best tariffs

What factors should you think about when choosing a new mobile phone?

Toolbox

You can use the **substitution method** to solve this pair of **simultaneous equations**.

$$x + y = 6 \quad \text{①}$$
$$2x + y = 10 \quad \text{②}$$

- Make one of the unknowns the subject of equation ①:

$$y = 6 - x$$

- Substitute this into equation ②:

$$2x + 6 - x = 10$$ ⟵ Solve to find the value of x.
$$x + 6 = 10$$
$$x = 4$$

- Make sure you find the value of both unknowns by substituting the found value into the other equation, in this case equation ①:

$$4 + y = 6$$
$$\text{so } y = 2$$

- Substitute the values back into equation ② to check your answer.

$$2 \times 4 + 2 = 10 \checkmark$$

Example – Solving simultaneous equations using the substitution method

Solve these simultaneous equations using the substitution method.

$$y = 3x - 8$$
$$y = 12 - x$$

Solution

$$y = 3x - 8 \quad \text{①}$$
$$y = 12 - x \quad \text{②}$$

$3x - 8 = 12 - x$ ← As both equations equal y, they are equal to each other.

$4x - 8 = 12$ ← Add x to both sides.

$4x = 20$ ← Add 8 to both sides.

$x = 5$ ← Divide both sides by 4.

$y = 3x - 8 \quad \text{①}$ ← Substitute the value of x you have just found into either equation to find the value of y.

$y = 3 \times 5 - 8$

$y = 15 - 8$

$y = 7$

Check: $y = 12 - x \quad \text{②}$

$7 = 12 - 5 \checkmark$

So the solution is $x = 5$, $y = 7$. ← You need the values of both x and y for the solution.

Check: $y = 12 - x \quad \text{②}$ ← Check your solution by substituting into the equation you didn't use to find the value of y.

$7 = 12 - 5$

$7 = 7 \checkmark$

Example – Solving a word problem involving simultaneous equations

At the local shop, birthday cards cost 5 times as much as postcards.
John buys 3 birthday cards and 6 postcards.
The shopkeeper charges him £8.40.
How much does each birthday card and postcard cost?

Solution

Let b stand for the cost of a birthday card in pence.
Let c stand for the cost of a postcard in pence.

$b = 5c \quad \text{①}$ ← Birthday cards cost five times as much as postcards.

$3b + 6c = 840 \quad \text{②}$ ← Three birthday cards and six postcards cost 840 pence.

$3b + 6c = 840 \quad \text{②}$ ← Substitute this value of b ($5c$) into equation ②.

$3 \times 5c + 6c = 840$

$15c + 6c = 840$ ← Solve the equation to find c.

$21c = 840$

$c = 40$

$b = 5c \quad \text{①}$

$b = 5 \times 40$ ← Substitute the value you found for c into equation ① to find b.

$= 200$

So a birthday card costs £2 ← Write 200 pence as £2 in your solution.
and a postcard costs 40 pence.

Practising skills

(1) Solve these simultaneous equations by substitution.

    a $x = 2y$
       $x + 3y = 15$

    b $x = 3y$
       $2x + y = 28$

    c $x = 2y - 1$
       $2x + 3y = 12$

    d $y = 3x + 5$
       $2x + 5y = 8$

(2) Solve these simultaneous equations by substitution.

    a $y = x - 2$
       $2x - 3y = 8$

    b $x = 3y - 2$
       $3x - 2y = 15$

    c $x = 5y + 3$
       $2x = 3y - 1$

    d $4x - 5y = 3$
       $x = 2y - 3$

(3) Solve these simultaneous equations by substitution.

    a $5x + 2y = 17$
       $y = 2x - 5$

    b $4x - y = -9$
       $y = 2x + 3$

    c $x = y - 6$
       $x + y = 14$

    d $y = 8x + 1$
       $x + y = 10$

(4) Solve these simultaneous equations.

    a $y = 6 - x$
       $2x + y = 11$

    b $x = 6 - y$
       $2x + y - 11 = 0$

    c $y = 11 - 2x$
       $x + y = 6$

    d $x = 5\frac{1}{2} - \frac{1}{2}y$
       $x + y - 6 = 0$

(5) Solve these simultaneous equations by substitution.

    a $x = 3y + 2$
       $4x - 5y = 22$

    b $2y = 3x + 14$
       $x = 5y + 4$

    c $x = y + 1$
       $2x - 5 = 3y - 6$

    d $y = 5x - 6$
       $3x - 2y = -2$

Developing fluency

(1) One number, x, is twice another number, y. The 2 numbers add up to give 15.

    a Write 2 equations for x and y.

    b Solve them to find the two numbers.

(2) The sum of two numbers is 6 and the difference is 1.
Write two equations and solve them to find the 2 numbers.

Exam-style

③ A hardback book costs £h and a paperback book costs £p.

Hardback books are twice the price of paperback books.

Jo buys 3 hardback books and 4 paperback books, and the total cost is £35.

   a Write this information as 2 equations for h and p.

   b Solve the equations.

   c Find the cost of 1 hardback book and 5 paperback books.

④ At a pet shop a rat costs £r and a mouse costs £m.

A rat costs £2 more than a mouse.

Billy buys 3 rats and 5 mice for £62.

   a Write 2 equations for r and m.

   b Solve the equations to find the costs of a rat and a mouse.

⑤ In a theatre a seat in the stalls costs £7 more than one in the circle.

Patrick buys 4 tickets for seats in the stalls and 7 tickets for seats in the circle, and the total cost is £523.

Write 2 equations and solve them to find the costs of the 2 types of ticket.

⑥ Mrs Jones organises a school trip to the theatre for 42 people.

She takes x children and y adults on the trip.

Each adult has paid £40 for their ticket.

Each child has paid £16 for their ticket.

The total cost of the tickets was £1080.

   a Write 2 equations for x and y.

   b How many adults went on the trip and how many children?

⑦ How can you solve these simultaneous equations by substitution?

   a $3x + y = 29$
       $x - y = 7$

   b $5x - 4y = 17$
       $x - 2y = 7$

⑧ **a** Make x the subject of the equation $x + 3y = 17$.

   b Solve these simultaneous equations by substitution.

     $x + 3y = 17$

     $5x - 2y = 0$

     Check your answer by substituting your values for x and y into both equations.

Problem solving

① Sadie thinks of two numbers, m and n.

   a Write this information as two equations for m and n.

   b Solve the equations. What are the values of m and n?

When I add my two numbers I get 27. One number is 15 more than the other.

② Charlie thinks of a two-digit number, XY.
The sum of the two digits is 12.

XY

    a Write this as an equation for X and Y.

    b Make Y the subject of the equation.

    c The difference between XY and YX is 18.
       Explain why this can be written as the equation
       $(10X + Y) - (10Y + X) = 18$.

    d Solve this equation with the equation you found in part **b**.

    e Show that Jim's number is 75.

③ Gerry organises a coach trip to the theatre.
There are a adults and c children.
The number of children is 5 greater than the number of adults.

    a Write this as an equation for a and c.

The cost of an adult ticket is £15 and the cost of a child's ticket is £10.
Gerry spends £550 on tickets.

    b Write another equation for a and c.

    c How many adults went on the trip and how many children?

④ A large tin of beans weighs l g and a small tin weighs s g.
A large tin of beans weighs 100 g more than a small tin of beans.
6 large tins of beans weigh the same as 10 small tins of beans.

    a Write this information as two equations for l and s.

    b Solve the equations.

    c Find the mass of 2 large tins and 5 small ones.

⑤ Josh is buying dog food.
Dog food is sold in small cans and large cans.
The small can of dog food weighs 140 g less than a large can.
5 large cans together weigh the same as 12 small cans.
A large can costs 90p and a small can costs 40p.
Explain which is the better buy.

90p   40p

Reviewing skills

1 Solve these simultaneous equations by substitution.

a $x = y + 6$
 $x + y = 12$

b $y = 3x - 4$
 $2x + 3y = 32$

c $x = 4y + 3$
 $3x - 5y = -5$

d $y = 6x + 2$
 $6x - 2y = 14$

2 Solve these simultaneous equations by substitution.

a $4x - 2y = -12$
 $x = 3y + 2$

b $y = 2x$
 $3x - 5 = 39 - 4y$

c $x = 5y + 9$
 $3x + y = 11$

d $y = x - 2$
 $2y + 3x = 1$

3 A train has f first-class coaches and s standard-class coaches.

The number of standard class coaches is 3 times the number of first-class coaches.

A first-class coach seats 40 passengers; a standard-class coach seats 80 passengers.

The train seats 560 passengers.

a Use this information to write 2 equations for f and s.

b Solve the equations.

c How many coaches does the train have?

Unit 4 • Solving simultaneous equations by elimination • Band h

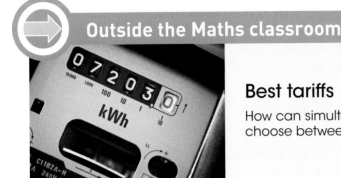

Best tariffs

How can simultaneous equations help you choose between two electricity providers?

Toolbox

A pair of simultaneous equations can be solved by **eliminating** one of the unknowns.

You either **add or subtract the equations** to form a third equation in just one unknown.

- To decide whether to add or subtract look at the signs of the unknown you wish to eliminate.

  If the signs are different, you add.

  If the signs are the same, you subtract.

- Sometimes you need to multiply each term in one (or both) equations by a constant so that one of the unknowns has the same coefficients.

When you have found one unknown, substitute in either equation to find the other.

To check your answer, substitute the values you have found into both equations.

Example – Subtracting simultaneous equations

Solve these simultaneous equations.

$$5x + 3y = 18$$
$$5x - 2y = 13$$

Solution

$$5x + 3y = 18 \quad \text{①}$$
$$5x - 2y = 13 \quad \text{②}$$

Subtract $\quad 0 + 5y = 5$

> Both equations have $5x$, so you can eliminate x.

> The signs in front of both $5x$ are the same $(+5x)$ so you subtract.

$$y = 1$$

> Divide both sides by 5.

Alternatively,

$$5x + 3y = 18 \quad \text{①}$$
$$-5x + 2y = -13 \quad \text{②}$$

Add $\quad 0 + 5y = 5$

> When subtracting one equation from another, you may find it helps to change the signs in the second equation and then add.

① $5x + 3y = 18$
$\quad 5x + 3 \times 1 = 18$ ← To find the value of x, substitute $y = 1$ into equation ①.
$\quad 5x + 3 = 18$
$\quad\quad 5x = 15$ ← Subtract 3 from both sides.
$\quad\quad\quad x = 3$ ← Divide both sides by 5.

So the solution is $x = 3$ and $y = 1$.

Check: $5x + 3y = 18$ ①
$\quad 5 \times 3 + 3 \times 1 = 18$
$\quad\quad 15 + 3 = 18$
$\quad\quad\quad 18 = 18$ ✓

$5x - 2y = 13$ ②
$5 \times 3 - 2 \times 1 = 13$
$\quad 15 - 2 = 13$
$\quad\quad 13 = 13$ ✓

Example – Multiplying simultaneous equations by a constant

Solve these simultaneous equations.
$\quad 3s + 2t = 13$
$\quad 5s - t = 13$

Solution

$\quad\quad 3s + 2t = 13$ ①
$\quad\quad 5s - t = 13$ ② ← Multiply equation ② by 2 to eliminate t.

① $\quad 3s + 2t = 13$
② × 2 $\quad 10s - 2t = 26$ ← The signs in front of the $2t$ are different ($+2t$ and $-2t$) so you add.
Add $\quad \overline{13s + 0 = 39}$
$\quad\quad\quad s = \dfrac{39}{13}$ ← Divide both sides by 13.
$\quad\quad\quad s = 3$

① $3s + 2t = 13$
$3 \times 3 + 2t = 13$ ← To find the value of t, substitute $s = 3$ into equation ①.
$\quad 9 + 2t = 13$
$\quad\quad 2t = 4$ ← Subtract 9 from both sides.
$\quad\quad\quad t = 2$ ← Divide both sides by 2.

So the solution is $s = 3$ and $t = 2$.

Check: $3s + 2t = 13$ ①
$\quad 3 \times 3 + 2 \times 2 = 13$
$\quad\quad 9 + 4 = 13$
$\quad\quad\quad 13 = 13$ ✓

$5s - t = 13$ ②
$5 \times 3 - 2 = 13$
$\quad 15 - 2 = 13$
$\quad\quad 13 = 13$ ✓

Example – Solving a word problem using simultaneous equations

Danni has £4.40 in 2p and 5p coins.
She has 100 coins altogether.
Write down 2 equations for this information.
How many of each type of coin does she have?

Solution

Let t = number of 2p coins and ⟵ | Choose letters to represent the unknowns.
f = number of 5p coins.

$t + f = 100$ ① ⟵ | There are 100 coins altogether.

$2t + 5f = 440$ ② ⟵ | Danni has 440 pence altogether.
This matches the 2 and 5 which are in pence.

$5 \times$ ① $\quad 5t + 5f = 500$ ⟵ | Make the coefficients of one of the unknowns the same in both equations.

② $\quad 2t + 5f = 440$ ⟵ | The signs on $5f$ are positive in both equations, so subtract.

Subtract $\quad 3t + 0 = 60$

$t = \dfrac{60}{3}$ ⟵ | Divide both sides by 3.

$t = 20$

① $t + f = 100$ ⟵ | To find the value of f, substitute $t = 20$ into equation ①.

$20 + f = 100$

$f = 80$

So Danni has 20 two-pence coins and 80 five-pence coins.

Check: $\quad t + f = 100$ ① $\qquad\qquad 2t + 5f = 440$ ②

$\qquad\quad 20 + 80 = 100 \qquad\qquad\quad 2 \times 20 + 5 \times 80 = 440$

$\qquad\qquad 100 = 100 \checkmark \qquad\qquad\qquad 40 + 400 = 440 \checkmark$

Practising skills

① Simplify these expressions.

a $5x - 9x$ **b** $3x + (-2x)$ **c** $4x + (-6x)$ **d** $2x - (-3x)$

e $-4x - (-4x)$ **f** $17 - 23$ **g** $18 - (-27)$ **h** $-15 - (-7)$

② Solve these simultaneous equations by adding them first.

a $x + 2y = 0$
$\quad x - 2y = 4$

b $3x + y = 18$
$\quad 2x - y = 7$

c $x - 5y = 2$
$\quad 3x + 5y = -14$

d $6x + 2y = 6$
$\quad x - 2y = 8$

e $-x + y = 1$
$\quad x + y = -5$

f $-2x + 3y = 10$
$\quad 2x + y = 6$

③ Solve these simultaneous equations by subtracting them first.

a $2x - 3y = 5$
$2x + 4y = 12$

b $x + 4y = 1$
$x + 2y = 3$

c $3x + 4y = 30$
$x + 4y = 26$

d $2x - 5y = 22$
$3x - 5y = 23$

e $5x - y = 12$
$3x - y = 8$

f $x + y = 2$
$3x + y = 12$

④ Solve these simultaneous equations. Decide for yourself whether to add them or subtract them.

a $3x + y = 7$
$2x - y = 8$

b $4x - 2y = 14$
$x - 2y = 11$

c $3x + 4y = 32$
$3x - 2y = 2$

d $-5x + 3y = 21$
$5x - 2y = -19$

e $6x - y = 21$
$3x + y = 15$

f $2x - 4y = 16$
$3x + 4y = 14$

⑤ Here are two simultaneous equations.

$3x + 4y = 18$ equation 1

$5x - 2y = 4$ equation 2

a Explain why you cannot eliminate either variable just by adding or subtracting.

b Which equation should be multiplied, and by which value, to ensure you can eliminate a variable?

c Solve the equations.

⑥ Solve these simultaneous equations by multiplying one equation first.

a $4x - y = 19$
$2x + 3y = -1$

b $3x + 4y = 7$
$x + 2y = 1$

c $5x - y = -20$
$4x + 3y = 3$

d $6x - 3y = 51$
$3x + 4y = 20$

e $x - 5y = 31$
$4x - 2y = 16$

f $3x - 2y = -2$
$2x - 4y = 12$

Developing fluency

① Here are two simultaneous equations.

$3x + 4y = 23$ equation 1

$2x + 3y = 16$ equation 2

a In this question you need to multiply each equation so that either x or y can be eliminated. Explain 2 ways that this can be done.

b Solve these 2 equations.

② Solve these simultaneous equations.

a $4a + 3b = 18$
$3a + 4b = 17$

b $3x + 2y = 20$
$2x + 5y = 17$

c $3p + 5q = -5$
$2p - 3q = 22$

d $7x - 4y = 39$
$3x + 5y = 10$

e $6x - 5y = 38$
$5x - 3y = 27$

f $-4m + 6n = -4$
$3m + 2n = 29$

Exam-style

3 In this diagram the perimeter of the triangle is 118 cm and the perimeter of the rectangle is 114 cm.

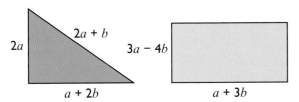

a Write two simultaneous equations for a and b.

b Solve them to find the values of a and b.

c Compare the areas of the triangle and the rectangle.

Exam-style

4 In one week, Trevor made 5 journeys to the supermarket and 3 journeys to the park. He travelled a total of 99 kilometres.

During the next week, he made 2 journeys to the supermarket and 4 to the park. He travelled a total of 62 kilometres.

a Write down 2 simultaneous equations. Use s for the distance to the supermarket and p for the distance to the park.

b Solve your equations.

c How far does Trevor travel in a week when he goes 7 times to the park and twice to the supermarket?

5 The price of tickets for a zoo are £a for adults and £c for children.

Rose buys 2 adult tickets and 3 children's tickets for £24.

Amanda buys 3 adult tickets and 5 children's tickets for £38.

a Write down two simultaneous equations.

b Solve them to find the price of each ticket.

c The Singhs have a family outing to the zoo. There are 9 adults and 21 children. How much do they pay?

6 Reya has these 2 equations.

$$5x - 4y = 18$$
$$x - 4y = -6$$

Her next step is to do a subtraction. She says,

'My rule is:

Change the signs on the bottom line and go on as if you were adding.'

a Carry out Reya's rule.

b Explain why Reya's rule works.

c Solve the equations.

Problem solving

① A banana costs b pence and an apple costs a pence.

Robin buys 4 bananas and an apple for 150p.

Marion buys 2 bananas and an apple for 100p.

   a Write this information as 2 simultaneous equations.

   b Solve the equations.

   c Find the cost of 7 bananas and 8 apples.

② In this diagram, the length and width of the rectangle are l cm and w cm respectively.

The equal sides of the isosceles triangle are also l cm and the base w cm.

The perimeter of the rectangle is 32 cm.

The perimeter of the triangle is 26 cm.

   a Write this information as two simultaneous equations.

   b Find the values of l and w.

③ Karen leaves her 2 dogs and 3 cats at The Pet Hotel for 7 days and it costs her £315.

Malcolm leaves his dog and 2 cats at The Pet Hotel for 7 days and it costs him £175.

One week The Pet Hotel looks after 15 dogs and 20 cats.

How much money do they collect from their customers in that week?

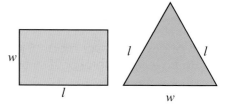

The Pet Hotel

Leave your pet in our expert care when you go on holiday.

④ Peter makes mountain bikes and sports bikes.

It takes him 4 hours to make a mountain bike and 6 hours to make a sports bike.

Each mountain bike costs him £45 to make and each sports bike costs him £60 to make.

One week Peter made m mountain bikes and s Sports bikes in 54 hours.

The cost of making these bikes was £570.

   a Write this information as a pair of simultaneous equations.

   b How many of each type of bike did he make?

⑤ A mobile phone company charges their pay-as-you-go customers c pence per minute for calls and t pence for each text message.

Ben is charged £7.30 for making 10 minutes of calls and sending 40 texts.

Alicia is charged £7.25 for making 5 minutes of calls and sending 50 texts.

   a Write this information as two simultaneous equations.

   b Solve the equations to find the values of c and t.

   c Ruby has £20 of credit. She makes 15 minutes of calls and sends 100 texts. How much credit does she have left?

⑥ **a** Write an equation for the angles in the triangle.

   b Write a second equation connecting the x and y.

   c Solve your equations to find the value of x and y. Show that, for these values, $x = 3y$.

   d To check your answers replace x by $3y$ in the triangle. Then write an equation for y and solve it.

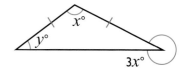

Reviewing skills

① Solve these simultaneous equations.

a $3x + 4y = 2$
$3x - 5y = 11$

b $2x - 3y = 2$
$5x - 3y = 14$

c $x - 4y = 15$
$2x + 4y = -6$

② Solve these simultaneous equations.

a $x - y = 7$
$5x + 3y = 75$

b $4x - 6y = 34$
$3x - 3y = 21$

c $7x + 4y = 27$
$3x + 2y = 11$

③ Solve these simultaneous equations.

a $3x + 2y = 6$
$2x + 3y = 4$

b $3x - 5y = 0$
$4x + 3y = 29$

c $4x - 5y = 17$
$3x - 2y = 18$

④ Cedric and Bethany go to a garden centre and buy some trees.
Cedric buys 4 peach trees and 3 apple trees for £75.
Bethany buys 3 peach trees and one apple tree for £45.

a Write this information as a pair of simultaneous equations.

b Solve the equations.

c Find the cost of 3 peach trees and 7 apple trees.

Unit 5 • Using graphs to solve simultaneous equations • Band h

Outside the Maths classroom

Best tariffs

Some households have a water meter fitted, so their water bill is worked out according to how much water is used. Other households are charged according to the value of their house.

Which system is fairer?

Toolbox

To solve these equations graphically:

$$y = 2x + 1$$
$$y = 4 - x$$

- Plot both equations on the same axes.
- If necessary, extend the lines so that they meet.
- Find the co-ordinates of the point where the two lines meet, in this case (1, 3).
- Make sure you write the solution as $x = \square$ and $y = \square$.
  In this case, the solution is $x = 1$ and $y = 3$.

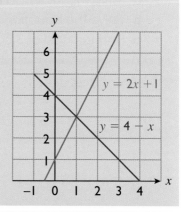

Example – Solving simultaneous equations graphically

Solve these simultaneous equations using a graph.

$$y = 2x$$
$$y = 6 - 2x$$

Solution

x	0	1	3
y = 2x	0	2	6

x	0	1	3
6	6	6	6
-2x	0	-2	-6
y = 6 - 2x	6	4	0

Find three points on each line.

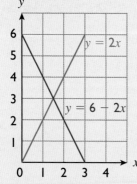

Plot the points for the two lines on the same graph.

The lines cross at the point (1.5, 3).

The solution is $x = 1.5$ and $y = 3$.

Practising skills

(1) a Write down the co-ordinates of the point of intersection of the 2 lines on this graph.

b Write down the solution of these equations.

$x + y = 4$
$y = x - 2$

c Check your answer by substituting values for x and y in the 2 equations.

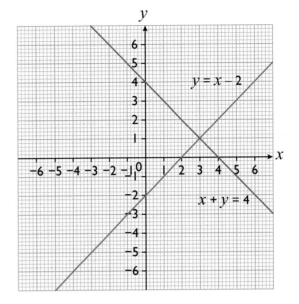

(2) a Write down the co-ordinates of the point of intersection of the 2 lines on this graph.

b Solve these equations in 2 ways.

$y = 4x - 3$
$4y = 3x + 1$

i By looking at the graph.

ii By algebra, using the substitution method.

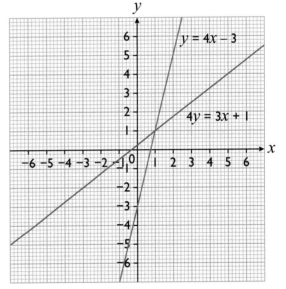

(3) a One of the lines on this graph is $y = x$ and the other is $3y = 4x - 1$. Which is which?

b Write down the co-ordinates of the point of intersection of the 2 lines.

c Solve these simultaneous equations.

$y = x$
$3y = 4x - 1$

i By looking at the graph.

ii By algebra, using the substitution method.

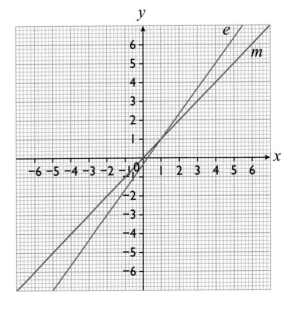

④ **a** One of the lines on this graph has equation $y = \frac{1}{3}x + 1\frac{2}{3}$.
The other has equation $y = -\frac{1}{2}x + 2\frac{1}{2}$.
Which is which?

b Write down the co-ordinates of the point of intersection of the 2 lines.

c Write down the 2 simultaneous equations for which this point is the solution.

d Check your solution by substituting your x- and y-values in both equations.

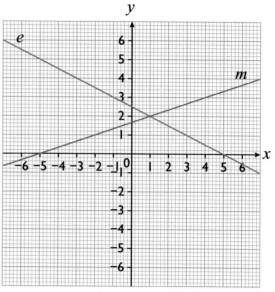

⑤ **a** Copy and complete this table of values for $y = 3x - 2$.

x	0	1	2	3
$3x$	0			
-2	-2			
$y = 3x - 2$	-2			

b Make a table of values for the line $y = 6 - x$.

c Draw the lines $y = 3x - 2$ and $y = 6 - x$ on the same graph.

d Use your graph to solve the simultaneous equations $y = 3x - 2$ and $y = 6 - x$.

e Use algebra to check your solution.

⑥ **a** Draw the lines $y = x + 3$ and $y = \frac{1}{4}x + 2\frac{1}{4}$ on the same graph.

b Use your graph to solve the simultaneous equations $y = x + 3$ and $4y = x + 9$.

⑦ **a** Copy and complete this table of values for $y = 8 - x$.

x	0	1	2	3
$y = 8 - x$	8			

b Make a table of values for the line $y = x + 4$.

c Draw the lines $y = 8 - x$ and $y = x + 4$ on the same graph.

d Use your graph to solve the simultaneous equations $y = 8 - x$ and $y = x + 4$.

e Check your answer using algebra to solve the equations.

⑧ **a** Draw the lines $y = 3x - 1$ and $y = x - 1$ on the same graph.

b Use your graph to solve the simultaneous equations $y = 3x - 1$ and $y = x - 1$.

c Use algebra to check your answer.

Developing fluency

① **a** Use algebra to solve these equations.

$$y = 4x$$
$$y = 2x^2$$

b Draw the lines $y = 4 - x$ and $y = 2x - 2$ on the same graph.

c Use your graph to check your answer to part **a**.

② **a** Use algebra to solve these equations.

$$y = 4x - 3$$
$$y = x + 3$$

b Draw the lines $y = 4x - 3$ and $y = x + 3$ on the same graph.

c Use your graph to check your answers to part **a**.

d Check your answer again, this time by substituting the x- and y-values in both equations.

③ **a** Use a graph to solve the simultaneous equations $y = 2x + 3$ and $x + y = 6$.

b Check your answer by solving these simultaneous equations by elimination.

$$-2x + y = 3$$
$$x + y = 6$$

④ **a** Try to use algebra to solve these simultaneous equations.

$$y = 2x + 3$$
$$y = 2x - 1$$

b What do you notice?

c Draw these two lines on the same axis.

d Use your graph to explain the result in part **a**.

⑤ **a** Draw the lines $2x + 3y = 24$ and $y = x + 3$ on the same graph.

b Use your graph to solve the simultaneous equations $2x + 3y = 24$ and $y = x + 3$.

c Check your answer by solving the equations algebraically.

d Find the area of the region bounded by the lines $2x + 3y = 24$, $y = x + 3$ and the x and y axes.

⑥ Two electricity companies advertise the following rates.

Green Power
Standing charge 30p per day
Cost of electricity 18p per unit

Sparkle
Standing charge 50p per day
Cost of electricity 16p per unit

a Write down an equation for the daily cost, C pence, of using u units of electricity for
  i Green Power
  ii Sparkle.

b On the same graph, draw two lines to illustrate the daily cost of electricity from each company for values of u from 0 to 15.

c **i** Use your graph to find the number of units for which both companies charge the same amount. How much do they each charge for this number of units?
  ii Check your answer to **ci** by solving your equations algebraically using the substitution method.

d The Watts family use an average of 12 units of electricity a day. Which company would you recommend?

(7) A quadrilateral is bounded by these 4 lines

$4y = x + 24$

$y + 4x = 23$

$y + 4x + 11 = 0$

$4y = x - 10$

a Draw the quadrilateral on a graph.

b Use your graph to find the co-ordinates of the vertices of the quadrilateral.

c Show how you can check your answer to **b** by substituting the x and y co-ordinates into the appropriate pair of equations.

d What is the name of the quadrilateral?

Problem solving

(1) Pete wants to hire a car. He wants to spend as little as possible.

He can hire it from one of two companies: U hire and Cars 2 go.

U hire	**Cars 2 go**
50p a mile	£60 plus 20p a mile

a Write down the equations for the cost £C of hiring a car for m miles from each company.

b On the same graph draw lines for your equations.

Use the vertical axis for C with a scale from 0 to 200 and the horizontal axis for m with a scale from 0 to 400.

c Pete expects to drive 250 miles. Which company would you advise him to use?

(2) Ros makes an accurate drawing of this diamond shape on graph paper.

The equations of the four lines are

$y = 3x - 3$

$y = 3x - 9$

$y = 3x + 15$

$y = 3x + 9$

a Make tables of values for these lines, taking values of x from 0 to 5.

b Draw a graph showing the parts of the lines that make the shape.

c Write down the co-ordinates of the four vertices, P, Q, R and S.

d Show how Ros could have used algebra to find the co-ordinates of the vertices.
Use this method to check your answers to part **c**.

e What is the mathematical name for this shape?

③ Catherine draws a triangle which is bounded by the lines $x + 2y = 12$, $2y = x + 4$ and $y = x - 3$.

a Draw the three lines on the same graph.

b i Write the coordinates of the vertices of the triangle.

ii Use your diagram to solve the following pairs of simultaneous equations.

A $x + 2y = 12$, $2y = x + 4$ **B** $x + 2y = 12$, $y = x - 3$ **C** $2y = x + 4$, $y = x - 3$

Catherine adds 2 horizontal and 2 vertical lines to her diagram to form a rectangle around her triangle. Each line passes through one of the vertices of the triangle.

c i Add these lines to your diagram.

ii State the equations of the lines that Catherine adds.

iii Find the area of the rectangle bounded by these 4 lines.

d Find the area of Catherine's triangle.

④ Look at these pay-as-you-go tariffs for 2 mobile phone companies.

Q-Mobile
30p per minute for calls
8p per text

Pear
20p per minute for calls
12p per text

Let m stand for the number of call minutes and t stand for the number of texts.

a Write down an equation for m and t for a bill of £5 with

i Q-Mobile **ii** Pear.

b Draw a graph of your equations.

Chloe uses Q-Mobile and Daisy uses Pear.

c One week they use the same number of call minutes as each other, and they send the same number of texts. They both use exactly £5 of credit.

How many call minutes and texts do they each use?

d Another week both girls make 4 minutes of calls and sent 40 texts.

i Mark a point on your graph to show this.

Both girls have £5 credit.

ii Who has to buy more credit? How much more credit does she need?

iii Who has credit left over? How much?

 ⑤ Here is the graph of the circle $x^2 + y^2 = 4$.
The line $y = 2x + 1$ cuts the circle at 2 points.
Find the co-ordinates of these 2 points.

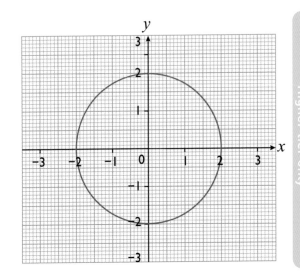

⑥ Here is the graph of the ellipse $\frac{x^2}{9} + \frac{y^2}{4} = 1$.

The line $x + y = 1$ cuts the ellipse at two points.
Find the co-ordinates of these two points.

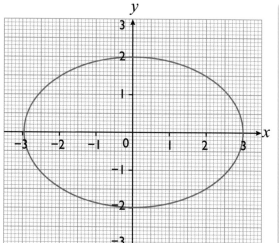

Reviewing skills

① a Draw the lines $y = 2x - 5$ and $y = 3x - 7$ on the same graph.

   b Use your graph to solve the simultaneous equations $y = 2x - 5$ and $y = 3x - 7$.

   c Check your solution by substituting the x- and y-values in both equations.

② a Use a graph to solve the simultaneous equations $y = 3x + 4$ and $y = x + 2$.

   b Check your answer algebraically by using the method of substitution.

   c Check your answer again, this time substituting the x and y values in both equations.

③ Avonford College compares the cost of two coach companies for a school trip.

Speedy Coaches
£150 per day
£2 per mile

Get-Aways!
£100 per day
£4 per mile

   a Write down an equation for the cost, £C, of hiring a coach for one day and for m miles for

     i Speedy Coaches

     ii Get-Aways!

   b On the same graph, draw 2 lines to illustrate the daily cost of hiring a coach from each company for values of m from 0 to 100.

   c i Use your graph to find the number of miles for which both firms charge the same amount. How much do they each charge for this number of miles?

     ii Check your answer to **ci** by solving your equations algebraically using the substitution method.

   d Avonford College are organising a coach for an 80-mile round trip.

     i Which company would you recommend?

     ii How much do Avonford College save by choosing this company?

Strand 5 Working with quadratics

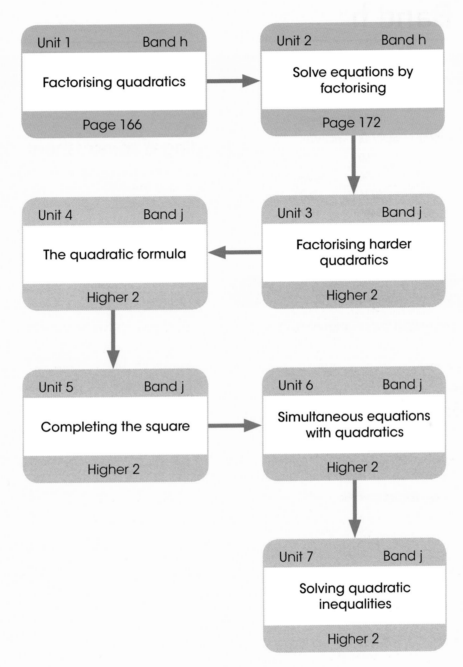

Unit 1   **Band h**

Factorising quadratics

Page 166

Unit 2   **Band h**

Solve equations by factorising

Page 172

Unit 4   **Band j**

The quadratic formula

Higher 2

Unit 3   **Band j**

Factorising harder quadratics

Higher 2

Unit 5   **Band j**

Completing the square

Higher 2

Unit 6   **Band j**

Simultaneous equations with quadratics

Higher 2

Unit 7   **Band j**

Solving quadratic inequalities

Higher 2

Unit 1 • Factorising quadratics • Band h

 Outside the Maths classroom

47,896.49	7130	3565	2139
54,815.62		4896	2448
5,253.16	#DIV/0!	#DIV/0!	#DIV/0!
8,397.00		750	375
101,519.73	15113	7556	4534
97,808.26		8736	4368
10,042.81	2990	1495	897
16,374.15		1463	731

Debugging a spreadsheet

How can altering formulae in a spreadsheet stop errors?

 Toolbox

A quadratic expression can sometimes be written as the product of two linear expressions, for example

$(x + 2)(x – 4)$

Expanding the brackets

$(x + 2)(x – 4) = x^2 + 2x – 4x – 8$
$= x^2 – 2x – 8$

Factorising means writing a number or expression as a product of 2 factors. It is the reverse of expanding brackets. So the expression $x^2 – 2x – 8$ factorises to $(x + 2)(x – 4)$.

$x + 2$ and $x – 4$ are **factors** of the original expression.

In general,

$(x + a)(x + b) = x^2 + ax + bx + ab$
$= x^2 + (a + b)x + ab$

> Multiply a and b to give the constant term.

> Add to a and b give the coefficient of the x term.

So to factorise $x^2 + 5x + 6$ first find numbers that multiply to give 6.

Possibilities are:

$1 × 6, 2 × 3, –1 × –6$ and $–2 × –3$

Of these, find the two numbers that add up to give 5:

$1 + 6 = 7$ ✗

$2 + 3 = 5$ ✔

$–1 + –6 = –7$ ✗

$–2 + –3 = –5$ ✗

So $x^2 + 5x + 6$ factorises to $(x + 2)(x + 3)$.

Check by expanding the brackets to get back to the original expression.

Special case

$(x + a)(x - a) = x^2 + ax - ax - a^2$
$= x^2 - a^2$

$x^2 - a^2$ is known as the **difference of two squares**.

Watch out for this when you need to factorise.

For example, $x^2 - 100$ is the difference of two squares $(100 = 10^2)$.

So $x^2 - 100 = (x + 10)(x - 10)$.

Example – Factorising quadratics

a Factorise $x^2 - 7x + 10$.
b Factorise $x^2 - x - 12$.

Solution

You need to reverse the process of expanding two brackets.

The first term to consider is the constant term or number 'on its own'.

a $x^2 - 7x + 10 = (x + \square)(x + \square)$
   You need two numbers that multiply to give +10.... ← | +2 and +5, –2 and –5, +10 and +1, –10 and –1 |
   ...and add up to give –7.
   $(+2) + (+5) = +7$, right number, wrong sign
   $(-2) + (-5) = -7$ ✔ ← | So the two numbers are –2 and –5. |
   Therefore, $x^2 - 7x + 10 = (x - 2)(x - 5)$

	x	-2
x	x^2	$-2x$
-5	$-5x$	$+10$

b $x^2 - x - 12 = (x + \square)(x + \square)$
   You need two numbers that multiply to give –12... ← | +12 and –1, –12 and +1, +6 and –2, –6 and +2, +4 and –3, –4 and +3 |

   ...and add to give –1. ← | $(+12) + (-1) = (+11)$ ✗ and $(-12) + 1 = (-11)$ ✗
$(+6) + (-2) = 4$ ✗ and $(-6) + (+2) = (-4)$ ✗ |

   $(+4) + (-3) = 1$, right number, wrong sign
   $(-4) + (+3) = -1$ ✔ ← | So the two numbers are –4 and +3. |
   Therefore, $x^2 - x - 12 = (x - 4)(x + 3)$

	x	-4
x	x^2	$-4x$
$+3$	$3x$	-12

Example – Difference of two squares

a Factorise $x^2 - 36$.
b Factorise $x^2 - 1$.

Solution

It is worth checking for the difference of two squares format when a quadratic expression has only 2 terms.

a The first square is x^2 so the brackets have x at the start:

$(x + \square)(x - \square)$

The second square is 36, so 6 fills in the other places.

$x^2 - 36 = (x + 6)(x - 6)$

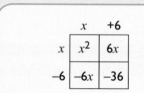

b The first square is x^2 so the brackets have x at the start:

$(x + \square)(x - \square)$

The second square is 1, so 1 fills in the other places.

$x^2 - 1 = (x + 1)(x - 1)$

Practising skills

① Expand and simplify where appropriate:

a $x(x + 3)$ **b** $x(x - 1)$ **c** $(x - 5)(x + 5)$ **d** $(x - 2)(x + 3)$

e $(x + 5)(x - 8)$ **f** $(x - 4)(x - 1)$ **g** $(x - 2)(x + 2)$

② The numbers –3 and 5 can be:

added together to give +2 $-3 + 5 = +2$

multiplied together to give –15 $-3 \times 5 = -15$.

Add up and multiply the following pairs of numbers.

a 3 and 4   **b** 2 and 6   **c** 1 and 4   **d** –1 and 5

e 3 and 3   **f** 8 and –2   **g** –3 and –4   **h** –2 and 2

③ Find pairs of numbers which do the following:

a add up to give 6 and multiply to give 8.

b add up to give 2 and multiply to give –8.

c add up to give –2 and multiply to give –8.

d add up to give –6 and multiply to give 8.

e add up to give 9 and multiply to give 8.

f add up to give 7 and multiply to give –8.

g add up to give –7 and multiply to give –8.

h add up to give –9 and multiply to give 8.

④ Find pairs of numbers which do the following:

a add up to give –5 and multiply to give 6. **b** add up to give 5 and multiply to give 6.

c add up to give –1 and multiply to give –6. **d** add up to give 1 and multiply to give –6.

e add up to give 7 and multiply to give 6. **f** add up to give 5 and multiply to give –6.

g add up to give –7 and multiply to give 6. **h** add up to give –5 and multiply to give –6.

⑤ Complete these simplifications.

a $2(a + 5) + 7(a + 5) = \square (a + 5)$ **b** $12(b – 6) – 3(b – 6) = \square (b – 6)$

c $8(c + 2) + (c + 2) = \square (c + 2)$ **d** $-2(d – 7) + (d – 7) = \square (d – 7)$

⑥ Complete these simplifications.

a $x(x + 5) + 7(x + 5) = (\square + \square) (x + 5)$ **b** $x(x – 6) – 3(x – 6) = (\square – \square) (x – 6)$

c $x(x + 2) + (x + 2) = (\square + \square) (x + 2)$ **d** $-x(x – 7) + (x – 7) = (\square x + \square) (x – 7)$

⑦ Complete these factorisations.

a

$x^2 + 6x + 8$ $2 \times 4 = 8$
                   $2 + 4 = 6$

$x^2 + 2x + \square x + 8$

$x(x + 2) + \square (x + 2)$

$(x + \square) (x + 2)$

b

$x^2 – 8x + 15$ $-3 \times -5 = 15$
                    $-3 + -5 = -8$

$x^2 – 3x – \square x + 15$

$x (x – 3) – \square (x – \square)$

$(x – \square) (x – \square)$

c

$x^2 – 2x – 24$ $4 \times -6 = -24$
                    $4 + -6 = -2$

$x^2 + 4x – \square x – 24$

$x(x + \square) – \square (x + \square)$

$(x – \square) (x + \square)$

d

$x^2 + x – 2$ $2 \times -1 = -2$
                  $2 + -1 = 1$

$x^2 + \square x – 1x – 2$

$x(x + \square) – 1(x + \square)$

$(x – \square) (x + \square)$

⑧ Factorise:

a $x^2 + 8x + 15$ **b** $x^2 – 9x + 20$ **c** $x^2 + 8x + 16$ **d** $x^2 + 4x – 21$

e $x^2 – x – 6$ **f** $x^2 + 17x + 16$ **g** $x^2 – 15x – 16$ **h** $x^2 – 8x – 20$

⑨ Factorise:

a $x^2 + 8x$ **b** $x^2 – 100$ **c** $x^2 – 16x$ **d** $x^2 – 16$

e $x^2 + 7x + 6$ **f** $x^2 – 1$ **g** $x^2 – 144$ **h** $x^2 – 5$

Developing fluency

① The diagram shows a rectangle PQRS divided up into 4 rectangular regions with dimensions a cm, b cm, c cm and d cm as shown.

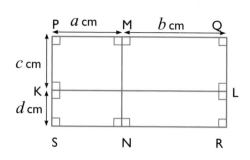

a Find the areas of the 4 regions.

b Which regions have areas

   i $a(c + d)$ **ii** $b(c + d)$

   iii $(a + b)(c + d)$?

c Factorise $ac + ad + bc + bd$.

② This rectangle is divided into 4 regions. One of them is a square of area x^2 cm^2. The others are rectangles. The diagram shows that one of the rectangles is 3 cm by 2 cm.

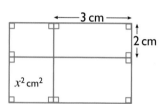

a Make a copy and mark the areas of the 4 regions on the diagram.

b Find the length and width of the whole rectangle.

c Use the diagram to factorise $x^2 + 5x + 6$.

d Use algebra to check your answer to part **c**.

③ This rectangle has an area of $x^2 + 6x + 8$ cm^2.

a Make a copy and divide the rectangle into four regions with areas x cm^2, $4x$ cm^2, $2x$ cm^2 and 8 cm^2.

b Show that the perimeter of the rectangle is $4x + 12$ cm and find its area.

c Use your diagram to factorise $x^2 + 6x + 8$.

d Use algebra to check your answer to part **c**.

④ Figure 1 shows a red square of side a cm.

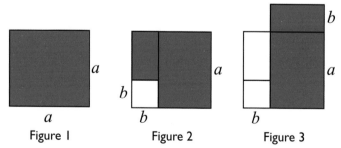

    Figure 1   Figure 2   Figure 3

In Figure 2 a smaller square of side b cm has been removed from the red square. A rectangle has been marked above the small square.

In Figure 3 the rectangle has been moved and turned so that it lies on the top.

a Find, in terms of a and b, the area of the red region in each of the 3 Figures.

b The red region in Figure 3 forms a large rectangle. Write down its dimensions in terms of a and b.

c Use the diagram to show that $a^2 - b^2 = (a + b)(a - b)$.

d Use algebra to show the same result.

Exam-style

5 **a** Expand:

    i $(x + 10)(x + 1)$

    ii $(x + 2)(x + 5)$

  b Simplify $(x + 10)(x - 1) - (x + 2)(x + 5)$.

  c Check your answer to part **b** by substituting $x = 2$.

6 **a** Expand:

    i $(x + 7)(x + 3)$

    ii $(x + 7)(x + 2)$

  b Simplify $(x + 7)(x + 3) - (x + 7)(x + 2)$.

  c How can you work out the answer to part **b** without expanding the brackets?

Problem solving

Exam-style questions that use skills developed in this unit are included in later units.

1 Without using a calculator, work out the area of the region that is shaded red.

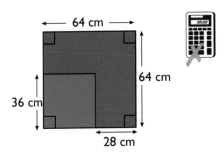

2 Pick an integer that is bigger than 3.

Square it and then subtract 4. Can the answer be a prime number? Explain.

Reviewing skills

1 Factorise these quadratics.

  a $x^2 - 6x + 8$ **b** $x^2 + x - 12$ **c** $x^2 - x - 12$ **d** $x^2 + 3x - 10$

  e $x^2 - 3x - 10$ **f** $x^2 - 8x + 16$ **g** $x^2 - 49$ **h** $x^2 - 3$

2 Show that $(x + 7)(x + 1) - (x + 2)(x + 6) + (x + 2)(x - 2) = (x + 3)(x - 3)$.

5 Unit 2 • Solving equations by factorising • Band h

Outside the Maths classroom

Discovering new numbers

How would you find the exact value of the hypotenuse of this triangle?

Toolbox

Here is a quadratic graph.

The parabola crosses the x axis at $(-2, 0)$ and $(3, 0)$. -2 and 3 are known as the **roots** of the equation $y = x^2 - x - 6$.

They are also the solution to the equation $x^2 - x - 6 = 0$.

This equation therefore has two solutions or roots, $x = -2$ and $x = 3$.

Quadratic functions can have 0, 1 or 2 roots, depending on where its curve crosses the x axis

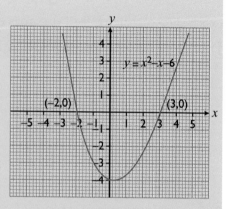

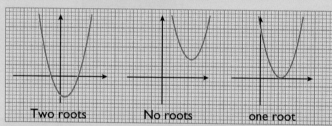

Two roots   No roots   one root

Some quadratic equations can be factorised and this gives an algebraic method for finding the **roots**.

It uses the fact that if 2 numbers multiply to give zero, then at least one of those numbers must be zero.

$x^2 + (a + b)x + ab = (x + a)(x + b)$ ⟵ [Factorising.]

$(x + a)(x + b) = 0$ ⟵

Either $x + a = 0$ [Roots are where its curve crosses the x axis, i.e. $y = 0$.]

$x = -a$ ⟵ [Rearranging.]

or $x + b = 0$

$x = -b.$ ⟵ [Rearranging.]

For our example, we can find the roots of $y = x^2 - x - 6$ by factorising.

$x^2 - x - 6 = 0$

$(x + 2)(x - 3) = 0$ ⟵ [Factorising, $2 - 3 = -1$, $2 \times -3 = -6$.]

Either $x + 2 = 0$ so $x = -2$

or $x - 3 = 0$ so $x = 3$.

You can check your answer by substituting back into the equation.

Example – Solving equations

The graph shows the function $y = x^2 + 7x + 12$.

a Solve $x^2 + 7x + 12 = 0$ algebraically.

b Solve $x^2 - 3x = 0$.

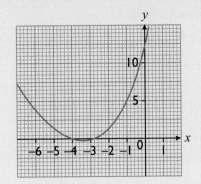

Solution

a $x^2 + 7x + 12 = 0$

Factorise first:

$(x + 3)(x + 4) = 0$ ← Two numbers that multiply to give +12 and add to give +7 are +3 and +4.

Either $x + 3 = 0$

$x = -3$ ← Check: $(-3)^2 + 7 \times (-3) + 12 = 9 - 21 + 12 = 0$ ✔

or $x + 4 = 0$

$x = -4$ ← Check: $(-4)^2 + 7 \times (-4) + 12 = 16 - 28 + 12 = 0$ ✔

b $x^2 - 3x = 0$

Factorise first:

$x(x - 3) = 0$ ← There is an 'x' in both terms

Either $x = 0$ ← Check: $0^2 - 3 \times 0 = 0$ ✔

or $x - 3 = 0$

$x = 3$ ← Check: $3^2 - 3 \times 3 = 9 - 9 = 0$ ✔

Example – Solving geometrical problems

A rectangle has width x metres, and length 1 metre more than its width. The area of the rectangle is $20\,\text{m}^2$.

a Form a quadratic equation for x.

b Solve the equation and find the length and width of the rectangle.

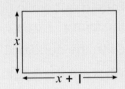

Solution

a Area of rectangle $= x(x + 1)$

So, $x(x + 1) = 20$ ← The area is 20 m². / Expanding.

$x^2 + x = 20$

$x^2 + x - 20 = 0$ ← You need to rearrange a quadratic equation into the form $ax^2 + bx + c = 0$ before you can solve it.

b $x^2 + x - 20 = 0$

$(x + 5)(x - 4) = 0$

Either $x + 5 = 0$, ← Two numbers that multiply to give –20 and add to give +1 are +5 and –4.

$x = -5$ ← Not a valid solution to this problem.

or, $x - 4 = 0$,

$x = 4$

The width of the rectangle is 4 metres.

The length of the rectangle is 5 metres. ← The length is 1 metre more than the width.

Check: $4 \times 5 = 20$ ✔

173

Practising skills

1 Solve these equations.

    a $(x + 4)(x + 1) = 0$ **b** $(x - 3)(x + 7) = 0$ **c** $(x - 1)(x - 1) = 0$ **d** $(x + 2)(x + 1) = 0$

2 Solve these equations.

    a $x^2 - 7x + 12 = 0$ **b** $x^2 - x - 2 = 0$ **c** $x^2 + 2x - 15 = 0$ **d** $x^2 + 6x + 5 = 0$

    e $x^2 - 4 = 0$ **f** $x^2 - 7x = 0$ **g** $x^2 + x - 12 = 0$ **h** $x^2 - 9 = 0$

3 Rearrange and solve these equations.

    a $x^2 + 4x = -3$ **b** $x^2 + 2x = 8$ **c** $x^2 = -x$

    d $x^2 = 3x + 4$ **e** $x^2 = 49$

4 Solve these equations.

    a $x^2 - 64 = 0$ **b** $x^2 = 9x + 36$ **c** $(x + 8)(x - 2) = 0$

    d $x^2 + x - 2 = 0$ **e** $x^2 - 9x = 0$

5 These are the solutions of quadratic equations. Write down each quadratic equation in the form $x^2 + bx + c = 0$.

    a 3 or 5   **b** −3 or −5   **c** 6 or −8

    d 1 or −1   **e** 9 or −10   **f** 0 or −6

Developing fluency

1 A rectangle measures x cm by $(x + 4)$ cm.
The area of the rectangle is 45 cm^2.

    a Write the area of the rectangle in terms of x.

    b Form a quadratic equation in x and rearrange it to the form $x^2 + bx + c = 0$.

    c Solve the quadratic equation.

    d What are the length and width of the rectangle?

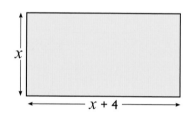

2 A rectangle measures x cm by $(x - 2)$ cm and has area 48 cm^2.

    a Form a quadratic equation in x and solve it.

    b What are the dimensions of the rectangle?

3 A triangle has height $(x + 6)$ cm and base x cm. The area of the triangle is 8 cm^2.
Form and solve a quadratic equation to work out the dimensions of the triangle.

Exam-style

④ The diagram shows the dimensions of a trapezium.
The area of the trapezium is $35\,\text{cm}^2$.

Form and solve a quadratic equation to work out the dimensions of the trapezium.

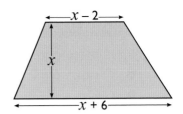

Problem solving

① The width of this rectangle is $(x - 8)\,\text{cm}$ and its area is $(x^2 - 64)\,\text{cm}^2$.

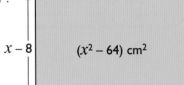

a Find an expression involving x for its length. The value of x will be different in each of the following parts **b**, **c** and **d**.

b The area of the rectangle is $36\,\text{cm}^2$. Find its length and width.

c Find the value of x for which it is possible to divide the rectangle into two equal squares.

d The rectangle has the same area as a square of perimeter $60\,\text{cm}$. Find the perimeter of the rectangle.

② Robin fires an arrow into the air.
The equation for the height, h metres, of the arrow at time, t seconds is $h = 45t - 5t^2$.

a Find the value of t when the arrow hits the ground.

b Find the times when the arrow is $100\,\text{m}$ above the ground.

③ Here is a rectangle with length $(x + 6)\,\text{cm}$ and width $(x - 5)\,\text{cm}$.
Find the length and the width of the rectangle.

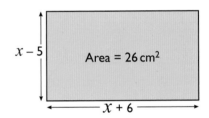

④

I think of a number.
I subtract 5 and square my answer.
My final answer is 4.

What numbers could Andy be thinking about?

⑤ A square of side $5\,\text{cm}$ is cut from a square of side $(x + 5)\,\text{cm}$.
The blue area remaining is $24\,\text{cm}^2$.

a Find the length of the original square.

b Explain why there is only one possible answer.

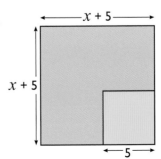

Reviewing skills

① Solve these equations.

a $x^2 + 5x + 6 = 0$ **b** $x^2 - 6x + 8 = 0$ **c** $x^2 - x - 2 = 0$ **d** $x^2 + 3x - 28 = 0$

e $x^2 + 5x = -4$ **f** $x^2 + 6 = 10$ **g** $x(x - 2) = 15$ **h** $x^2 - 10 = 0$

② A rectangle has width 3cm less than its length.

The area of the rectangle is 54cm^2.

Form and solve a quadratic equation to work out the dimensions of the rectangle.

Strand 1 Units and scales

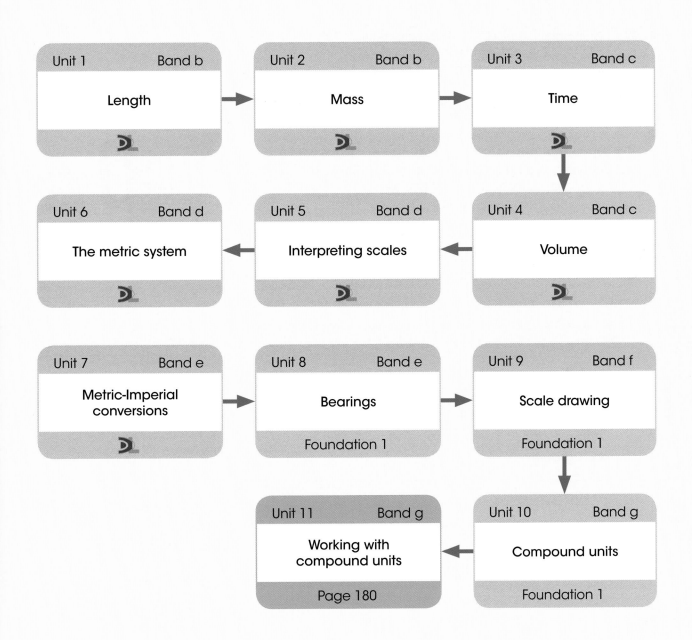

| Unit 1   Band b | Unit 2   Band b | Unit 3   Band c |
| Length | Mass | Time |

| Unit 6   Band d | Unit 5   Band d | Unit 4   Band c |
| The metric system | Interpreting scales | Volume |

Unit 7 Band e	Unit 8 Band e	Unit 9 Band f
Metric-Imperial conversions	Bearings	Scale drawing
	Foundation 1	Foundation 1

Unit 11 Band g	Unit 10 Band g
Working with compound units	Compound units
Page 180	Foundation 1

Units 1–10 are assumed knowledge for this book. They are reviewed and extended in the Moving on section on page 178.

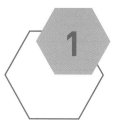

Units 1–10 • Moving on

Reasoning

① Peter and Hans are having a race on a track.

Peter is riding a motorbike at 90 miles per hour.

Hans is driving his car at 40 metres per second.

Who is travelling faster?

② Jess is making jugs of squash for a meeting of 60 people.
The squash is made using 1 part orange to 4 parts water.

The orange comes in cartons of 330 ml. Jess thinks she
needs 1 jug of squash for every 3 people.

How many cartons of orange will she need?

③ There are 35 grams of salt in a litre of seawater.

Work out the number of metric tonnes of salt in one cubic kilometre of seawater.

Exam-style

④ Nadia wants to make some rock cakes for a school fête. She has:

1.5 kg of flour

$\frac{3}{4}$ kg of butter

1 kg of sugar

675 g of dried fruit

Here is a list of the ingredients needed to make 12 rock cakes.

| 225 g flour |
| 110 g butter |
| 60 g sugar |
| 150 g dried fruit |

Does Nadia have enough ingredients to make 60 rock cakes?

5 This conversion graph can be used to exchange between gallons and litres.

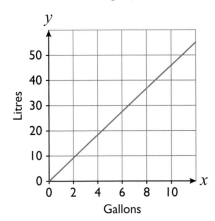

Art has oil-fired central heating. His oil tank holds 280 gallons of oil when full.

Art's tank is only $\frac{1}{4}$ full.

Oil costs 50p per litre.

Work out an estimate for the cost of filling the oil tank.

6 The smallest postage stamp ever was square, with sides measuring 10 millimetres.

The biggest stamp ever was rectanglar measuring 2 inches by $3\frac{1}{2}$ inches.

How many times bigger is the area of the rectangular stamp than the area of the square stamp?

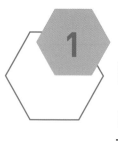
Unit 11 • Working with compound units • Band g

Outside the Maths classroom

Making boats

Why does a stone sink but a piece of wood float?

Toolbox

Common compound measures are:

Measure	Description	Common units
Speed	Distance travelled in 1 unit of time	m/s, km/h
Acceleration	Change in speed over 1 unit of time	m/s^2, km/h^2
Density	Mass of 1 unit of volume	g/cm^3, kg/m^3
Unit price	The price of an item for one unit of weight, area or volume	pence/gram, £/kg, pence/litre, £/gallon, $£/m^2$
Population density	Number of people in 1 unit of area	$people/km^2$

The units tell you the calculation to perform to calculate the compound measure.

For example, speed in m/s is calculated as:

metres (distance) ÷ seconds (time).

So, to convert from one compound unit to another, e.g. convert $6.7\,g/cm^3$ into kg/m^3:

$6.7\,g = 0.0067\,kg$ ← [1 kg = 1000 g]

$1\,cm^3 = 0.000001\,m^3$ ← [$1\,cm^3$ is 0.01 m by 0.01 m by 0.01 m]

$$\text{Density} = \frac{6.7\,g}{1\,cm^3} = \frac{0.0067\,kg}{0.000001\,m^3} = 6700\,kg/m^3$$

Speed and acceleration are also known as **rates of change.** They can often be found from the gradient of a graph.

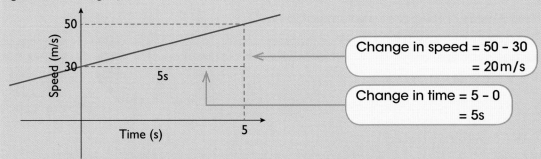

Change in speed = 50 − 30
= 20 m/s

Change in time = 5 − 0
= 5s

Acceleration is the gradient of a graph of speed against time.

Acceleration = $\left(\dfrac{20}{5}\right) = 4\,\text{m/s}^2$

Example – Electricity bills

Totals from SuLin's last four electricity bills are given below.

A 1070 kWh   Total cost £145.00
B 850 kWh   Total cost £119.30
C 600 kWh   Total cost £90.09
D 750 kWh   Total cost £107.61

SuLin wants to find out how much she pays per kWh.

Use a graph to find this information.

Solution

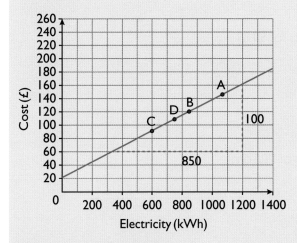

Cost per kWh = $\dfrac{100\ (\pounds)}{850\ (\text{kWh})}$

= £0.12 per kWh

= 12p per kWh

Example – Problems involving density

A brass block has a mass of 187 g and a volume of 22 cm^3.

a Calculate the density of brass in g/cm^3.

A brass cylinder has a mass of 53 g.

b Calculate the volume of the cylinder.

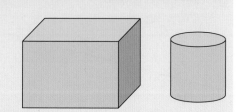

Solution

a Density = mass ÷ volume

$= 187 \div 22$

$= 8.5\,\text{g/cm}^3$

b Density $= \dfrac{\text{mass}}{\text{volume}}$

$8.5 = \dfrac{53}{v}$

$8.5v = 53$ ← ⟨Multiply both sides by v.⟩

$v = \dfrac{53}{8.5} = 6.2$ ← ⟨Divide both sides by 8.5.⟩

So the volume is 6.2 cm^3.

Practising skills

① Which is better value?

   a 1.5 litres of lemonade for 65p or 1 litre for 44p?

   b 15 pencils for 99p or 12 for 75p?

   c 3 kg of grass seed for £4.20 or 85 g for 96p?

   d 650 g of dog food for £2.15, 1.5 kg for £4.65 or 5 kg for £18?

② Lucy swims 500 m in 2 minutes and 20 seconds.

Calculate her speed in

   a metres per second

   b kilometres per hour.

③ A block of metal has a mass of 475 g and a volume of 225 cm^3.

Calculate the density in

   a g/cm^3 **b** kg/m^3.

④ A cube has sides of 16.4 cm.

Its mass is 1.2 kg.

Calculate its density in g/cm^3.

⑤ Dave runs n metres in t seconds. Write his speed in

   a m/s   **b** km/h.

6 The mass of this block of silver is 1260 g.

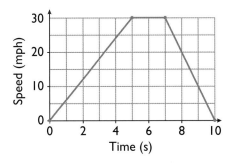

    a Calculate the density of silver in g/cm³.

    b Find the mass of a 20 centimetre cube of silver in kilograms.

7 This graph shows the way that the speed of one car changes in a certain 10 second period.

    a What is happening to the car between 5 and 7 seconds into its journey?

    b What is the rate of change of speed during the first 5 seconds?

    c What term describes the rate of change of speed?

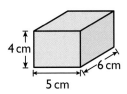

Developing fluency

1 Jean is driving from the south of France to Paris.
She sees a road sign.
She knows that it takes her 1 hour to travel 60 miles.
The time now is 10 pm.
Jean wants to get to Paris by 2.30 am.
Will she be able to get to Paris by 2.30 am?

2 Alex buys a 150 g bar of chocolate for £1.75 in the UK.
He knows that a $\frac{1}{2}$ pound bar will cost the equivalent of £2.75 in the USA.
Where is it better value, in the UK or in the USA?

3 Salima knows that the fuel tank on her car has a capacity of 9 gallons.
When she was in France she filled up the tank from half full at a cost of €30.
£1 = €1.25
Work out the cost in pounds of a litre of fuel in France.

4 Match the following descriptions with the graphs.

    a An object travels at a constant speed of 15 metres per second for five seconds.

    b An object travels 15 metres in five seconds without accelerating.

    c An object accelerates at a constant rate and reaches a speed of 15 metres per second in five seconds.

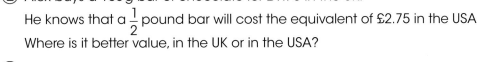

Reasoning

5 Andy says that these two graphs are for the same car at the same time.
Is Andy correct?
Explain how you know.

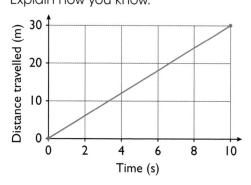

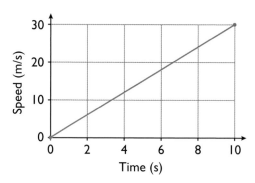

Exam-style

6 A £1 coin has a mass of 9.5 g.
Its diameter is 22.5 mm and its thickness is 3.15 mm.
Calculate the density of a £1 coin in g/cm^3.

Reasoning

7 **a** A block of metal A weighs 486 g and has a volume of 180 cm^3.
A block of metal B weighs 26 700 kg and has a volume of 3 m^3.
Use the formula density $= \dfrac{\text{mass}}{\text{volume}}$ to calculate the density of each block.
b Ben has a block of metal A and a block of metal B.
Both blocks are identical sizes.
Which block is heavier?

8 The pressure exerted by an elephant's foot is f N/m^2 (newtons per square metre).
Write this in newtons per square centimetre.

9 A concrete block has a volume of v cm^3 and a mass of m g.
Write the density in kg/m^3.

10 Show that V metres per second is about the same speed as $2.25V$ miles per hour.

Problem solving

Exam-style

1 A car is travelling at 50 kilometres per hour.

a Work out how long it will take the car to travel 24 metres.

A bridge is 24 metres long.

b When you calculate the time a car takes to cross the bridge that is 24 metres long, why could your answer be different from your answer to part **a**?

② Bob is following a fitness programme. He wears a device that monitors his calorie burn.
The graph shows some information about his calorie burn during a period of 15 minutes.

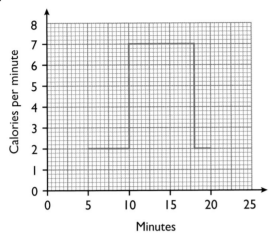

a Work out the number of calories Bob burned over the first 5 minutes of the 15-minute period.

b Work out the average rate at which he burned calories over the 15 minutes.

Bob found that his average rate of calorie burn was 2.5 calories per minute when he was awake and 1.5 calories per minute when he was asleep.

c Work out the total number of calories Bob burned during a 24-hour period when he spent 8 hours asleep.

③ The diagram shows two bottles of the same make of shampoo.

1.8 litres
£4

2.5 litres
£5.80

Which bottle gives the better value for money?
You must show your working to support your choice.

④ The density of wood is 0.9 g/cm.

a Work out the density of the wood in kg/m^3.

x litres of oil have a mass of y grams.

b Work out an expression for the density of the oil in kg/m^3.

⑤ Jim uses a water meter in his house.
The cost of the water he uses during one year is the sum of the meter charge + the charge for the water used.
The meter charge is £41.
The charge for the water used is £2.10 per 1000 litres.
On average Jim uses 170 litres of water per day.
Work out the cost of the water Jim uses in one year.

⑥ The BMI of a person is calculated using the rule
$$BMI = mass\ in\ kg \div (height\ in\ m)^2$$
Ideal BMIs lie between 18 and 25.
Bill weighs 154 pounds and has a height of 183 cm.
Does Bill have an ideal BMI? Give a reason for your answer.

⑦ Brass alloy is made by melting together copper and zinc in the ratio 3:2 by mass.
The density of copper is 8.94 g/cm³.
The density of zinc is 6.57 g/cm³

  a Find the mass of copper and the mass of zinc in 100 grams of the alloy.

  b Work out the density of brass alloy.

⑧ A company sells gold bars in the shape of cuboids.
The measurements of a bar are 80 mm by 40 mm by 16 mm.
The density of gold is 19.32 g/cm³.
Midas thinks that the mass of the block is over 1 kilogram.
Is he correct? Explain your answer.

⑨ Here is a graph that shows the costs of hiring a cement mixer and a concrete leveller.

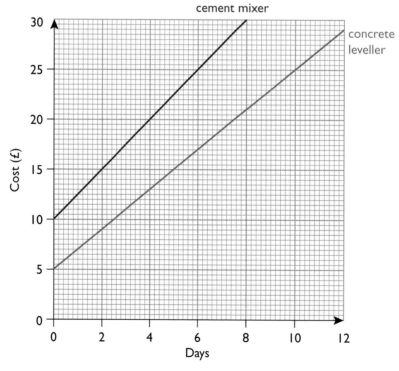

  a Find the difference in the daily rate of hiring each item of equipment.

  b Find the equations of the two graphs.

Reviewing skills

① Peter is driving in France.

At 10 am he sees a road sign which says Calais 308 km.

Peter knows that he can drive at a maximum speed of 55 miles per hour.

Work out the earliest time Peter can get to Calais.

② A 275 cm^3 block of expanded polystyrene has a mass of 15 g.

What is the density of expanded polystyrene in kg/m^3?

③ Peter's water is unmetered. His water company provides the graph below so residents can work out how much they will be charged. The chargeable value of Peter's house is £140.

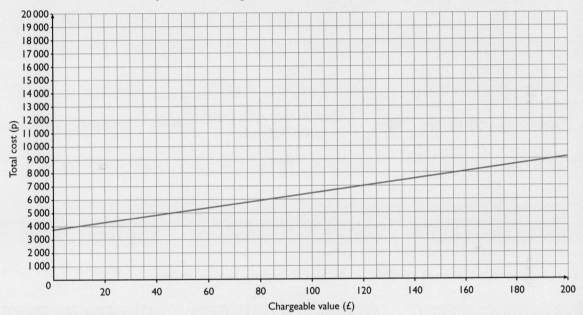

a How much will Peter be charged? Give your answer in £.

b How much does the water company charge per £ of chargeable value?

Strand 2 Properties of shapes

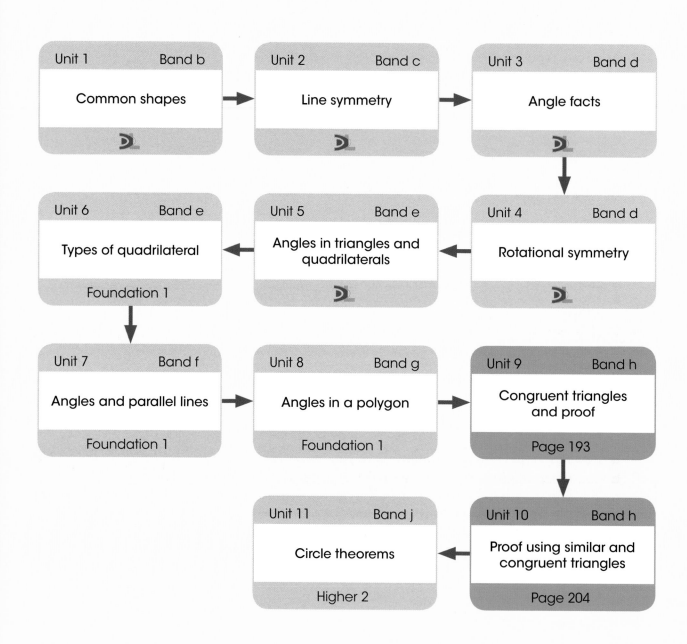

Unit 1 Band b	Unit 2 Band c	Unit 3 Band d
Common shapes	Line symmetry	Angle facts

Unit 6 Band e	Unit 5 Band e	Unit 4 Band d
Types of quadrilateral	Angles in triangles and quadrilaterals	Rotational symmetry
Foundation 1		

Unit 7 Band f	Unit 8 Band g	Unit 9 Band h
Angles and parallel lines	Angles in a polygon	Congruent triangles and proof
Foundation 1	Foundation 1	Page 193

Unit 11 Band j	Unit 10 Band h
Circle theorems	Proof using similar and congruent triangles
Higher 2	Page 204

Units 1–8 are assumed knowledge for this book. They are reviewed and extended in the Moving on section on page 189.

Units 1–8 • Moving on

① Anna wants to make a logo for her company.

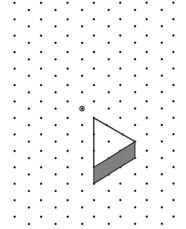

She wants to rotate this shape about the centre C, to make a logo that has rotational symmetry of order 3.

a Draw a possible logo.

b Describe the transformations of your logo.

② Design a logo with rotational symmetry of order 6.
Use the shape already on the grid of dots.

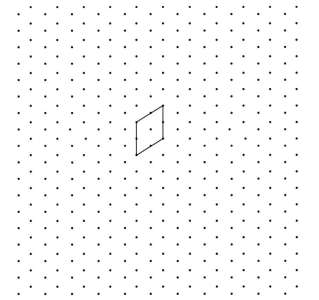

③ In a quadrilateral, the smallest angle is acute.
Each of the other angles is 20° more than the smallest angle.
Find the size of each of the three equal angles.

④ Here is a shape with rotational symmetry of order 4.

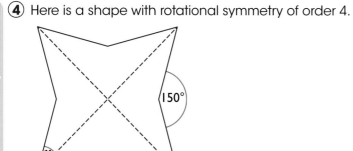

Work out the value of x.

⑤ ABCD is a parallelogram.

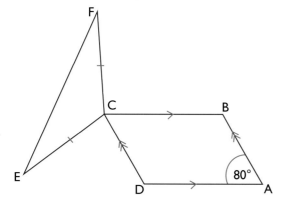

$\angle DAB = 80°$.

Triangle ECF is an isosceles triangle with EC = FC.

$\angle BCF = \angle DCE = 90°$.

Find the sizes of the equal angles in triangle EFC.

Give reasons at each stage of your working.

⑥ ABCD is a quadrilateral.

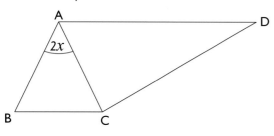

AB = AC

AD is parallel to BC.

$\angle BAC = 2x$

$\angle ACD = 90°$

Show that $\angle ADC = x$.

Give reasons at each stage of your working.

Exam-style

7 The diagram shows two identical triangles.

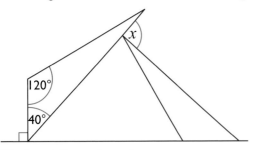

Work out the value of x.

Exam-style

8 Annie thinks she can draw a quadrilateral where:
three of the angles are each double the smallest angle, and
each angle is a whole number of degrees.
Is Annie correct?
You must give a reason for your answer.

Exam-style

9 Here are 3 identical triangles.

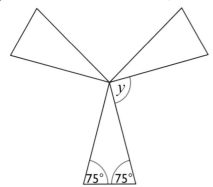

The diagram has rotational symmetry of order 3.
Work out the value of y.

Exam-style

10 Here are two identical kites. The smallest angle is 40°; the angle opposite it is 90°.

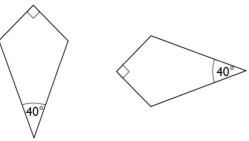

In this diagram one of the kites has been translated.

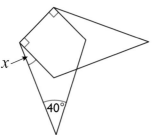

Work out the value of x.

11 Find the size of each lettered angle in these diagrams.
For each one write down the angle fact(s) that you use.

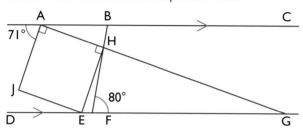 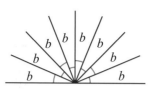

12 The diagram shows two parallel lines ABC and DEFG.
A and E are vertices of a square AHEJ.

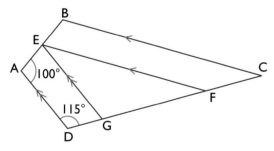

AHG and BHF are straight lines.
EH is perpendicular to AG.
Work out the size of ∠EHF.

13 ABCD is a kite.
EF is parallel to BC.
AD is parallel to EG.
Calculate the size of ∠GEF.

2

Unit 9 · Congruent triangles and proof · Band h

Outside the Maths classroom

Triangular supports

Why do builders use triangular supports?

Toolbox

A **proof** is a water-tight argument that cannot be disputed. A mathematical proof starts from a position that is known to be true. Each step is justified. The explanation is often written in brackets. The proofs in this unit involve angle facts and congruent triangles.

Congruent shapes are exactly the same shape and size.

There are four sets of conditions that prove two triangles are congruent.

1 **SSS.** The three sides of one triangle are equal to the three sides of the other.

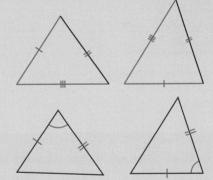

2 **SAS.** Two sides of one triangle are equal to two sides of the other, and the angles between those sides are equal.

3 **SAA.** Two angles of one triangle are equal to two angles of the other, and a pair of corresponding sides are equal.

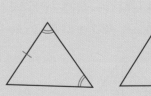

4 **RHS.** Two right-angled triangles have equal hypotenuses and another pair of equal sides.

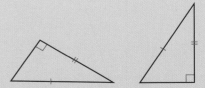

Note that three angles being equal in a pair of triangles (AAA) is not proof of congruence. One triangle may be bigger than the other. It does, however, prove they are similar.

Example – Recognising congruence

These four triangles have two sides and one angle equal.

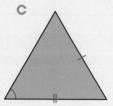

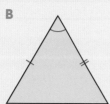

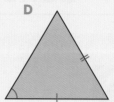

a Are any of the triangles congruent?
b Which triangle is congruent to this one?

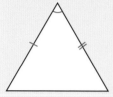

Solution

a **A** and **D** are congruent. If you reflect **D** in the line bisecting the marked angle you get **A** (SAS).

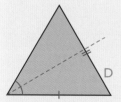

b The yellow triangle (**B**) is congruent to the white one (SAS).

Example – Using congruent triangles

In this kite, AB = AC and BD = CD.
Prove that angles ABD and ACD are equal.

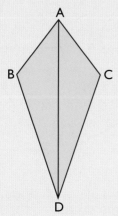

Solution

In triangles ABD and ACD:

AB = AC ⟵ Given

BD = CD ⟵ Given

AD is common.

Therefore triangles ABD and ACD are congruent. ⟵ SSS

So, ∠ABD = ∠ACD ⟵ Corresponding angles of congruent triangles.

Example – Angle proofs

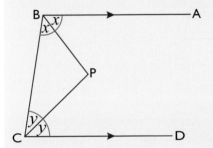

In the diagram, BA and CD are parallel.

The bisectors of ∠ABC and ∠BCD meet at P.

Prove that ∠BPC = 90°.

Solution

Let ∠ABC = 2x and ∠BCD = 2y as shown in the diagram.

∠ABP = ∠CBP = x ⟵ BP bisects ∠ABC.

∠BCP = ∠DCP = y ⟵ PC bisects ∠BCD.

∠ABC + ∠BCD = 180° ⟵ Interior angles on parallel lines.

$$2x + 2y = 180°$$

$$x + y = 90°$$ ⟵ Dividing both sides by 2.

∠CBP + ∠BCP + ∠BPC = 180° ⟵ Angle sum of triangle BPC.

$$x + y + ∠BPC = 180°$$

$$90° + ∠BPC = 180°$$ ⟵ Since $x + y = 90°$.

$$∠BPC = 90°$$

Practising skills

① Say why the angles in each of the following pairs are equal.
In each case choose a reason from this list.

Alternate angles	Corresponding angles	Vertically opposite angles

Angles in an isosceles triangle	Opposite angles of a parallelogram

a
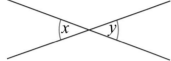

b

c

d
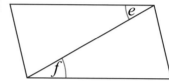

e
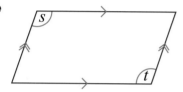

f
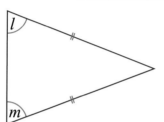

g
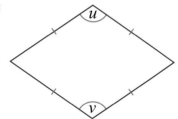

h
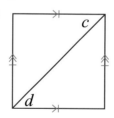

i
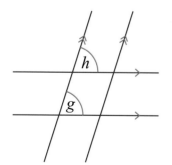

j
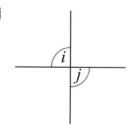

② Say why the lines in each of the following pairs are equal.

a

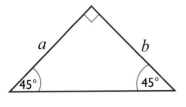

b

c

d

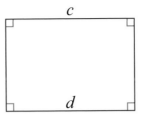

e

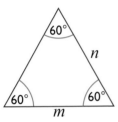

③ **a** State two pairs of equal angles in this diagram.

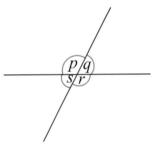

b State four different pairs of angles that add up to 180°.

c Copy and complete this statement.

$p + q + r + s =$ _____ (angles round a ....)

④ **a** State, giving reasons, three pairs of equal angles in this diagram.

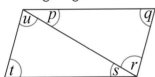

b State, giving reasons, four different sets of three angles that add up to 180°.

5 Say whether the triangles in each pair are congruent. If they are, give a reason (SSS, SAS, ASA, RHS).

a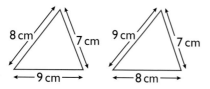

b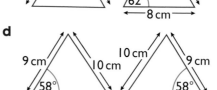

c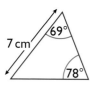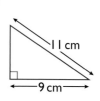

d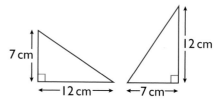

e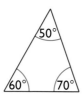

f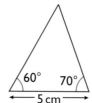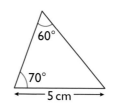

g

h

6 In the diagram, O is the centre of the circle.
The ∠ZOY is 50° as shown.

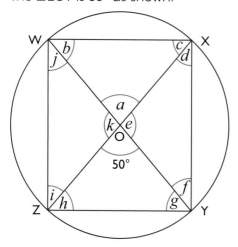

a Find the sizes of the angles marked $a, b, c, d, e, f, g, h, i, j$ and k.
In each case give your reasons.

b Use your answers to prove that WXYZ is a rectangle.

c How many pairs of congruent triangles are there in the diagram?

⑦ ABC is an isosceles triangle with AB = AC.
AP bisects ∠BAC.
Prove that PB = PC.

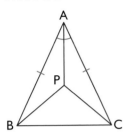

Developing fluency

① In the diagram, AB and DE are parallel.
AC and CE are both 8 cm long.

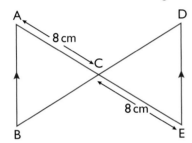

a Copy and complete this proof that triangles ABC and CDE are congruent.

In triangles ABC and EDC

AC = ☐ (both given as 8 cm)

∠ACB = ∠ECD (☐)

∠BAC = ☐ (alternate angles)

So triangles ABC and EDC are congruent (☐).

b What does this tell you about lines AB and DE?

② The diagram shows a rhombus, ABCD.

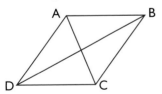

a Copy and complete this proof that triangles DAB and DCB are congruent.

In triangles DAB and DCB

AB = CB (a rhombus has equal sides)

AD = CD (☐)

BD is common to both triangles.

So triangles DAB and DCB are congruent (☐).

b What does this tell you about ∠ADB and ∠CDB?

③ AB is a chord of a circle, centre O.
ON is perpendicular to AB.

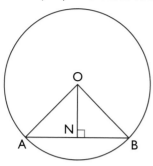

a Prove that triangles OAN and OBN are congruent.

b What does this tell you about point N?

④ Peter has given reasons why the triangles below are congruent.
Explain his errors.

a SAS

b ASA

c RHS

d AAA

⑤ In this diagram, angles DAB and CBA are equal and AD = BC.
Prove that BD = AC.

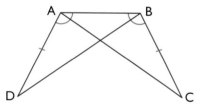

⑥ In this diagram AQ and BP are perpendicular to AB.
AQ = BP
Prove that AB bisects PQ.

7 In this diagram, D is the mid-point of the line AB.

DM and DN are perpendiculars from D to AC and BC.

DM = DN

Prove that triangle ABC is isosceles.

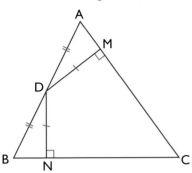

8 ABCD is a quadrilateral. The diagonal AC bisects the angles BAD and BCD.

Prove that the quadrilateral is a kite.

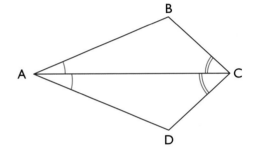

Problem solving

1 ABCDE is a regular pentagon.

  a What does this tell you about its sides?

  b What does this tell you about its interior angles?

  c Use congruent triangles to prove that BE = BD.

  d Which other lines are diagonals of this pentagon?
  Explain how you know that all the diagonals are equal in length.

2 In triangle ABC, AB = AC and D is a point on BC.
The line AD bisects the angle at A.

  a Prove that the triangles ABD and ACD are congruent.

  b Prove that
    i D is the mid-point of BC
    ii $\angle ADC = 90°$.

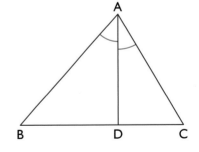

③ In this diagram, ∠PQS = ∠PRS.
PS bisects ∠QPR.

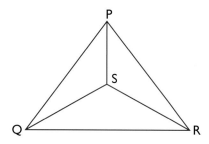

a Prove that triangle PQR is isosceles.

b Hence prove that ∠SQR = ∠SRQ.

④ In the diagram, ADB, BCE, AFC and DFE are all straight lines.
∠DBC is a right angle.
AB = BE and AC = DE.
Prove that AD = CE.

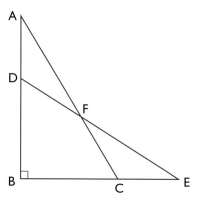

⑤ PQRS is a parallelogram.
N and M are points on QS such that PM and RN are perpendicular to QS.

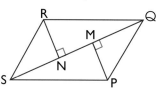

a Prove that triangles PMQ and RNS are congruent.

b Prove that SM = QN.

⑥ All four sides of a rhombus are equal.

a Taking this as a starting point and using congruent triangles, prove that the opposite sides are parallel.

b Prove, using congruent triangles, that the diagonals of a rhombus intersect at right angles.

Reviewing skills

① Say why the following pairs of triangles are similar.
In each case choose a reason from this list.

| Alternate angles | Corresponding angles | Vertically opposite angles |

| Angles in an isosceles triangle | Opposite angles of a parallelogram |

a

b
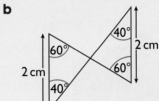

c
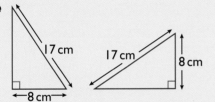

d
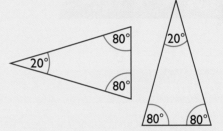

e
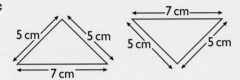

f
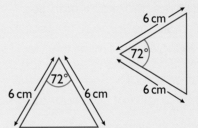

② CDE is an isosceles triangle with CE = DE.
ABCD is a rectangle, and EF is perpendicular to CD.

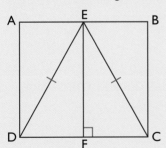

a Prove that triangles ADE and BCE are congruent.

b What does this tell you about point E?

③ ABCD is a parallelogram. Therefore its opposite sides are equal and parallel.
Prove that the diagonals AC and BD bisect each other.

Unit 10 • Proof using similar and congruent triangles • Band h

Outside the Maths classroom

Understanding concepts

How did Pythagoras help Roman builders get perfect right angles in their buildings?

Toolbox

You have met quite a lot of standard geometry results. These can be proved using angle facts, congruent triangles and similar triangles.

Similar triangles are the same shape but not necessarily the same size.

To prove two triangles are similar, you need to show two pairs of angles are equal (AA). Since the angles of each triangle add up to 180°, the third pair must be equal.

The ratios of the lengths of corresponding sides of similar triangles are equal.

You will also meet two other ways of proving triangles are similar.

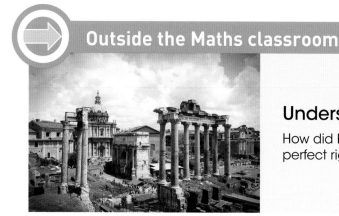

a The ratios of all three corresponding sides are the same.

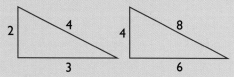

b The ratios of two corresponding sides are the same and the angles between these sides are equal.

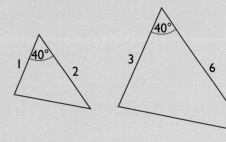

Example – Using congruent triangles to prove a standard result

ABC is an isosceles triangle with AB = AC.
Prove that ∠ABC = ∠ACB.

Solution

Mark the mid-point of BC as M.

Join AM.

In the triangles ABM and ACM

AB = AC (Given)

BM = CM (M is mid-point of BC)

AM is common.

Therefore triangles ABM and ACM are congruent (SSS).

So ∠ABM = ∠ACM (Corresponding angles of congruent triangles)

These are the required angles.

∠ABC = ∠ACB

Example – Proof using similar triangles

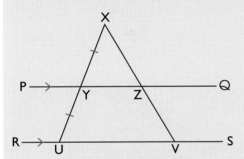

In the diagram, PQ and RS are parallel lines.

XYU and XZV are straight lines.

XY = YU

Prove that UV = 2YZ.

Solution

In the triangles XYZ and XUV

∠XYZ = ∠XUV (Corresponding angles)

∠YXZ is common.

> This is because lines PQ and RS are parallel.

Therefore triangles XYZ and XUV are similar (AA).

So, the sides are in ratio.

$$\frac{XU}{XY} = \frac{UV}{YZ} = \frac{VX}{ZX}$$

Since XY = YU (given), XU = 2XY and $\frac{XU}{XY} = 2$.

Therefore $\frac{UV}{YZ} = 2$ and UV = 2YZ.

Practising skills

① Here are 25 triangles. They are 12 pairs and 1 odd one out.
The pairs are either similar or congruent.
Identify the pairs (and the odd one out).
For each pair, justify why you are linking them.

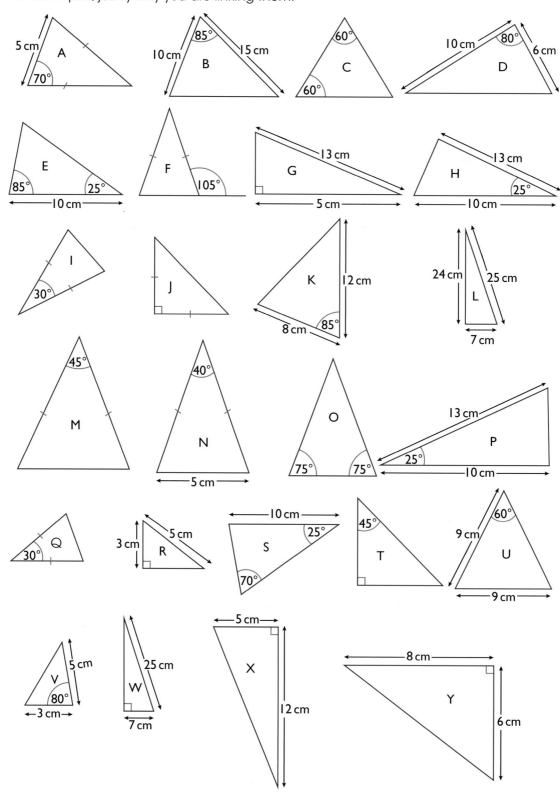

Developing fluency

① ABCDEF is a regular hexagon.
Use congruent triangles to prove that BDF is an equilateral triangle.

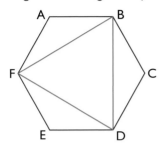

② ABCD is a quadrilateral.
AB = CD and AD = BC
The angles at A, B, C and D are all 90°.

  a What sort of quadrilateral is ABCD?

  b Prove triangles ADB and BCA are congruent.

  c Hence show that AC = BD.

  d What general result have you proved?

③ ABCD is a kite. The diagonals meet at X.

  a Prove triangles ABC and ADC are congruent.

  b Hence prove triangles ABX and ADX are congruent.

  c Show that X is the mid-point of BD.

  d State this as a general result that is true for all kites.

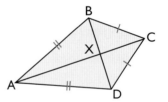

④ In the diagram, the lines AB and DE are parallel.
AC = 2CE

  a Copy and complete this proof that triangles ABC and DEC are similar.
    In triangles ABC and DEC
    $\angle$ACB = $\angle$☐ (vertically opposite)
    $\angle$ABC = $\angle$☐ (alternate)
    Therefore the triangles are similar (☐).

  b Write down the value of the ratio $\dfrac{AC}{EC}$.

  c What fraction of the way along AE is the point C?

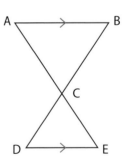

⑤ ABC is a triangle.

X is the mid-point of AB.

Y is a point on AC such that XY is parallel to BC.

Prove that Y is the mid-point of AC and $XY = \frac{1}{2}BC$.

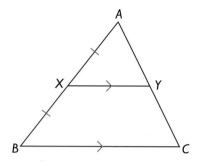

⑥ In the diagram,

L, M and N are the mid-points of the sides of triangle ABC

X, Y and Z are the mid-points of the sides of triangle LMN.

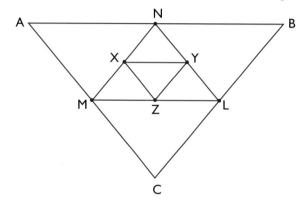

a Prove that triangles ABC and ANM are similar.

b What can you say about triangles ABC, LMN and XYZ?

c Find the ratio of the sides of triangle XYZ to those of triangle ABC.

Problem solving

Exam-style questions that require skills developed in this unit are included in later units.

① The diagram shows the pentagon ADBCE.

ABE is an equilateral triangle.

∠DAB = 90°

∠CEB = 90°

DB = BC.

a Prove that triangles DAB and CEB are congruent.

b Prove that ∠DBE = ∠CBA.

c Explain whether the result in part **a** is still true if triangle ABE is isosceles.

2 ABCD and CEFG are parallelograms.
BCG and DCE are straight lines.

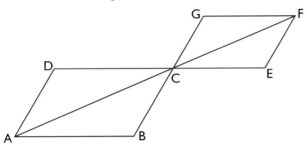

a Prove that triangle CFG is similar to triangle CBA.
Write down reasons at each stage of your working.

b Given that DC : CE = 3 : 2, find the value of AF : AC.

3 In this diagram, ABCD is a parallelogram.
So the diagonals AC and BD bisect each other at O.
OP is parallel to DA and OQ is parallel to DC.

a Prove that triangles OPB and DAB are similar.

b Write down another pair of similar triangles.

c Prove that P is the mid-point of AB.

d Prove that $PQ = \frac{1}{2} AC$.

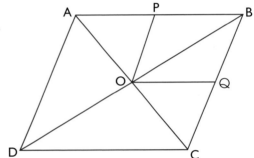

4 PQR is a right-angled triangle. QRS is an isosceles triangle with SQ = SR.
ST is parallel to QP.

a Prove that triangles SQU and SRU are congruent.

b Write down the ratio QR : UR.

c Prove that triangles PQR and TUR are similar.

d Show that PQ = 2TU.

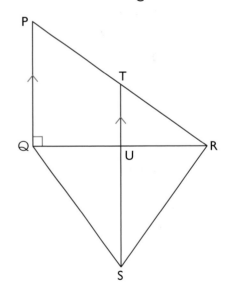

⑤ In the diagram, ABC is an isosceles triangle with AB = AC.

CF and AB are parallel.

M is the mid-point of BC.

DEMF and DAC are straight lines.

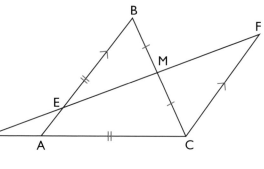
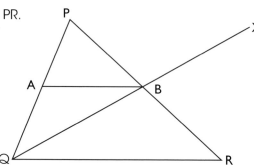

  a Prove that triangles DEA and DFC are similar.

  b Prove that triangles BME and CMF are congruent.

  c Hence show that $\dfrac{EA}{EB} = \dfrac{DE}{DF}$.

⑥ In this diagram, A and B are the mid-points of PQ and PR.

QBX is a straight line with QB = BX.

  a Prove triangles PAB and PQR are similar.

   What does this tell you about lines AB and QR?

  b Prove triangles QAB and QPX are similar.

   What does this tell you about lines PX and QR?

  c Have you done enough to prove that PXRQ is a parallelogram?

   Explain your answer fully.

Reviewing skills

① In the diagram, AC and BD are two straight lines that bisect each other at X.

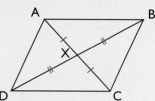

  a Prove that AB = CD and ∠BAX = ∠DCX.

  b What does this tell you about the quadrilateral ABCD? Give reasons for your answer.

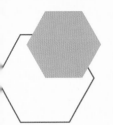

Strand 3 Measuring shapes

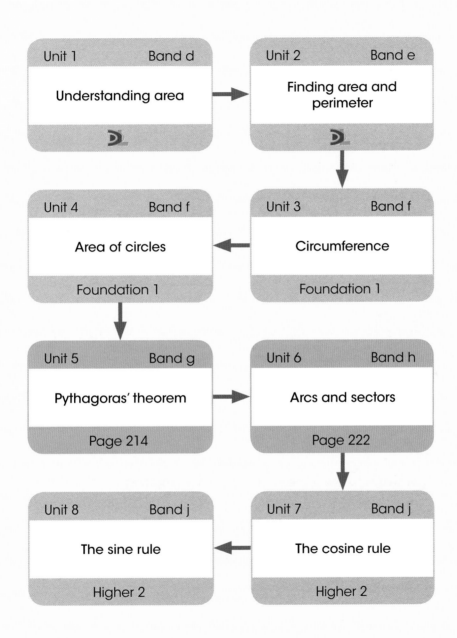

Unit 1 — Band d	Unit 2 — Band e
Understanding area	**Finding area and perimeter**

Unit 4 — Band f	Unit 3 — Band f
Area of circles	**Circumference**
Foundation 1	Foundation 1

Unit 5 — Band g	Unit 6 — Band h
Pythagoras' theorem	**Arcs and sectors**
Page 214	Page 222

Unit 8 — Band j	Unit 7 — Band j
The sine rule	**The cosine rule**
Higher 2	Higher 2

Units 1–4 are assumed knowledge for this book. They are reviewed and extended in the Moving on section on page 212.

Units 1–4 • Moving on

① Lisa wants to make this path in her garden.

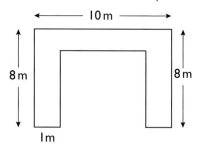

The path is 1 m wide.

She wants to make the path from wood chippings.

The wood chippings she likes are sold in bags costing £6.99 each.

A bag of wood chippings is enough to make $\frac{3}{4}$ m² of path.

Work out the total cost of the wood chippings.

② This is a plan of a symmetrical stage floor in a theatre.

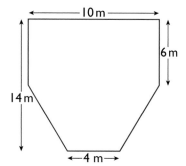

The stage manager wants to cover the floor with special matting.

The matting costs £6.50 for a square metre. The manager has a budget of £1200.

Can he afford matting for the whole stage floor? You must give a reason for your answer.

③ This is a diagram of a field in the shape of a trapezium.

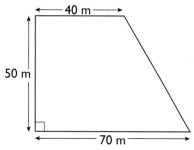

The lengths of the parallel sides of the field are 40 m and 70 m.

The sides are 50 m apart

The farmer wants to put fertiliser on the field.

He knows that 8 grams of fertiliser will treat 5 m² of field.

Work out the total amount of fertiliser he will need.

Exam-style

④ This is a diagram of a children's playground. The playground consists of a trapezium with a square inside.

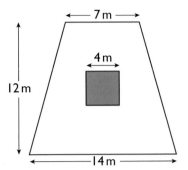

The trapezium has parallel sides of lengths 7 m and 14 m.

The parallel sides are 12 m apart.

The square has sides of length 4 m.

The region outside the square is to be covered with a rubber surface.

The rubber costs £17.99 per square metre.

Work out the cost of the rubber needed.

Exam-style

⑤ The diagram shows a picture frame.

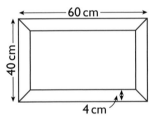

The total width of the frame is 60 cm and the total height is 40 cm.

The width of the frame is 4 cm.

Roger wants to cover the frame with gold leaf.

There is enough gold leaf in a packet to cover 1600 cm^2.

Will one packet be enough? You must give a reason for your answer.

Exam-style

⑥ Gill has 18 square tiles each of width 2 cm.

Gill makes a rectangle 6 cm wide using all the tiles.

a What is the length of the rectangle?

Rory uses all Gill's tiles to make a different rectangle.

b Show that Rory can make a rectangle that has a larger perimeter than Gill's.

Exam-style

⑦ Will is designing a large logo for his company office.

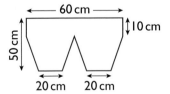

The logo has a single line of symmetry.

Will needs to know the area of the logo.

Work out the area of the logo.

Unit 5 • Pythagoras' theorem • Band g

Outside the Maths classroom

Buildings

Why do most buildings have corners that are right angles?

Toolbox

The longest side of a right-angled triangle (the side opposite the right angle) is called the **hypotenuse**, the side marked h on the diagram.

Pythagoras' theorem says that for a right-angled triangle, the square on the hypotenuse is equal to the sum of the squares on the other two sides.

Pythagoras' theorem allows the third side of a right-angled triangle to be calculated when the other two sides are known.

Pythagoras' theorem:

$$a^2 + b^2 = h^2$$

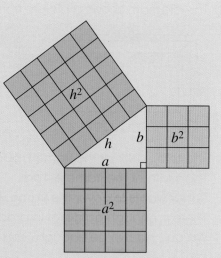

Example – Finding the length of the hypotenuse

Find the length of the side labelled h in this triangle.

Solution

Let $a = 10$ and $b = 6$ ⟵ It could be $a = 6$ and $b = 10$.

$a^2 + b^2 = h^2$ ⟵ Pythagoras' theorem.

$10^2 + 6^2 = h^2$ ⟵ Substitute in the lengths.

$100 + 36 = h^2$

$136 = h^2$

$h = 11.661...$

$h = 11.7\,cm$ (to 1 d.p.)

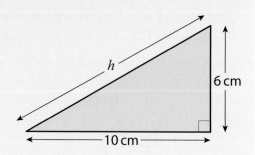

Example – Solving a problem involving a right-angled triangle

Gill is a decorator.

She uses a ladder 6 m long.

The safety instructions on the ladder say that the foot of the ladder must be at least 1.75 m from the base of the wall on horizontal ground.

What is the maximum height her ladder will reach up a vertical wall?

Solution

$$1.75^2 + y^2 = 6^2$$ ← Pythagoras' theorem rewritten for this problem.

$$3.0625 + y^2 = 36$$

$$y^2 = 36 - 3.0625$$ Draw a sketch and label it
y stands for the height reached by the ladder.

$$y^2 = 32.9375$$

$$y = \sqrt{32.9375}$$ ← Take the square root of both sides.

$$y = 5.739\ldots$$

Maximum height of ladder = 5.74 m (to the nearest centimetre)

Practising skills

① For each triangle, write down which is the longest side (the hypotenuse).
Then write Pythagoras' theorem in terms of the letters given.

a

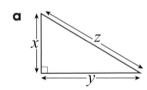

b

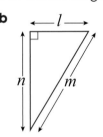

c

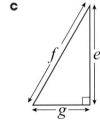

d

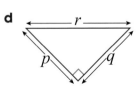

(2) Find the length of the hypotenuse of each triangle.
Copy and complete each calculation.

a $x^2 = 5^2 + 12^2$

$x^2 = 25 + \square$

$x^2 = \square$

$x = \sqrt{\square}$

The hypotenuse is $\square$ cm

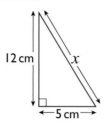

b $y^2 = 6^2 + 8^2$

$y^2 = \square + \square$

$y^2 = \square$

$y = \sqrt{\square}$

The [＿＿＿＿＿]

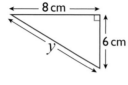

c $z^2 = \square + \square$

$z^2 = [＿＿＿＿]$

$z^2 = [＿＿＿＿]$

$z = \sqrt{\square}$

The [＿＿＿＿＿＿＿＿]

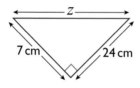

(3) Find the length of the unknown side in each triangle. Give each answer correct
to 1 decimal place.

a

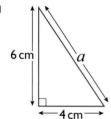

b

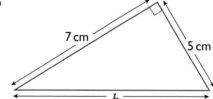

c

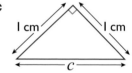

(4) Find the length of the hypotenuse in each of these triangles.

a

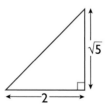

b

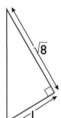

c

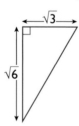

Why did you not need a calculator to answer this question?

⑤ Find the length of the unknown side of each triangle. Copy and complete each calculation.

a $x^2 + 4^2 = 5^2$
$x^2 + 16 = 25$
$x^2 = 25 - 16$
$x^2 = \Box$
$x = \sqrt{\Box}$
The base of the triangle is $\Box$ cm

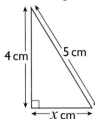

b $y^2 + 15^2 = \Box$
$y^2 + \Box = \Box$
$y^2 \Box = \Box$
[ ]
[ ]

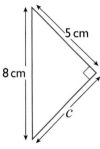

c $z^2 + \Box = \Box$
[ ]
[ ]
[ ]
[ ]

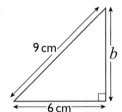

⑥ Find the length of the unknown side in each triangle. Give the answer correct to 1 decimal place.

a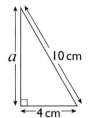

b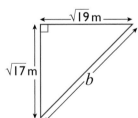

c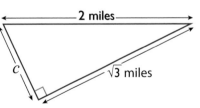

⑦ Without using a calculator, find the length of the unknown side in each triangle.

a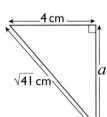

b

c

Developing fluency

① Calculate the perimeter and the area of this triangle.

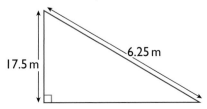

(2) The sides of triangle A are 7 cm, 9.4 cm and 12.2 cm.
The sides of triangle B are 7.2 cm, 9.6 cm and 12 cm.
The sides of triangle C are 7.4 cm, 9 cm and 12.4 cm.
Which of the three triangles are right-angled triangles? Explain your answer.

(3) A ladder is placed on horizontal ground
and leans against a vertical wall.
It reaches a height of 3.2 m up the wall.
The foot of the ladder is 2.4 m from the base of the wall.
Calculate the length of the ladder.

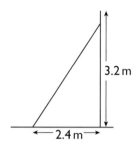

(4) Harry is making a wooden gate with
three horizontal lengths, three vertical lengths
and one diagonal length as shown.
Work out the total length of
timber he needs to make the gate.

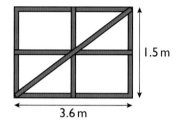

(5) A hiker leaves camp and walks south for 8 km, then east for 19.2 km where she stops for a rest.
Then she walks directly back to camp. How much shorter is her return journey?

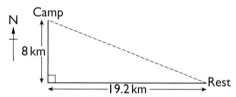

(6) In this diagram, find
  a the length CD
  b the perimeter of triangle ABC
  c the area of triangle ABC.

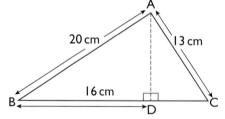

(7) Find the perimeter and area of the quadrilateral PQRS.

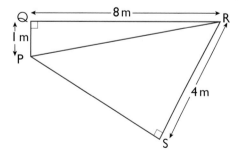

Exam-style

(8) KLMN is a rhombus. Its perimeter is 52 cm.
The diagonal LN is 24 cm long.
Find the area of KLMN.

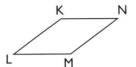

(9) A square is drawn with its vertices on the circumference
of a circle of radius 5 cm.

a What is the length of each side of the square?

b The regions between the square and circle
are four segments.
Find the area of each segment, giving your answer
to 3 significant figures.

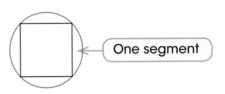

One segment

Problem solving

Exam-style

(1) This is a field in the shape of a right-angled triangle.
Fencing is going to be put around the field.
The fencing costs £17.50 for a 2-metre length.
Work out the cost to put fencing round the field.
Give your answer correct to the nearest £10.

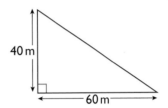

40 m

60 m

(2) The diagram shows a garden in the shape of a trapezium.

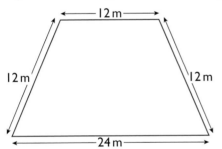

12 m

12 m 12 m

24 m

Turf is going to be put down in the garden.
Turf costs £2.50 per m^2.
Work out the total cost of the turf for the garden.

Exam-style

(3) Two boats leave a port at the same time.
The *Sirius* sails due north at 10 km per hour.
The *Polaris* sails due east at 24 km per hour.
By how much does the distance between the boats increase each hour?

④ The diagram shows the end of a modern building.

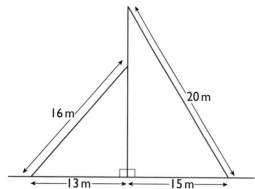

At a certain wind speed, the wind exerts a force on the building of 128 newtons per square metre.
Norman says that the total force on the end of the building is more than 20 000 newtons.
Rodney says that the total force on the end of the building is less than 20 000 newtons.
Who is correct? You must show all your working.

⑤ This is a field in the shape of a rectangle ABCD.
The rectangle has a width of 57 m and a length of 76 m.
Ali starts from A and runs once around the field.
He goes from A to B to C to D and back to A.
Beth starts from A and runs along AC and back again.
They both run at the same speed.
They start at the same time.
Show that when Beth gets back to A, Ali is still at D.

⑥ In the diagram, AD and BC are vertical posts.

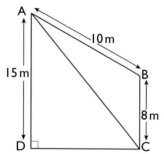

The posts are joined by cables AB and AC.
Sally needs to replace the cables with new ones.
She has 25 m of new cable.
Does she have enough new cable to replace both AB and AC?
Explain your answer fully.

⑦ The diagram shows the design of an electronic component in the shape of a rectangle.
The rectangle has a total length of 64 mm.
The isosceles triangles are identical and each of the sloping sides has length 20 mm
The parts of the rectangle shown shaded have to be coated.
Calculate the total area of the shaded parts.

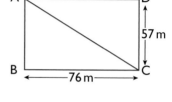

Reviewing skills

① Calculate the length of the unknown side in each triangle.

a
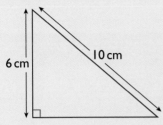

b
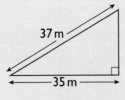

c
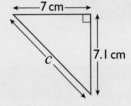

② Calculate the length of the unknown side in each triangle. Give your answer correct to one decimal place.

a
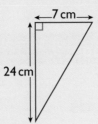

b
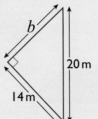

c
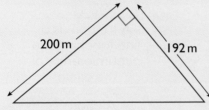

③ Calculate the perimeter and area of this field.

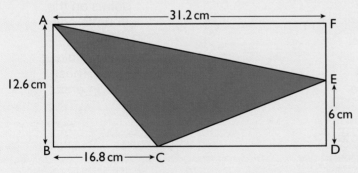

④ ABCDEF is a rectangle. Calculate the perimeter of triangle ACE.

Unit 6 • Arcs and sectors • Band h

Outside the Maths classroom

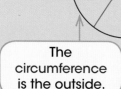

Flower beds

Why would a gardener need to work out areas and perimeters of sectors?

Toolbox

Here are some of the words used with circles.

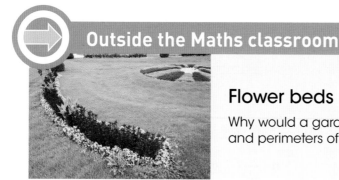

The centre is the middle of the circle.

A diameter goes across the circle, through the centre.

A tangent is a line touching the circumference of the circle.

The circumference is the outside.

A radius goes from the centre to the circumference.

A chord joins two points on the circumference.

A chord divides the circle into two regions. These are called segments.

The yellow region of this circle is a **sector**.
The sector is bounded by two radii and an arc.
The sector makes an angle $x°$ at the centre of the circle.
The arc length,

$$l = \frac{x}{360} \times \pi d$$

The area of the sector,

$$A = \frac{x}{360} \times \pi r^2$$

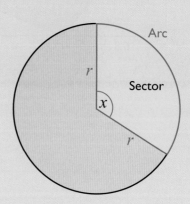

Example – Arcs

A sector has a radius of 9 cm and an angle at the centre of 120°.

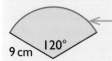

The arc is marked in red.

9 cm   120°

a Calculate the length of the arc.
b Find the perimeter of the sector.
c Another arc has the same radius and a length of 9.4 cm.
   Calculate the angle at the centre.

Solution

a Length of arc $= \dfrac{x}{360} \times \pi d$

$$= \dfrac{120}{360} \times \pi \times 18$$ The radius is 9 cm so $d = 18$ cm.

$$= 6\pi$$ You will often give your answer like this, as a multiple of π.

$$= 18.8 \text{ cm}$$ To 1 decimal place.

b The perimeter of the sector is made up of two radii and the arc.

Perimeter $= 9 + 9 + 6\pi$

$$= (18 + 6\pi) \text{ cm}$$ Leaving the answer in terms of π.

$$= 36.8 \text{ cm}$$ To 1 d.p.

c Arc length $= \dfrac{x}{360} \times \pi d$

$$9.4 = \dfrac{x}{360} \times \pi \times 18$$ Replace are length 9.4 and d with 18.

$$9.4 \times 360 = x \times \pi \times 18$$ Multiply both sides by 360.

$$\dfrac{3384}{18\pi} = x$$ Divide both sides by 18 π.

$$x = 59.8$$

So the angle at the centre is 59.8°.

Example – Area of a sector

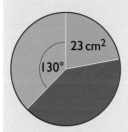

A circle of radius 6 cm is divided into 3 sectors as shown.
a The blue sector has an angle of 130°.
   Calculate the area of the blue sector.
b The green sector has an area of 23 cm^2.
   Calculate the angle of the green sector.
c Show that the area of the red sector is 23$(\pi - 1)$ cm^2.

Solution

a Area of blue sector

$$A = \frac{x}{360} \times \pi r^2$$

$$= \frac{130}{360} \times \pi \times 6^2 \quad\longleftarrow\quad \boxed{\text{Replace } x \text{ with 130 and } r \text{ with 6.}}$$

$$= \frac{130 \times 36}{360} \times \pi \quad\longleftarrow\quad \boxed{\text{Simplifying.}}$$

$$= 13\pi \quad\longleftarrow\quad \boxed{\text{This is the answer in terms of } \pi \text{ To 1 d.p.}}$$

$$= 40.8 \text{ cm}$$

b Area of red sector

$$A = 23 = \frac{x}{360} \times \pi \times 6^2 \quad\longleftarrow\quad \boxed{\text{Replace } A \text{ with 23 and } r \text{ with 6.}}$$

$$23 \times 360 = x \times \pi \times 36 \quad\longleftarrow\quad \boxed{\text{Multiply both sides by 360.}}$$

$$\frac{8280}{36 \times \pi} = x \quad\longleftarrow\quad \boxed{\text{Divide both sides by } 36\pi.}$$

$$x = 73.2$$

The angle of the yellow sector is 73.2°.

c Area of red sector = area of whole circle – area of blue sector – area of green sector.

$$= \pi \times 6^2 - 13\pi - 23 \quad\longleftarrow\quad \boxed{\text{Area of blue sector is } 13\pi \text{ from part } \mathbf{a}.}$$

$$= 36\pi - 13\pi - 23$$

$$= 23\pi - 23$$

$$= 23(\pi - 1) \text{ cm}^2 \quad\longleftarrow\quad \boxed{\text{Factorising.}}$$

Practising skills

1 Calculate the lengths of these arcs.
Give your answers correct to 1 decimal place.

a

8 cm 56°

b
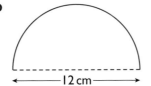
—12 cm—

c
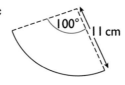
100° 11 cm

d

252°

2 a The diagram shows a quadrant. Find
  i the perimeter
  ii the area of this sector.

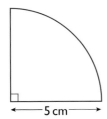
—5 cm—

Find the perimeter and area of each of these shapes.

b

—10 cm—

c

5 cm

d

5 cm

e

5 cm

3 Calculate the areas of these sectors.
Give your answers correct to 1 decimal place.

a
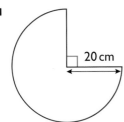
20 cm

b
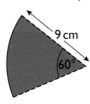
9 cm 60°

c
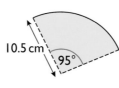
10.5 cm 95°

d
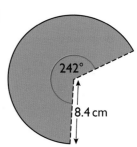
242° 8.4 cm

4 For each sector shaded red find the
  a arc length and
  b area.

i
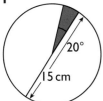
20° 15 cm

ii
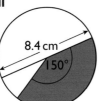
8.4 cm 150°

iii
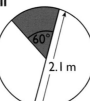
60° 2.1 m

iv
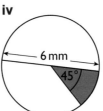
—6 mm— 45°

Give your answers correct to 1 decimal place.

⑤ **a** An arc has a length of 35 cm and a radius of 8 cm.
Calculate the reflex angle at the centre.
Give your answer to the nearest degree.

b An arc has a length of 4π cm and a radius of 12 cm.
Calculate the acute angle at the centre.
Give your answer to the nearest degree.

c This sector has a radius of 7 cm and an area of 30 cm².
Calculate the obtuse angle at the centre.

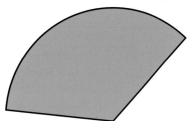

Developing fluency

① The arcs in these three sectors have the same length.

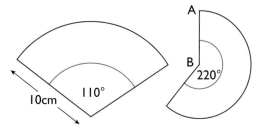

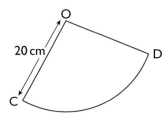

Calculate

a the radius AB

b the size of ∠COD.

② The shape of a flower bed is a sector of radius of 2.4 m.
The angle at the centre is 115°. Find

a the perimeter of the flower bed

b the area of the flower bed,

giving your answers correct to 1 decimal place.

③ This shape is made from sectors of circles. Show that the perimeter of this shape is (7π + 18) cm.

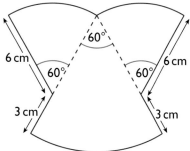

Exam-style

④ A sector has an angle of 64° and an area of 10π cm².
Calculate the radius of the sector.

⑤ This sector has arc length of 3.42π cm and angle of 114°.
Calculate the area of the sector, giving your answer in terms of π.

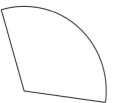

⑥ Here is a cone.
The net of the cone consists of a sector and a circle.
The circumference of the red circle is equal to the length of the yellow arc.
Calculate the angle at the centre of the sector.

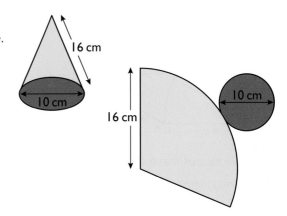

⑦ This creature is made from three sectors.
Each sector has an angle at the centre of 130°.
The two green sectors each have a radius of 7.5 cm.
The yellow sector has a radius of 9.7 cm.
Calculate the total area of the creature, giving your answers in cm², correct to 1 decimal place.

⑧ AB is a diameter of a circle.
O is the centre of the circle.
CD is an arc, equal in length to the diameter AB.
Calculate the size of ∠AOB.

Problem solving

① The diagram represents the design for part of the hallway of a hotel.
The hallway is in the shape of a quarter circle.
An architect wants the shaded region to be specially made.

   a Calculate the perimeter of the shaded region.

   b Calculate the area of the shaded region.

② The diagram represents a framework for a greenhouse.
The cross-section of the framework is a quarter-circle of radius 4 metres.
The length of the greenhouse is 8 metres.

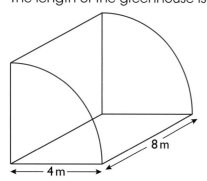

   a Work out the total amount of the framework required.

   b Investigate whether the volume enclosed will be over 100 m³.

③ Here is a design for a company logo.
The logo is the region between 2 semicircles.
The semicircles have the same centre.
The width of the logo is 2 m.
The diameter of the larger semicircle is 8 m.
The company wants to put wire all along the edges of the logo.

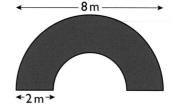

   a Calculate the length of wire required.

   The company wants to paint the logo.

   b Calculate the area of the region.

④ **a** Use Pythagoras' theorem to work out the perpendicular height of this triangle.
      Hence work out the area of the triangle.

   b The diagram represents the cross-section of a circular tunnel.
      The radius of the tunnel is 4 m.
      The base of the tunnel is filled with concrete to make a pathway
      of width 4 m.

      i Calculate the area of the sector OAB.

      ii Calculate the area of the segment between AB and the circle.

   c The tunnel is 30 m long. Work out the volume of concrete needed.

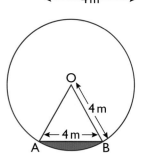

Exam-style

⑤ The perimeter of a semicircle is 100 + 50π cm.
Work out the area of the semi-circle.
Give your answer as a multiple of π.

⑥ The diagram represents the plan for a scented garden.
The scented garden will be planted in the sector AOB.
The sector has a radius of 10 m.
The scented garden has to be fenced all round.
The gardener uses 40 m of fencing.
Work out the value of *x*.

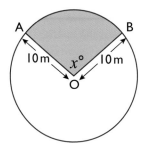

⑦ The diagram shows the design for a gear wheel.
The gear wheel is in the shape of part of a circle, centre O.
The area of the part of the circle is 240 cm².
The edges of the gear wheel have to be specially treated to harden them.
Work out the length that has to be specially treated.

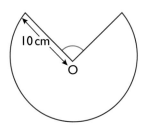

Reviewing skills

① The length of the minute hand on a clock is 4.2 cm.
Find the distance moved by the tip of the minute hand between
  a 3 pm and 3:15 pm
  b 3:15 pm and 3:45 pm
  c 3:45 pm and 4:30 pm
  d 4:30 pm and 4:40 pm
Give your answers to the nearest mm.

② Find
  a the perimeter
  b the area of each of the shaded regions.
Give your answers correct to 2 decimal places.

i   ii   iii   iv

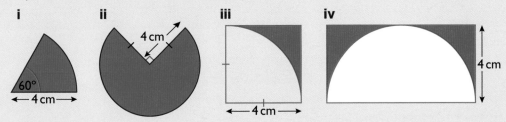

③ A throwing area on a sports field is a 30° sector of a circle with radius of 80 m.
Calculate the perimeter and area of the throwing area in terms of π.

Strand 4 Construction

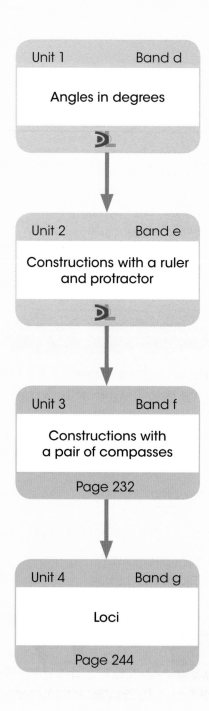

Unit 1	Band d
Angles in degrees	

Unit 2	Band e
Constructions with a ruler and protractor	

Unit 3	Band f
Constructions with a pair of compasses	
Page 232	

Unit 4	Band g
Loci	
Page 244	

Units 1–2 are assumed knowledge for this book. They are reviewed and extended in the Moving on section on page 231.

1 A and B represent two telescopes 400 m apart each pointing north (N).

The telescope at A turns 50° clockwise to point towards a tower, T.

The telescope at B turns 60° anticlockwise to point towards the tower T.

Use a suitable drawing to find the distance of the tower from the telescope at A.

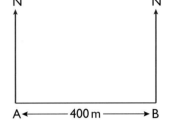

2 X and Y are two direction-finding radio receivers.

X is 60 km due north of Y.

The operator at X detects a signal from a ship on a bearing of 060°.

The operator at Y says he detects the same signal on a bearing of 062°.

The operator at X is correct.

a Explain why the operator at Y cannot be correct.

The operator at Y then says that he detects the same signal on a bearing of 026°.

b Use a suitable drawing to find the distance from X to the ship.

3 A ship is sailing due east.

At 2 a.m. the captain sees a lighthouse on a bearing of 065°.

By 4 a.m. the captain sees the lighthouse on a bearing of 330°.

The ship sails at a rate of 30 km per hour.

Use a suitable drawing to find the least distance from the ship's path to the lighthouse.

4 A structure consists of girders fitted together to make right-angled triangles.

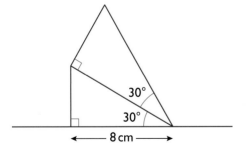

The lowest triangle has a base of length 8 m and angles of 30° and 90°.

Triangles are then made on top, with the base of the next triangle being the hypotenuse of the triangle below and with angles of 30° and 90°.

A third triangle is added to the two already shown.

Use a suitable diagram to find the height of the top of this triangle above ground level.

Unit 3 • Constructions with a pair of compasses • Band f

Outside the Maths classroom

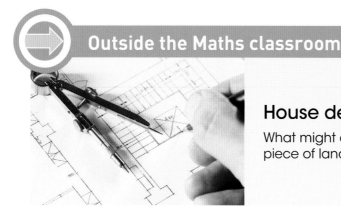

House design

What might affect where a house is built on a piece of land?

Toolbox

A circle has a very useful property.
All the points on the circumference are the same distance from the centre.
That distance is the **radius** of the circle.

Part of a circle is called an **arc**.

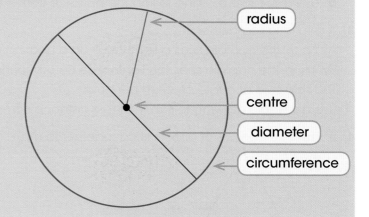

You use a pair of compasses to draw a circle.
You can construct many other things with compasses:

- triangles, given their sides
- line bisectors
- angle bisectors
- perpendicular from a point **to** a line
- perpendicular from a point **on** a line.

Example – Bisecting a line

Bisect the line AB.

A ———————————— B

Solution

- Open your compasses.
  Put the point on A.
  Draw arcs above and below the line.

- Do not adjust the compasses.
  Put the point on B.
  Draw two more arcs to cut the first two.

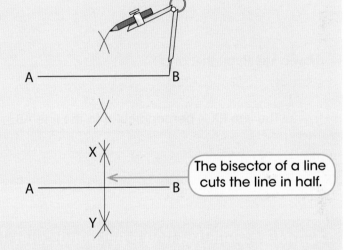

- The arcs meet at X and Y.
  Draw the line XY.

> The bisector of a line cuts the line in half.

Example – Constructing a perpendicular from a point to a line

Construct the perpendicular from the point R to the line.

Solution

- Draw a line. Mark point R away from the line.

- Put the point of the compasses on R.
  Draw an arc.
  It intersects the line at A and B.

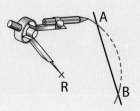

- With the point on A, draw an arc on the opposite side of the line from R.

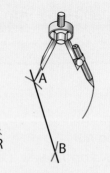

- Do not adjust the compasses.
  With the point on B, draw another arc.
  The arcs intersect at X.

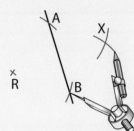

- Draw a line through R and X.

The line RX is perpendicular to the line AB.

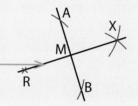

Example – Constructing a perpendicular from a point on a line

Construct a perpendicular from the point T on this line.

Solution

- Put the point of the compasses on T.
- Mark two points, A and B on the line.
  Each point is the same distance from T.

- Open the compasses wider.
  With the point on A draw an arc.

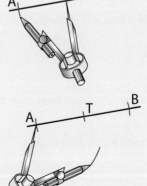

- Do not adjust the compasses.
  With the point on B draw an intersecting arc.

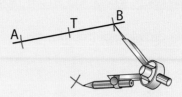

- Draw a line through T and the intersection X.

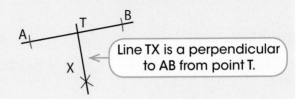

Line TX is a perpendicular
to AB from point T.

Example – Bisecting an angle

Bisect this angle.

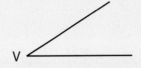

Solution

- Put the point of the compasses on V.
  Draw an arc cutting both lines at points A and B.
- Put the point of the compasses on A.
  Draw an arc.
  Do not adjust the compasses.
  Put the point of the compasses at B.
  Draw an arc.

These two arcs meet at C.

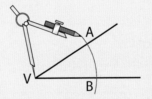

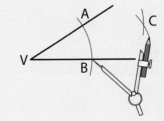

- Join V to C.

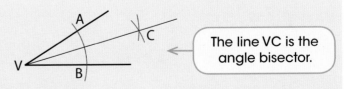

The line VC is the
angle bisector.

Example – Constructing a triangle

Make an accurate drawing of this triangle.

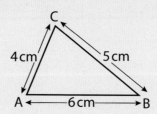

Solution

- Draw a line 6 cm long.

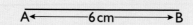

- Draw an arc of radius 4 cm and centre A.
  The point C is on this arc.

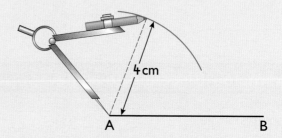

- Now draw an arc of radius 5 cm and centre B.
  C is on this arc too.

- The two arcs meet at C.
  Join AC and BC to form the triangle.

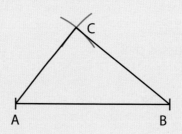

Practising skills

① Use a ruler and a pair of compasses to construct each triangle accurately.
Then measure its angles.

a
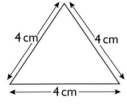
4 cm 4 cm
4 cm

b
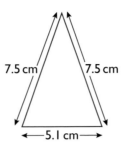
7.5 cm 7.5 cm
5.1 cm

c
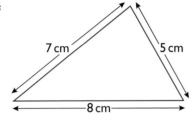
7 cm 5 cm
8 cm

d
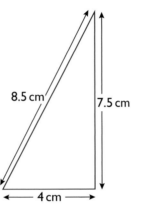
8.5 cm 7.5 cm
4 cm

e
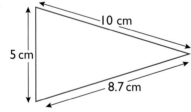
10 cm
5 cm
8.7 cm

f
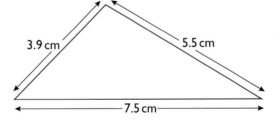
3.9 cm 5.5 cm
7.5 cm

② **a** Draw this triangle accurately. (You may use a protractor for the right angle.)

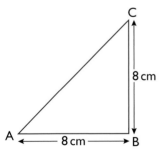

C

8 cm

A ← 8 cm → B

Using a ruler and a pair of compasses, draw the perpendicular bisectors of AB and BC.
What do you notice about the point where they meet?

b Repeat part **a** for the following right-angled triangles.
Do you always notice the same thing?

i

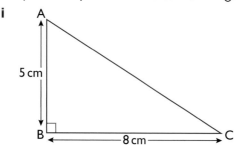

ii

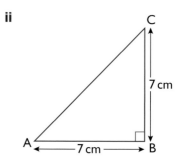

iii

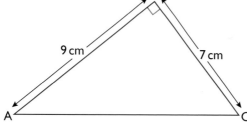

③ **a** Draw this triangle accurately.

Using a ruler and a pair of compasses, draw the perpendicular bisector of each of the three sides.

You should find that the three lines you have just drawn all go through a point.

Call this point O.

If your lines do not go through a point, start again. You have not done the drawing accurately!

Now draw a circle with centre O and radius OP. What do you notice?

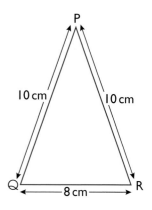

b Repeat part **a** for the following triangles. Do you always notice the same things?

i

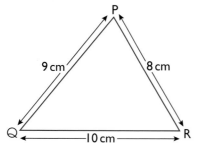

ii

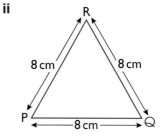

iii

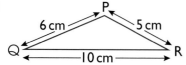

iv

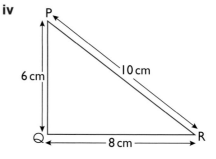

④ a Draw this triangle accurately.

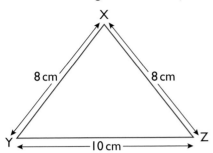

Using a ruler and a pair of compasses (but no protractor), draw the bisectors of the three angles.

You should find that your three lines go through a point. Call it C.

If your lines do not go through a point, start again. You have not done the drawing accurately.

Now draw a circle with centre C. Set your compasses so that the circle just touches the line XY. What do you notice?

b Repeat part **a** for the following triangles. Do you always notice the same things?

i

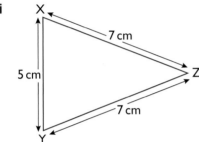

ii

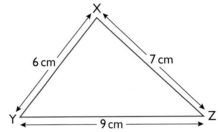

iii

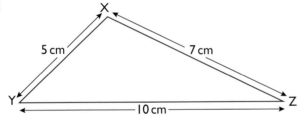

iv

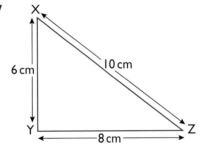

⑤ **a** The diagram shows a triangle ABC. You are to find its area.

A line has been drawn through point A perpendicular to BC.

Copy and complete this working.

By measurement

BC = □ cm

AD = □ cm

So the area of triangle

ABC = $\frac{1}{2}$ × □ × □ cm^2

= □ cm^2 (to 1 decimal place)

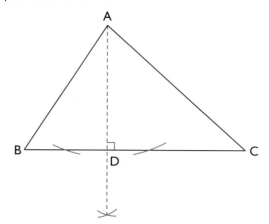

b Now draw the following triangles. Then use the method in part **a** to find their areas.

You should use only a ruler and a pair of compasses.

i Triangles XYZ where XY = 8 cm, YZ = 10 cm and ZX = 7 cm

ii Triangle LMN where LM = 5 cm, MN = 6 cm and NL = 8 cm

iii Triangle PQR where PQ = 7 cm, QR = 10 cm and RP = 5 cm

Developing fluency

① Draw a horizontal line AC 10 cm long. Mark the point T on the line 3 cm from A.

Construct a line perpendicular to AC that passes through T.

On one side of this line mark a point B such that BT = 4 cm.

On the other side mark a point D such that DT = 4 cm.

Join ABCD to make a quadrilateral.

Describe this quadrilateral.

② **a** Draw a vertical line PR 8 cm long.

Construct the perpendicular bisector of PR. Mark the mid-point of the line PR as M.

Mark points Q and S on the perpendicular bisector of PR, on either side of the line, where QM = SM = 6 cm.

Join PQRS to make a quadrilateral.

Describe this quadrilateral.

b Repeat part **a** but this time let QM = SM = 4 cm.

What sort of quadrilateral do you have now?

③ **a** Use a ruler and a pair of compasses to construct a triangle LMN with LM = 8 cm, MN = 4 cm and NL = 6 cm.

b Construct the line through N perpendicular to LM.

c Work out the area of the triangle LMN.

4 a Construct the trapezium MNOP accurately.
Mark the point Q 2 cm from point M.

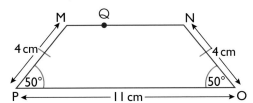

b Construct a line perpendicular to PO that passes through Q.

c Make suitable measurements and work out the area of the trapezium.

5 a Draw a circle of radius 10 cm.

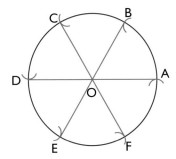

With your compasses still set at 10 cm, mark 6 points round its circumference, as shown.
Call these points A, B, C, D, E and F and the centre of the circle O.

Join AD, BE and CF to make three diameters.

Now draw the bisectors of all the angles at the centre (∠AOB, ∠BOC, …). These give you three more diameters. Mark the points where they cross the circumference.

Now do the same again to get six more diameters. Mark the points where they cross the circumference.

b You now have 24 points on the circumference. Join them up to make a regular 24-sided polygon.

c By joining suitable points on the circumference you can construct other regular polygons.
Which polygons can you make? Draw one example of each. (You may find it helpful to use different colours.)

d Now look at the angles at the centre.
List of all the angles you can identify between 0° and 360°.

Problem solving

1 Here is a line AB.

A•————————•B

a Using only a straight edge and a pair of compasses, draw
  i a triangle ABC where the angles at A and B are both 45°
  ii an equilateral triangle ABD.

b Name the two possible shapes for the quadrilateral ACBD.

② Jim has a triangular garden. The lengths of the sides of his garden are 20 m, 16 m and 14 m. Draw a suitable scale diagram of the garden, using only a ruler and a pair of compasses. Construct a line through one vertex of the triangle perpendicular to the opposite side. Now make a suitable measurement and calculate the area of Jim's garden.

 ③ Here is a square.

Using only a straight edge and a pair of compasses, construct

a a triangle that has the same area as the square

b a rectangle that has the same area as the square, but half the height

c a rhombus with the same area as the square.

④ Alice is designing a logo for her company. It is the shaded region in this sketch.

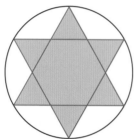

Diagram **not** accurately drawn.

The circle has radius 4 cm.
The logo must have rotational symmetry of the order 6.

a Using only a ruler and a pair of compasses, construct an accurate drawing of the logo.

b Measure the lengths of one side of the large equilateral triangles.

c Without doing any further measurements, work out the area of the logo.

⑤ P and Q are two lighthouses 10 miles apart. P is due north of Q.
At 08:00 the *Whinlatter* is at point R, 14 km from P and 6 km from Q.

a Show the information on a scale drawing.
At 08:30 the *Whinlatter* is at point S, 8 km from P and 9 km from Q.

b Add this to your scale drawing.

c How far is it from R to S?

d How fast is the *Whinlatter* sailing?

Reviewing skills

① Use a ruler and a pair of compasses to draw triangle ABC accurately.

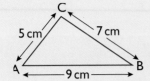

    a Measure the angles of the triangle.

    b Construct a line through C perpendicular to AB.

    c Make a suitable measurement and use it to work out the area of the triangle.

② **a** Use a ruler and a pair of compasses to construct triangle ABC.

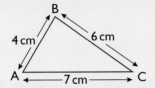

    b Construct the perpendicular bisector of each of the three sides.

    c Mark the point M where the three perpendicular bisectors meet.

    d Draw a circle with centre M which passes through the points A, B and C.

    e Measure the circle's radius.

Outside the Maths classroom

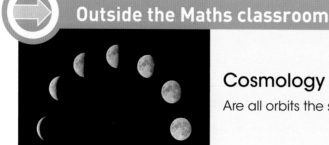

Cosmology

Are all orbits the same shape?

Toolbox

A **locus** is the path of all the points which obey a rule.

In two dimensions:

- The locus of all the points which are the **same distance from one point** is a circle.

- The locus of all the points which are the **same distance from two points** is the perpendicular bisector of the line which joins those two points.

- The locus of all the points which are the **same distance from a line segment** is two parallel lines with semicircles joining the ends.

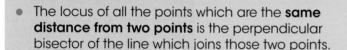

- The locus of all the points which are the **same distance from two lines that cross** is the angle bisector of the angles formed by the two lines.

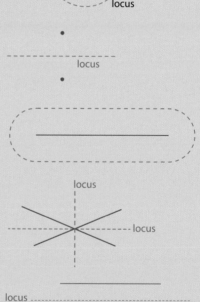

- The locus of all the points which are **the same distance from two lines that do not cross** is a line parallel to them, and midway between them.

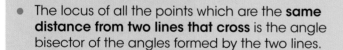

Note:

- Construct means do it accurately using instruments.
- Sketch means do it by eye illustrating the important features.
- Draw means somewhere between constructing and sketching. You should use your judgement to decide what is required.

Example – Loci equidistant from two points

A and B are the positions of two radio beacons.

An aeroplane flies so that it is always the same distance from each beacon.

Draw two crosses to represent the beacons.

Construct a line to represent the aeroplane's path.

A x

B x

Solution

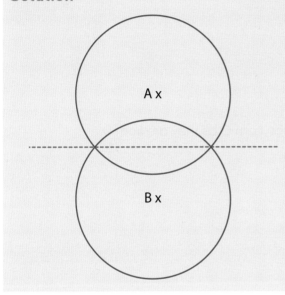

Practising skills

① Mark a point P on your page.

   a Make an accurate drawing of the locus of points that are 4 cm from the point P.

   b What name is given to this locus?

② Mark a point P on your page.

   Shade the locus of the points that are more than 4.5 cm from P but less than 6.5 cm from P.

③ Find, by constructing and measuring lines through P, the distance of point P from each of the sides of the rectangle ABCD.

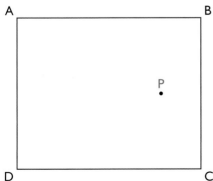

④ **a** Draw a straight line across your page.

b Draw the locus of points on your page that are 2 cm from your line.

⑤ **a** Copy this diagram.

C

5 cm

D

b Draw the locus of points that are the same distance from C as they are from D.

 ⑥ **a** Make a full size copy of this diagram.

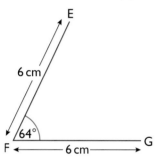

E

6 cm

64°

F ←— 6 cm —→ G

b Make an accurate drawing of the locus of points that are the same distance from EF and FG.

c What is the name given to this locus?

 ⑦ **a** Draw the square HIJK. Its sides are 5 cm long.

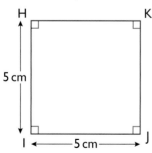

H   K

5 cm

I ←— 5 cm —→ J

b Draw the locus of points that are the same distance from HK and HI.

8 a Copy this diagram on to squared paper.

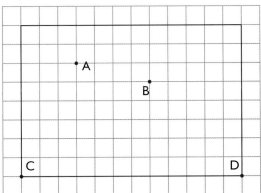

b Shade these regions.

   i Points that are at most 2 cm from A.

   ii Points that are at least $2\frac{1}{2}$ cm from point B.

   iii Points that are less than 1 cm from the line CD.

c Are there any points in all three regions?

Developing fluency

1 Hassan designs a logo.

He starts with an equilateral triangle with sides of length 6 cm.

He splits the triangle into 6 regions by drawing 3 lines. Each line is the locus of points inside the triangle that are the same distance from two of its sides.

Make an accurate full-size drawing of the logo.

2 PQRS is a square. Its sides are 6 cm long. T is the centre point.

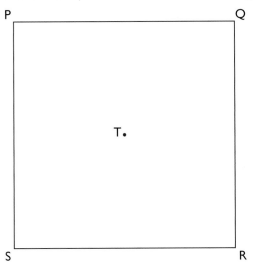

a Draw the square accurately.

b Shade the locus of points on the diagram that are

   • inside the square

   • and more than 3 cm from T

   • and closer to PQ than any of the other sides of the square

   • and closer to QR than PS.

③ This is a scale drawing of a mural called 'The hole in the wall'.
The full size of the mural is 9m by 6m.

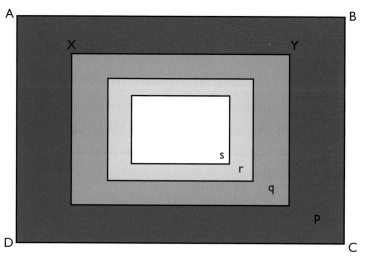

a Describe the line XY as a locus, using ABCD as a reference.

b A point is 3 metres from BC and 4 metres from AD. Which region is it in: p, q, r or s?

c Describe the locus of points in the regions using ABCD as a reference.
   i s   ii r

④ a Construct triangle XYZ accurately.

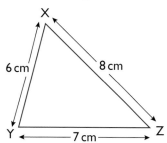

b Draw the locus of points that are the same distance from X and Z.

c Draw the locus of points that are the same distance from X and Y.

d Mark the point Q that is the same distance from X, Y and Z. Measure QX.

Exam style

5 The diagram shows 2 goats tied to a rectangular shed. One goat, Misty, is attached to point B by a rope that is 4m long. The other goat, Billy, is attached to point D by a rope that is 8m long.

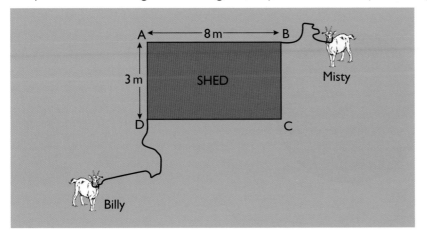

The shed measures 8m by 3m and is located in the middle of a large field.

a Draw the diagram accurately, using a scale of 1cm = 1m.

b Using different colours, shade the areas where

  i Only Misty can graze

  ii Only Billy can graze

  iii Both goats can graze

Reasoning

6 a Draw a rectangle KLMN with side LM longer than side KL.

  Now draw the locus of points in the rectangle that are the same distance from KL and KN.

b Draw also the locus of points that are the same distance from LM and LK.

c How many points are the same distance from the three lines LM, LK and KN?

d Explain why there are no points that are the same distance from all four edges of the rectangle.

e In a different rectangle PQRS there is a point O that is the same distance from all four edges. What can you say about the rectangle PQRS?

⑦ Here is a part of a local chart for ships entering the port of Avonford.

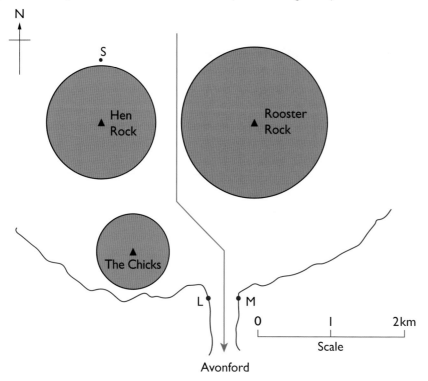

Ships follow the green route.

There are three dangerous areas round rocks, marked by the red circles.

The river entrance is marked by lights at L and M.

a Describe each of the three parts of the green route as a locus.

b Describe each of the red regions.

c A ship is at point S. It is going to Avonford.
    Advise its captain what course to steer.

Problem solving

① PQRS is a field in the shape of a rectangle.

PQ = 100 m and QR = 80 m.

There is a path crossing the field. All points on the path are the same distance from PS and PQ.

There is a different path crossing the field. All points on this path are the same distance from PS and QR.

These two paths cross at the point X.

Use a suitable drawing to find the distance of X from S.

② A, B and C are three towns.

C is 20 miles due east of B.

A is 16 miles due north of B.

A mobile phone tower, T, is to be built such that it is the same distance from A and B, and it is 10 miles from C.

a Draw a scale diagram. Use it to locate the two possible positions of the tower.

b Find the shorter distance of the tower from A.

③ ABCD is the plan of a house.

AB = DC = 8 m

BC = 6 m

A path of width 2 m is to be made round three sides of the house.

The path starts at A, goes along AB, then BC and then CD.

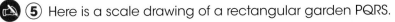

a Make an accurate scale drawing of the path.

b What is the total area of the path?

c Jake says, 'The outside of the path is the locus of the points that are 2 m away from house.'
Give two reasons why Jake's statement is not right.

④ A pitch for five-a-side football is 32 m long and 16 m wide.

a Draw a diagram of the pitch, using a scale 1 cm = 4 m.
Lights are placed at the 4 corners of the pitch and at the mid-points of the two longer sides.
A light can light all points up to 10 m away.

b Show that the 6 lights are not enough to light the whole football pitch.

c Show how some of the lights could be moved to light the whole pitch.

⑤ Here is a scale drawing of a rectangular garden PQRS.

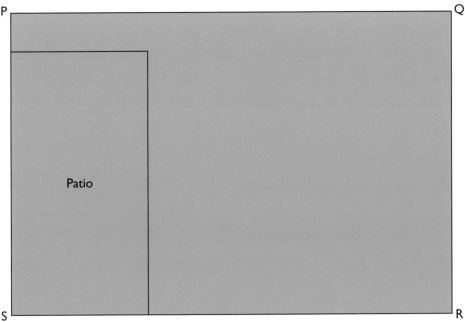

Scale: 1 cm represents 2 m.

Jane wants to plant a tree in the garden at least 10 m from the corner R, nearer to PQ than to PS and less than 6 m from SR.

The tree cannot be planted on the patio.

On the diagram, shade the region where Jane can plant the tree.

6 PQRS is the plan of an enclosure at a zoo.

Its shape is an isosceles trapezium.

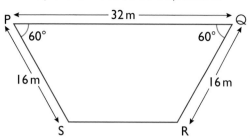

a Make an accurate scale drawing of the enclosure.

The enclosure is divided up into four regions: p, q, r and s, by wire netting.

Region p is those points that are nearer to vertex P than to any other vertices, region q is those points that are nearer to vertex Q and so on.

b Draw lines on your diagram to show where the wire netting goes.

c Make suitable measurements and work out the total length of wire netting. Give your answer to the nearest metre.

d Work out the area of each region. Answer to the nearest square metre.

e Show that with another 32 m of wire netting the enclosure can be divided up into 6 regions of equal area.

Reviewing skills

1 Describe the loci represented by the red lines or curves in the following diagrams.

a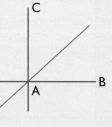

b

c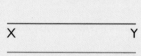

d

2 Describe the regions shaded in these diagrams.

a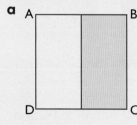

b

c

d

3 A watering pipe is laid in the shape of a circle of radius 40 m.

The region of the garden within 10 m of the pipe can be watered from the pipe.

a Draw a scale diagram to show this region.

b What is the area of the garden that can be watered from the pipe?

Strand 5 Transformations

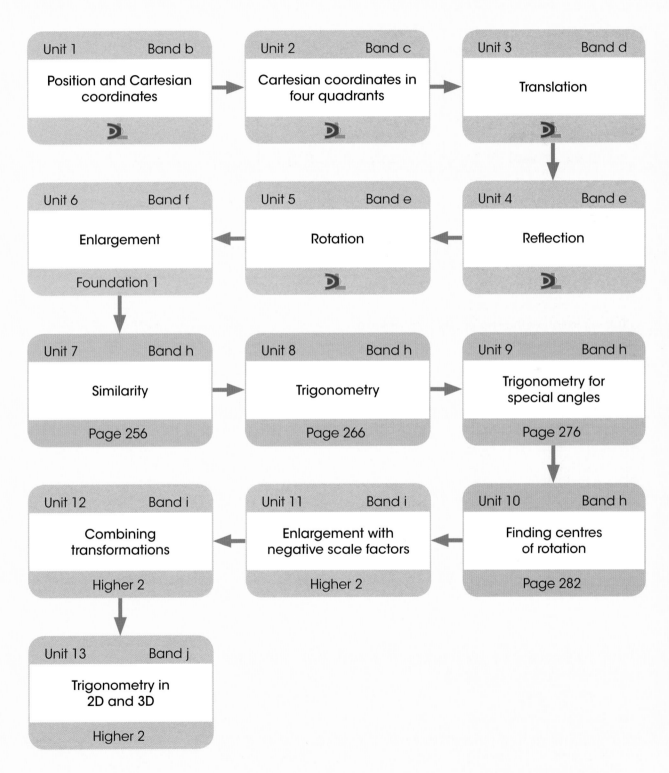

Unit 1	Band b
Position and Cartesian coordinates	

Unit 2	Band c
Cartesian coordinates in four quadrants	

Unit 3	Band d
Translation	

Unit 6	Band f
Enlargement	
Foundation 1	

Unit 5	Band e
Rotation	

Unit 4	Band e
Reflection	

Unit 7	Band h
Similarity	
Page 256	

Unit 8	Band h
Trigonometry	
Page 266	

Unit 9	Band h
Trigonometry for special angles	
Page 276	

Unit 12	Band i
Combining transformations	
Higher 2	

Unit 11	Band i
Enlargement with negative scale factors	
Higher 2	

Unit 10	Band h
Finding centres of rotation	
Page 282	

Unit 13	Band j
Trigonometry in 2D and 3D	
Higher 2	

Units 1–6 are assumed knowledge for this book. They are reviewed and extended in the Moving on section on page 254.

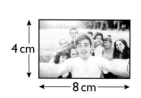

Exam-style

① Here is a picture and a frame.

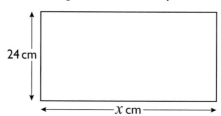

Diagram **not** accurately drawn.

4 cm

8 cm

24 cm

x cm

John wants to enlarge the picture to fit the frame.
The length of the shorter side of the large picture is 24 cm.
Work out the perimeter of the frame.

Exam-style

② A and B are points that are images of each other under a reflection.
P has coordinates $(4, b)$
Q has coordinates $(4, 2b)$
The equation of the line of reflection is $y = 6$
Find the value of b.

Exam-style

③ The diagram shows a trapezium A drawn on a grid.

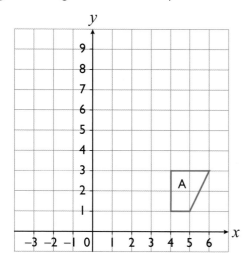

a Copy the diagram.

b Reflect trapezium A in the line $y = x$. Label the image B.
Trapezium C is the image of trapezium A under a reflection in the equation $y = x + 2$.

c Describe the transformation that will map trapezium B to trapezium C.

④ Two shapes, S and T have been drawn on a grid.

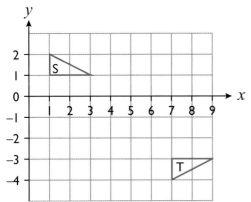

Shape S is mapped to shape T by a translation followed by a reflection.

a Describe fully both the translation and the reflection.

b Describe whether carrying out the reflection on S first followed by the translation gives shape T.

⑤ A shape has been drawn on a grid. Copy the diagram.

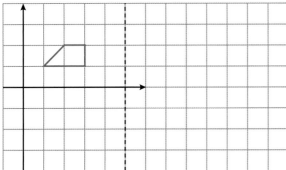

The shape is translated by $\begin{pmatrix} a \\ b \end{pmatrix}$, and then reflected in the dotted line.

a What could a and b be, given that when the shape is first reflected in the dotted line and then translated by $\begin{pmatrix} a \\ b \end{pmatrix}$ the image is **different**?

The shape is translated by $\begin{pmatrix} c \\ d \end{pmatrix}$, and then reflected in the dotted line.

b What could c and d be, given that when the shape is first reflected in the dotted line and then translated by $\begin{pmatrix} c \\ d \end{pmatrix}$ the image is the **same**?

⑥ Pat wants to practise designing a wallpaper pattern.
He rotates triangle B 90° clockwise about (2, 0) to give triangle C.
He rotates triangle C 90° anticlockwise about (4, 0) to give triangle D.

a Describe the single transformation that maps B to D.

b What type of single transformation is also equivalent to a rotation of 90° clockwise about a point, followed by a rotation of 90° anticlockwise about a different point?

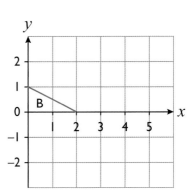

Unit 7 • Similarity • Band h

Using shadows

What does the length of your shadow depend upon?

⬇️ **Toolbox**

When you enlarge a figure with a scale factor of 3, all the lengths are made three times longer but the corresponding angles remain the same.

They are the same shape but different sizes.

The figures are **similar**.

The angles in the two figures are the same and the lengths of the sides are all in the same ratio.

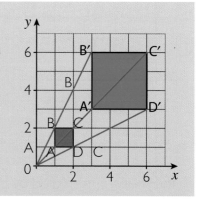

Example – Similar and congruent figures

Sarah has drawn the stars on this grid.

a Which stars are congruent to A?

b Which stars are similar to A?

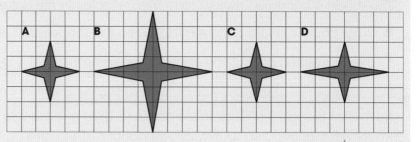

Solution

a Congruent figures are the same shape and size.

Only A and C are congruent.

b Similar figures are the same shape but they may be different sizes.

A, B and C are all similar.

> Notice that D is a different shape.

Notice that congruent figures are always similar but similar figures need not be congruent.

Example – Using ratios of similar figures

These triangles are similar.

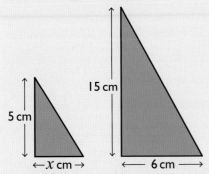

15 cm

5 cm

←x cm →

←— 6 cm —→

What is the value of x?

Solution

Method 1

The ratio of the vertical sides, small:large is 5:15 = 1:3.

So the sides of the large triangle are three times as long as those of the small triangle.

For the bases

$3x = 6$

$x = 2$ ← The base of the small triangle is 2 cm long.

Method 2

In the large triangle the ratio of the sides,

base:height is 6:15 = 1:2.5.

So the height of each triangle is 2.5 times the base.

For the small triangle

$2.5x = 5$

$x = 2$ ← The base of the small triangle is 2 cm long.

Practising skills

① P is a rectangle 3 cm by 1 cm.
Q is a rectangle 5 cm by 2 cm.

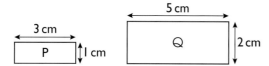

Say whether the following rectangles are similar to P or to Q or to neither.

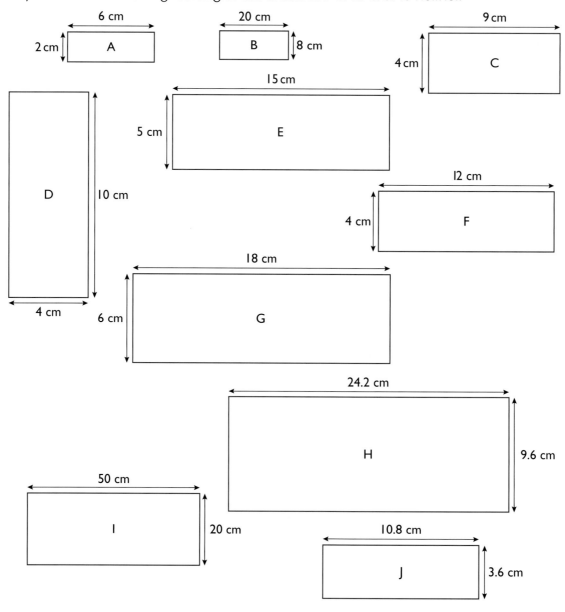

② Triangle C is enlarged to give triangle D. The scale factor of the enlargement is 3.

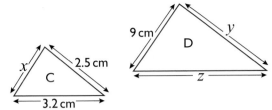

    a Find the value of y.

    b Find the value of z.

    c Find the value of x.

    d Are triangles C and D congruent or similar?

③ Triangle A is enlarged to give triangle B. The scale factor is 4.

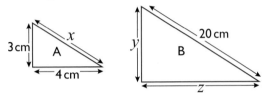

    a Find the value of y.

    b Find the value of z.

    c Find the value of x.

    d Are triangles A and B congruent or similar?

    e What is special about both triangles?

④ Triangle E is enlarged to give triangle F.

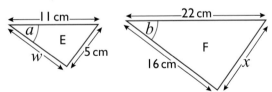

    a What is the scale factor of enlargement?

    b Find the value of x.

    c Find the value of w.

    d What do you know about the size of the angles labelled a and b?

    e What is the relationship between triangles E and F?

⑤ Shapes A and B are given below. In each case decide if shapes A and B are similar or not similar. You must explain your answer.

a

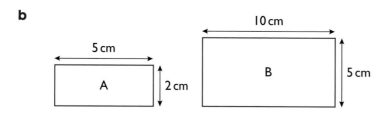

b

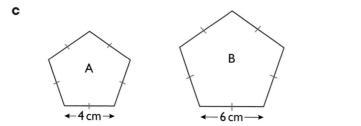

c

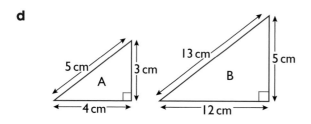

d

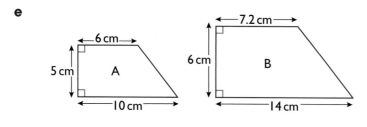

e

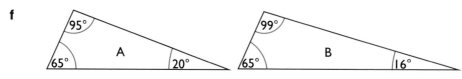

f

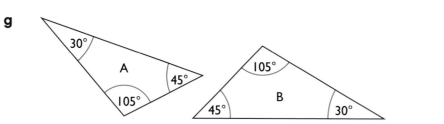

g

⑥ For each pair of parallelograms, decide if P and Q are similar or not similar. You must explain your answer fully.

a

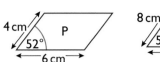 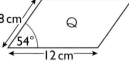

b

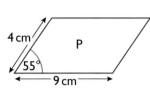 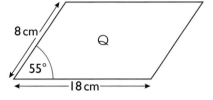

c

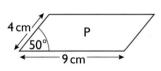 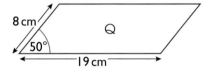

Developing fluency

① A photograph is 6 inches by 4 inches. Which of these are similar to it?

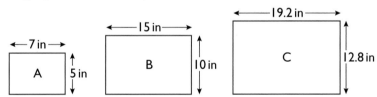

② The diagram shows part of the landing stage for a ferry. The two triangles are similar.

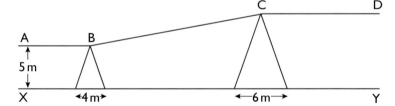

AB, CD and XY are horizontal.
AB is 5 m above the sea.
The bases of the triangles are 4 m and 6 m.
How much higher above sea level is CD than AB?

③ The trapezia M and N are similar.

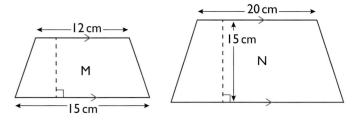

    a Work out the area of trapezium M.

    b Work out the area of trapezium N.

④ In the diagram, ABCDEF is a 6-pointed star with rotational symmetry of order 6.

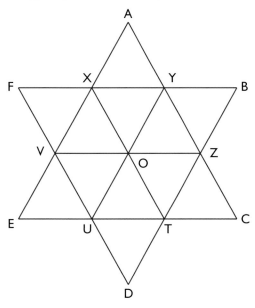

AXY is an equilateral triangle.

    a How many triangles can you see that are congruent to AXY?

    b Which triangles are similar to AXY but not congruent to it? Place them in groups that are congruent to each other.

    c The perimeter of the star is 36 cm. What is its area?

⑤ Triangles A and B are similar.

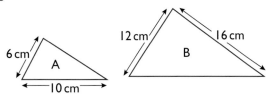

    a Work out the perimeter of triangle A.

    b Work out the perimeter of triangle B.

    c Work out the areas of both triangles.

Exam-style

Exam-style

⑥ Shape P is reflected to give shape A.

Shape P is rotated to give shape B.

Shape P is translated to give shape C.

Shape P is enlarged to give shape D.

a Which shapes are congruent?

b Which shapes are similar?

Problem solving

Exam-style

① The diagram shows a set of supports of two sizes made to support shelves.

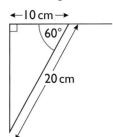 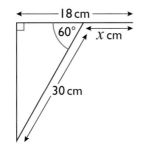

a Explain how you know that the triangular parts of the supports are similar.

b Find the value of x.

Exam-style

② The diagram shows a step ladder on horizontal ground. DE is a horizontal bar inserted for stability.

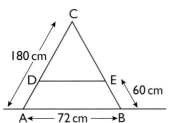

What is the length of DE?

Exam-style

③ The diagram shows a support for a vertical wall. The ground is horizontal and the strut DE is perpendicular to AC.

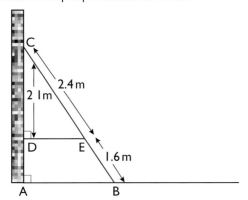

a Show that triangles CDE and CAB are similar.

b Work out the height of the point D above the floor AB.

④ Here is a design for a fold-up seat.

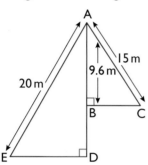
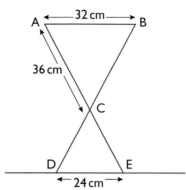

AB = 32 cm

AC = 36 cm

DE = 24 cm

The design has a vertical line of symmetry.

Work out the length of the leg AE.

⑤ In the diagram, the straight line DBA bisects ∠EAC.

BC and DE are perpendicular to DBA.

AC = 15 m, AE = 20 m and AB = 9.6 m

Find the length of BD.

⑥ The diagram shows a framework used to support the top of a building. It is made of rods. The dimensions are marked on the diagram.

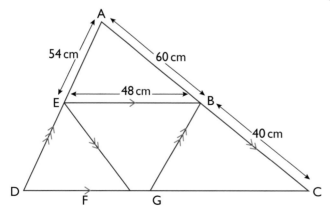

EB is parallel to DFGC, EF is parallel to BC and DE is parallel to GB.

Work out the total length of all the rods.

Reviewing skills

① Rectangles P and Q are similar. Find the value of x in each case.

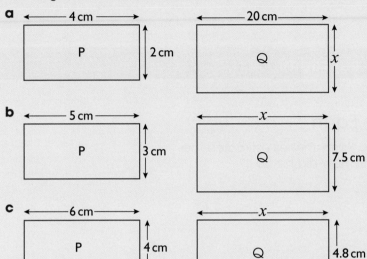

a

4 cm — P — 2 cm

20 cm — Q — x

b

5 cm — P — 3 cm

x — Q — 7.5 cm

c

6 cm — P — 4 cm

x — Q — 4.8 cm

② **a** Prove triangles T and V are similar.

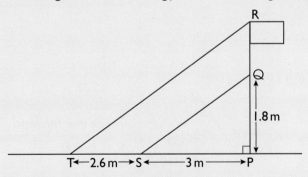

6 cm
3 cm
110°
30°
T
y

40°
9 cm
V
x
110°
7.5 cm

b Find the value of x.

c Find the value of y.

③ The diagram shows a flagpole PR standing on horizontal ground PST.

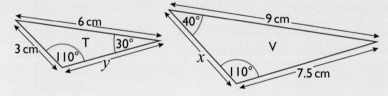

R

Q

1.8 m

T ←2.6 m→ S ←—— 3 m ——→ P

PQ is a vertical rod of length 1.8 m.

PS and PT are the shadows of the rod and the flagpole.

Work out the height of the flagpole.

Unit 8 · Trigonometry · Band h

Outside the Maths classroom

Size of the Earth

In about 240 BC, Eratosthenes estimated the size of the Earth. How did he do it?

Toolbox

Each side in a **right-angled triangle** has a name.

- The longest side is called the **hypotenuse (H)**.
- The side opposite the marked angle is called the **opposite (O)**.
- The remaining side, next to the marked angle, is called the **adjacent (A)**.
- The ratio of the lengths of the sides are given special names.

$$\text{cosine (cos) } \theta = \frac{\text{adjacent}}{\text{hypotenuse}}$$

$$\text{tangent (tan) } \theta = \frac{\text{opposite}}{\text{adjacent}}$$

$$\text{sine (sin) } \theta = \frac{\text{opposite}}{\text{hypotenuse}}$$

These ratios are constant for similar right-angled triangles.

You can use this information to find angles and lengths in triangles.

hypotenuse
17 cm

opposite
15 cm

adjacent
8 cm

For this triangle

$$\cos \theta = \frac{8}{17}$$

$$\sin \theta = \frac{15}{17}$$

$$\tan \theta = \frac{15}{8}$$

You will find keys for sin, cos and tan on your calculator.

hypotenuse

opposite

adjacent

Example – Using trigonometry to find a length

John is a window cleaner. His ladder is 6 m long.
The angle between the ladder and ground is 70°.
Find the height that his ladder reaches up the wall.

Solution

$$\sin \theta = \frac{\text{opposite}}{\text{hypotenuse}}$$

$$\sin 70° = \frac{y}{6}$$

so $y = 6 \times \sin 70°$ ← Multiply by 6.

$= 6 \times 0.94$

$= 5.64 \, \text{m}$

sin 70° = 0.94 from a calculator.

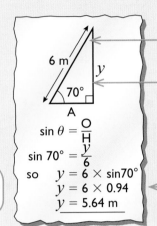

The ladder is the hypotenuse. It is 6 m long.

The height the ladder reaches up the wall is the opposite side to the angle of 70°.

$$\sin \theta = \frac{O}{H}$$

$$\sin 70° = \frac{y}{6}$$

so $y = 6 \times \sin 70°$
$y = 6 \times 0.94$
$y = 5.64 \, \text{m}$

The distance from the bottom of the ladder to the wall is the adjacent side.

Example – Using trigonometry to find an angle

a Look at the diagram. Which ratio would you use to find the value of θ?
b Find the value of θ.

Solution

a Use $\cos \theta = \frac{\text{adjacent}}{\text{hypotenuse}}$

The adjacent side is 6 cm.

The hypotenuse is 11 cm.

b $\cos \theta = \frac{6}{11}$

$\theta = \cos^{-1}\left(\frac{6}{11}\right)$

$\theta = 56.9°$

You can write $\theta = \cos^{-1}\left(\frac{6}{11}\right)$

or $\theta = \arccos\left(\frac{6}{11}\right)$.

Find this using your calculator.

Practising skills

① Look at these triangles.

a

b
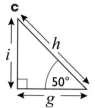

c

d
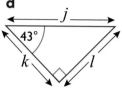

e
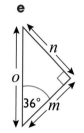

f
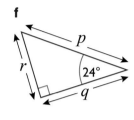

For each triangle, write down which side is

i the hypotenuse

ii opposite

iii adjacent.

② Look at this triangle.

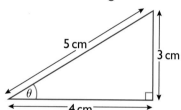

Which of these are true?

a $\sin \theta = \dfrac{3}{4}$ $\sin \theta = \dfrac{3}{5}$ $\sin \theta = \dfrac{5}{3}$

b $\cos \theta = \dfrac{3}{4}$ $\cos \theta = \dfrac{4}{5}$ $\cos \theta = \dfrac{4}{3}$

c $\tan \theta = \dfrac{3}{5}$ $\tan \theta = \dfrac{3}{4}$ $\tan \theta = \dfrac{4}{3}$

③ Look at this triangle.

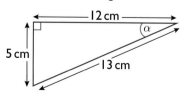

Which of these are true?

a $\tan \alpha = \dfrac{5}{12}$ $\sin \alpha = \dfrac{13}{12}$ $\cos \alpha = \dfrac{12}{5}$

b $\sin \alpha = \dfrac{5}{12}$ $\cos \alpha = \dfrac{5}{13}$ $\sin \alpha = \dfrac{12}{13}$

c $\cos \alpha = \dfrac{5}{12}$ $\tan \alpha = \dfrac{12}{5}$ $\tan \alpha = \dfrac{5}{13}$

④ Look at these triangles. In each case you are going to find the value of x.

a
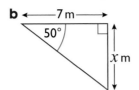

b
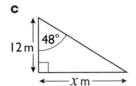

c

d
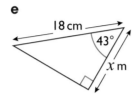

e
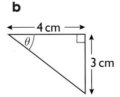

For each triangle
i   sketch the triangle
ii label the sides H, O and A
iii decide whether to use sin, cos or tan
iv work out the value of x correct to 1 decimal place.

⑤ Use your calculator to find the value of θ to the nearest degree.

a $\sin \theta = 0.5$ **b** $\tan \theta = 1$ **c** $\cos \theta = 0.5$

d $\tan \theta = 0.839$ **e** $\sin \theta = 0.951$ **f** $\cos \theta = 0.139$

g $\sin \theta = \dfrac{4}{5}$ **h** $\cos \theta = \dfrac{2}{3}$ **i** $\tan \theta = \dfrac{9}{5}$

⑥ For each triangle
i   sketch the triangle
ii label the sides H, O and A
iii decide whether to use sin, cos or tan
iv work out the value of θ correct to 1 decimal place.

a   **b**   **c**

d
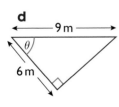
e
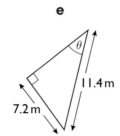
f
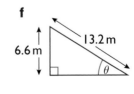

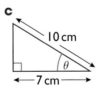

7 For each triangle

    i sketch the triangle

    ii label the sides H, O and A

    iii decide whether to use sin, cos or tan

    iv work out the value of x correct to 1 decimal place.

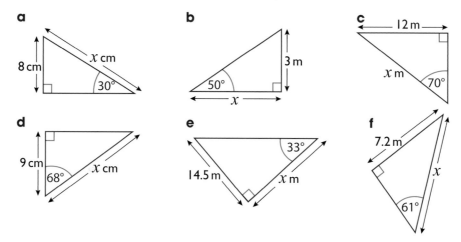

Developing fluency

1 **a** Work out the perpendicular height, h m, of this triangle.

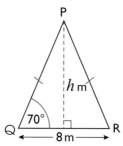

    b Calculate the triangle's area.

    c Calculate the triangle's perimeter.

2 Work out the area and perimeter of this triangle.

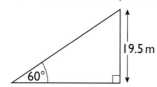

3 Joshua has made a 5-barred gate. The diagonal is 4 m long and makes an angle of 30° with the horizontal. What length of wood did he need?

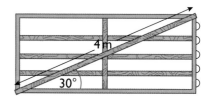

④ Alice has lost her cat Truffles. After some searching she finds Truffles up a tree.
When Alice is 30 m from the tree she sees Truffles at an angle of elevation of 25°.

a Alice's eye is 1.5 m above the ground.
How high up the tree is Truffles?

The dog barks and Truffles climbs a further 5 m up the tree.

b Now what is the angle of elevation at which Alice sees Truffles?

⑤ Robin is standing on top of a vertical cliff looking at a small boat.

He sees it at an angle of depression of 18°. The top of the cliff is 50 m above the sea and Robin's eye height is 1.5 m.

a How far from the base of the cliff is the boat?

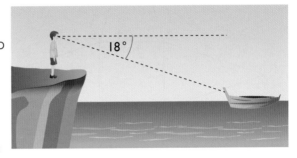

The boat then sails directly out to sea.

b How much further is it from the cliff when Robin sees it at an angle of depression of 10°?

⑥ Look at triangle ABC.
You are given the lengths of AB and AC.
There are two different ways to find the length of BC.

a i Use trigonometry to work out ∠ABC.

ii Use trigonometry again to calculate the length of BC.

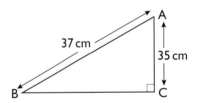

b Without using any trigonometry, use Pythagoras' theorem to find the length of BC.

c Do the two methods give the same answer?

⑦ Point X is 1800 m due west of point Y.

T is the base of a tower.

The bearing of T from X is 040° and the bearing of T from Y is 320°.

Floella walks from X to T and then from T to Y.

Work out how far she walks.

⑧ The diagram is the net of a square-based pyramid. The points V_1, V_2, V_3 and V_4 all come together at the vertex V when it is folded up.

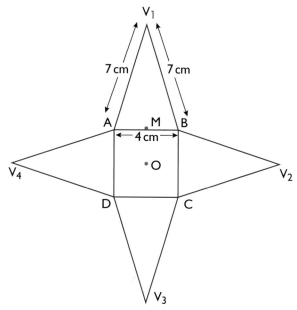

The four triangles in the net are all isosceles with sides 7 cm, 7 cm and 4 cm.

M is the mid-point of AB.

O is the middle of the base ABCD.

a Show that the length V_1M is $\sqrt{45}$ cm.

b Draw the triangle VMO when the net is folded up. Mark the right angle in your triangle.

c Work out the angle VMO to the nearest 0.1 degrees. This is the slant angle of the sloping faces of the pyramid.

d Calculate the height of the pyramid.

Problem solving

① The diagram shows a ramp for wheelchair access to a building.

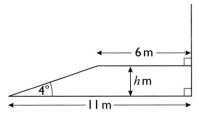

The slope of the ramp is $4°$.
The top of the ramp is 6 m from the building.
The bottom of the ramp is 11 m from the building.
Find the value of h.

② A ship leaves a port P and sails on a bearing of $040°$.
There is a lighthouse L which is 36 km from P on a bearing of $035°$.
Work out the distance of the ship from L when it is at its closest.

③ The diagram shows the side view of a solar panel in a field.

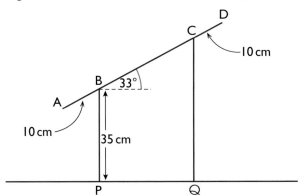

The straight line ABCD represents the panel edge.
PB and QC are vertical supports.
PQ is horizontal.
AB = CD = 10 cm
AD = 102 cm
PB = 35 cm
To get the maximum efficiency the panel must be tilted at $33°$ to the horizontal.

a Work out the distance PQ.

b Work out the distance QC.

④ A supermarket has a moving walkway between the ground floor and the first floor.
The top of the walkway is 3.5 m above the ground floor.
The walkway makes an angle of $10°$ with the horizontal.

a Work out the horizontal distance covered by the walkway.

b Find the length of the walkway.

⑤ The diagram shows a set of steps with a rail PQ.

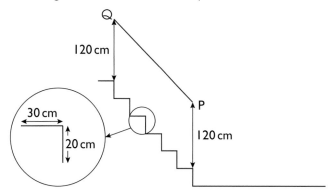

The height of each step is 20 cm.
The width of each step is 30 cm.
P is 120 cm above the first step.
Q is 120 cm above the last step.
There are 6 steps.

a Work out the angle that PQ makes with the horizontal.

b Explain why the angle you found in part **a** will always be the same no matter how many steps there are.

⑥ The diagram represents a framework that is going to support a vertical wall. It consists of 4 rods.

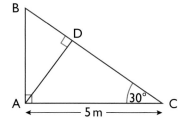

The dimensions are shown.
Work out the total length of the rods in the framework.

Reviewing skills

① Look at these triangles. In each case you are going to find the length of the side marked x.

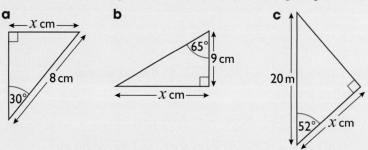

For each triangle, write down which side is
  i the hypotenuse   **ii** opposite   **iii** adjacent.

Then choose the best ratio to use to work out the value of x.

② For each triangle
   i sketch the triangle
   ii label the sides H, O and A
   iii decide whether to use sin, cos or tan
   iv work out the value of θ correct to 1 decimal place.

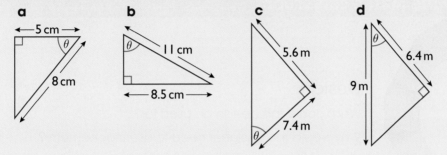

③ For each triangle, find the value of x correct to 1 decimal place.

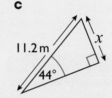

④ For each triangle, find the value of x correct to 1 decimal place.

⑤ The diagram shows the end view of a house, ABCDE.

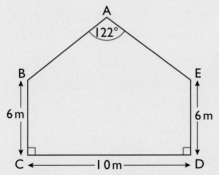

The dimensions are as shown. There is a line of symmetry through A.
Find the height of point A.

Unit 9 • Trigonometry for special angles • Band h

Outside the Maths classroom

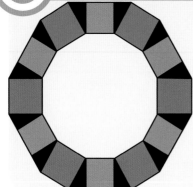

Design

What could this design be used for?

Why would the designer need to use trigonometry?

Toolbox

Using exact values of some sines, cosines and tangents avoids rounding errors.

$\sin 45° = \cos 45° = \dfrac{1}{\sqrt{2}}$

$\tan 45° = 1$

$\sin 30° = \cos 60° = \dfrac{1}{2}$

$\sin 60° = \cos 30° = \dfrac{\sqrt{3}}{2}$

$\tan 30° = \dfrac{1}{\sqrt{3}}$

$\tan 60° = \sqrt{3}$

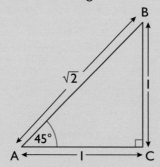

$\sin 90° = 1$

$\cos 90° = 0$

Remember when working with surds:

$\dfrac{1}{\sqrt{2}} = \dfrac{\sqrt{2}}{\sqrt{2} \times \sqrt{2}} = \dfrac{\sqrt{2}}{2}$

$\dfrac{1}{\sqrt{3}} = \dfrac{\sqrt{3}}{\sqrt{3} \times \sqrt{3}} = \dfrac{\sqrt{3}}{3}$

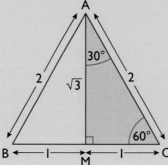

Example – Using exact values

In the diagram, triangle ABC has angle B = 60° and angle C = 45°.
AC = 16 cm and AD is perpendicular to BC.

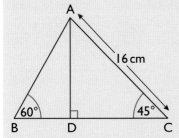

a Calculate the exact length of AD.
b Calculate the exact area of the triangle ABC.

Solution

a $\dfrac{AD}{16} = \sin 45°$

$\dfrac{AD}{16} = \dfrac{1}{\sqrt{2}}$ ← $\sin 45° = \dfrac{1}{\sqrt{2}}$

$AD = \dfrac{16}{\sqrt{2}}$ ← multiplying by 16

$AD = \dfrac{16\sqrt{2}}{2}$ ← $\left(\dfrac{1}{\sqrt{2}} = \dfrac{\sqrt{2}}{2}\right)$

$AD = 8\sqrt{2}$ cm

b Area of triangle ABC = area of triangle ABD + area of triangle ACD.

Triangle ABD

Area $= \dfrac{1}{2} \times BD \times AD$

To find BD, use

$\dfrac{BD}{AD} = \tan 30°$

$\dfrac{BD}{8\sqrt{2}} = \dfrac{1}{\sqrt{3}}$

$BD = 8 \times \sqrt{2} \times \dfrac{\sqrt{3}}{3}$

Area of triangle ABD

$= \dfrac{1}{2} \times 8 \times \sqrt{2} \times \dfrac{\sqrt{3}}{3} \times 8 \times \sqrt{2}$

$= 64\dfrac{\sqrt{3}}{3}$

Triangle ACD

Area $= \dfrac{1}{2} \times DC \times AD$

To find DC, use

$\dfrac{DC}{AD} = \tan 45°$

$\dfrac{DC}{8\sqrt{2}} = 1$

$DC = 8 \times \sqrt{2}$

Area of triangle ACD

$= \dfrac{1}{2} \times 8 \times \sqrt{2} \times 8 \times \sqrt{2}$

$= 64$

Total area of triangle ABC $= 64\dfrac{\sqrt{3}}{3} + 64$

$= 64\left(\dfrac{\sqrt{3}}{3} + 1\right) cm^2$

Practising skills

Give all answers exactly.

(1) Calculate the length of

    a BC

    b AB.

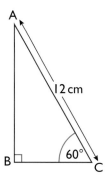

(2) Calculate the length of

    a PQ

    b RQ.

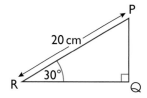

(3) Calculate

    a the length of BC

    b the length of AB

    c the area of triangle ABC.

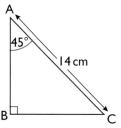

(4) Calculate the length of

    a BC

    b AC.

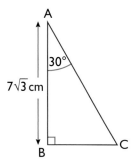

(5) Calculate the length of

    a AC

    b BC.

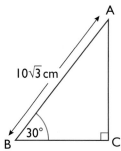

Developing fluency

Give all answers exactly.

(1) The length of the diagonal of a square is 26 cm.
Calculate the length of each side.

(2) An equilateral triangle has a base of 16 cm.
Calculate the area of the triangle.

(3) ABC and ACD are right-angled triangles.
Calculate the length of AD.

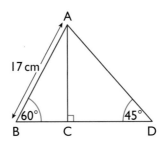

(4) A regular hexagon is constructed from 6 congruent equilateral triangles.
The height of the hexagon is 64 cm.
Calculate

   a the perimeter

   b the area of the hexagon.

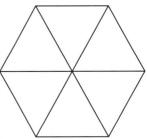

(5) In the diagram ABC is an equilateral triangle with sides of length 10 cm.
M is the mid-point of BC.
Triangle BMD is isosceles.

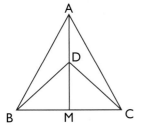

   a Find the sizes of the angles of triangle ABD.

   b Find the lengths of the sides of triangle ABD.

   c Find the area of triangles ABC and BDC.

   d Find the area of triangle ABD.

   e Find the perpendicular distance of D from the line AB.

⑥ The diagram shows a symmetrical roof beam.
AB = 3 m and ∠BAG = 30°

   a Find the lengths of AG and BG.

   b Show that the width, AE, of the beam is 8 m.

   c Find the total length of the sloping sides, AH + HE.

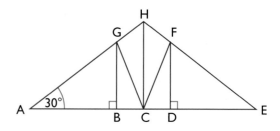

Problem solving

Give all answers exactly.

① ABCDE is a pentagon made of 3 similar right-angled triangles.
∠BAE = 90° and ∠ABC = 90°
BC = 3 cm

   a Show that ∠BAC = 30°.

   b Calculate the length of AE.

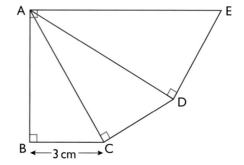

② Triangle ABC has a square drawn on each side.

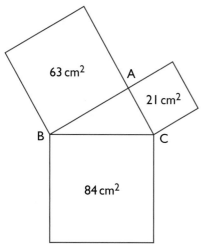

The areas of the squares are 63 cm², 21 cm² and 84 cm².
Show that

   a ∠BAC = 90°   **b** ∠ABC = 30°.

③ A kite is made of an isosceles right-angled triangle and an equilateral triangle.

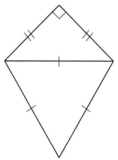

Calculate

   a the ratio of the kite's width to its height

   b the ratio of the area of the isosceles triangle to the area of the equilateral triangle.

④ The diagram shows a circle of radius 5 cm sandwiched between two squares, ABCD and PQRS.

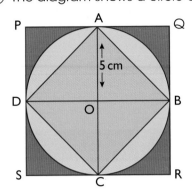

a Use the perimeters of the squares to show that the circumference of the circle lies between $20\sqrt{2}$ cm and 40 cm.

b Hence show that $2\sqrt{2} < \pi < 4$.

c Copy the diagram and draw two regular hexagons on it. One is outside the circle and touching it. The other has its points on the circumference of the circle. Find the circumferences of the two hexagons.

d Use your answers to show that $3 < \pi < 2\sqrt{3}$.

Reviewing skills

① Calculate

a the lengths of AB and AC

b the area of triangle ABC

c the length of BD

d the area of triangle ABD

e the area of triangle ADC.

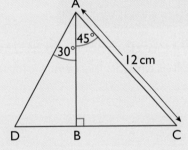

Unit 10 • Finding centres of rotation • Band h

Outside the Maths classroom

Wallpaper patterns

How do wallpaper designers use transformations?

Toolbox

The **centre of rotation** is the point that does not move as a result of the rotation.
During a rotation, an object revolves around the centre of rotation to form the image.

To find the centre of rotation that maps triangle A onto triangle B:

- join the corresponding points on the two shapes
- draw the perpendicular bisectors of the joining lines
- the centre of rotation is where the perpendicular bisectors meet.

In this example, the rotation that maps triangle A onto triangle B is a 90° clockwise rotation about (0, –1).

Example – Finding the centre of rotation

Quadrilateral Q is the image of quadrilateral P under a rotation.

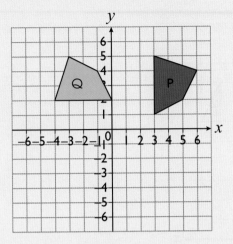

a   Find the centre of rotation.

b   Describe fully the transformation that maps P onto Q.

Solution

a   Join each vertex of Q to the corresponding vertex of P.
Draw the perpendicular bisector of each of these lines.
The bisectors meet at the centre of rotation.

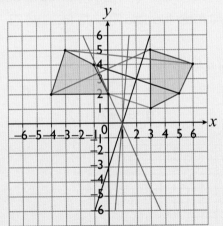

So the centre of rotation is $(1, 0)$.

b   The transformation is a 90° anti-clockwise rotation about $(1, 0)$.

> Don't forget to state angle, direction and centre.

Practising skills

① Copy and complete the diagram and statements.

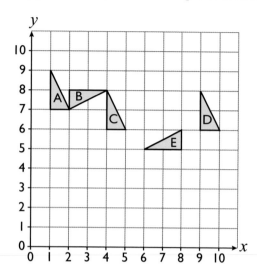

a When triangle A is rotated ☐° clockwise about (☐, ☐), it moves to position B.

b When triangle B is rotated 90° ☐ about (4, 8), it moves to position ☐.

c When triangle C is rotated 90° ☐ about (☐, ☐), it moves to position E.

d When triangle ☐ is rotated 90° clockwise about (9, 4), it moves to position ☐.

e When triangle B is rotated 180° about (☐, ☐), it moves to position E.

f There is no rotation that will map triangle ☐ onto triangle ☐.

② Copy the diagram.
Find the centre and angle of rotation for

a A → B   b B → C   c C → D   d D → E

e E → F   f F → G   g G → A.

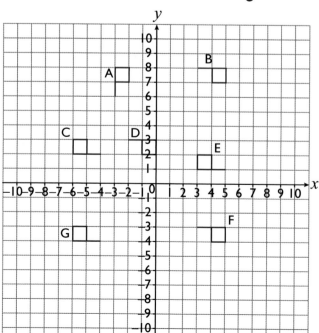

Developing fluency

 1 Copy the diagram.

    a Find the centre of rotation for

      i A → X   **ii** A → Y   **iii** A → Z.

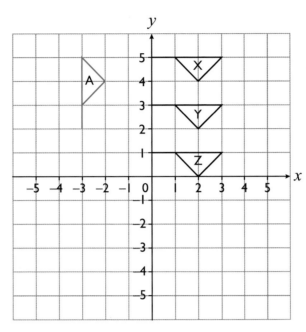

    b Say what you notice about the centres of rotation.

2 Here are five transformations.

    a The blue triangle is a 180° clockwise rotation of the green triangle.

    b The orange triangle is a 90° anticlockwise rotation of the green triangle.

    c The purple triangle is a 90° anticlockwise rotation of the orange triangle.

    d The purple triangle is a 180° clockwise rotation of the green triangle.

    e The orange triangle is a 90° clockwise rotation of the blue triangle.

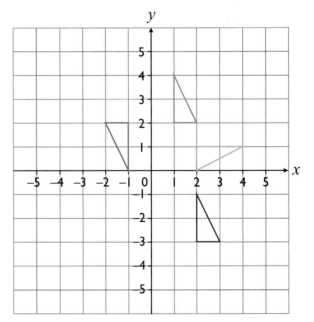

The five centres of rotation are:

    i P(4, −1)

    ii Q(0, 2)

    iii R(1, 1)

    iv S(0.5, −0.5)

    v T(1, 3)

Match the transformations with the correct centres of rotation.

285

③ Describe fully the rotations that map

    a shape A onto shape B.

    b shape B onto shape A.

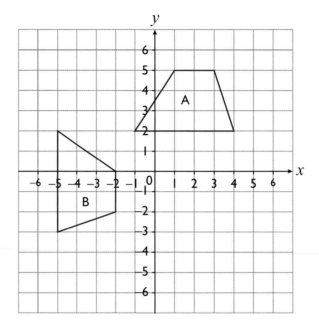

④ Copy the diagram.

    a Rotate the triangle X 90° anticlockwise about (−1, 2). Label the new triangle A.

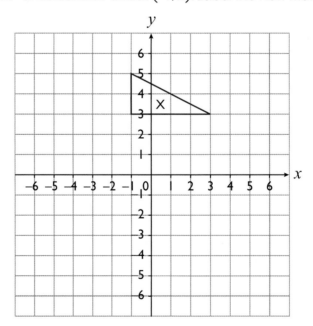

    b Rotate the triangle X 90° clockwise about (1, 0). Label the new triangle B.

    c Describe fully the rotation that maps triangle A onto triangle B.

Exam-style

⑤ The diagram shows four congruent shapes A, B, C and D.

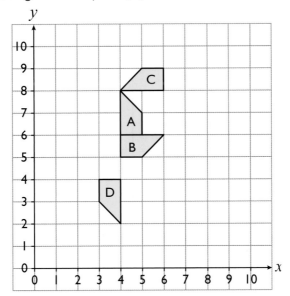

Describe the rotation that maps

a shape A → shape B
b shape B → shape C
c shape C → shape D
d shape D → shape A.

⑥ Copy the diagram.

a The quadrilateral C is the reflection of B in the x axis. Draw C on the diagram.

b Sally tries to find the centre of rotation from A to C. Show that she is unsuccessful and explain why.

c Describe the transformation that maps quadrilateral A onto quadrilateral B.

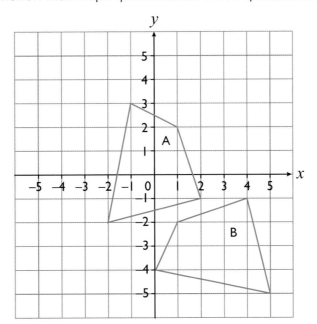

⑦ This diagram shows five congruent triangles.

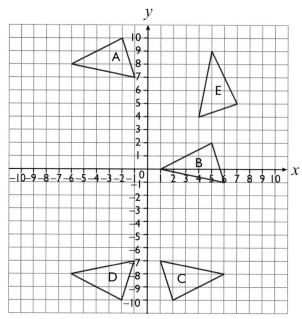

a Describe fully the single transformation that maps

    i A → B   **ii** B → C   **iii** C → D   **iv** D → A

    v A → E   **vi** E → C   **vii** C → B   **viii** B → A.

b State which pairs of triangles cannot be mapped onto each other by a single transformation.

Problem solving

① Copy the diagram.

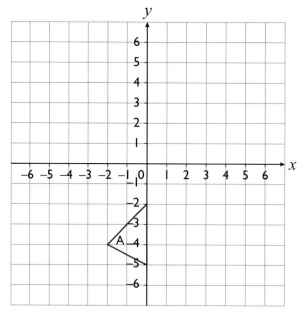

a Rotate triangle A through 180° about the origin. Label the image B.

b Rotate triangle B through 90° anticlockwise about (0, 1). Label the image C.

c Describe fully the single transformation that maps triangle C directly to triangle A.

Exam-style

② Shape L_1 is drawn on a grid. Copy the diagram.

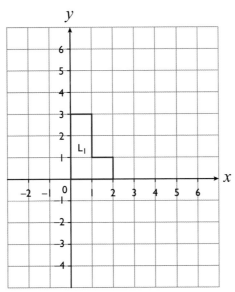

a Translate L_1 by the vector $\begin{pmatrix} 2 \\ 2 \end{pmatrix}$. Label the image L_2.

b Rotate L_2 through 90° anticlockwise about (6, 1). Label the image L_3.

c Describe fully the single transformation that maps L_3 directly to L_1.

Reviewing skills

① This diagram shows three congruent triangles A, B and C.

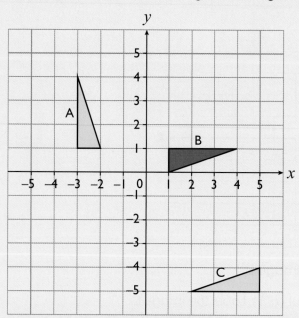

Describe fully the rotations that map

a A → B   **b** B → A
c C → A   **d** B → C

② This diagram shows three congruent trapeziums.

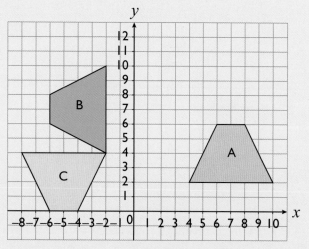

a Describe the transformation that maps trapezium A to trapezium B.
b Describe the transformation that maps trapezium B to trapezium C.
c Describe the transformation that maps trapezium C to trapezium A.

Strand 6 Three-dimensional shapes

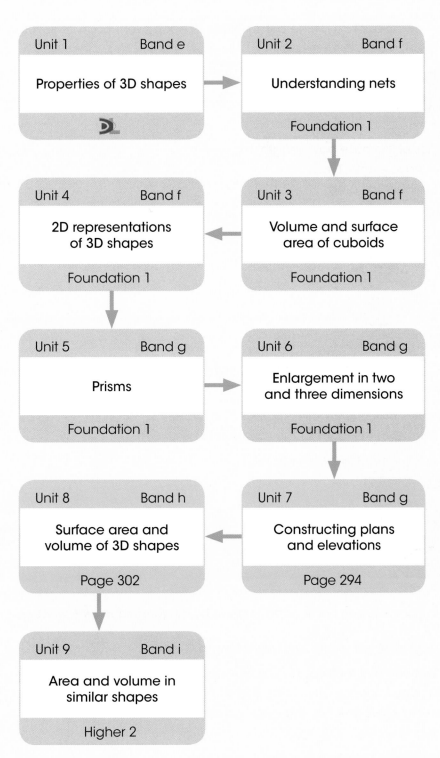

Unit 1	Band e		Unit 2	Band f
Properties of 3D shapes			Understanding nets	
			Foundation 1	

Unit 4	Band f		Unit 3	Band f
2D representations of 3D shapes			Volume and surface area of cuboids	
Foundation 1			Foundation 1	

Unit 5	Band g		Unit 6	Band g
Prisms			Enlargement in two and three dimensions	
Foundation 1			Foundation 1	

Unit 8	Band h		Unit 7	Band g
Surface area and volume of 3D shapes			Constructing plans and elevations	
Page 302			Page 294	

Unit 9	Band i
Area and volume in similar shapes	
Higher 2	

Units 1–6 are assumed knowledge for this book. They are reviewed and extended in the Moving on section on page 292.

1 The diagram shows a podium for the first 3 people in each event of an athletics competition.

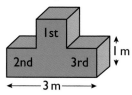

Two of the edges of the base have length 3 m.
All other edges have length 1 m.
Work out the total surface area.

2 Write down the name of the solid that each net will make.

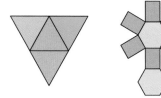

Draw a sketch of each solid.

3 By referring to a net or otherwise, explain why the sum of the angles at any vertex of a solid must be less than 360°.

4 Draw a solid shape that has exactly 5 planes of symmetry.
Describe the shapes of the faces of the solid you have drawn.

5 A scientist is studying heat loss from hot bricks.

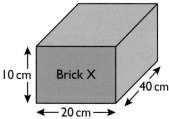

The rate of heat loss R, joules per second, is given by the formula $R = kA$, where k is a constant and $A \, \text{cm}^2$ is the total surface area.
Brick X has height of 10 cm, width 20 cm and length 40 cm.

a Work out the value of A for Brick X.

The scientist then makes Brick Y. It has the same volume as Brick X.
Brick Y is twice the height and half the length of Brick X.

b Find the value of A for Brick Y.

c Which brick loses heat faster?

(6) The diagram shows a wooden block with a hole drilled all the way through.

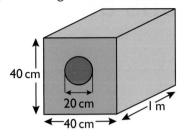

40 cm

20 cm

40 cm

1 m

The block is a cuboid with height 40 cm, width 40 cm and length 1 m. The diameter of the hole is 20 cm.

The block is immersed in a trough. The trough is a cuboid with width 60 cm and length 1.5 m.

By how much will the water level in the trough rise?

(7) The measurements of the edges of a cuboid are in the ratio 3:4:5.

The area of the largest face is 240 cm^2.

Work out the area of the smallest face with the smallest area.

Unit 7 • Constructing plans and elevations • Band g

Outside the Maths classroom

Architecture

How do architects use constructions?

Toolbox

The most common types of 3-dimensional drawing are

a **isometric** drawings

b **plans and elevations**.

An **isometric drawing** is often made on a triangular grid.

Vertical edges are drawn vertically, but horizontal edges are not drawn horizontally.

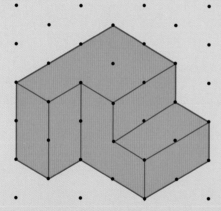

Plans and elevations show the view from above, the front and the side.

Plan   Front elevation   Side elevation

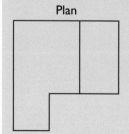
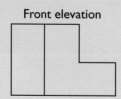
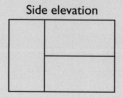

Example – Isometric drawings

Here are the plan, front and side elevations of a shape.

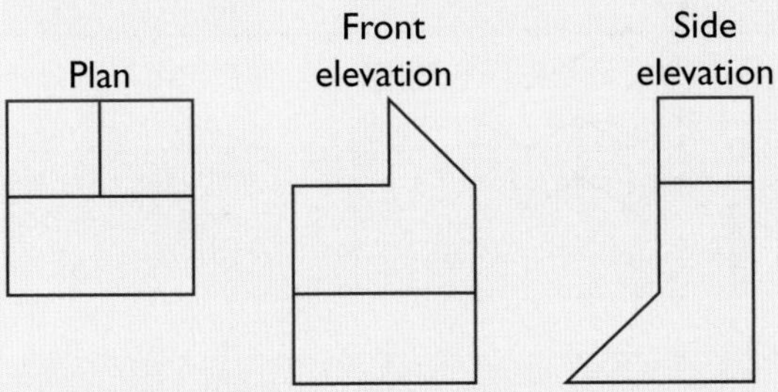

Plan | Front elevation | Side elevation

Make an isometric drawing of the shape.

Solution

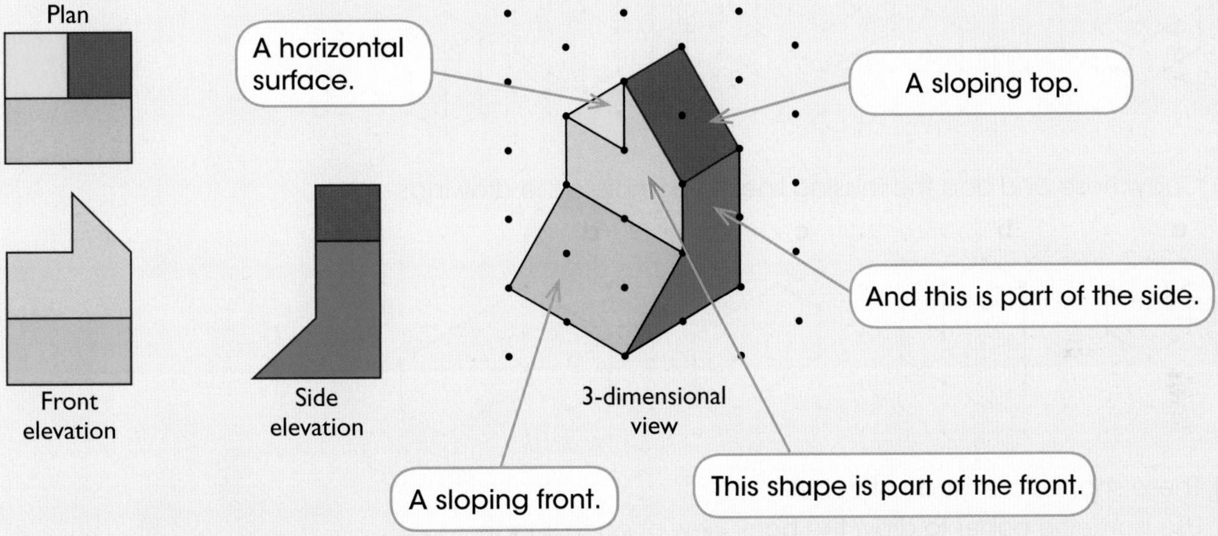

Plan

Front elevation

Side elevation

A horizontal surface.

A sloping top.

And this is part of the side.

3-dimensional view

A sloping front.

This shape is part of the front.

Practising skills

① Match each shape at the top with the same shape at the bottom.

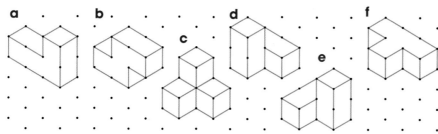

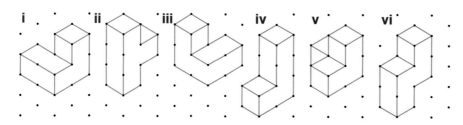

② Copy these and add the missing lines to complete the drawings.

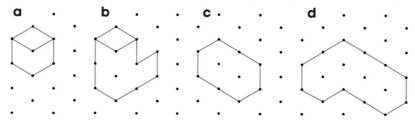

③ These shapes are made of cubes.
Use isometric paper to draw the back view of each shape.

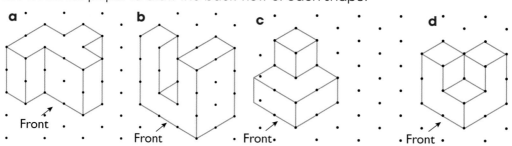

④ Copy and complete the table by matching these isometric drawings to the views.

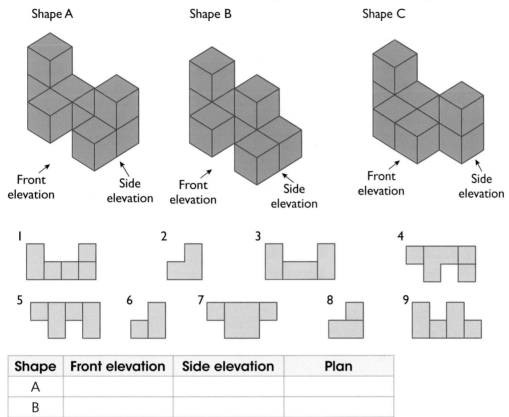

Shape A

Shape B

Shape C

Front elevation   Side elevation   Front elevation   Side elevation   Front elevation   Side elevation

1   2   3   4

5   6   7   8   9

Shape	Front elevation	Side elevation	Plan
A			
B			
C			

⑤ Sketch the plan, front elevation and side elevation of each of these shapes.

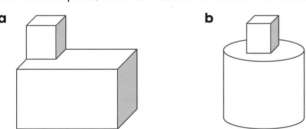

a   b

Developing fluency

1 Make isometric drawings of the shapes shown in these views.

a

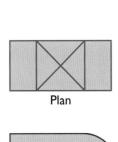
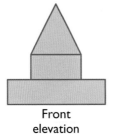
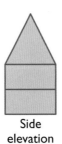

Plan   Front elevation   Side elevation

b

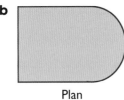

Plan   Front elevation   Side elevation

2 Each of these shapes is made of 8 cubes.
Draw the plan, front and side elevations of the shapes.

a

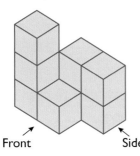

Front   Side

b

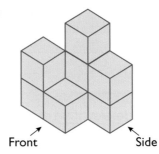

Front   Side

3 Draw plans, front and side elevations of these shapes.

a

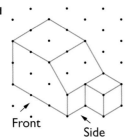

Front   Side

b

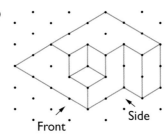

Front   Side

4 Draw the plan, front elevation and side elevation of this shape.

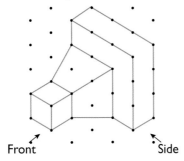

Front   Side

Exam-style

5 Make an isometric drawing of this shape.

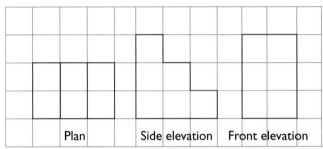

Plan   Front elevation   Side elevation

6 Here are the plan and elevations of a 3D shape.

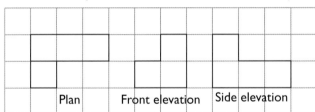

Plan   Side elevation   Front elevation

a Make an isometric drawing of this 3D shape.
The solid is made from centimetre cubes.

b Find the
  i volume   **ii** surface area of the solid.

Reasoning

7 Here are the plan and elevations of a 3D shape.

Plan   Front elevation   Side elevation

a Make an isometric drawing of this 3D shape.
The solid is made from centimetre cubes.

b Add 1 more cube to your drawing, so that the drawing has plane symmetry.
Find two different answers.

c Add 2 more cubes to your drawing from part a, so that the drawing has plane symmetry.
How many different answers can you find?

Problem solving

① Here is the plan view and elevations for a 3D shape.

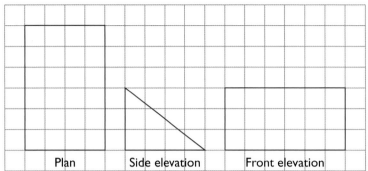

Plan   Side elevation   Front elevation

    a Draw the 3D shape. What is the mathematical name for this shape?

    b Find the volume of the 3D shape.

    c Construct an accurate drawing of the net for the shape.

    d Work out the surface area of the shape.

② A child builds a shape out of multi-link cubes.
Here are the plan and elevations of the shape.

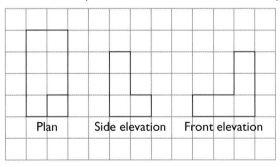

Plan   Side elevation   Front elevation

    a Draw the 3D shape on isometric paper.

    b Add one cube to your diagram so that the resulting shape has a plane of symmetry.

③ **a** Draw the plan, front and side elevations of this 3D shape.

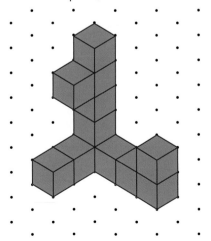

    b Copy the 3D shape on isometric paper.
       Add 3 cubes to your diagram so that the resulting shape has a plane of symmetry.

Reviewing skills

① This shape is made of cubes.
Draw the shape viewed from the back.

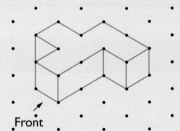

Front

② Make an isometric drawing of the shape shown in these views.

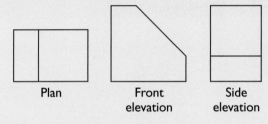

Plan   Front   Side
              elevation   elevation

③ This shape is made of 8 cubes.
Draw the plan, front and side elevations of this shape.

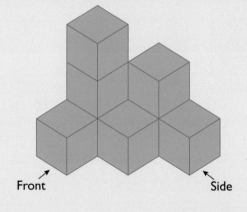

Front   Side

Unit 8 • Surface area and volume of 3D shapes • Band h

Outside the Maths classroom

Domes

How could you estimate the amount of gold leaf needed to cover this dome?

 ## Toolbox

The volume of a pyramid $= \frac{1}{3}$ base area × height.

Pyramid

The volume of a cone $= \frac{1}{3}\pi r^2 h$.

The surface area of a cone = area of base + area of curved surface
$$= \pi r^2 + \pi r l.$$

The volume of a sphere $= \frac{4}{3}\pi r^3$.

The surface area of a sphere $= 4\pi r^2$.

Sphere

The volume of a cylinder $= \pi r^2 h$.

The surface area of a cylinder $= 2rh + 2\pi r^2$.

Example – Using formulae

A cone has a radius of 7.5 cm and a height of 18 cm.

a Calculate the volume of the cone.

b Calculate the surface area of the cone.

Solution

a Volume $= \frac{1}{3}\pi r^2 h$

$= \frac{1}{3}\pi \times 7.5^2 \times 18$ ($r = 7.5$ and $h = 18$)

$= 1060 \, \text{cm}^3$ to the nearest cm^3

b By Pythagoras[3] theorem, $l^2 = r^2 + h^2$ ← [First find the slant height of the cone.]

$l^2 = 7.5^2 + 18^2 = 380.25$

$l = \sqrt{380.25} = 19.5 \, \text{cm}$

Surface area $= \pi r^2 + \pi r l$ ← [$r = 7.5$ and $l = 19.5$.]

$= \pi \times 7.5^2 + \pi \times 7.5 \times 19.5$

$= 636 \, \text{cm}^2$ ← [To the nearest cm^2.]

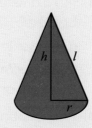

Example – Leaving π in the answer

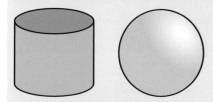

A cylinder has diameter 16 cm and height 16 cm.

A sphere has diameter 16 cm.

Which shape has the greater volume and by how much?

Give your answer in terms of π.

Solution

Volume of cylinder $= \pi r^2 h$ ← [Diameter is 16 cm so radius is 8 cm and height is 16 cm.]

$= \pi \times 8^2 \times 16$

$= 1024\pi$

Volume of sphere $= \frac{4}{3}\pi r^3$ ← [Diameter is 16 cm so radius is 8 cm.]

$= \frac{4}{3}\pi \times 8^3$

$= \frac{2048}{3}\pi$

The cylinder has a larger volume by $1024\pi - \frac{2048}{3}\pi$

$= \frac{3072 - 2048}{3}\pi$ ← [$1024\pi = \frac{3072}{3}\pi$]

$= \frac{1024}{3}\pi \, \text{cm}^3$

Practising skills

① A pyramid has a square base with sides of 11 cm.
Its vertical height is 15 cm.
Calculate the volume of the pyramid.

② A cone has a radius of 9 cm, a vertical height of 12 cm and a slant height of 15 cm.
Calculate

   a the volume

   b the surface area of the cone, including its base.
Give your answers correct to the nearest whole unit.

③ The diameter of a sphere is 25 cm.
Calculate

   a the volume

   b the surface area of the sphere.
Give your answers correct to the nearest whole unit.

④ A square-based pyramid has volume 147 cm^3 and height 9 cm.
Calculate the length of a side of the base.

⑤ Calculate

   a the volume

   b the surface area (including the base) of this shape.
Give your answers in terms of π.

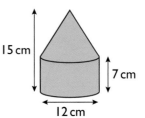

Developing fluency

① This is a solid wooden hemisphere.

The radius is 14 cm.
Calculate

   a the surface area

   b the volume.
Give your answers to the nearest whole unit.

② A cone has volume 784π cm^3 and height 12 cm.
Calculate the radius of the base.

Exam-style

③ A cone has radius 11 cm and slant height 28.6 cm
Calculate

  a the surface area

  b the volume.
Give your answers in terms of π.

④ A sphere has surface area 576π cm².
Calculate the volume of the sphere.
Give your answers in terms of π.

⑤ A cat's toy is made to look like a mouse.

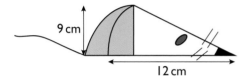

It is made of a quarter sphere with radius 9 cm and half a cone of radius 9 cm and
length 12 cm.
The underside is flat.
Calculate

  a the volume

  b the surface area of the toy.
Give your answers in terms of π.

⑥ A truncated cone has a base diameter of 30 cm and a top diameter of 24 cm.

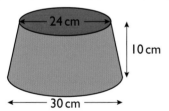

The height of the truncated cone is 10 cm.
Calculate the volume, giving your answer in terms of π.

⑦ A cone and a sphere have equal radii, r cm. The height of the cone is h cm.
The volume of the sphere is double the volume of the cone.

  a Show that $h = 2r$.

  b Show that the slant length, l cm, of the cone is given by $l = \sqrt{5}r$.

  c Show that the ratio of their surface areas is $4 : (1 + \sqrt{5})$.

Problem solving

① 71% of the Earth's surface is covered in water.

    a Treating the Earth as a sphere of radius 6371 km, work out an estimate for the area of the surface area of the Earth that is covered in water.

    b Is it possible to judge whether your answer to part **a** is an overestimate or an underestimate?

② An architect is considering these two designs, A and B, to cover a new arena.

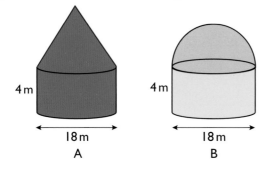

A   B

Each has a cylindrical base of diameter 18 m and height 4 m.

Design A has a conical roof of height 9 m.

The roof of design B is a hemisphere.

Work out how much more volume is enclosed by design B than by design A.

③ A cone fits into a hemisphere.

The base of the cone is also the base of the hemisphere.

The apex of the cone lies on the surface of the hemisphere.

    a Show that the volume of the hemisphere is twice the volume of the cone.

    b Show also that the ratio of the curved surface areas is $\sqrt{2}:1$.

④ Craig makes wedding cakes.

Here is a cake with 3 tiers.

Each tier is 10 cm high.

The diameter of tier 1 is 60 cm.

The diameter of tier 2 is 40 cm.

The diameter of tier 3 is 30 cm.

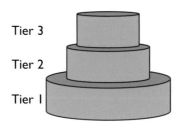

Tier 3

Tier 2

Tier 1

    a Work out the total volume of the cake.

The surfaces of the cake are covered in icing. This includes the complete tops of the tiers but not their underneath.

    b Work out the area of icing needed.

Exam-style

⑤ A factory makes hollow capsules.

Each capsule consists of two hemispherical ends and a central cylinder, with dimensions shown in the diagram.

The factory makes the capsules and then puts aspirin into 200 000 capsules each hour.

Each capsule is 80% full.

Work out the volume of aspirin required each hour. Give your answer in m³.

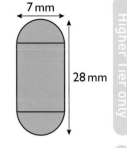

7 mm

28 mm

⑥ A factory makes steel ball bearings.

The steel is delivered to the factory in ingots.

Each ingot is a cylinder with a radius 12 cm and length 2 metres.

Each ball bearing is a sphere of diameter 1 cm.

Work out the number of ball bearings that can be made from 1 ingot of steel.

⑦ The diagram shows a pile of sand. It is a cone with base radius 5 m.

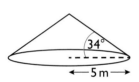

34°

5 m

Its angle of slope is 34°.

Work out the volume of sand in the pile.

Reviewing skills

① The diagram shows a square-based cuboid with a hemisphere stuck on the top. The dimensions are as shown.

The hemisphere just meets the edges of the cuboid.

Calculate the surface area of the shape giving your answer correct to the nearest cm².

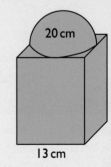

20 cm

13 cm

② A cone has a radius of 15 cm and a height of 20 cm.

Calculate

a the volume of the cone

b the surface area of the cone.

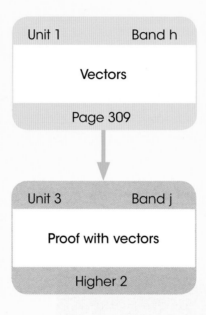

Unit 1 • Vectors • Band h

Outside the Maths classroom

Computer games

Why do computer game designers use vectors?

Toolbox

A **vecto**r is a quantity that has size (or magnitude) and direction.

A **translation** is a vector.

A vector can be described in 3 ways.

The vector from A to B can be written as

$\overrightarrow{AB}$ or **x** or $\begin{pmatrix} 3 \\ 1 \end{pmatrix}$.

Vectors can be added.

$\overrightarrow{AB} + \overrightarrow{BC} = \overrightarrow{AC}$

$\begin{pmatrix} 3 \\ 1 \end{pmatrix} + \begin{pmatrix} 5 \\ -2 \end{pmatrix} = \begin{pmatrix} 8 \\ -1 \end{pmatrix}$

Vectors can be subtracted.

$\overrightarrow{AB} - \overrightarrow{BC} = \overrightarrow{AD}$

$\begin{pmatrix} 3 \\ 1 \end{pmatrix} - \begin{pmatrix} 5 \\ -2 \end{pmatrix} = \begin{pmatrix} -2 \\ 3 \end{pmatrix}$

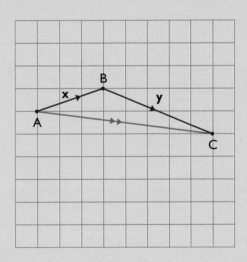

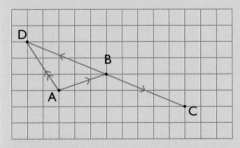

← As $\overrightarrow{BD}$ is the same as $-\overrightarrow{BC}$.

Vectors can be multiplied by a **scalar**. ← A scalar is a number with size but no direction.

$2\begin{pmatrix} 5 \\ -2 \end{pmatrix} = \begin{pmatrix} 10 \\ -4 \end{pmatrix}$

This gives a parallel vector, $\begin{pmatrix} 10 \\ -4 \end{pmatrix}$, which is twice as long and parallel to $\begin{pmatrix} 5 \\ -2 \end{pmatrix}$.

Example – Adding and subtracting vectors

$$\overrightarrow{AB} = \begin{pmatrix} 3 \\ 3 \end{pmatrix}, \overrightarrow{BC} = \begin{pmatrix} 4 \\ -2 \end{pmatrix}.$$

a Draw vectors representing $\overrightarrow{AB}$ and $\overrightarrow{BC}$ on a grid.

b Work out the column vector for $\overrightarrow{AB} + \overrightarrow{BC}$.
Draw the answer on a grid.

c Work out the column vector for $\overrightarrow{BC} - \overrightarrow{AB}$.
Draw the answer on a grid.

Solution

a

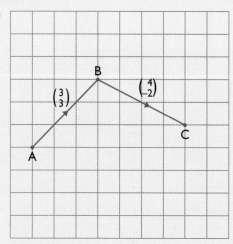

b $\overrightarrow{AB} + \overrightarrow{BC}$

$$= \begin{pmatrix} 3 \\ 3 \end{pmatrix} + \begin{pmatrix} 4 \\ -2 \end{pmatrix} = \begin{pmatrix} 7 \\ 1 \end{pmatrix}$$
 ⟵ | 3 + 4 = 7 and 3 + –2 = 1. |

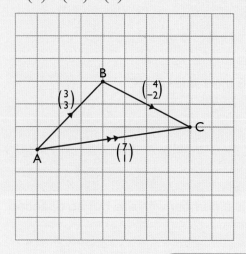

$\overrightarrow{AC} = \overrightarrow{AB} + \overrightarrow{BC}$ ⟵ | You can add vectors by drawing them end-to-end. |

c $\overrightarrow{BC} - \overrightarrow{AB}$

$= \begin{pmatrix} 4 \\ -2 \end{pmatrix} - \begin{pmatrix} 3 \\ 3 \end{pmatrix} = \begin{pmatrix} 1 \\ -5 \end{pmatrix}$ ← This is $\overrightarrow{BD}$ on the diagram.

← 4 – 3 = 1 and –2 – 3 = –5.

$\overrightarrow{CD} = -\overrightarrow{AB}$

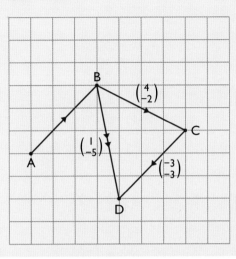

This is the same as BC + (–AB). ←

Example – Multiplying a vector by a scalar

The diagram shows the vector **b**.

a Write **b** and 3**b** as column vectors.

b Draw the vector 3**b** and describe its relationship to **b**.

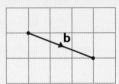

Solution

a $\mathbf{b} = \begin{pmatrix} 3 \\ -1 \end{pmatrix}$.

$3\mathbf{b} = 3 \begin{pmatrix} 3 \\ -1 \end{pmatrix} = \begin{pmatrix} 9 \\ -3 \end{pmatrix}$ ← Multiply both numbers in the vector by 3.

b The red vector.

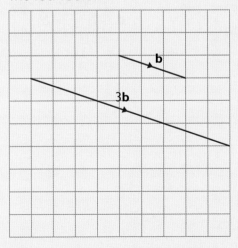

3**b** is three times the length of **b** and is parallel to it.

Notice that **b** and 3**b** can be drawn anywhere on the grid.

Practising skills

① Match the vectors on the grid with the column vectors.

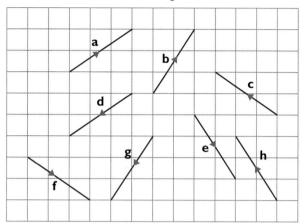

i $\begin{pmatrix} 3 \\ -2 \end{pmatrix}$ ii $\begin{pmatrix} 2 \\ 3 \end{pmatrix}$ iii $\begin{pmatrix} -3 \\ -2 \end{pmatrix}$ iv $\begin{pmatrix} -2 \\ 3 \end{pmatrix}$

v $\begin{pmatrix} -2 \\ -3 \end{pmatrix}$ vi $\begin{pmatrix} 3 \\ 2 \end{pmatrix}$ vii $\begin{pmatrix} 2 \\ -3 \end{pmatrix}$ viii $\begin{pmatrix} -3 \\ 2 \end{pmatrix}$

② Work out these vector additions. In each case draw a diagram on squared paper to show the vectors.

a $\begin{pmatrix} 4 \\ 2 \end{pmatrix} + \begin{pmatrix} 3 \\ 4 \end{pmatrix}$ b $\begin{pmatrix} 5 \\ -1 \end{pmatrix} + \begin{pmatrix} 2 \\ 3 \end{pmatrix}$ c $\begin{pmatrix} 4 \\ 2 \end{pmatrix} + \begin{pmatrix} 3 \\ -4 \end{pmatrix}$ d $\begin{pmatrix} 0 \\ -4 \end{pmatrix} + \begin{pmatrix} -3 \\ -7 \end{pmatrix}$

③ Work out these vector subtractions.

a $\begin{pmatrix} 4 \\ 6 \end{pmatrix} - \begin{pmatrix} 3 \\ 4 \end{pmatrix}$ b $\begin{pmatrix} 3 \\ -1 \end{pmatrix} - \begin{pmatrix} 2 \\ 3 \end{pmatrix}$ c $\begin{pmatrix} -2 \\ -3 \end{pmatrix} - \begin{pmatrix} -5 \\ 5 \end{pmatrix}$ d $\begin{pmatrix} 0 \\ -2 \end{pmatrix} - \begin{pmatrix} -3 \\ -4 \end{pmatrix}$

④ Work out these vectors.

a $3\begin{pmatrix} 2 \\ 3 \end{pmatrix}$ b $4\begin{pmatrix} 3 \\ -1 \end{pmatrix}$ c $4\begin{pmatrix} 2 \\ -3 \end{pmatrix} + 3\begin{pmatrix} -2 \\ 1 \end{pmatrix}$ d $-7\begin{pmatrix} 2 \\ -3 \end{pmatrix} - 3\begin{pmatrix} -2 \\ 4 \end{pmatrix}$

⑤ **a** Which vector is parallel to **d**?

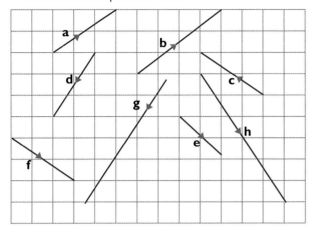

b Find another set of parallel vectors.

c Which vector is perpendicular to **a**?

⑥ Put these vectors into pairs of parallel vectors.

$\begin{pmatrix} 9 \\ 12 \end{pmatrix}$ $\begin{pmatrix} 6 \\ -8 \end{pmatrix}$ $\begin{pmatrix} 15 \\ 20 \end{pmatrix}$ $\begin{pmatrix} 2 \\ -3 \end{pmatrix}$ $\begin{pmatrix} -8 \\ -12 \end{pmatrix}$ $\begin{pmatrix} 8 \\ -12 \end{pmatrix}$ $\begin{pmatrix} 12 \\ -16 \end{pmatrix}$ $\begin{pmatrix} 10 \\ 15 \end{pmatrix}$

  A   B   C   D   E   F   G   H

Developing fluency

① Plot a path through this maze.

You can only move up, down or sideways, not diagonally.

You can only move onto squares with an answer of $\begin{pmatrix} 8 \\ 12 \end{pmatrix}$, $\begin{pmatrix} 4 \\ -6 \end{pmatrix}$, $\begin{pmatrix} 8 \\ -6 \end{pmatrix}$, or $\begin{pmatrix} -4 \\ 12 \end{pmatrix}$.

Record your path on an empty 6 × 6 grid.

START	$3\begin{pmatrix} 2 \\ 0 \end{pmatrix} - \begin{pmatrix} 2 \\ 12 \end{pmatrix}$	$\begin{pmatrix} -2 \\ 14 \end{pmatrix} - 2\begin{pmatrix} 1 \\ 2 \end{pmatrix}$	$\begin{pmatrix} -2 \\ 13 \end{pmatrix} + \begin{pmatrix} -2 \\ -1 \end{pmatrix}$	$\begin{pmatrix} 3 \\ 3 \end{pmatrix} - \begin{pmatrix} -5 \\ -9 \end{pmatrix}$	$\begin{pmatrix} -2 \\ 3 \end{pmatrix} + \begin{pmatrix} 6 \\ -3 \end{pmatrix}$
$4\begin{pmatrix} 2 \\ 3 \end{pmatrix}$	$-2\begin{pmatrix} -2 \\ -3 \end{pmatrix}$	$-2\begin{pmatrix} 2 \\ 3 \end{pmatrix} + \begin{pmatrix} 8 \\ 0 \end{pmatrix}$	$\begin{pmatrix} -2 \\ 3 \end{pmatrix} + 3\begin{pmatrix} 2 \\ 3 \end{pmatrix}$	$\begin{pmatrix} -1 \\ -7 \end{pmatrix} + \begin{pmatrix} 9 \\ 1 \end{pmatrix}$	$6\begin{pmatrix} 2 \\ 0 \end{pmatrix} - \begin{pmatrix} 4 \\ 6 \end{pmatrix}$
$\begin{pmatrix} 3 \\ -1 \end{pmatrix} - \begin{pmatrix} -1 \\ 5 \end{pmatrix}$	$\begin{pmatrix} -1 \\ -2 \end{pmatrix} + \begin{pmatrix} 9 \\ 4 \end{pmatrix}$	$\begin{pmatrix} -4 \\ 2 \end{pmatrix} + \begin{pmatrix} 12 \\ -8 \end{pmatrix}$	$-4\begin{pmatrix} 2 \\ -3 \end{pmatrix}$	$\begin{pmatrix} -2 \\ 10 \end{pmatrix} - 2\begin{pmatrix} 1 \\ 1 \end{pmatrix}$	$-4\begin{pmatrix} 1 \\ -3 \end{pmatrix}$
$\begin{pmatrix} -4 \\ 7 \end{pmatrix} + \begin{pmatrix} 0 \\ 5 \end{pmatrix}$	$2\begin{pmatrix} 2 \\ 3 \end{pmatrix} + \begin{pmatrix} 4 \\ 0 \end{pmatrix}$	$\begin{pmatrix} -2 \\ -3 \end{pmatrix} + \begin{pmatrix} 6 \\ -3 \end{pmatrix}$	$\begin{pmatrix} -3 \\ -3 \end{pmatrix} - \begin{pmatrix} -7 \\ 3 \end{pmatrix}$	$3\begin{pmatrix} 2 \\ 3 \end{pmatrix} + \begin{pmatrix} -2 \\ 3 \end{pmatrix}$	$5\begin{pmatrix} 2 \\ 3 \end{pmatrix} + \begin{pmatrix} -2 \\ -3 \end{pmatrix}$
$3\begin{pmatrix} -2 \\ 3 \end{pmatrix} + \begin{pmatrix} 2 \\ 3 \end{pmatrix}$	$7\begin{pmatrix} 2 \\ 3 \end{pmatrix} - 3\begin{pmatrix} 2 \\ 3 \end{pmatrix}$	$3\begin{pmatrix} -2 \\ -3 \end{pmatrix} + \begin{pmatrix} 2 \\ 3 \end{pmatrix}$	$4\begin{pmatrix} -1 \\ 3 \end{pmatrix}$	$4\begin{pmatrix} 2 \\ 0 \end{pmatrix} + \begin{pmatrix} 4 \\ -6 \end{pmatrix}$	$\begin{pmatrix} -1 \\ -2 \end{pmatrix} - \begin{pmatrix} -5 \\ 4 \end{pmatrix}$
$\begin{pmatrix} -1 \\ -7 \end{pmatrix} + \begin{pmatrix} 9 \\ -1 \end{pmatrix}$	$\begin{pmatrix} 5 \\ -2 \end{pmatrix} - \begin{pmatrix} -3 \\ 4 \end{pmatrix}$	$-2\begin{pmatrix} -2 \\ 3 \end{pmatrix}$	$\begin{pmatrix} 2 \\ 3 \end{pmatrix} + 3\begin{pmatrix} 2 \\ -3 \end{pmatrix}$	$\begin{pmatrix} -1 \\ -2 \end{pmatrix} + \begin{pmatrix} 9 \\ 8 \end{pmatrix}$	**FINISH**

Reasoning

② $\mathbf{a} = \begin{pmatrix} 2 \\ 3 \end{pmatrix}$, $\mathbf{b} = \begin{pmatrix} 4 \\ -1 \end{pmatrix}$, $\mathbf{c} = \begin{pmatrix} 1 \\ 5 \end{pmatrix}$, and $\mathbf{d} = \begin{pmatrix} -3 \\ -2 \end{pmatrix}$

   a Calculate these as column vectors

     i 2**a**　　　　**ii** **a** + **c**　　　**iii** **b** − **d**

     iv 2**b** − **a**　　　**v** 3**b** − 2**d**　　**vi** **a** − **b** + **c** − **d**

   b Show that 3**a** − **b** is parallel to **c**.

③ A and B are hikers. They start together at the origin, O, on their map.

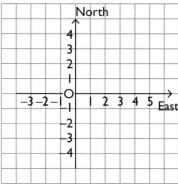

Units are in kilometres

   During the morning, A moves through $\begin{pmatrix} 4 \\ 2 \end{pmatrix}$ and B moves through $\begin{pmatrix} -2 \\ 3 \end{pmatrix}$.

   a Mark their positions on the map.

   They have agreed to meet in the afternoon at the point $\begin{pmatrix} 0 \\ -4 \end{pmatrix}$.

   b Mark their afternoon journeys on the map and write them as column vectors.

   c Who has the longer journey in the afternoon?

④ A shape is translated through $\begin{pmatrix} 1 \\ -5 \end{pmatrix}$.

   It is then translated from its new position through $\begin{pmatrix} 2 \\ 3 \end{pmatrix}$.

   What translation will return the shape to its original position?

⑤ Find the value of the letters in these equations.

   a $\begin{pmatrix} 2 \\ 3 \end{pmatrix} + \begin{pmatrix} a \\ b \end{pmatrix} = \begin{pmatrix} 1 \\ -5 \end{pmatrix}$　　　　　　　　**b** $2\begin{pmatrix} 2 \\ -1 \end{pmatrix} - \begin{pmatrix} c \\ 3 \end{pmatrix} = \begin{pmatrix} 3 \\ d \end{pmatrix}$

   c $4\begin{pmatrix} e \\ -3 \end{pmatrix} + 3\begin{pmatrix} -1 \\ f \end{pmatrix} = \begin{pmatrix} 5 \\ -3 \end{pmatrix}$　　　　**d** $g\begin{pmatrix} 4 \\ -2 \end{pmatrix} - 3\begin{pmatrix} 2 \\ h \end{pmatrix} = \begin{pmatrix} -14 \\ 13 \end{pmatrix}$

⑥ Ben is at an adventure playground.

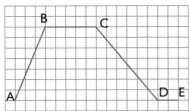

Scale: 1 square = 0.5 m

He climbs a ladder (AB), walks along a balance beam ($\overrightarrow{BC}$) and then goes down a slide ($\overrightarrow{CD}$ and $\overrightarrow{DE}$).

a Write down a vector for each part of Ben's journey.

b i Work out $\overrightarrow{AB} + \overrightarrow{BC} + \overrightarrow{CD} + \overrightarrow{DE}$.

   ii Write down the vector $\overrightarrow{AE}$. What do you notice?

There is a larger slide at the playground, OPQRS.
The sloping part of the slide, QR, is parallel to CD.
QR is 4 times as long as CD.
The horizontal section of the slide, RS, is 3 times as long as DE.

c i Write down the two vectors, $\overrightarrow{QR}$ and $\overrightarrow{SR}$, to describe Ben's journey down this slide.

   ii Write down a single vector $\overrightarrow{QS}$ to describe Ben's journey from the top of the slide to the end.

d i Given that $\overrightarrow{PQ} = \begin{pmatrix} 4 \\ 0 \end{pmatrix}$ and $\overrightarrow{OS} = \begin{pmatrix} 48 \\ 0 \end{pmatrix}$ find a vector for the ladder $\overrightarrow{OP}$.

   ii Are the ladders AB and OP parallel?

       Explain how you know.

⑦ Carla is playing a game on her phone.

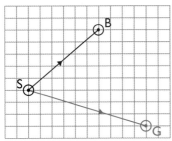

She needs to fire each ball from the Start, S, into the correct hole.

a Write down a vector to show the trajectory of a

   i blue ball, $\overrightarrow{SB}$

   ii green ball, $\overrightarrow{SG}$

Carla accidentally fires a blue ball into the green hole.
She has to fire the blue ball from the green hole to the blue hole.

b Write down a vector for

   i $\overrightarrow{GB}$ **ii** $\overrightarrow{SB} - \overrightarrow{SG}$ **iii** $\overrightarrow{GS} + \overrightarrow{SB}$

   What do you notice about your answers?

A red hole, R, is exactly halfway between the blue and green holes.

c Write down a vector for

   i $\frac{1}{2}\overrightarrow{GB}$ **ii** $\overrightarrow{SG} + \frac{1}{2}\overrightarrow{GB}$ **iii** $\overrightarrow{GR}$

   What do you notice about your answers?

Problem solving

① The diagram shows five places A, B, C, D and O on a map.

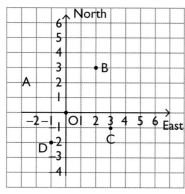

The scale is 1 unit = 1 kilometre.

Ali walks from A to B, then to C, then to D and then back to A.

a Write down translation vectors for the four legs of Ali's journey: $\overrightarrow{AB}$, $\overrightarrow{BC}$, $\overrightarrow{CD}$ and $\overrightarrow{DA}$.

b Work out $\overrightarrow{AB} + \overrightarrow{BC} + \overrightarrow{CD} + \overrightarrow{DA}$.

Explain your answer.

c What shape is ABCD?

How do you know this from the four vectors?

② Alfie starts walking from a point O.

He walks to a point P where the translation vector from O to P is $\begin{pmatrix} 3 \\ 4 \end{pmatrix}$ in kilometres.

He then turns and walks to a point Q where the translation vector from P to Q is $\begin{pmatrix} 1 \\ -7 \end{pmatrix}$.

a Draw a diagram on a grid to show this situation.

b Alfie then walks from Q to O.

Show this journey on your diagram and describe it as a translation vector.

c Find the lengths of the three legs of Alfie's journey.

③ On this diagram $\overrightarrow{OA}$ and $\overrightarrow{OB}$ represent the vectors **a** and **b**.

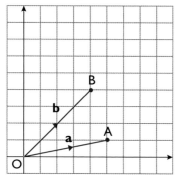

Copy the diagram, then draw these vectors.

    i $\overrightarrow{OC}$ where **c** = **a** + **b**   **ii** $\overrightarrow{OD}$ where **d** = 2**a** + **b**

    iii $\overrightarrow{OE}$ where **e** = −**a** − **b**   **iv** $\overrightarrow{OF}$ where **f** = **a** − **b**.

4 $\mathbf{p} = \begin{pmatrix} 1 \\ 1 \end{pmatrix}$, $\mathbf{q} = \begin{pmatrix} 1 \\ -1 \end{pmatrix}$ are vectors representing two translations.

a Work out $\mathbf{p} + \mathbf{q}$ and $\mathbf{p} - \mathbf{q}$.

b Find the combination of the vectors $\mathbf{p}$ and $\mathbf{q}$ that gives a translation of

i $\begin{pmatrix} 6 \\ 0 \end{pmatrix}$ **ii** $\begin{pmatrix} 3 \\ 4 \end{pmatrix}$ **iii** $\begin{pmatrix} -3 \\ -4 \end{pmatrix}$

5 $\mathbf{p}$ and $\mathbf{q}$ are translations.

$\mathbf{p} = \begin{pmatrix} 2 \\ 1 \end{pmatrix}$, $\mathbf{q} = \begin{pmatrix} 1 \\ -2 \end{pmatrix}$

a Find a combination of $\mathbf{p}$ and $\mathbf{q}$ that gives a translation

i parallel to the y axis

ii parallel to the x axis.

b Find a combination of $\mathbf{p}$ and $\mathbf{q}$ that gives a translation $\begin{pmatrix} 20 \\ 15 \end{pmatrix}$.

6 $\mathbf{p} = \begin{pmatrix} 2 \\ -1 \end{pmatrix}$, $\mathbf{q} = \begin{pmatrix} 1 \\ 1 \end{pmatrix}$

a Work out $\mathbf{p} + \mathbf{q}$ and $2\mathbf{q} - \mathbf{p}$.

b Deduce values of n and m for which $n\mathbf{p} + m\mathbf{q}$ is equal to the vector $\begin{pmatrix} 3 \\ 6 \end{pmatrix}$.

Reviewing skills

1 Work out these vector additions. In each case draw a diagram on squared paper.

a $\begin{pmatrix} 2 \\ 6 \end{pmatrix} + \begin{pmatrix} -3 \\ 2 \end{pmatrix}$ **b** $\begin{pmatrix} -4 \\ -3 \end{pmatrix} + \begin{pmatrix} -5 \\ 2 \end{pmatrix}$

2 Work out each of the following.

a $\begin{pmatrix} 1 \\ 2 \end{pmatrix} - \begin{pmatrix} 3 \\ -4 \end{pmatrix}$ **b** $\begin{pmatrix} -3 \\ -3 \end{pmatrix} - \begin{pmatrix} -3 \\ 2 \end{pmatrix}$ **c** $-2\begin{pmatrix} 3 \\ -4 \end{pmatrix}$ **d** $3\begin{pmatrix} -3 \\ 1 \end{pmatrix} + \begin{pmatrix} 3 \\ 2 \end{pmatrix}$

Strand 1 Statistical measures

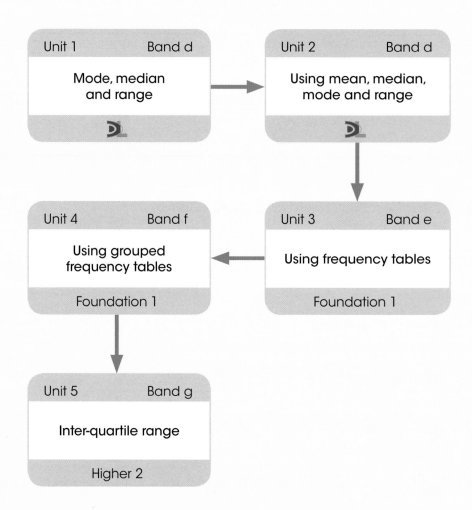

Units 1–4 are assumed knowledge for this book. The skills are reviewed and extended in the Moving on section on page 319.

Knowledge and skills from these units are used within other Strands in this book.

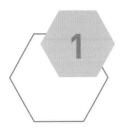

1 Here are the marks for 18 teams at a sports club quiz night. Nine teams consisted of tennis players and nine teams consisted of football players.

    Football: 35, 32, 12, 55, 32, 60, 40, 35, 32.

    Tennis: 60, 15, 80, 45, 16, 85, 40, 77, 36.

Compare the scores of the football team and tennis team.

2 A score from 0 to 20 is given in each round of a TV quiz show.

Here are the marks one team obtains in the first five rounds.

16	17	12	13	17

There are two more rounds.

Work out the smallest possible value that the median could be for all seven rounds.

3 John plays basketball. His current team play in red.

He has been asked to join a team that play in blue.

The table shows the scores of each of the current players in both teams when taking 10 attempts to score a basket.

    Red team: 1, 3, 5, 9, 2.

    Blue team: 3, 3, 4, 5, 5.

  a Which team is better at scoring? Explain your answer.

  b John is the player in the red team who scored 5 baskets. Based on these scores, would you recommend that John changes teams? Explain why.

  c What other information might John wish to know before making a decision?

4 Katherine has a clothes shop.

She records the numbers of dresses she sold each month last year.

Month	Jan	Feb	Mar	Apr	May	June	July	Aug	Sept	Oct	Nov	Dec
Number of dresses sold	12	15	13	16	17	15	17	18	15	16	18	20

Katherine wants to compare the number of dresses sold last year with this year to see whether her sales are increasing.

Katherine decides to use the mean.

  a Calculate the mean number of dresses Katherine sold last year.

  b Is this the best average to use? You must explain your answer.

5 The mean mass of ten adults is 76 kg.

Another adult joins the group. Their mean mass is now 78 kg.

What is the mass of the adult who joins the group?

⑥ A fish breeder is testing two new types of food.

Two hatchings of baby fish are fed the different foods.

After two months the masses of the baby fish are measured, to the nearest 0.1 gram.

Batch A

0.9	1.2	1.3	2.2	0.9	1.3	1.2	0.9	1.6
1.5	2.2	2.1	1.9	2.8	1.4	1.8	2.0	1.7
2.2	1.7	1.2	1.2	1.5	2.6			

Batch B

2.5	1.4	0.3	3.5	1.2	1.5	2.2	1.4	2.4
1.9	2.4	1.9	1.8	2.9	3.1	1.6	0.2	1.2
3.6	1.4	0.6	0.5	2.2				

Which fish food do you think is more effective? Give a reason for your answer.

⑦ A council is considering new parking restrictions. One day they record the length of time that cars are parked in five parking bays.

Length of time (mins)	10 or less	11–30	31–60	61–120	121+
Number of cars	20	7	15	11	4

a Calculate the mean time that cars parked in these bays.

b Say whether you think the mean is representative of the data, giving your reasons.

Higher tier only

Strand 2 Draw and interpret statistical diagrams

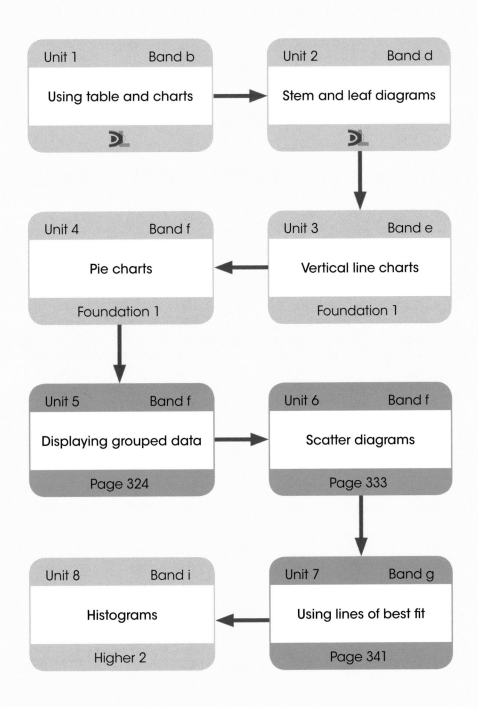

Unit 1 Band b	Unit 2 Band d
Using table and charts	**Stem and leaf diagrams**

Unit 4 Band f	Unit 3 Band e
Pie charts	**Vertical line charts**
Foundation 1	Foundation 1

Unit 5 Band f	Unit 6 Band f
Displaying grouped data	**Scatter diagrams**
Page 324	Page 333

Unit 8 Band i	Unit 7 Band g
Histograms	**Using lines of best fit**
Higher 2	Page 341

Units 1–4 are assumed knowledge for this book. They are reviewed and extended in the Moving on section on page 322.

Units 1–4 • Moving on

① Look at this graph.

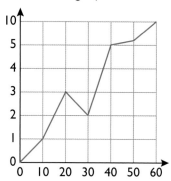

Give two reasons why the graph is misleading.

② Emily collects the ages of 60 people taking their driving test over one week at the local test centre.

> 40, 24, 32, 17, 18, 21, 29, 18, 39, 17, 20, 30, 17, 19, 17, 18, 21, 30, 46,
> 17, 26, 19, 17, 21, 18, 19, 28, 18, 21, 37, 19, 31, 40, 18, 21, 18, 25, 18,
> 40, 18, 33, 18, 21, 18, 44, 19, 21, 19, 19, 25, 19, 20, 21, 22, 23, 27, 30,
> 31, 39, 50

a Draw a stem-and-leaf diagram for this data set.

b Why aren't any of the ages less than 17?

c What is the modal age? Why do you think this might be?

d What do you notice about the shape of your stem-and-leaf diagram? Explain your answer.

e What percentage of people who took their test were over 20?

③ This graph shows the temperature at 3 p.m. in degrees centigrade, for ten days in August in Sudbury.

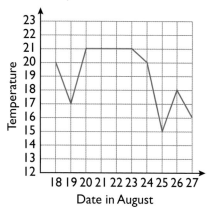

a Describe what is wrong with the graph.

b Use the graph to predict the temperature on 28 August. Give a reason why your prediction may be wrong.

④ A branch of a bank records the number of new accounts it opens each week over a two-month period.

Week	1	2	3	4	5	6	7	8	9
Number of accounts	10	7	15	6	8	2	3	12	9

    a In which week did they open the fewest accounts?

    b Draw a vertical line chart to show the number of accounts opened each month.

    c The branch manager joins the tops of the vertical lines to make it easier to see any trends. Explain to the manager why this is wrong.

⑤ A paperback publisher carries out a survey in a busy high street about reading habits.
One of the questions asks where people buy their paperbacks.
Here are the results.

In a book shop	16
Purchase online	45
Download electronic versions to a tablet	33
Second-hand purchase	17
Have a free source	3
Don't read paperbacks	8
Other	2

    a Draw a pie chart to illustrate the data.

    b What percentage of those surveyed do not buy physical copies of paperbacks?

    c The publisher has a small budget to market a new title being published next month. Where do you think they should advertise? Explain why.

⑥ George works for a group of health and fitness clubs.
He wants to compare the ages of the club members at two different clubs.

Club A					
36	32	55	28	31	36
32	27	33	40	21	29
45	51	60	38	43	25
41	41	35	31	38	41
57	45	29	51	37	32
37					

Club B					
35	22	48	51	43	37
34	56	62	43	35	26
34	72	51	30	43	29
23	48	52	44	38	32
41	22	43	38	53	27
26					

    a Display this information in a back-to-back ordered stem-and-leaf diagram.

    b George thinks that Club B has a better mix of age ranges. Is he correct? You must explain your answer.

    c George also thinks that most people who use Club A are in their 30s. Is this true? Explain your answer.

Unit 5 • Displaying grouped data • Band f

Outside the Maths classroom

Investigating population trends

When a government looks at trends within a population the data it uses is usually grouped.

What are the advantages of grouping data for display?

Toolbox

How many pets have you got?

0	2	3	0	1
4	2	0	1	6
5	0	3	2	2
1	0	0	3	4
2	4	3	1	1

14 s	13.5 s	20 s	16.7 s	14.96 s
15 s	19 s	16.75 s	14.8 s	17.63 s
13.9 s	17.2 s	18 s	21 s	15.87 s
18.2 s	17.3 s	20 s	14.24 s	13.1s
16 s	18.12s	14 s	16.4 s	17s

Coley times his classmates running 100 m.

Ava's data are **discrete**. Each value must be a whole number. You cannot own 4.2 pets!

Coley's data values are **continuous**. Any sensible value is possible. The time taken to complete 100 metres could be 14 seconds, 15.2 seconds or 13.98 seconds.

You can group both types of data in a frequency table.

A time of 14 seconds is included in the group $14 \leqslant t < 16$.

This frequency diagram shows the data in the table.

Time, t seconds	Frequency
$12 \leqslant t < 14$	3
$14 \leqslant t < 16$	7
$16 \leqslant t < 18$	8
$18 \leqslant t < 20$	4
$20 \leqslant t < 22$	3

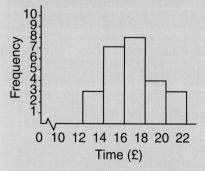

Use a jagged line to show the scale on an axis that does not start at zero. Sometimes just one axis has a broken scale, sometimes it is both. A broken scale can make it easier to plot a graph but it can also mislead you occasionally.

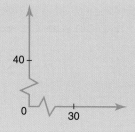

Example – Plotting a frequency diagram

Alex and Emily measured heights, h m, of girls in their athletics club.

1.45	1.57	1.60	1.48	1.60	1.77	1.56	1.55	1.66	1.66
1.70	1.62	1.60	1.42	1.52	1.55	1.59	1.72	1.52	1.62
1.80	1.52	1.75	1.55	1.70	1.63	1.44	1.73	1.50	1.54
1.36	1.62	1.54	1.64	1.55	1.82	1.47	1.68	1.55	1.70
1.60	1.75	1.63	1.75	1.44	1.60	1.60	1.42	1.58	1.80

a Display this information in a grouped frequency table.
b Use your grouped frequency table to plot a frequency diagram.
c Describe the distribution of the data.

Solution

a

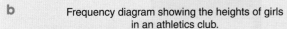

Height, h m	Frequency
$1.30 \leqslant h < 1.40$	1
$1.40 \leqslant h < 1.50$	7
$1.50 \leqslant h < 1.60$	15
$1.60 \leqslant h < 1.70$	15
$1.70 \leqslant h < 1.80$	9
$1.80 \leqslant h < 1.90$	3

b

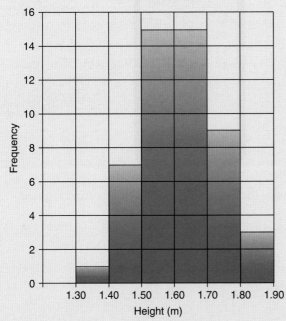

Frequency diagram showing the heights of girls in an athletics club.

c Most of the girls are between 1.5 and 1.7 m tall. A few are shorter than this and some are taller.

Practising skills

① State whether each type of data is discrete or continuous.

    a   **i**   The number of cars passing a camera on a motorway.

        ii   The speed of cars passing the camera on a motorway.

       iii   The numbers of people in the cars.

       iv   The numbers on the cars' registration plates.

    b   **i**   The number of passengers on an aeroplane.

        ii   The masses of the passengers.

       iii   The average age of the passengers.

       iv   How long the aeroplane flight lasts.

② Pam wants to investigate the heights, in cm, of rushes beside a river.
These are her ideas for the class intervals on her data collection sheet.

Option A	**Option B**
$140 \leqslant \text{height} \leqslant 150$	$140 < \text{height} < 150$
$150 \leqslant \text{height} \leqslant 160$	$150 < \text{height} < 160$
Option C	**Option D**
$140 - 150$	$140 \leqslant \text{height} < 150$
$150 - 160$	$150 < \text{height} \leqslant 160$

Criticise these suggestions and write a better one.

③ Trevor has recorded the masses of some people.
Here are the results, in kg.

    a   Copy and complete the tally chart.

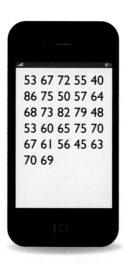

53 67 72 55 40
86 75 50 57 64
68 73 82 79 48
53 60 65 75 70
67 61 56 45 63
70 69

Mass, w kg	Tally	Frequency
$40 \leqslant w < 50$		
$50 \leqslant w < 60$		
$60 \leqslant w < 70$		
$70 \leqslant w < 80$		
$80 \leqslant w < 90$		

    b   Which class has the highest frequency?

    c   Draw a frequency diagram to show Trevor's data.

    d   Which shows the data most clearly, the tally chart, the frequency diagram or the original information?

④ These are the numbers of people visiting a gym on each of 21 days.

23, 45, 31, 37, 63, 54, 36, 64, 60, 49, 50, 32, 45, 40, 38, 37,
41, 53, 71, 57, 62

a Copy and complete the tally chart.

Number attending, n	Tally	Frequency
$20 \leqslant n < 30$		
$30 \leqslant n < 40$		
$40 \leqslant n < 50$		
$50 \leqslant n < 60$		
$60 \leqslant n < 70$		
$70 \leqslant n < 80$		

b Which is the modal class?

c On how many days did fewer than 40 people attend?

d What can you say about the numbers of people who went to the gym over this period?

Developing fluency

① Sally records the reaction times for a group of people.
Here are her results, in seconds.

0.34	0.56	0.72	0.20	0.65	0.57	0.36	0.43
0.81	0.73	0.27	0.30	0.52	0.48	0.61	0.59
0.28	0.28	0.44	0.62	0.64	0.50	0.28	0.33
0.58	0.46	0.44	0.51	0.26	0.38		

a Make a grouped frequency table using class intervals $0.20 \leqslant n < 0.30$,
   $0.30 \leqslant n < 0.40$, and so on.

b Draw a frequency diagram to show the data.

c What percentage of the group have a reaction time of less than 0.30 seconds?

d Describe the shape of the distribution.

2 Henry plays a computer game and keeps a record of his scores.

    a Make a grouped frequency table using class intervals
$20 \leqslant n < 30$,
$30 \leqslant n < 40$, and so on.

    b Draw a frequency diagram to show the data.

    c What is the median? What is the easiest way to find it?

    d Describe the shape of the distribution. Is it easier to use the original data or the grouped data?

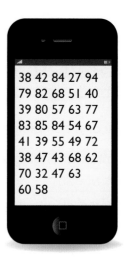

38 42 84 27 94
79 82 68 51 40
39 80 57 63 77
83 85 84 54 67
41 39 55 49 72
38 47 43 68 62
70 32 47 63
60 58

3 Here are the lengths of the tails of a group of rats, in mm.

156	184	157	173	165	180	191	186
169	170	173	153	147	168	154	166
182	145	153	160	152	185	159	166
155	176	158	153	147	172		

    a Make a grouped frequency table. Choose your own class intervals.

    b Draw a frequency diagram to show the data.

    c How many of the rats have tails longer than 169 mm?

    d Which of your groups is the modal group?

4 Sam recorded the ages of people using the local swimming pool. His results are in this frequency diagram.

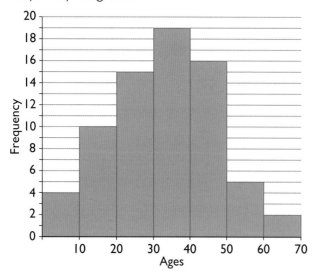

    a How many people in the survey were aged 40 to 60?

    b Make and complete a frequency table for the data.

    c Explain why it is likely that this survey was taken in the evening.

    d Sketch a frequency diagram to show what it might look like if the survey was taken in the day time.

Exam-style

Exam-style

⑤ The junior members of a cricket club record how long they can stay underwater, t seconds.

Boys	24	15	21	18	9	0	45	33	54	31	7	25	27	31	30	24	42
Girls	48	36	24	16	42	50	44	28	30	20	16	35	42	52	34		

a Make grouped tally charts to show
  i the boys' data
  ii the girls' data.
  Use the groups $0 \leqslant t < 10$, $10 \leqslant t < 20$, and so on.

b Find the medians for boys and for girls.

c Draw separate frequency diagrams for the boys and the girls.

d Who can stay underwater longer, boys or girls? Explain your answer.

⑥ Gok is collecting data about the heights of adult men and women for a clothing company.
He records the data in a back-to-back stem-and-leaf diagram.

Men		Women
	13	9
	14	3 8
9 6 4	15	1 2 6 7 7
9 9 8 8 7 6 5 5 3 3 2 2 1	16	0 0 1 1 2 2 3 3 4 4 4 5 5 5 5 5 6 6 7 7 7 8 8 9 9
9 9 8 8 8 7 7 6 6 5 5 4 4 4 3 3 3 3 2 2 0 0	17	0 0 0 1 1 2 3 4 4 5 5 6 7 9
8 6 5 5 4 4 2 2 1 0 0	18	0 1 5
4 1	19	

Key: 3|16|1 means a man of height 163 cm and a women of height 161 cm

a How many men and women did Gok survey?

b Find the modal height for
  i men
  ii women.

c State the modal class for
  i men
  ii women.

d Draw frequency diagrams with 5 cm intervals for the men's and women's heights.

e Use your frequency diagram to give the modal class for
  i men
  ii women.

f Which representation is more useful for the clothing company?

⑦ Explain whether you think the following variables should be treated as discrete or continuous.

a The numbers of hairs on human heads.

b People's ages.

c The world's population.

Problem solving

(1) In an investigation, each of the 30 students in a biology class counts the number of poppies in a different patch of a meadow. All the patches have the same area.

Pat records their results as follows.

72	67	47	65	55	52
58	15	74	69	66	31
22	91	48	84	82	73
150	71	33	44	65	15
52	50	64	49	88	76

a One of the values is an outlier. Which one is it?

Give one reason why the students might exclude it and one reason why they might accept it.

Boris says the figure was his and it should have been 15. So they change it to 15.

b Make a grouped frequency table, using intervals of class width 10, starting at 0.

c Draw the frequency diagram.

d Find the mode and the median of the data. Which of them is more representative of the data? What about the modal class?

e The meadow is said to be "in good heart" where there are 60 or more poppies per patch. Estimate the percentage of the meadow that is "in good heart".

(2) Zubert is a diver. He holds a competition to find out how far his friends can swim underwater without taking a breath.

He records the results in a frequency table.

Distance, metres		Frequency
At least	Less than	
0	10	2
10	20	11
20	30	4
30	40	2
40	50	1

a Display this information as a frequency diagram.

b Describe the distribution.

c Calculate the percentage of people in the modal group.

Zubert shows his friends some techniques and then tests them again.

This is the frequency diagram now.

d Describe the effect that Zubert's teaching has had.

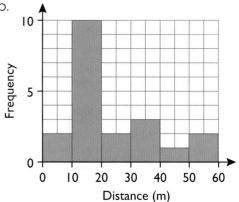

3 It can be very difficult to tell whether a newly hatched chicken is male or female.

Owen keeps a particular rare breed of chicken and he does an experiment to see if newly hatched cockerels are heavier than newly hatched hens. He weighs and marks newly hatched chickens and then records whether each one turns out to be a cockerel or a hen.

Owen's measurements are summarised in this table.

a Draw frequency diagrams for females and males.

b Say what your diagrams show you.

Owen says, 'As a rule of thumb, any chick under 45 grams will turn into a hen and any chick over 45 g will turn into a cockerel.'

c Estimate the percentages of

i female chicks that Owen would judge to be male

ii chicks overall that he would be right about.

Mass, m g	Female	Male
$25 \leqslant m < 30$	1	0
$30 \leqslant m < 35$	6	0
$35 \leqslant m < 40$	18	2
$40 \leqslant m < 45$	23	10
$45 \leqslant m < 50$	7	27
$50 \leqslant m < 55$	3	26
$55 \leqslant m < 60$	2	13
$60 \leqslant m < 65$	0	2
Total	**60**	**80**

4 Poppy asks her school friends to record how many minutes they spend playing computer games during one week in February.

Here are her results.

25	150	485	30	525	537	55	370	520	60
540	490	76	500	66	140	40	170	74	130
45	125	350	220	472	143	0	90	96	132
477	185	89	167	68	515	160	82	50	468

a Display the data in a grouped frequency table.

b Draw a frequency diagram to show this information.

c Describe the distribution. What does it tell you about the way Poppy's friends spend their time?

d Poppy plans to ask the same question in August. Predict the shape of the new diagram.

5 Stephen and his sister Anna share a computer.

Stephen and Anna each keep a record of the length of time, in minutes, that they use the computer each day for one month.

Stephen
35 84 66 47 94 77 63 58 42
55 62 74 46 43 28 67 40 51
58 64 45 72 53 46 68 62 53
25 38 46 69

ANNA
38 0 0 64 95 22 83 0 10
53 76 104 86 17 0 47 23 76
64 93 81 23 0 32 95 84 52
0 0 86 115

a Compare the distributions of the length of time Stephen and the length of time Anna use the computer this month.

b Stephen and Anna want their parents to buy them a second computer. They say, 'We often have to stay up late to do our work on the computer.' Comment on what they say.

Reviewing skills

① The frequency diagram shows the masses of cats taken into a vet's surgery one week.

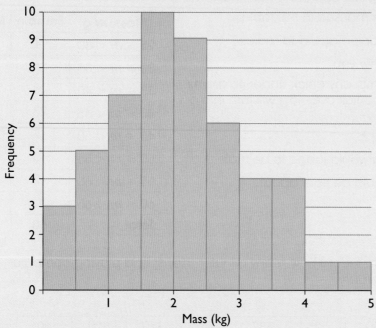

a Tabby weighs 832 g. Which group is she in?

b Which is the modal group?

c Make and complete a grouped frequency chart for these data.

d How many cats were taken in to see the vet that week?

Unit 6 • Scatter diagrams • Band f

Outside the Maths classroom

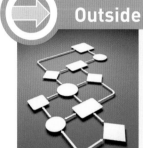

Looking for links

A statistician says, 'Correlation does not imply causation.'

What does this mean?

Toolbox

Scatter diagrams are used to investigate possible relationships between two variables affecting the same data (called bivariate data).

You do not join up the points on a scatter diagram.
If the variables increase together there is **positive correlation**.
If one variable decreases when the other increases there is **negative correlation**.
If there is **correlation** between the variables, you can draw a **line of best fit** through the points.
This is a straight line that best represents the data.

The word 'correlation' describes the relationship between the values of the two variables.

Positive correlation	Negative correlation	No correlation

Example – Plotting a scatter diagram

Matthew and Aneesa are having an argument.

I think that people with long legs can jump further than people with short legs.

*Rubbish!
The length of a person's legs does not affect how far they can jump.*

They decide to collect data from their friends to find out who is right.

	Alan	Barry	Claire	Dipak	Ernie	Flora	Gurance	Habib	Ivan
Inside leg measurement (cm)	60	70	50	65	65	70	55	75	60
Standing jump distance (cm)	85	90	65	90	80	100	80	95	70

a Draw a scatter diagram.

b i Describe the correlation in the scatter diagram for Matthew's and Aneesa's data.

ii Does the scatter diagram support Matthew or Aneesa?

c i Draw a line of best fit.

Jemima has an inside leg measurement of 70 cm.

ii Use your graph to estimate what distance she is likely to jump.

d Have they got enough data to be certain about their findings?

Solution

a

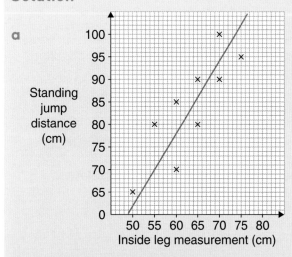

b i The graph shows positive correlation: as the inside leg measurement increases, so does the distance jumped.

ii This supports Matthew's claim.

c i A line of best fit is drawn on the graph.
The line of best fit leaves an even distribution of points on either side of the line.
The line of best fit may go through some points or none at all.

ii From the graph we can see that Jemima should jump about 93 cm.

d They do not have enough data to be certain. More points on the graph would help.

Practising skills

① Give a description of the correlation shown in each of these scatter diagrams.

② A number of people go on a hiking trip. The scatter graph shows the distances some of them walked in one day and the loads they carried.

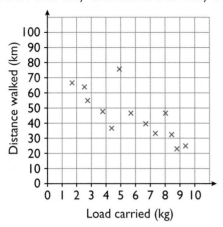

a Describe the correlation shown in the diagram.

b Copy the diagram and draw the line of best fit.

c Use the line of best fit to estimate the distance walked by someone with a 6 kg load.

d Use the line of best fit to estimate the load carried by someone who walked 70 km.

③ A car salesman draws three scatter graphs to show information about the cars on his forecourt. The axes on the scatter graphs have no labels.

i   ii   iii

a How many cars does the salesman have on his forecourt?

b From the box below, choose an appropriate label for each axis.

> Age of car (years).
> Length of car (m).
> Petrol tank capacity (litres).
> Mileage (1000s of miles.)
> Mass of car (kg.)
> Value of car (£).

c Describe the correlation for each scatter graph.

d Two of the scatter graphs have an outlier. Give a possible explanation for the outlier in each case.

Reasoning

④ The table shows the marks (out of 10) given by two judges at a local flower show.

Entrant	A	B	C	D	E	F	G	H	I	J	K	L
Judge 1	10	7	2	4	8	4	6	7	0	2	9	3
Judge 2	9	8	3	5	6	4	7	7	1	4	8	3

a Draw a scatter diagram to show the marks of both judges.

b Describe the correlation between the two judges.

c Draw the line of best fit.

d Use the scatter diagram to estimate Judge 2's score for an entrant awarded 5 by Judge 1.

⑤ This data shows the scores from two assessments taken by some school leavers who want a career in the media.

Assessment 1	Assessment 2
68	52
69	58
43	45
57	60
38	27
41	38
83	76
27	27

a Plot the data and draw a line of best fit for the graph.

b Fauzia scored 50% in the first assessment, but she missed the second assessment. Use your graph to predict what score she might have achieved.

Developing fluency

① A group of language students took oral and written tests.

Oral (%)	16	30	65	32	62	55	45	74	63	33	67
Written (%)	27	32	62	47	73	57	43	82	76	32	51

a Draw a scatter diagram to show the data.

b Describe the correlation between the two tests.

c How many got a higher mark in the oral test than the written test?
How can you tell this easily from your graph?

d Draw the line of best fit.

e Use the line of best fit to estimate
i   the oral mark for a pupil scoring 60 in the written test
ii the written mark for a pupil who scores 40 in the oral test.

Exam-style

② These data are from a football league. They show the numbers of goals some of the teams scored and the numbers of points they received.

Goals	79	36	63	50	54	81	31	58	46	68
Points	31	28	42	24	37	72	16	51	42	61

a Draw a scatter diagram to show the data.

b Describe the correlation between the goals scored and points received.

c Draw the line of best fit.

d Use the line of best fit to estimate the number of
   i points for a team scoring 60 goals
   ii goals for a team gaining 45 points.

Exam-style

③ Paula is looking at some crime statistics.

She records the numbers of police officers in a small sample of police forces and the numbers of reported crimes in one month, in their areas.

Number of police officers	58	38	16	72	34	57	78	12	33	42
Number of reported crimes	68	110	125	177	107	93	48	146	134	83

a Draw a scatter diagram to show the data.

b Which point represents a large police force operating in a high crime area?

c Describe the correlation between the number of police officers and the number of reported crimes.

d Draw the line of best fit.

e Estimate the likely number of reported crimes if a police force employs 50 police officers.

Reasoning

④ A health visitor is investigating the relationship between a mother's height and the height of her daughter.

Height of mother (cm)	165	152	164	158	169	164	174	170	155	158	163	177	161	159	162
Height of daughter (cm)	167	154	161	159	173	160	177	169	161	160	164	175	162	162	164

a Draw a scatter graph to illustrate the data.

b Describe the correlation shown.

c **i** Explain how you can use your scatter graph to find the median height of the group of mothers and find the median height of the group of mothers.
   ii Does the mother who is of median height have a daughter of median height?

⑤ Here are some data about the members of a junior football team.

Name	Height (cm)	Goals this season
Nabil	138	16
Lee	150	11
Loamia	123	2
Younis	141	7
Lorraine	140	0
Chantel	152	3
Heidi	129	14
Sabrina	137	9
David	141	0
Jody	138	17
Youssu	164	0
Patricia	149	2
John	128	15
Stuart	137	1
Crystal	125	22

a Display this information on a scatter diagram.

b Which players are likely to be goal-keepers? Explain your reasoning.

The coach says, 'I always put the tall players in defence or in goal. Shorter players tend to be nippier and so are good in attack.'

c Is the scatter diagram consistent with the coach's policy? Explain your answer carefully.

Problem solving

① An athletics coach thinks that athletes who are good at running are also good at high jump. The coach collects some data from his club.

Time to run 200 m (s)	25.3	27.4	26.4	27.5	29.0	30.2	27.3	26.6	30.1	32.0	28	28.3	29.4	27.0	31.3	31.7
High jump (m)	2.24	2.15	2.18	2.01	1.89	1.76	1.90	2.10	2.06	2.26	2	1.96	1.92	2.00	1.80	1.75

a Draw a scatter diagram to show the coach's data.

b Describe the correlation. Is the coach right?

c Find the median running time.

d Find the median height jumped. Is this the same person as in part **c**?

e The coach decides the top 25% of athletes in each sport should form an elite squad. How many athletes make it on to the squad?

② Here is a scatter diagram it shows the mass and cost of 11 books in a shop.

Julie says, 'You can see that heavier books cost more.'

Robert says, 'There is no correlation between a book's mass and its cost.'

Assess the validity of the two statements. You must explain your reasoning.

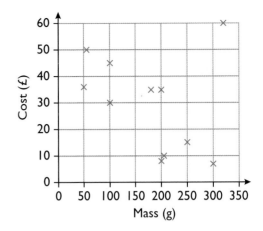

③ Mrs Jones collects information about how many hours students spent watching television in the week before a biology exam and their exam mark.

The scatter diagram shows the information.

Mrs Jones thinks that there is a connection between the number of hours spent watching television and the biology exam mark.

a Does the scatter diagram support this statement?

Describe the correlation shown.

Mrs Jones collects some more data and finds that there is strong positive correlation between number of hours spent revising and the mark achieved in the test.

b i Sketch a scatter graph to illustrate this.

ii Mrs Jones says, 'This shows you either watch television or you revise for biology, and you know which will definitely get you the better mark.'

Is Mrs Jones right? Explain your reasoning.

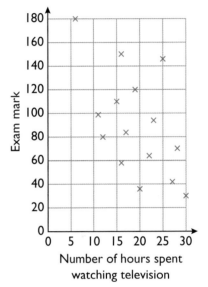

④ The table gives data for a number of diesel cars. For each car it shows the engine size and the distance it travels on 1 litre of diesel.

Engine size (litres)	3.0	.6	1.2	1.8	2.8	1.5	1.0	2.5
Distance (km)	6	15	13	10	7	11	12	9

a Draw a scatter diagram for the data.

b Comment on the correlation.

c Draw a line of best fit.

d Estimate the distance travelled for a car with an engine size of 1.4 litres.

5 The table shows the marks (out of 10) given by two judges for each of ten dancers in a competition.

Judge 1	2	7	1	8	6	3	9	4	5
Judge 2	3	8	2	10	8	3	7	6	5

  a Draw a scatter graph to illustrate the data.

  b Do you think the judges are consistent? Give a reason for your answer.

  c Add a line of best fit to your scatter graph.

Judge 1 gives another competitor a mark of 3.

  d Use your line of best fit to estimate the mark Judge 2 would give this competitor.

A twelfth competitor is judged.

Judge 1 gives him a mark of 7.

Judge 2 gives him a mark of 3.

The contestant objects and says, 'Judge 2 is being unfair as this makes this mark an outlier and is inconsistent with the other pairs of marks.'

  e Comment on the validity of this argument.

Reviewing skills

1 Avonford Swimming Club keeps a record of the age of each swimmer and how many lengths they can swim in one go. This table shows the data for a few of the swimmers.

Age	16	38	53	36	63	46	22	55	58
Number of lengths	58	45	68	30	12	33	46	34	21

  a Draw a scatter diagram to show the data.

  b Describe the correlation between the age of the swimmer and the number of lengths they can swim.

  c Draw the line of best fit.

  d Use the scatter diagram to estimate

    i the number of lengths that a person aged 50 may swim

    ii the likely age of a person who can swim 40 lengths.

Unit 7 • Using lines of best fit • Band g

➡ **Outside the Maths classroom**

Making predictions

How can statistics help us predict outcomes of future events?

⬇ **Toolbox**

Scatter graphs are used to show the relationship between **bivariate data** – this means the data contains pairs of values.

A **line of best fit** shows the overall trend of the data. It does not have to go through the origin.

An **outlier** is a pair of values that does not fit the overall trend.

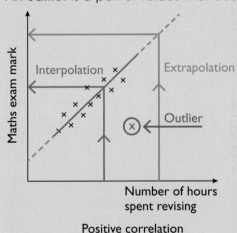

Positive correlation

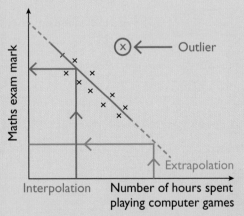

Negative correlation

Interpolation: this is where you use your line of best fit to estimate a value within the range of the data. Interpolation is reliable if there is a strong correlation.

Extrapolation: this is where you extend your line of best fit to estimate a value beyond the range of the data. Extrapolation is not very reliable because you cannot tell whether the trend will continue.

A strong correlation does not prove **causation.**

Spending more time revising will **cause** your maths mark to go up.

Computer games do not **cause** people to do badly in a maths test but they might cause them to revise less!

Example – Extrapolation and causation

Country	Life Expectancy at birth	Birth rate per 1000
Australia	82.0	12.2
Barbados	75.0	12.0
Cambodia	63.8	24.4
Canada	81.7	10.3
Czech Republic	78.3	9.8
Guatemala	71.7	25.4
India	67.8	19.9
Italy	82.0	8.8
Libya	76.0	18.4
Samoa	73.2	21.3
Syria	68.4	22.8
Tajikistan	67.1	25.0
Uganda	54.5	44.2
Uruguay	76.8	13.2

a Draw a scatter diagram to show the figures for life expectancy and birth rate in different colours.

b Describe the correlation.

c Draw a line of best fit.

d Are either of these two statements true?

> The scatter diagram shows that a high life expectancy causes a low birth rate.

> You can see that a high birth rate causes low life expectancy.

e Someone looking at the line of best fit says, 'It shows that when the life expectancy in a country reaches 88, people will stop having children.' Comment on this statement.

Solution

a and **c**

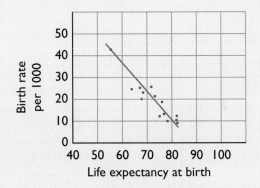

b The graph shows there is negative correlation between life expectancy and birth rate.

d A high life expectancy does not cause a low birth rate. Neither does a low birth rate cause a high life expectancy, although it could be true that more care can be given to older people if there are fewer babies to look after! It is more the case that both high life expectancy and low birth rate are the result of better access to medication and education.

> Notice that *Correlation does not imply Causation.* In this case a common underlying factor, economic development, seems to lie behind both the observed effects of low birth rate and high life expectancy.

e Common sense tells us this is definitely not true. We should not therefore **extrapolate** the line of best fit beyond the values given in the data. We can be fairly certain the relationship exists within the region of evidence but we cannot assume the relationship will exist outside of that region.

Practising skills

① This table gives the power (in horsepower) and the fuel consumption (in miles per gallon) of a number of cars.

a Find the smallest and greatest values of the power and of the fuel consumption.

Use them to decide on suitable scales for a scatter diagram.

b Draw the scatter diagram.

c Draw a line of best fit.

d Use your line of best fit

   i To describe the relationship between power and fuel economy.

   ii To predict the power of a car that travels 15 miles on one gallon of petrol.

   iii To predict the fuel economy of a car that produces 450 horsepower.

Power	Fuel consumption	Power	Fuel consumption
195	24.5	305	21.4
185	27.7	278	21.6
145	31.5	173	27.9
182	31.2	270	25.3
178	28.7	268	24.8
182	23.5	301	18.9
290	19.5	360	15.9
360	15.9	470	14.9
285	19.8	355	18.6
355	18.6	420	17
302	17.5	360	15.9
360	15.9	411	13.4
305	19.7	395	17.3
159	19.2	236	17

e Formula 1 racing cars produce around 800 horsepower. Can you use your graph to find their typical fuel consumption? Explain your answer.

Developing fluency

Reasoning

① Look at these four lines of best fit. They are all drawn for the same data.
Rank them in order from what you consider to be the best line of best fit, to the worst.
Explain why you've ordered them in this way.

A
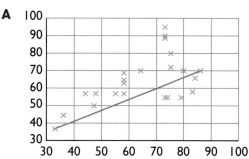

B
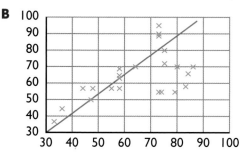

C
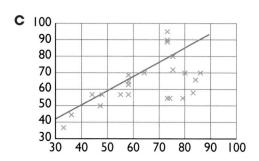

D
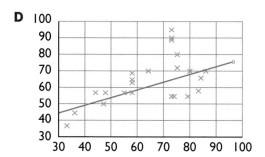

② Here are the personal best performances of some athletes in a club.

Time to run 100m (s)	11.57	11.12	10.88	11.54	11.25	10.73	11.92	11.24
Time to run 1500m (s)	275	328	326	296	316	345	266	299
Distance jumped (m)	4.49	5.56	5.52	4.95	5.33	5.92	4.31	5.02

The data can be written as these pairs: 100m and 1500m; 100m and long jump; 1500m and high jump.

a Investigate the correlations shown by the data.

b What do these correlations tell you about who is good at these events?

c How could you tell if the correlations hold for athletes in general?

d Comment on these statements from the team coach.

   i 'One of these days we'll get a team member who can run the 100m in 10 seconds. He'll be able to do 7m in the long jump.'

   ii 'Being able to run the 100m in a low time makes you able to run the 1500m in a low time.'

③ This scatter diagram shows the science and maths marks of a class in two tests.

   a Describe the correlation between the two sets of marks.

   The science teacher says, 'This shows that doing well at science makes you good at maths.'

   The maths teacher says, 'This shows that doing well at maths makes you good at science.'

   b Which of them (if either) is right? Give your reasons.

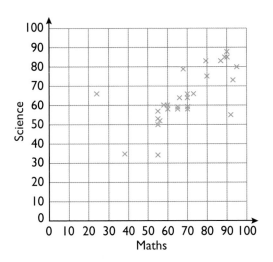

Problem solving

① A life guard kept a daily record of the highest temperature and the number of people swimming in the sea at 3 p.m.

The results are shown below.

Temperature (°C)	32	30	31	34	27	26	25	24	25	23	22	23	24	22
Number of people swimming	203	180	188	144	171	164	155	140	145	135	120	132	129	110

   a Show these data on a scatter diagram.

   b Describe any correlation between the two variables.

   c There is an outlier in the data. State which it is and suggest a reason for it.

   d Draw a line of best fit on your scatter graph.

One day the temperature is forecast to be around 15 °C.

   e Use your line of best fit to predict the number of swimmers.

   Comment on the reliability of your estimate, giving a reason for your answer.

An ice-cream vendor records number of people in the sea at 3 p.m. and number of ice-creams sold each day.

Here is the ice-cream vendor's graph.

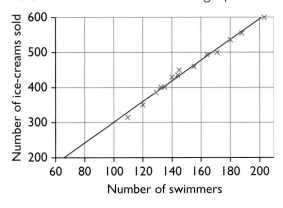

   f The ice-cream vendor says, 'My graph proves that swimming causes people to eat more ice-cream.'

   Explain why the vendor is not correct.

② Archie thinks that older people take less exercise.

He carries out a survey.

He chooses 20 adults of different ages.

They each keep a record of how much exercise they take during one week.

Here are his results.

Age	18	17	22	25	32	37	42	50	55	60	57	45	23	42	27	45	37	54	19	29
Hours of exercise	14	12	13	10	8	7	5	6	2	5	1	7	13	7	11	15	5	3	8	7

a Draw a scatter diagram of Archie's results.

b Is there any correlation between age and the amount of time spent exercising? What does this mean?

c Identify any outliers.

d Draw a line of best fit on your scatter diagram.

e Archie takes 8 hours of exercise per week. Estimate his age.
Comment on the reliability of your estimate, giving a reason for your answer.

f Mary is 72 years old. Estimate how much exercise she takes.
Comment on the reliability of your estimate, giving a reason for your answer.

③ The table gives some information about different types of aircraft.

Aircraft	A320	A318	B747	A350	B747	MD-11	A310	B737	AN225
Wingspan (m)	35.8	34.1	64.8	65	38	52	44	36	88
Maximum landing mass (tonnes)	66.0	57.5	251	205	88	185	124	66	640

a Draw a scatter diagram to show the data.

b Is there evidence from the scatter diagram to suggest there is a correlation between the wingspan of an aircraft and the maximum landing mass of the aircraft? You must explain your answer.

c Draw a line of best fit.

d Use your line of best fit to estimate the maximum landing mass of an aircraft with wingspan 58 m.

e Peter has an aircraft with a wingspan of 12 metres. Would it be sensible for him to use the line of best fit to estimate the maximum landing mass of his aircraft? Explain your answer.

④ Megan is carrying out a science experiment.

She hangs a weight from a spring and measures the final length of the spring.

Megan repeats the experiment for different masses.

Here are Megan's results.

Mass (g)	50	100	150	200	250	300	350	400	450	500	550	600
Length of spring (cm)	6.5	8.3	10.1	12.2	14.3	20.1	18.3	20.3	22.6	24.1	26.5	28.7

a Draw a scatter diagram to show the data.

b Megan has made a mistake when she wrote down one of the results.

The correct result should be 16.2 cm.

Identify and correct the mistake.

c Draw a line of best fit.

d Use your line of best fit to estimate the length of the spring when a mass of 180 g is hung from it.

e Comment on the reliability of using your line of best fit to estimate the length of the spring when a 1 kg mass is hung from it.

f Estimate the original length of the spring.

Reviewing skills

① This table shows the height in metres above sea level and the temperature in Celsius, on one day at 8 different places in Europe.

Height (m)	1300	275	800	360	580	540	1300	690
Temperature (°C)	10	20	14	20	27	17	12	17

a Plot a scatter diagram and describe the correlation.

b Identify any outliers and suggest a reason for them.

c Use your diagram to estimate the temperature at a height of 400 m.

d Use your diagram to estimate the height of a place with a temperature of 25°C.

e Comment on the reliability of your answers in parts **c** and **d**.

Strand 4 Probability

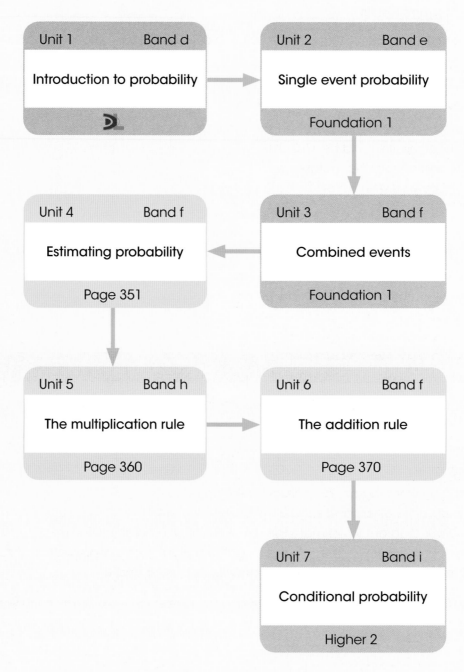

Unit 1	Band d
Introduction to probability	

Unit 2	Band e
Single event probability	
Foundation 1	

Unit 4	Band f
Estimating probability	
Page 351	

Unit 3	Band f
Combined events	
Foundation 1	

Unit 5	Band h
The multiplication rule	
Page 360	

Unit 6	Band f
The addition rule	
Page 370	

Unit 7	Band i
Conditional probability	
Higher 2	

Units 1–3 are assumed knowledge for this book. They are reviewed and extended in the Moving on section on page 349.

Units 1–3 • Moving on

1 A bag contains 7 red and 3 yellow counters.
A counter is drawn out of the bag then replaced before a second counter is drawn out.
What is the probability that the counters are

a the same colour.

b different colours?

2 A die is rolled.

a Find the probability that the score is 2 or more.

b Find the probability that the score is 2 or less.

c Explain why adding the answers to part **a** and part **b** does not give you 1.

d Find the probability that the score is either 2 or more or is 2 or less.

3 Jenny is trying to raise money for a local charity. She has a board set out as shown.

Each square on the grid is covered by a label that has the name of a football team on it.

She sells the labels for 50p per team to the students in her school. Each student writes their name on their chosen label.

When all the teams are sold Jenny takes off the labels and finds where the £10 prize is hidden.

a How much does the full card raise?

b Find the probability of winning, if a student buys

  i one team

  ii a column of teams

  iii a row of teams.

4 Roberto is staying in a ten-storey hotel. He enters a lift on the fourth floor and, without looking, presses a button at random.

a Calculate the probability of the lift

  i going up

  ii going down.

b Add up your answers from part **a**. Why is the answer not 1?

⑤ In a game show, contestants spin a wheel of fortune and pick a card to seal their fate. Calculate:

  a P(winning £100)

  b P(losing £400)

  c P(no money is lost or won)

  d P(wheel lands on £400)

  e P(winning some money).

⑥ Samil and Phil go on a Duke of Edinburgh camping expedition. They take two packets of soup, three packets of rice and two packets of dried fruit. The packets are all exactly the same size and shape.

  a Phil chooses one at random, without looking. What is the probability it is soup?

  After they have used one of the packets of soup, it rains heavily and all the labels come off the other packets. When they open the next packet, what is the probability that it contains:

  b soup

  c rice

  d dried fruit?

⑦ Here are descriptions of ten events.

    A: Next Saturday will have 24 hours in it.
    B: Dopey and Bashful will be the two dwarfs picked randomly from 7.
    C: Not rolling a 1 with a fair six-sided die.
    D: Picking a club from a full set of 52 playing cards.
    E: Tossing a coin and getting a head.
    F: Picking any weekday randomly from the days of the week.
    G: Rolling an odd number with a fair six-sided die.
    H: Not choosing winter randomly from all of the seasons.
    I: Rolling an 8 with a fair six-sided die.

  a Pair them up so the total probability for each pair is 1. There will be one left over.

  b The description left over pairs with this card to give a total probability of 1:
    Randomly picking Pittsburgh airport from a list of some international airports.
    How many international airports are there on the list?

Unit 4 • Estimating probability • Band f

Outside the Maths classroom

Insurance

What factors affect the cost of insurance?

Toolbox

A **population** is everything or everyone with some characteristic, for example

- All people over 100 years old
- All red squirrels
- All the students in a school
- All cars of a particular model.

A **sample** is a small set that is chosen from the population to provide information about it.

Samples are often used to **estimate** population probabilities.

> In a random sample every item in the population has the same probability of being selected, so is equally likely.

To be useful a sample must be representative of the population. This is often achieved by choosing a **random** sample, but this is not always possible. The larger the sample, the more accurate it is likely to be.

Probability is estimated from what has been observed, using **relative frequency**.

Sometimes you need to carry out an experiment with **trials**.

$$\text{Estimated probability (or relative frequency)} = \frac{\text{number of successful trials}}{\text{total number of trials}}$$

You can estimate the number of times an outcome will occur using the formula

Expected number = P (a successful outcome) × number of trials

Example – Using a sample

It is believed that a rare bird species has more males than females. After a long search, a team of scientists find a colony of these birds. 16 of them are male and 4 are female.

a Estimate the probability that a bird of this type is male.

b Comment on the sampling method.

Solution

a The total number of birds is 16 + 4 = 20.

The estimated probability that a bird in the population is male is $\frac{16}{20} = 0.8$.

> This is an example of an opportunity sample.

b The sample is not random. It is just one group of the birds.

The sample is small so the estimate is unlikely to be accurate. If the scientists can find more birds, and so have a larger sample, the estimate should be more reliable.

Example – Relative frequency

An insurance company investigates a number of speeding convictions in a country. It classifies them according to the age and gender of the offender and then summarises the data in this table.

		Age	
		Under 25	25 and over
Gender	Male	455	284
	Female	120	141

a Calculate the probability that a speeding conviction belongs to

  i a male person

  ii someone under 25.

b Do the data show that males drive faster than females?

Solution

Start by adding a Total row and column to the table

a

		Age		Total
		Under 25	25 and over	
Gender	Male	455	284	739
	Female	120	141	261
	Total	575	425	1000

i $P(\text{male}) = \frac{739}{1000}$

> There are 739 convictions for males.
> There are 1000 convictions in total.

ii $P(\text{under 25}) = \frac{575}{1000}$

> There are 575 convictions for under 25s.

b No. The data do not tell you how many male and how many female drivers there are.

It is possible that in that country there are only a few female drivers but they drive fast and get convictions.

It is also possible that there are about equal numbers of male and female drivers and the males do drive faster.

You do not have the information to draw a conclusion.

Practising skills

1 A shop sells newspapers.

Here are the results for a few days.

Newspaper	Daily Post	Gazette	The News	The Tribune
Frequency	186	84	216	105

a Estimate the probability that the next newspaper sold will be *The News*.

b The owners open a new shop in the same area. They expect to sell 1000 newspapers each day. How many of each one should they stock?

2 A computer repair company keeps a record of the faults in the computers it repairs.

Component	Motherboard	Power supply	Hard drive
Frequency	67	215	103

a Millie is called out to do a repair. Estimate the probability that she will find the fault is in the

   i motherboard   **ii** power supply   **iii** hard drive.

b The engineers say that it is more likely than not that the fault will be in the power supply. Are they correct?

c The computer company normally repair 5000 computers each year. Estimate how many of each component they will need.

3 Ben has a gold coin. It is going to be used for the toss in the World Cup Final.

Ben wants to be sure his coin is unbiased.

He throws his coin and records how many heads he gets.

Number of throws	20	50	100	400	1000	2000	5000
Number of heads	12	27	46	211	486	982	2516
Relative frequency	0.6						

a Copy and complete the relative frequency line of the table.

b Do you think his coin is unbiased? Give a reason for your conclusion.

4 During a local election a radio station conducts an exit poll. They ask people who they have voted for, as they came out of one polling station.

Here are the results.

Party	Blue Party	Red Party	Orange Party
Number of voters	84	72	33

a Work out the probability that one voter selected at random voted for

   i the Blue Party   **ii** the Red Party   **iii** the Orange Party.

b There are 20 000 voters in the community.

   i Estimate how many vote for the Orange Party.

   ii Comment on the reliability of your answer.

(5) The police force in a large city select vehicles at random for road-worthiness checks.
The table shows the results of a traffic survey at a particular road junction.

Vehicle	Lorry	Van	Bus or coach	Car
Frequency	15305	2411	1064	24792

   a Estimate the probability of each type of vehicle being selected on one occasion.

   b In one week the police carry out checks on 190 vehicles at the same road junction.
Estimate how many of these vehicles are buses or coaches.

   c On one occasion, across the whole city, the police select 2400 vehicles for checks.
Comment on the accuracy of using the data from the table to estimate the total number of lorries checked.
Give a reason for your answer.

Developing fluency

(1) A bag contains some coloured balls. They are red, blue or green.
Eleanor takes a ball out at random, notes its colour and replaces it.
She does this 40 times.
Here are her results.

Colour	Red	Blue	Green
Frequency	12	18	10

   a Estimate the probability that the next ball she draws is

     i red   **ii** blue   **iii** green.

   b There are 12 balls in the bag.
Estimate how many there are of each colour.
What could Eleanor do to make her estimate more reliable?

(2) A school conducts a small survey among its students to see if they like their uniform or if they want to change it.
Here are their results.

Decision	Frequency
Like it/Keep it	42
Change it	29
Don't know	16

   a Use the data to estimate the probability that a student selected randomly will answer:

     i *Keep it*

     ii *Change it*

     iii *I do not know.*

   b The governors say that if there are at least 400 students in the school who want to change the uniform then they will discuss it at their next meeting. There are 1240 students in the school. Are they governors likely to discuss school uniform at their next meeting?

(3) The table lists the births in a maternity hospital one week.

	Boys	Girls
Monday	5	3
Tuesday	2	4
Wednesday	6	3
Thursday	4	7
Friday	5	1

A baby is selected at random and called 'the baby of the week'.

a What is the probability that the baby of the week on this occasion is

  i male

  ii female?

b During one year, how many babies of the week would you expect to be male and how many female?

(4) Kwame and Kofi are investigating a type of moth.

There are two varieties of this moth: light and dark.

They collect moths at different sites, A and B, and record which variety each moth is that they collect.

Kwame (Site A)					Kofi (Site B)			
Light	Dark	Dark	Light		Dark	Light	Light	Light
Dark	Light	Dark	Dark		Light	Dark	Dark	Light
Light	Dark	Dark	Dark		Light	Light	Light	Light
Light	Light	Dark	Dark		Dark	Light	Light	Dark
Dark	Dark	Dark	Dark		Light	Dark	Light	Light

a Estimate the probability that a moth is dark:

  i using all the data

  ii using only Kwame's data

  iii using only Kofi's data.

b Kwame says he thinks the moths are different at the two sites.
  Explain why he says this.

c Kofi says, 'To be sure, we need to …'. Complete Kofi's sentence.

(5) Tim has a normal die.

Sara says that she normally throws a six every 3 throws.

Pete says he takes at least 20 throws to get a six.

Ian says that he never gets a six.

a Who is correct?

b Tim throws the dice 20 times and gets 5 sixes.

  i Is the die definitely biased?

  ii Alfie then throws the dice 100 times and gets 15 sixes. Is the die biased?

c How can they check that the die is unbiased?

⑥ Dan has an unbiased coin. He says that if he throws the coin twice he should get one head. Is he correct? Explain your answer.

⑦ Jane, Katie and Len want to know the probability that a letter in written English is an E. (It can be upper case E or lower case e.) They each take a sentence as a sample to estimate this probability.

   a In each case, use the sample sentence to estimate the probability that a letter in written English is an E.

      i Jane: *The quick brown fox jumps over the lazy dog.*

      ii Katie: *To be or not to be, that is the question.*

      iii Len: *Never in the field of human conflict have so many owed so much to so few.*

   b The probability of a letter being E is actually 0.12.

      i Which of the sentences gave the closest estimate?

      ii Explain why Jane's sentence cannot be regarded as random.

   c Suggest how they can obtain a more accurate estimate.

   d In a *Scrabble* set there are 100 tiles. Two of them are blank and the other 98 have letters on them. How many tiles would you expect to have the letter E in a set designed for players using English?

     Find out how many Es there are in a standard *Scrabble* set.

Problem solving

① Here is the result of a traffic survey a council did over one week on a busy road.
It shows the numbers of lorries, buses and cars that used the road.

	Lorries	Buses	Cars	Motorbikes
Frequency	16 000	10 000	240 000	9000

   a Keith stands at the side of this road.

     Estimate the probability that the next vehicle to go past Keith is

     i a car

     ii a motorbike

     iii not a lorry.

   b In one day, 15000 vehicles go past a particular point.

     Estimate the number of buses to pass that point.

② A biased tetrahedral die has 4 sides numbered 1, 2, 3 and 4.
The die is thrown 20 times and the number it lands on is recorded.

1 3 4 2 4 4 3 2 2 1 1 2 2 4 3 2 1 1 1 2

a Copy and complete the relative frequency table.

Lands on	1	2	3	4
Relative frequency				0.2

These are the relative frequencies after the die is thrown 100 times.

Lands on	1	2	3	4
Relative frequency	0.3	0.4	0.15	0.15

b Which of the two relative frequencies for 'lands on 4' is the better estimate of the probability of the die landing on 4?

Give a reason for your answer.

The die continues to be thrown.

c Estimate the number of times it will land on '1' in 1000 throws.

③ A school is consulting students about changing the length of the school lunch time from 45 minutes to 30 minutes.
A sample of students gave the following opinions.

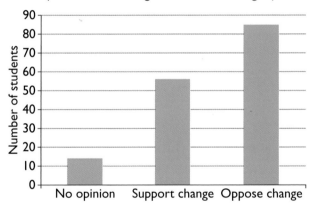

a Estimate the probability that a randomly chosen student will support the change.

The school has 1200 students.

b Use these sample results to estimate how many of the 1200 students are likely to oppose the change.

④ A four-sided spinner has the numbers 1, 3, 5 and 7 on it.
The table shows the probability that it will land on each number.

Number	1	3	5	7
Probability	0.15	0.4	0.25	0.2

Harry spins the spinner 150 times.

a Work out how many times he expects to get

i 3   **ii** 5.

b How many times does he expect **not** to get 3?

c What is the probability that he does not get 3?

⑤ At a charity fete there is a stall selling tickets.

The probability of winning £1 with one ticket is $\frac{1}{8}$.

Tickets cost 20p each.

The charity would like to make a profit of £120.

How many tickets do they need to sell?

⑥ Mr Thomas wants to find out how fit the students at his school are.

A bleep test involves running between two points that are 20 m apart.

Each stage consists of several laps and a bleep signifies the start of the next stage. The bleeps get progressively closer together so the student has to run faster to complete the next level.

Mr Thomas asks a group of randomly chosen Year 9 students to perform a bleep test.

Here are the results.

Stage achieved	1	2	3	4	5	6	7	8	9	10
Girls	4	5	7	13	23	15	9	2	1	1
Boys	2	3	5	7	16	23	14	5	3	2

a Estimate the probability that a randomly chosen

   i boy achieves stage 10

   ii girl achieves stage 6 or better

   iii student achieves stage 4.

b Mr Thomas says a student is unfit if they achieve stage 3 or lower.

There are 190 girls and 200 boys in Year 9.

Estimate the number of

   i girls that are unfit

   ii boys that are unfit.

c There are 180 boys in Year 7, Mr Thomas says, 'I expect that about 36 Year 7 boys will achieve stage 5.'

Is Mr Thomas's estimate too low, too high, or about right? Give a reason for your answer.

Reviewing skills

A doctors' surgery keeps a record of how early or late patients are seen.

The results are recorded in the table below.

At least $\frac{1}{4}$ hour early	4
Up to $\frac{1}{4}$ hour early	20
On time	8
Up to 5 minutes late	4
5 minutes to 10 minutes late	3
more than 10 minutes late	1

a Use the table to find the probability that a patient selected at random will be seen

　i   up to 5 minutes late

　ii 5 minutes to 10 minutes late

　iii more than 10 minutes late.

b The next day the surgery sees 124 patients. Estimate how many of them will be seen more than 10 minutes late.

　There is a larger doctors' surgery in the same town. In one day, the larger surgery sees 438 patients.

c Comment on the accuracy of using the data from the table to estimate the probability that a patient is seen late at the larger surgery.

　Give a reason for your answer.

Unit 5 • The multiplication rule • Band h

 Outside the Maths classroom

Game shows

Why do so many game shows involve chance?
How can contestants use the laws of probability
to help them win?

 Toolbox

Events are **independent** if the outcome of one does not affect the outcomes of the other.
For two independent events, A and B, then
P(A and B) = P(A) × P(B)

When a coin is flipped and a die is rolled then the score on the die does not change the likelihood of getting heads on the coin. So 'rolling a 6' and 'heads' are **independent**.

P('*6*' and '*heads*') = $\frac{1}{6} \times \frac{1}{2} = \frac{1}{12}$.

Events are **dependent** if the outcome of one event affects the outcomes of the other.

The events '*first marble is red*' and '*second marble is red*' without replacement are **dependent events**.

The first event has had an impact on the probability of the second event.

A **tree diagram** can be used to show all the possible outcomes of an event or sequence of events.

This tree diagram shows the possible outcomes of taking marbles (without replacement) from a bag containing 3 red marbles and 2 green marbles.

First marble   Second marble

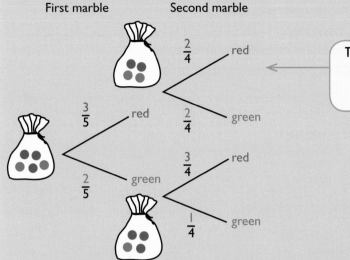

The probability of the second marble being red depends on what colour the first marble was. The events are dependent.

You can multiply the probabilities as you move along the branches to find the probability of combined events.

P(red marble followed by a green marble) = $\dfrac{3}{5} \times \dfrac{2}{4} = \dfrac{6}{20} = \dfrac{3}{10}$

Example – Independent events

A coin is flipped and a die is rolled.
a The coin is flipped 10 times and each time shows a tail.
   What is the probability that the 11th time it will also show a tail?
b A die is rolled 100 times and a six has not yet been rolled.
   What is the probability that the next roll will give a six?
c What is the probability of getting a 'tail' and a '6' together?

Solution

a Each flip of a coin is an independent event. What has happened in previous flips does not affect it so the probability is $\dfrac{1}{2}$.

Wrongly believing that a head is more likely to turn up as it is 'overdue' is known as the 'Gamblers fallacy'.

b Each roll of a die is an independent event so the probability of scoring a six on each roll is exactly the same. The probability of scoring a six on the 100th roll is $\dfrac{1}{6}$.

c The events are independent, so P(tail and 6) = P(tail) × P(6)

$$= \frac{1}{2} \times \frac{1}{6} \qquad \left(\frac{1}{2} \times \frac{1}{6} = \frac{1 \times 1}{2 \times 6} = \frac{1}{12} \right)$$

$$= \frac{1}{12}$$

Example – Without replacement

In an office there are 30 employees. Nine of them wear glasses.
Two employees are chosen at random from the group.
  a What is the probability that the second employee chosen wears glasses?
  b What is the probability that exactly one of the employees wears glasses?

Solution

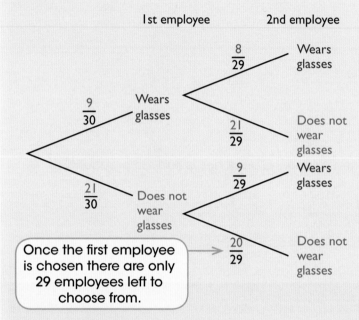

1st employee   2nd employee

$\frac{9}{30}$ Wears glasses

$\frac{8}{29}$ Wears glasses

$\frac{21}{29}$ Does not wear glasses

$\frac{21}{30}$ Does not wear glasses

$\frac{9}{29}$ Wears glasses

$\frac{20}{29}$ Does not wear glasses

> Once the first employee is chosen there are only 29 employees left to choose from.

a The second employee wears glasses in two of the paths on the tree diagram.

P(1st wears glasses and 2nd wears glasses) $= \frac{9}{30} \times \frac{8}{27} = \frac{72}{870}$.

> The probability that the second employee chosen wears glasses is found by adding these two probabilities together.

P(1st does not wear glasses and 2nd wears glasses) $= \frac{21}{30} \times \frac{9}{29} = \frac{189}{870}$.

So, P(2nd employee wears glasses) $= \frac{72}{870} + \frac{189}{870} = \frac{261}{870} = \frac{87}{290}$.

> Simplify to $\frac{87}{290}$ by dividing the 'top' and 'bottom' by 3.

b There are two paths through the tree diagram that lead to exactly one employee wearing glasses.

P(1st wears glasses and 2nd does not wear glasses) $= \frac{9}{30} \times \frac{21}{29} = \frac{189}{870}$.

P(1st does not wear glasses and 2nd does wear glasses) $= \frac{21}{30} \times \frac{9}{29} = \frac{189}{870}$.

So, P(exactly one wears glasses) $= \frac{189}{870} + \frac{189}{870} = \frac{378}{870} = \frac{63}{145}$.

Practising skills

(1) Matilda is playing *Snakes and ladders* with Sarah. They use one die.

a Matilda rolls the die first. What is the probability that she rolls a 6?

b Sarah rolls the die. What is the probability that she rolls a 6?

c Matilda rolls the die again. What is the probability that she rolls a 6?

d Sarah rolls the die again. What is the probability that she rolls a 6?

e After a while Matilda needs to roll a 3 to win. What is the probability that Matilda rolls a 3 on her next turn?

(2) Two dice are rolled.

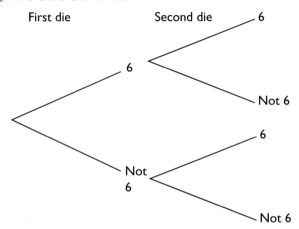

a Copy and complete the tree diagram.

Use this tree diagram to calculate the probability that

b both dice show a 6

c neither die shows a 6

d at least one die shows a 6

e exactly one die shows a 6.

(3) Arlo and Bekah are playing cards. There are 52 cards in the pack; 4 of them are aces. They deal the cards and they are not replaced.

a Bekah deals the first card. What is the probability that it is an ace?

b Bekah's card is not an ace. Arlo gets the next card. What is the probability that it is an ace?

c Arlo's card is not an ace. Bekah deals the next card. What is the probability that it is an ace?

d Bekah's card **is** an ace. Arlo deals the next card. What is the probability that it is an ace?

④ A coin is tossed and a die is rolled.

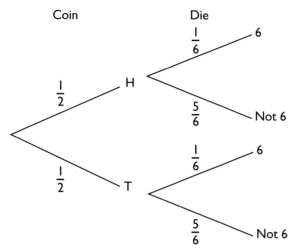

Use this tree diagram to calculate the probability of scoring

a a head and a six

b a head and not a six

c a tail and a six

d a tail and not a six.

⑤ 12 coloured counters are placed into a bag. Seven are red and five are blue.

A counter is drawn out of the bag. The counter is not replaced. A second counter is then drawn out of the bag.

a Copy and complete this tree diagram.

First counter   Second counter

Red Red ☐ x ☐ = ☐

Red Blue ☐ x ☐ = ☐

Blue Red ☐ x ☐ = ☐

Blue Blue ☐ x ☐ = ☐

b Another time the first counter is replaced.
Draw the tree diagram for this situation.

⑥ Della has these coloured counters in a bag.

   a She takes out a counter without looking.
What is the probability that it is red?

   b The first counter was red. Della does
not put it back.
How many red counters and how many yellow counters are left in the bag?

   c Della shakes the bag and takes out another counter.
What is the probability that it is red?
This counter too is red and again Della does not put it back.
She takes out another counter from the bag.
What is the probability that it is
   i red   **ii** yellow?

Developing fluency

① A class of students has 16 girls and 13 boys.
Two names are chosen at random from the register.

   a Draw a tree diagram to show the possible outcomes.

   b Use your tree diagram to find the probability that
   i both students are girls

   ii both students are boys

   iii at least one of the students is a boy

   iv exactly one of the students is a boy.

② In each case, state whether P and Q are independent or dependent.

   a P: I toss a coin and record how it lands.
Q: I roll a die and record its score.

   b P: It rains some time today.
Q: It rains some time tomorrow.

   c P: A person lives to be 100 years old.
Q: A person smokes.

   d P: A pet cat is ginger.
Q: A pet cat wears a collar.

③ Lucie has two dice. One is blue and has eight sides numbered from 1 to 8. The other is red and is a normal, six-sided die.

    a Lucie rolls both dice.

       i What is the probability that she rolls a six on the blue die?

       ii What is the probability that she rolls a six on the red die?

    b Lucie rolls both dice again.

       i What is the probability that she rolls a six on the blue die?

       ii What is the probability that she rolls a six on the red die?

    c Lucie rolls both dice again. She rolls a six on the red die.

       What is the probability that she rolls a six on the blue die?

    d Are the outcomes on the two dice independent or dependent?

④ At the start of a game, a cricketer has a probability of 0.6 of holding a catch.

    If he holds the first catch he becomes more confident and the probability of holding the next catch goes up to 0.75.

    On the other hand, if he drops the first catch he becomes nervous and the probability of holding the next catch goes down to 0.5.

    In one match the cricketer receives two catches.

    a Draw a tree diagram to represent this situation.

       Fill in all the probabilities.

    b Use your tree diagram to find the probabilities that, out of the two catches, he holds

       i none   **ii** one   **iii** both.

⑤ The probability that Seb has toast for breakfast is 0.4.

    The probability that Seb has toast for lunch is 0.05.

    The events are independent.

    Select the right calculation for each of the following.

    a The probability that Seb doesn't have toast for lunch.

    b The probability that Seb doesn't have toast for breakfast.

    c The probability that Seb has toast for breakfast and lunch.

    d The probability that Seb has toast at least once a day.

$1 - 0.05$	0.95×0.4	
$1 - 0.95 \times 0.6$	$1 - 0.4$	
0.05×0.4	$1 - 0.05 \times 0.4$	

6 James says that he tossed a coin 20 times and got tails every time.
Joe says that this is impossible and that James is not telling the truth.
Explain why Joe is wrong.

Problem solving

1 20 counters are placed into a bag. Seven are red and the rest are blue. A counter is drawn out of the bag and then replaced. A second counter is then drawn out of the bag.

   a Draw a tree diagram to show the possible outcomes and use it to calculate the probability of drawing out

     i two blue counters

     ii two red counters

     iii one of each colour

     iv at least one blue counter.

2 A box contains two white balls and one black ball.
A bag contains yellow and green balls in the ratio 2 : 3.
Mary takes a ball at random from the box.
She then takes a ball from the bag.
What is the probability that she will take

   a a white ball and a yellow ball

   b a black ball and a yellow ball

   c a black ball and a yellow or green ball?

3 A manager wants to select two people to look after a stand at a conference. They are chosen from eight female staff, including Mrs Bell, and six male staff, including her husband Mr Bell.

   a His first plan is to select the two people at random from all 14 staff.
What is the probability that Mr and Mrs Bell are both chosen?

   b He then decides he should select one woman and one man.
What is the probability that Mr and Mrs Bell are both chosen now?

4 On the way to work, Millie has to pass through two sets of traffic lights.
The probability that the first set of lights is red is 0.8 and the probability that the second set of lights is red is 0.3.
Over a 25-day period Millie has to stop at both sets of lights 6 times on her way to work.

   a Millie thinks the lights work independently.
Do you agree? Given a reason for you answer.

   b If Millie is right, how often would you expect her to have to stop at just one set of lights?

⑤ Naela takes the train to work. When it is raining the probability the train is late is 0.3. When it is not raining, the probability the train is late is 0.05.

In January, she worked on 22 days. It rained as she went to work on 8 of those days.

a Find the probability that the train was late on a day in January.

b The railway company advertised that fewer than 10% of their trains were late during January. Could this claim be true for Naela's train? Explain your answer.

⑥ Geoff has a pack of 10 light bulbs of which 3 are faulty.

He takes 3 of the bulbs at random and fits them into 3 lamps.

a Draw a tree diagram to represent this situation.

b Use your tree diagram to find the probabilities that
   i none of the lamps works   **ii** 1 of the lamps works
   iii 2 of the lamps work   **iv** all 3 of the lamps work.

c Add all 4 of yours answers to part **b** together. What does your answer tell you?

⑦ There are 6 blue socks and 4 red socks in a drawer.

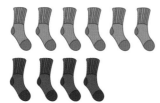

Freddie takes out 2 socks at random.

a Work out the probability that Freddie takes out 2 socks of the same colour.

b What is the maximum number of socks he would need to take out at random to ensure he had a red pair?

⑧ Jamil has a bag containing 5 counters. 4 are blue and 1 is red.

Jamil wants the red counter. He takes them out one at a time until he comes to the red one. If he picks a blue counter, he does not replace it.

a Copy and complete this tree diagram.

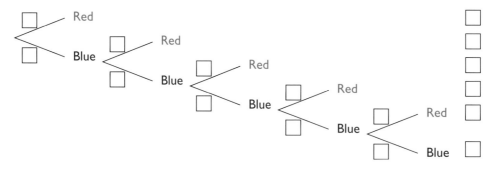

b Jamil can take 1, 2, 3, 4 or 5 attempts to get the red counter. Before he starts, what is the probability that he will take each of these numbers of attempts?

What does the total of these 5 probabilities tell you?

Now investigate the situation if Jamil replaces any blue counters he takes out.

c How does this affect the tree diagram?

d What is the probability that he gets the red counter in his first 5 attempts?

Reviewing skills

1. 15 counters are placed in a bag. Five are red and the rest are green. Two counters are drawn from the bag in succession, without replacement. What is the probability of drawing out
   a two red counters
   b two green counters
   c one of each colour
   d at least one green counter?

2. The probability that it will rain today is 0.2. If it rains today, the probability that it will rain tomorrow is 0.15. If it is fine today, the probability it is fine tomorrow is 0.9.
   a Draw a tree diagram and calculate the missing probabilities.
   b What is the probability that at least one of the two days will be fine?

Unit 6 · The addition rule · Band f

Outside the Maths classroom

Games of chance

Which games involve probability? How can probability improve your strategy when you play a game of chance?

Toolbox

Mutually exclusive events

Two events or outcomes are **mutually exclusive** if they cannot both happen.

(When you toss a coin the outcomes '*heads*' and '*tails*' are mutually exclusive – you cannot get both heads and tails!)

When two events or outcomes are mutually exclusive then the probability that one or the other of them happens can be found by **adding** their individual probabilities.

The events must be mutually exclusive for the **Addition Rule** to work.

You can use **Venn diagrams** to show possible outcomes.

This Venn diagram shows 2 mutually exclusive events.

> There is no intersection as A and B can never both happen!

> $P(A \text{ or } B) = P(A) + P(B)$

For example, event A is '*throwing a dice and getting an odd number*' and event B is '*throwing a dice and getting 2*'.

Events that are not mutually exclusive

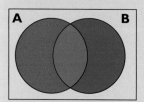

> The intersection shows that A and B can happen at the same time:
>
> $P(A \text{ or } B) = P(A) + P(B) - P(A \text{ and } B)$

For example, event A is '*someone owning a cat*' and event B is '*someone owning a dog*', the intersection is '*someone owning a cat and a dog*'.

Set notation: $E = \{x : x \text{ is a factor of } 24\}$ means E is the set of all the numbers that are factors of 24, i.e. 1, 2, 3, 4, 6, 12, 24.

Example – Mutually exclusive events

A bag contains 20 counters. Five of them are blue, two are green and the rest are other colours.

a Draw a Venn diagram showing this information.

b A counter is selected at random. What is the probability that it is

  i blue

  ii green

  iii blue or green

  iv neither blue nor green?

Solution

a

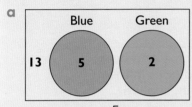

b i $P(\text{blue}) = \dfrac{5}{20} = 0.25$

  ii $P(\text{green}) = \dfrac{2}{20} = 0.1$

  iii Choosing a blue counter and choosing a green counter are mutually exclusive, so you add their probabilities.

     $P(\text{blue or green}) = P(\text{blue}) + P(\text{green})$

     $= \dfrac{5}{20} + \dfrac{2}{20}$

     $= \dfrac{7}{20} = 0.35$

  iv Choosing a counter that is neither blue nor green is the opposite of choosing one that is either blue or green.

     So $P(\text{neither blue not green}) = 1 - 0.35 = 0.65$. ← The total probability is 1.

     Another way of doing this is to look at the Venn diagram.

     There are $20 - 5 - 2 = 13$ other colours.

     So the required probability is $\dfrac{13}{20} = 0.65$.

Example – Events that are not mutually exclusive

A fair die is rolled.

a Draw a Venn diagram to show the events A and B, where A = {*prime numbers on a die*} and B = {*even numbers on a die*}

b Use your Venn diagram to find

  i P(score is prime) **ii** P(score is even)

  iii P(score is prime and even) **iv** P(score is prime or even).

Solution

a The prime numbers on a die are 2, 3 and 5. So A is {2, 3, 5}
The even numbers on a die are 2, 4 and 6. So B is {2, 4, 6}

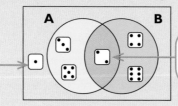

1 is neither prime nor even so it goes outside of the circles.

2 is prime and even, and goes in the intersection.

b i P(score is prime) = $\frac{3}{6} = \frac{1}{2}$ ← 3 out of the 6 possible scores are prime.

  ii P(score is even) = $\frac{3}{6} = \frac{1}{2}$ ← 3 out of the 6 possible scores are even.

  iii P(score is prime and even) = $\frac{1}{6}$ ← 2 is the only even prime.

  iv P(score is prime or even) = $\frac{3}{6} + \frac{3}{6} - \frac{1}{6} = \frac{5}{6}$ ← 2, 3, 4, 5 and 6 are prime or even.

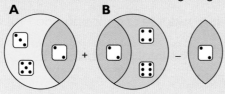

Practising skills

① A bag contains 15 counters. Three are red, two are blue and the rest are yellow.
A counter is chosen at random. Find the probability that the counter is

  a red

  b blue

  c red or blue.

② A raffle has tickets numbered from 1 to 300. Richard has 5 tickets and Sue has 7 tickets. One ticket is drawn to find the winner of the star prize.

What is the probability that

a Richard wins the star prize

b Sue wins the star prize

c Either Richard or Sue win the star prize?

③ Pete is listening to his music on shuffle.

He has 600 songs. He has rated 57 of them as 5 star songs and 72 of them as 4 star songs. What is the probability that the next song he plays is

a a 5 star song

b a 4 star song

c either a four star or five star song

d rated with 0, 1, 2 or 3 stars?

④ A die is rolled. What is the probability that the number that comes up is

a 2 or less

b 5 or more

c either 2 or less, or five or more?

⑤ In a survey 50 students were asked whether they liked soccer or rugby.

21 liked soccer.

10 liked both.

8 liked neither soccer nor rugby.

a Draw a Venn diagram showing this information.

b What is the probability that a student chosen at random from this group liked only rugby?

⑥ In a class of 30 students, 8 own a dog, 11 own a cat and 4 own both a cat and a dog.

a Copy the Venn diagram. Add numbers to complete the Venn diagram to show this information.

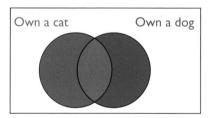

b Find the probability that a randomly chosen student has

i a dog

ii a dog and a cat

iii a dog or a cat or both

iv no pets.

7 Emily has cards numbered from 1 to 15.

    a Write each number from 1 to 15 in the correct place in the Venn diagram.

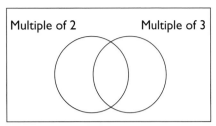

    b Find the probability that a card Emily selects at random is

      i a multiple of 2

      ii a multiple of 3

      iii a multiple of 2 and a multiple of 3

      iv a multiple of 2 or a multiple of 3

      v neither a multiple of 2 nor a multiple of 3.

Developing fluency

1 There are 52 cards in a pack. Each card is equally likely to be chosen.
What is the probability that a card chosen at random is

    a a club

    b not a club

    c a spade, heart or diamond

    d a 2 or a 3

    e neither a 2 nor a 3?

2 The probability that there will be rain in London on a day in November is 60%.
The probability that there will be sun in London on a day in November is 70%.
Explain why the probability that there will be either rain or sun on a day in November in London is not 130%.

3 This two way table shows how many students in a class fit certain descriptions.

	Blonde hair	Brown hair	Black hair	Total
Wears glasses	3	4	0	
Does not wear glasses	9	10	3	

    a Copy the table and complete the cells in the Total column.

    b Use the table to find the probability that a student chosen at random has

      i blonde hair

      ii blonde hair or black hair

      iii blonde hair or wears glasses, but not both

      iv black hair or wears glasses, but not both

      v black hair and wears glasses.

Reasoning

④ Rosie always eats a bowl of cereal for breakfast.

The probability that Rosie eats cornflakes is $\frac{1}{4}$.

The probability that Rosie eats muesli is $\frac{5}{12}$.

Calculate the probability that

a Rosie has cornflakes or muesli today

b Rosie has neither cornflakes nor muesli today.

⑤ Ryan writes down each of the numbers from 1 to 20 on a separate card.

He then decides which cards belong in the following sets:

A = {x: x is a factor of 18}

B = {x: x is an odd number}

a Draw a Venn diagram to show the two sets A and B.

b Ryan shuffles his cards and selects a card a random.

Find the probability that a number on a card selected at random is:

i odd

ii a factor of 18

iii an odd number and a factor 18

iv an odd number or a factor of 18

v neither an odd number nor a factor of 18.

⑥ A vet is investigating the possible effects of inbreeding in a breed of pedigree dog.

Two possible effects are bad eyesight and weak hips.

The vet looks at a sample of 80 dogs and finds that 44 have neither condition, 24 have bad eyesight and 32 have weak hips.

a Show this information in a Venn diagram.

b Estimate the probability that a dog of this breed suffers from both defects.

Say why your answer is an estimate and not necessarily accurate.

c Find the probability that a dog of this breed suffers from at least one of the defects, by using

i the formula P(A or B) = P(A) + P(B) – P(A and B)

ii the numbers on the Venn diagram.

Problem solving

① 100 patients take part in a trial of new medicines.

36 patients receive medicine X only.

25 patients receive medicine Y only.

15 patients receive both medicine X and medicine Y.

The remaining patients receive a placebo.

a Draw a Venn diagram showing this information.

b What is the probability that a patient chosen at random receives a placebo?

2 100 people belong to a health spa club. It has a swimming pool and a gym.

70 use the swimming pool only.

10 use both the swimming pool and the gym.

1 uses neither the swimming pool nor the gym.

a Draw a Venn diagram showing this information.

Members are chosen at random to take part in a survey.

b What is the probability that someone chosen for the survey uses the gym?

c What is the probability that someone chosen for the survey uses one (but not both) of the club's facilities?

3 At a supermarket, 80% of customers bring their own carrier bags and 25% of customers have loyalty cards.

15% of customers have both their own bags and a loyalty card.

a Draw a Venn diagram to show this information.

b Find the probability that a randomly chosen customer has

    i a loyalty card but no carrier bag

    ii a carrier bag but no loyalty card

    iii a carrier bag or a loyalty card or both

    iv neither a carrier bag nor a loyalty card.

4 Ben always cycles, walks or drives to work.

On any day the probability that Ben cycles to work is $\frac{1}{3}$ and the probability that he drives is $\frac{1}{4}$. Calculate the probability that

a Ben walks to work

b Ben either walks to work or he cycles.

5 There are 80 A-level students at a college. 40 of them do at least one science.

28 students do physics.

28 students do chemistry.

3 students do physics and biology only.

14 students do physics and chemistry only.

1 student does chemistry and biology only.

5 students do all three sciences.

One of the 80 students is chosen at random, to meet a visiting television science presenter.

a Identify the sets in this Venn diagram.

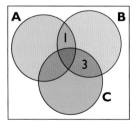

b Fill in all the missing numbers.

c Find the probability that the student chosen does 2 or 3 science subjects.

d Which is more likely: that the student chosen does some science or that the student does no science?

Reviewing skills

① **a** A die is rolled. What is the probability that the number that comes up is
  i even
  ii 3 or less
  iii either even, or is 3 or less.

  b Are the outcomes 'even' and '3 or less' mutually exclusive?
  Explain your answer.

② In a group of 30 students
  8 study history only.
  5 study both history and geography.
  2 study neither history nor geography.

  a Draw a Venn diagram showing this information.

  b A student is chosen at random from this group. Find the probability that the student studies one out of history and geography but not both.

Index

3D shapes *see* three-dimensional shapes

A

acceleration 180–1
accuracy 11–17
  assumed knowledge 11
  bounds 13
  examples 13
  limits of 13–17
addition
  addition rule 370–7
  inverse 68
  simultaneous equations 151
  standard form 5
  vectors 309–11
addition rule 370–7
  mutually exclusive events 370–2
  probability 370–7
  Venn diagrams 370–2
adjacent side of triangle 266–7
algebra 66–176
  assumed knowledge 66
  complex formulae 86–92
  functions 113–36
  graphs 113–36
  identities 93–8
  inequalities 138–44
  methods 137–64
  sequences 99–112
  simplifying expressions 80–5
  starting 66–98
  see also equations; quadratics
angles
  bisection 235
  corresponding 195, 205
  cosine ratio 267
  proofs 195
  special 276–81
  see also trigonometry
arcs 222–9
  construction 232–6
  drawing with compasses 232–6
  examples 223
area
  right-angled triangle 277
  sectors 224
  surface area 302–7
  trapezium 87
asymptotes 129

B

balance method, equations 68
base numbers 61
best fit lines 333–4, 341–7
birth rate data 342–3
bisection of angle 235
bisection of line 232, 233
bivariate data 341
bounds 13

brackets
  equations with 74–9
  factorising quadratics 166–7
  index notation 50–1
  see also expanding brackets

C

calculating
  number 1–2, 5–10
  standard form 5–10
calculators, cos/sin/tan keys 266–7
causation 341, 343
centre of circle 222, 232
centre of rotation 282–90
  examples 283
  finding centre 283
chord of circle 222
circles
  arcs 222–9
  construction 232
  loci 244
  sectors 222–9
circumference of circle 222, 232
coefficients of terms 166
coin flipping 360, 361, 370
common ratio 108–9
compasses, pair of 232–43
compound interest 27–8
compound units 180–7
cones 302–3
congruency
  similarity 256
  triangles 193–203
congruent triangles 193–203
  examples 194–5
  proofs 193–203, 205
  recognising congruency 194
  RHS proof 193
  SAA proof 193
  SAS proof 193
  SSS proof 193
  use of 194–5
consecutive integers 93–4
constant of proportionality 35–40
constants
  multiplication by 151, 152
  proportionality 35–40
  quadratics 166–7
  simultaneous equations 151, 152
construction 230–52
  angle bisection 235
  assumed knowledge 230
  circles 232
  elevations 294–301
  examples 233–6
  line bisection 232, 233
  loci 244–52
  with pair of compasses 232–43
  perpendicular from point on line 232, 234–5

perpendicular from point to line 232, 233–4
  plans 294–301
  triangle 236
continuous data 324
conversion graphs 35–6
conversion of units 180
correlation
  lines of best fit 341–3
  scatter graphs 333–4
corresponding angles 195, 205
cosine (cos) ratio 266–7, 276
cost price 23
cube numbers 62
cubic functions 130
curves
  asymptotes 129
  definition 115
  leading terms 129
  parabolas 122, 128, 172
  powers of 128–9
  reciprocal graphs 130
cylinders 302–3

D

data
  birth rates 342–3
  bivariate 341
  continuous 324
  discrete 324
  grouped 324–32
  life expectancy 342–3
decimals 86
density 180, 182
dependent events 360–2
depreciation 27
diameter of circle 222, 232
die rolling 360, 361, 370, 372
differences, sequences 101–2
difference of two squares 167–8
direction of vectors 309
direct proportion 35
discrete data 324
division
  index notation 50–1
  inverse 68
  standard form 5–6
drawing
  adding vectors 310
  conversion graphs 36
  graphs 36, 129
  isometric 294–5

E

electricity bills 181
elevations 294–301
elimination method, simultaneous equations 151–7

enlargement 256
equations
  balance method 68
  with brackets 74–9
  complex 68–73
  definition 93
  examples 69, 75
  roots 122–3, 172
  solving equations 69, 74–9, 172–6
  solving quadratics 172–6
  straight-line graphs 115–21
  unknowns 68–9, 75, 145, 151
  word problems 69
  see also simultaneous equations
equivalent amounts 51
estimated probability 351–9
even numbers 372
expanding brackets
  equations 74
  inequalities 139
  pairs of brackets 81, 166
  quadratics 166–7
  simplifying expressions 80–1
expressions
  definition 93
  examples 81
  expanding brackets 80–1
  laws/rules of indices 80–1
  quadratics 166
  simplification 80–5
extrapolation 341, 343

F

factorisation
  consecutive integers 94
  prime 55–60
  quadratics 166–76
  sector area 224
factorising quadratics 166–76
  difference of two squares 167–8
  examples 167–8, 173
  geometrical problems 173
  solving equations 172–6
factors, prime 55–7
factor trees 55–6
formulae
  complex 86–92
  cone surface area 302–3
  cone volume 302–3
  constant of proportionality 35
  creating a formula 35
  definition 93
  examples 87–8
  negative numbers 86–7
  pyramid volume 302
  rearranging 86, 88
  rectangle perimeter 88
  sphere surface area 302
  sphere volume 302–3
  straight-line graph 115–17
  subject of formula 86
  trapezium area 87
  using 303
  working with 87
fractions 18–19
frequency
  diagrams 324–5
  relative 351–2
  tables 324–5
front elevations 294–5

function machines 88
functions 113–36
  assumed knowledge 113
  polynomial 128–36
  quadratic 122–7, 130
  reciprocal 128–36

G

'Gamblers fallacy' 361
geometrical problems 173
geometric progressions 108–12
  common ratio 108–9
  contexts used 108
  examples 109
  generation of 109
geometry 177–317
  construction 230–52, 294–301
  measuring shapes 211–29
  properties of shapes 188–210
  3D shapes 291–307
  transformations 253–90
  units/scales 177–87
  vectors 308–17
gradients 115–17, 181
graphs 113–36
  assumed knowledge 113
  conversion graphs 35–6
  drawing 36, 129
  electricity bills 181
  examples 130–1
  identifying 130
  parabolas 122, 128, 172
  quadratic 172–3
  reciprocal 130
  scatter 333–40, 342–3
  shape and powers of 128–9
  simultaneous equations 158–64
  straight lines 115–21
grouped data 324–32
  displaying 324–32
  examples 325
  frequency diagrams 324–5

H

highest common factor (HCF) 55–7
hypotenuse 193, 214, 266–7

I

identities 93–8
  definition 93
  examples 94
  whole numbers 93–4
image mapping 282–3
independent events 360–1
index notation 50–4
  brackets 50–1
  division 50–1
  equivalent amounts 51
  example 51
  multiplication 50–1
indices
  base numbers 61
  cube numbers 62
  examples 62
  laws/rules 61–5, 80–1
  negative powers 61
  notation 50–4

square numbers 62
inequalities 138–44
  changing direction of sign 138, 140
  examples 138–40
  negative numbers 138, 140
  number lines 138–9
  signs 138, 140
  solving 139–40
  word problems 138
integers 93–4, 138–9
intercepts 116, 123
interest, compound 27–8
interpolation 341
intersections 57, 370
inverse proportion 41–7
  examples 41–2
  recognition of 42
  solving problems 41–2
  variables increasing/decreasing 41
inverses 68
investments 27
isometric drawings 294–5

L

laws of indices 61–5, 80–1
LCM (lowest common multiple) 56–7
leading terms 129
'less than or equal to' sign 138
life expectancy data 342–3
limits of accuracy 13–17
linear inequalities *see* inequalities
line bisection 232, 233
lines of best fit 341–7
  bivariate data 341
  causation 341, 343
  correlation 341–3
  examples 342–3
  extrapolation 341, 343
  interpolation 341
  outliers 341
  scatter graphs 333–4, 342–3
  use of 341–7
lines of symmetry 122–3
loci 244–52
  equidistant from two points 245
  examples 245
  types 244
lower bounds 13
lowest common multiple (LCM) 56–7

M

magnitude of vectors 309
mapping images 282–3
mass 181
measuring shapes 211–29
multiples
  LCM 56–7
  whole numbers 93–4
multiplication
  index notation 50–1
  inverse 68
  laws/rules of indices 61
  multiplication rule 360–9
  simultaneous equations 151, 152
  standard form 5–6
  vectors by scalars 309, 311

multiplication rule 360–9
  dependent events 360–2
  independent events 360–1
  probability 360–9
  tree diagrams 361, 362
  without replacement 360–2
mutually exclusive events 370–2

N

negative correlation 333, 341, 343
negative gradients 117
negative numbers 86–7, 138, 140
negative powers 61
th term of sequence 101–2
number 1–65
  accuracy 11–17
  assumed knowledge 1, 3
  calculating 1–2, 5–10
  fractions 18–19
  percentages 20–32
  properties 48–65
  proportion 33–47
  ratio 33–47
  standard form 5–10
  using system 3–10
number lines 138–9
number properties
  assumed knowledge 48
  index notation 50–4
  laws/rules of indices 61–5
  prime factorisation 55–60

O

opportunity samples 352
opposite side of triangle 266–7
original price of article 22
outcomes 351
outliers 341

P

pairs of compasses 232–43
parabolas
  quadratic functions 122, 128
  solving equations 172
  throwing ball 128
parallel vectors 309, 311
patterns and sequences 102
percentages 20–32
  assumed knowledge 20
  compound interest 27–8
  examples 22–3, 27–8
  increases 23, 27–32
  original price 22
  reductions 22, 27–32
  repeated increases/decreases
    27–32
  reverse 22–6
perimeter 13, 88
perpendiculars 233–5, 244
pi (π) 222–4, 302–3
plans 294–301
plotting
  frequency diagrams 325
  points on graphs 129, 131

scatter graphs 333–4
  simultaneous equations 158
polynomials 128–36
population density 180
populations 351
positive correlation 333–4, 341
powers
  graph shapes 128–9
  laws/rules of indices 61
  standard form 5
  see also indices
price
  cost 23
  original 22
  sale 22–3
prime factorisation 55–60
  examples 56–7
  factor trees 55–6
  highest common factor 55–7
  lowest common multiple 56–7
  prime factors 55–7
  Venn diagrams 56–7
prime numbers 372
probability 348–77
  addition rule 370–7
  assumed knowledge 348
  estimating 351–9
  examples 351–2
  multiplication rule 360–9
  mutually exclusive events 370–2
  relative frequency 351–2
  samples 351–2
product of prime factors 55–6
profit 23
proofs
  angle proofs 195
  congruent triangles 193–203, 205
  identities 94
  similar triangles 204–10
properties of number 48–65
properties of shapes 188–210
proportion 33–47
  assumed knowledge 33
  constant of proportionality 35–40
  conversion graphs 35–6
  direct 35
  examples 35–6
  inverse 41–7
  sign 41
pyramids 302
Pythagoras' theorem 214–21
  cone surface area 303
  examples 214–15
  length of hypotenuse 214
  solving problems 215

Q

quadratics 122–7, 165–76
  examples 123
  factorising 166–76
  functions 122–7, 130
  intercepts 123
  lines of symmetry 122–3
  parabolas 122, 128
  roots of equations 122–3, 172
  sequences 101–7
  solving equations 172–6
  turning points 123
  working with 165–76

quadratic sequences 101–7
  differences 101–2
  generating terms 101
  th term 101–2
  square numbers 101

R

radius of circle 222, 232
random samples 351
rates of change 181
ratio 33–47
  assumed knowledge 33
  common ratio 108–9
  similarity 204, 256, 257
  similar triangles 204
rearranging formulae 86, 88
reciprocal functions 128–36
rectangles 88
reductions 22, 27–32
relative frequency 351–2
reverse percentages 22–6
RHS (right angle/hypotenuse/side)
    congruency proof 193
right-angled triangles
  area 277
  congruency proof 193
  Pythagoras' theorem 214–21
  trigonometry 266–81
right angle/hypotenuse/side (RHS)
    congruency proof 193
roots of equations 122–3, 172
rotation, centre of 282–90
rules of indices 61–5, 80–1

S

SAA (side/angle/angle) congruency
    proof 193
sale price 22–3
samples 351–2
SAS (side/angle/side) congruency
    proof 193
satisfying inequalities 138
scalars 309, 311
scale factors 256
scales 177–87
scatter graphs 333–40
  correlation 333–4
  examples 333–4
  lines of best fit 333–4, 342–3
  plotting 333–4
sectors 222–9
  area 224
  examples 224
segment of circle 222
sequences 99–112
  and patterns 102
  assumed knowledge 99
  geometric progressions 108–12
  quadratic 101–7
set notation 370
shapes 188–229
  arcs 222–9
  assumed knowledge 188, 211
  congruency 193–203, 256
  of graphs 128–9

measuring 211–29
proofs 193–210, 205
properties 188–210
Pythagoras' theorem 214–21
sectors 222–9
similarity 204–10, 256–65
3D 291–307
side/angle/angle (SAA) congruency
    proof 193
side/angle/side (SAS) congruency
    proof 193
side elevations 294–5
side/side/side (SSS) congruency
    proof 193, 205
similarity 256–65
    congruency 256
    examples 257
    ratio 204, 256, 257
    transformations 256–65
    triangles 204–10
similar triangles 204–10
    examples 205
    proof of similarity 204
    proof using similarity 205
simplifying expressions 80–5
simultaneous equations 145–64
    elimination method 151–7
    examples 145–6, 151–3, 158
    graphical solutions 158–64
    multiplying by constant 151, 152
    substitution method 145–50
    subtraction 151–2
    word problems 146, 153
sine (sin) ratio 266–7, 276–7
sketching graphs 117, 129
special angles 276–81
speed 180–1
spheres
    surface area 302
    volume 302–3
square numbers
    indices 62
    Pythagoras' theorem 214
    sequences 101
square roots 215
SSS (side/side/side) congruency
    proof 193, 205
standard form 5–10
    addition 5
    calculating with 5–10
    division 5–6
    examples 6
    large numbers 6
    multiplication 5–6
    small numbers 6
    subtraction 5–6
statistics 318–77
    assumed knowledge 318, 321
    diagrams 321–32
    grouped data 324–32
    lines of best fit 333–4, 341–7
    measures 318–20
    probability 348–77
    scatter graphs 333–40, 342–3

straight-line graphs 115–21
    equations 115–21
    examples 116–17
    formula 115–17
    gradient and one point 115–16
    gradients 115–17
    simultaneous equations 158–64
    two points defining 115, 117
subject of formula 86
substitution
    checking solutions 75, 146, 152, 163
    into formulae 86–7
    simultaneous equations 145–50
    to find unknowns 145, 151
subtraction
    inverse 68
    simultaneous equations 151–2
    standard form 5–6
    vectors 309–11
surface area 302–7
    cones 302–3
    cylinders 302
    examples 303
    spheres 302
    3D shapes 302–7
    using formulae 303
symmetry, lines of 122–3

T

tangent (tan) ratio 266, 276–7
tangent to circle 222
terms
    coefficients 166
    definition 93
    geometric progressions 108–9
    leading 129
    quadratic sequences 101–2
three-dimensional (3D) shapes
        291–307
    assumed knowledge 291
    elevations 294–301
    plans 294–301
    surface area 302–7
    volume 302–7
transformations 253–90
    assumed knowledge 253
    centre of rotation 282–90
    similarity 256–65
    trigonometry 266–81
translations 309
trapeziums 87
tree diagrams 361, 362
trees, factor 55–6
trials 351
triangles
    congruency 193–203, 205
    construction 236
    see also right-angled triangles
trigonometry 266–81
    angles, finding 267
    cosine ratio 266–7, 276
    exact values 277

examples 267, 277
lengths, finding 267
sine ratio 266–7, 276–7
special angles 276–81
tangent ratio 266, 276–7
turning points 123, 128–9

U

unit price 180
units 177–87
    acceleration 180–1
    assumed knowledge 177
    common examples 180
    compound 180–7
    electricity bills 181
    examples 181–2
    speed 180–1
unknowns 68–9, 75, 145, 151
upper bounds 13

V

value-added tax (VAT) 22
variables
    proportion 35, 41
    rearranging formulae 86
VAT (value-added tax) 22
vectors 308–17
    addition 309–11
    examples 310–11
    multiplication by scalars 309, 311
    subtraction 309–11
Venn diagrams
    addition rule 370–2
    prime factorisation 56–7
volume 302–7
    cones 302–3
    cylinders 302–3
    density 180, 182
    examples 303
    leaving pi (π) in answer 303
    pyramids 302
    spheres 302–3
    3D shapes 302–7
    using formulae 303

W

whole numbers 93–4, 138–9
word problems
    complex equations 69
    inequalities 138
    simultaneous equations 146, 153

X

x-intercepts 123

Y

y-intercepts 116, 123